W9-BZU-645

THE PEN IS MIGHTIER

THE PEN IS MIGHTIER

The Muckraking Life of
Charles Edward Russell

ROBERT MIRALDI

palgrave
macmillan

070.92

m i r

21590722

THE PEN IS MIGHTIER

Copyright © Robert Miraldi, 2003.
All rights reserved. No part of this book may be used or reproduced in
any manner whatsoever without written permission except in the case of
brief quotations embodied in critical articles or reviews.

First publish   2003 by PALGRAVE MACMILLAN™
175 Fifth Avenue, New York, N.Y. 10010 and
Houndmills, Basingstoke, Hampshire, England RG21 6XS.
Companies and representatives throughout the world.

PALGRAVE MACMILLAN is the global academic imprint of the
Palgrave Macmillan division of St. Martin's Press, LLC and of Palgrave
Macmillan Ltd. Macmillan® is a registered trademark in the United
States, United Kingdom and other countries. Palgrave is a registered
trademark in the European Union and other countries.

ISBN 0-312-29292-9 hardback

Cataloging-in-Publication Data Available from the Library of Congress.

A catalogue record for this book is available from the British Library.

Design by Letra Libre, Inc.

First edition: February 2003
10 9 8 7 6 5 4 3 2 1

Printed in the United States of America.

To Charles Pfeiffer,
a good man

CONTENTS

More than a Muckraker

In the voluminous clippings, letters, and diaries of Charles Edward Russell (1860–1941) in the Library of Congress in Washington, D.C. is a reference to Howard University, a small coeducational college founded in 1867 to educate newly emancipated slaves. The university had once given a testimonial dinner for Russell late in his life, honoring him for the many causes he championed and crusades he mounted in a fifty-year career in journalism, politics, diplomacy, and letters. While Russell was most famous during his life for his work as a "muckraking" or exposé journalist in the first two decades of the twentieth century, he was also well known in the African American community for his support of equal rights for blacks. In fact, in 1909 he was one of the three founding members of the National Association for the Advancement of Colored People. When he died in 1940, a black community newspaper in Washington said: "Mr. Russell was one of the best loved figures in this section and proved himself a genuine friend of the Negro race."[1]

When I called Howard University to find files related to Russell, I was transferred to the Moorland–Springarn Collections, where historical materials on African American literature and history are housed. A librarian told me that there were indeed materials on Russell. Not knowing that I was many years into my research, she began to tell me who Russell was. "Let's see," she said. "He was a poet and publicist. And, from what I see here, he was a great friend of the black people. He was a white man, you know."[2] That I knew, but what surprised me was that from the university's point of view, Russell was a poet, publicist, and friend of blacks. Here was a man who edited and published two of the greatest newspapers in the world, who was one of the most prolific, well known, and effective of the investigative reporters during the early part of the twentieth century, who ran four times for national and state office from New York and was almost nominated as the Socialist Party's presidential candidate in 1916, who wrote hundreds of magazines articles and thirty-one books, and who won the Pulitzer Prize for biography in 1927. And yet, to Howard University, he was remembered for his gentler side—for his four books of poetry, his love of Shakespeare, and his tireless efforts to associate himself with and promote good causes. When Russell died in 1941, befuddled obituary headline writers did not know what to call him; he was alternately labeled as a writer, reformer, socialist, poet, journalist, muckraker, and newspaper editor.[3]

Charles Edward Russell was a lifelong journalist bent on raising the public consciousness; a muckraking provocateur exposing the excesses of industrialism; a crusading progressive reformer seeking to make things better; a brooding poet; a biographer with a penchant for finding righteous lives to unfurl; a fighter for civil rights; a left-wing orator and politician who believed that cooperation needed to replace competition in America; and a diplomat and patriot who wanted to help America fight the forces of authoritarianism in the world. Russell was all of those things in a remarkably diverse, productive career that spanned sixty years. Unfortunately, his has tended to fall into the shadows of history, partly because of the difficulty of pinning down and defining the man who was Charles Edward Russell.

Born in the Midwest in 1860, Russell moved to New York City as a young man and became one of America's most famous newspaper reporters. Next he edited the two largest newspapers in America under Joseph Pulitzer and William Randolph Hearst during the "yellow journalism" phase of American newspapers. After the turn of the twentieth century, he joined with a group of other journalists who became famous as the muckrakers, attacking political corruption and industrial excess and urging reform. Unlike his colleagues, however, Russell turned for solutions, like millions of other Americans, to socialism. He ran four times for political office as a Socialist, twice nearly receiving the party's presidential nomination. Despite his anti-capitalist sentiments, Russell became a fierce patriot who argued for American entry into World War I. His pro-war stance prompted the Socialists to throw him out of the party, but it led President Woodrow Wilson to enlist him as a diplomat to fight the threat of German authoritarianism. When the war ended, Russell turned to various new causes and to writing biographies, for which he won a Pulitzer Prize in 1927.[4]

To trace Russell's life is to brush up against all of the great reform causes of the late nineteenth and early twentieth centuries—Populism, Progressivism, racial integration, and Socialism. In the process it becomes clear that many of the issues that engaged Russell are prevalent today. As this book was being finished, a scandal emerged concerning a Texas energy giant, the Enron Corporation. Reports of inflated stock prices, corporate profiteering, and political-influence peddling made national headlines, prompting criminal and congressional investigations. Beginning in 1904 and for twenty years thereafter, Russell routinely exposed these same problems, arguing that American companies were regularly inflating their profits in order to sell stock at higher prices and arguing that both political parties could be "bought" by the big corporations. Reform and regulation, he argued, would never cure the problem, because wily company heads, spurred by the natural desire for maximum profit, would always find a way around government regulators. Moreover, he argued, finding loopholes in regulations is the natural thing to do in a competitive system that forces even good people to behave in a way that enhances the bottom line at the expense of other priorities—and the law. Until the day he died, Russell felt that capitalism was at the root of many of America's ills, and his major journalistic efforts—exposing the slum landlord Trinity Church, the tyranny of America's meatpacking monopoly, the cruelty of a prison labor-capitalism cabal, and the octopus-like powers of various industrial combines—were directed to show how unregulated capitalism would breed evil. If Russell were alive today he would be writing many of his same stories, especially the ones that pointed to a growing gap between the wealthy and the poor, the issue that most turned him to Socialism as a cure.

As he crusaded against a variety of evils and muckraked America's problems, Charles Edward Russell became one of the most well-known writers and journalists in America. It was impossible not to encounter Russell in a headline or byline in the first twenty years of the twentieth century. But Russell's work and impact have been largely forgotten today.[5] While all of the major muckrakers have had biographies—more than one for Lincoln Steffens, Ida Tarbell, Upton Sinclair, Ray Stannard Baker, and David Graham Phillips—little has been written about Russell.[6] This is odd given that he muckraked on more topics and wrote more exposé articles for a longer period of time than any of the others. Nonetheless, he had no one "smoking gun" issue that won him fame. Tarbell's history of Standard Oil immortalized both her and John D. Rockefeller, Sinclair created *The Jungle* and touched millions of readers, and Steffens's "Shame of the Cities" still appears in high school textbooks.[7] In addition, Russell's turn to Socialism in 1908 and his foray into elective office isolated him from the more conventional and popular reformers of his day, as well as muddied the waters between his roles as journalist and activist. Have historians resented Russell for leaving the conventional political fold and embracing radicalism? If so, they would be unfair. Russell's politics were always democratic. Frankly, much of what he wanted—from old-age insurance to government control of the railroads to stricter rules for the workplace—is accepted as social policy today, and hardly radical. Russell the person may have also diminished his standing in history. Formal, private, and almost austere, he has failed to capture the imagination of biographers. Indeed, finding the personal side of Russell has been near impossible for this writer. When they can be found, his letters are almost always on social issues and deal little with passion, love, or family. The diaries he kept during World War I discuss the war, and never his emotions.

As a public figure, however, Russell was not difficult to locate. He was everywhere in the early twentieth century—in newspapers, magazines, and books and on the lecture circuit. One summer I was in a New York University library looking at microfilmed material on socialism. A young man at an adjacent microfilm reader struggled with his machine. I helped him adjust his focus, and almost magically a large black-and-white photograph appeared of Charles Edward Russell, who was surrounded by Yiddish headlines. The man was reading Abraham Cahan's *Forward*, a daily newspaper whose crusades for social justice profoundly influenced the Jewish community. A story about Russell's 1912 race for New York governor—and his progressive platform—was the lead item in that day's *Forward*. It was ironic, of course, that Russell popped up in the center of page one of the *Forward* on an adjacent screen just as I was researching his life. But it was also fitting: he was a pervasive figure who deserves to be front and center in any discussion of twentieth-century social justice, investigative journalism, and progressive publicity.

Re-creating a life is never an easy task, and many people have helped me discover Charles Edward Russell. I would like to acknowledge and thank the following: the National Endowment for the Humanities for two grants; the State University of New York's College at New Paltz for various financial assistance; librarians at the Davenport (Iowa) Public Library, the Library of Congress in Washington, D.C., the New York State Library in Albany, and Ulster County Community College in Stone Ridge, New York. I am particularly grateful to William A. Vasse, A. David Kline, David Lavallee, Gerald Benjamin, Lynn Spangler, Howard Good, Deanna Lorenzo, Gerlinde Barley, and various librarians at New Paltz's Sojourner Truth Library. Many others helped, too, including James Boylan, Paul R. Baker, Susan Ciani, Martin Gottlieb, Janet Graham Gottlieb, Terrence Kivlan, Edith Miraldi, Lawrence Miraldi, Alan Silverman, and Bob Villelm. Special thanks to my editor, Deborah Gershenowitz. My children, Robert Michael and Sara Elspeth, always listened to my tales of research woes and glories. And my wife, Mary Beth Pfeiffer, patiently and endlessly talked me through this book, helped edit it, and made possible its completion. Finally, I dedicate this book to my father-in-law Charles Pfeiffer, who died just as the book was completed and who always encouraged me about the importance of history and a dedicated life.

THE PEN IS MIGHTIER

CHAPTER ONE

THE JOHNSTOWN FLOOD: "ALMOST IMPOSSIBLE TO DESCRIBE"

I. GETTING THERE AT ANY COST

FOR THE TWENTY-NINE-YEAR-OLD CHARLES EDWARD RUSSELL, May 31, 1889 was one of those mundane working days that young newspaper reporters are forced to bear. He was assigned to cover the New York City police department's annual parade, a pompous ritual with little substance. Nonetheless, he pronounced it "the best effort the police ever made" and signed off on an eight-inch story for the *New York Herald*, one of the city's great newspapers and his employer for four years. Although the uneventful day seemed over for the blue-eyed Iowa native, it had barely begun. At 10:00 P.M., as he prepared to head for his Brooklyn flat, news flashed over the telegraph wire that would change Russell's standing as a journalist, test his mettle to survive, and begin to shape his view of the profession on which he would make his mark over the next four decades. A dam had burst twenty miles north of Johnstown, an industrial city of twelve thousand in western Pennsylvania. At least twelve people were dead in a flood that roared through the Conemaugh River Valley.[1]

New York City has always been—for better or worse—the greatest hotbed of journalistic competition in America. Ever since the 1830s, when the one-cent newspaper emerged, the New York dailies battled fiercely for readers. In their effort to make circulations soar, publishers avidly pursued gruesome murders, juicy divorces, and natural disasters.[2] But while editors might revel in the latest crime or crisis, reporters often cringed at their next assignment. Such was the case for Russell, whose editor now told him that he would have to trek 370 miles to the disaster scene.

By the time he was ready to depart, more telegrams had arrived; perhaps as many as forty people were now dead in Johnstown. Russell doubted the figures. Such things as forty fatalities in a dam burst do not happen, he thought. Exaggeration, he figured, was "the pure embroidery of the bulletin writer." A decade earlier, while working at his father's small newspaper in Davenport, Iowa, Russell had been in charge of the newspaper's telegraph office. He knew full well "how the country correspondent always loses his head in the presence of a story." Russell was expecting a simple assignment—"a night of rest in my lower berth [on the train], a column story filed early, and back to-morrow night."[3] Little did he know that he was about to undertake an exhausting and perilous journey that would put his life at risk, bring him to the scene of the worst flood in American history, and offer him his first great newsgathering adventure—and social lesson—in what would be a lengthy and remarkable journalism career.

The same telegrammed news that came to the *Herald* also went to all the other New York newspapers, most likely initiated by an Associated Press correspondent in the area of the flood. The world's largest earthworks dam, perched 400 feet above Johnstown, holding back a 100-foot lake with 20 million tons of water, had been unleashed. Given the potential magnitude of this story, Russell was not surprised to find that when he went to the station a special newspaper car had been arranged to bring him and three other reporters, William J. Kenney of the *New York Times*, Richard A. Farrelly of the *New York World*, and Ervin Wardman of the *New York Tribune*, to the flood scene. The rival *New York Sun*, the *Herald*'s bitter penny-press rival, was not invited.[4]

Despite stormy weather, all went well on the ride south to Philadelphia, where the New York press corps learned that reporters from the City of Brotherly Love were also pursuing the story. A fierce competition to get to Johnstown first had begun. Once they were out of Philadelphia, the weather worsened, and three miles before Harrisburg torrential spring rains flooded the train tracks. Water came to within one inch of the train's firebox, terrifying the passengers as the train swayed from side to side. The train sloshed into Harrisburg at 8:00 A.M. where bad news awaited: the Pennsylvania Railroad had shut down all operations. With miles of track under water, the trains could go no further. The reporters were stuck hundreds of miles from Johnstown, where the Philadelphia newspapers were now reporting that the death toll might reach the thousands. But the challenge of outwitting a rampaging storm—and the rest of the press corps—had gotten Russell's competitive juices flowing. He needed to find a way to get to the biggest story of his life. "We must rush on at any cost," he declared, even if it meant going on foot.[5]

The New Yorkers found a train heading directly south into West Virginia's Cumberland Valley, in the opposite direction from where they wanted to go; but from Virginia they could head west again, and then back north directly to Johnstown. The rampaging waters intervened once more, this time at Hagerstown, Maryland, where at 11:00 A.M. their train was forced to halt near a bridge across the overflowing Potomac River, a bridge too shaky to allow a train to cross. A railroad official, seeing how desperate this band of reporters was to get to the scene of the burst dam, told them that a wrecking car (a small vehicle about the size of a modern automobile) could take the reporters to the edge of the bridge. From there—if they dared—they could walk across. When Russell and his group arrived at the bridge, it was obvious why the train could not proceed: "The bridge was visibly trembling," Russell wrote. The rails were twisted out of shape and one of the bridge's main center supports was missing, swept away by the canal boats that had pummeled the support structure. Russell witnessed a completely intact farmer's barn in the morass. "I had a small taste for the crossing of that bridge and yet the thing had to be done," Russell later recalled. Using umbrellas and canes to steady themselves, Russell and his colleagues walked the plank. The key to not falling off the bridge, the reporters knew, was to avoid looking at the rushing water below. The first reporter put a cigar in his mouth and watched its tip; the man behind watched the feet of the man in front. "The river was roaring below us," Kenney recalled. To look down "was to throw away our lives." But the reporters made it across, after which Russell concluded dryly: "I have taken much pleasanter walks." Twenty minutes later the bridge was swept away into the river.[6]

Now the fun really began for the reporters, who plodded over to a nearby farmer's house and pleaded for help. They got it. After a dinner of corn pone, salt pork, and potatoes, the farmer took them by wagon to the nearby Martinsburg train station where again the news was all bad. No trains would be leaving for a week; the reporters were stuck again, "completely shut off from the rest of the world as [if] we had been on a desert island." They were "frantic," Russell reported, not only that the Philadelphia pressmen would beat them but that somehow other New Yorkers would outrace them to Johnstown.[7] As they studied maps and plotted ways out, blind luck entered the chase. An influential train superintendent, also stranded, took pity on the frazzled reporters and helped map a route to Johnstown. His plan: to take a special engine that would leave at daybreak, hire a carriage at Chambersburg, Maryland, and then walk the rest of distance. The plan sounded fine until the train official disclosed that he had given the same advice to the reporters from Philadelphia, also in hot pursuit of the story. The Philadelphians were to arrive in Chambersburg at the exact moment as the New Yorkers, with a carriage and horses awaiting them also. "May the best side win," the train official declared. Journalistic Rule Number 1, a rule Russell grew to hate, was now invoked: being first to the story is more important than anything else. Scoop the opposition by any means necessary.[8]

Arriving at Chambersburg, the reporters were greeted at the train station by half the town, curious to see what the press knew. But the townspeople, it turned out, knew more than the reporters, who were told that the Philadelphia press corps was due at any moment. This sent the New Yorkers on a wild chase through town to find the lone available carriage. It had already been reserved by the Philadelphia reporters.

> "This carriage is engaged for Mr. Brown," the driver told them.
> "Right," said Wardman of the *Tribune*. "I'm Mr. Brown."
> But, the driver protested, "I heard them call you Wardman."

Just a nickname, Wardman responded.[9] By two in the morning they had gone as far as the carriage would take them, and they had to plead again with a nearby farmer to show them the road to Johnstown. Startled and wary in the early morning hours, the farmer held a gun to the reporters' heads until they convinced him that the grizzled and by now dirty quartet really were esteemed representatives of the press, not robbers. Once convinced, the farmer agreed to help; he immediately fed the reporters—their last good meal for a number of days. The farmer stopped in the small village of Bedford where a telegram from New York awaited the reporters: "No one is ahead of you. Go for it."[10]

II. "Too Awful to Talk About"

By four o'clock in the morning on Sunday the reporters had reached the summit of the Allegheny Mountains, which was as far as the farmer's buggy could travel. Although only two hours from Johnstown, Russell knew that "the most perilous and difficult part of our journey" had begun. The farmer showed them a logger's path that would lead to the Conemaugh Valley. It was barely a path, forcing them to slog through ankle-deep mud, wade through bogs, and slide downhill over jagged rocks. "If any one of us had missed his footing," Russell remembered, "we would have fallen and been killed or seriously injured." In a dispatch to the *Herald* nine days later, Russell described how they felt: "dismal, cheerless, splashed with mud, fagged out with loss of sleep and sick at heart with the expectation that other men [from Philadelphia] had got through before us." One eyewitness who observed Russell and his colleagues enter Johnstown described them as "utterly exhausted by the hardship of the journey. The poor fellows were in far better condition for a hospital than for the tyrannic work which the situation demanded."[11]

By 1:00 P.M. on Monday, nearly 60 hours after leaving New York, they finally reached the road that led directly to Johnstown. It was thronged with curious people from nearby towns as well as with refugees from the valley, people who had lost families, friends, and homes. "We were wet to the skin, covered with mud, and dog tired, " Russell wrote, "but so strange are the ways of the human mind that every sense of discomfort vanished at the almost incredible news that awaited us." Everyone they encountered on the road to Johnstown gave them the same response: "Boys, it is too awful to talk about."[12] At fifteen minutes before two o'clock, they got their first view of the flooded city, which, Russell wrote, looked like dominoes set on end, then toppled. In a story filed two days later, Russell repeated: "The best way to get an idea of the wreck is to take a number of children's blocks, place them closely together and draw your hand through them."[13] The New York reporters had beaten the Philly reporters. Reporters from the *Sun* arrived that evening. Russell, leading his group, was the first reporter from the east to set foot in Johnstown. But that accomplishment mattered little as he began to observe the scene of destruction.

Seven towns had been virtually wiped out when the dam burst. Constructed by a group of wealthy Pittsburgh industrialists who wanted a pristine place to fish, the dam had long been neglected by its owners and called unsafe. Hundreds of houses, many with people in them, had been washed down through the valley, collecting at a great stone arch bridge over the Conemaugh River. With people screaming, the houses crashed upon each other, and the wooden structures were caught up in a massive blaze. People stood helpless on the shoreline as they watched their neighbors burn to death. Piecing together the story, the reporters were overwhelmed. "Probably nowhere outside of a battlefield and not always there would such sights assail one," Russell recollected as he—and the reporters from Pittsburgh already on the scene—began to describe the disaster, trying to figure out what had happened, how many had died, and what could be done to bring relief and comfort to the victims of the great Johnstown Flood of 1889. Over the next ten days Russell wrote thousands of words, at times filling the first four pages of the *Herald*.[14]

Still wearing a borrowed blue overcoat that had now become a muddy brown mess, Russell began to wander about and retrieve information to wire back to his editors who waited anxiously in New York. Russell telegraphed on Saturday, apparently from a train station, reporting, "On my way to the scene of the disaster I learned that 119 bodies had been counted in the flood." The following day, while Russell was wading through mud, the *Herald* joined the rest of the New York press in wild estimates about the loss of life. "Ten thousand may have perished," one headline blared. "Never before in this country has there happened a disaster of such appalling proportions," it reported. That was true; the eventual death toll was not.[15]

The *Herald's* first two pages were filled with stories on the disaster. Some were obviously the product of a writer sitting in the Ann Street office in Manhattan, imagining, as a novelist would, what the flood was like. Waiting for Russell's facts, the *Herald* took dispatches from Pittsburgh correspondents who exaggerated the disaster and then either made up or used unreliable sources to allege, for example, that Hungarian immigrants were stealing jewelry from the dead. When Russell finally began to report on June 4, he did not mention Hungarian thieves.[16] In writing that reflected a man moved by the events around him, Russell struggled for the appropriate words. "The horrors that are seen every hour, who can attempt to describe," he wrote in his first day at the scene. "It is impossible to describe the appearance of Main Street," he added at another point. "No pen can adequately depict the horrors of this twin disaster—holocaust and deluge," he wrote in one of his four stories of June 4. Yet Russell did effectively and graphically describe horrors over the next few days. There was, for example, John Jordan of the town of Conemaugh whom he spotted wandering the valley in search of his lost family. At daylight Jordan found his wife's sewing machine in the mud. Workmen helping him dig at the site first unearthed his little boy and then his wife and daughter, with the mother's arms clinging to the children. Wrote Russell, "The white haired old man sat down in the ashes and caressed the dead bodies and talked to them just as if they were alive until some one came and led him quietly away."[17] In one place Russell saw a human foot protruding from the mud; in another he watched workers remove "burned and mangled bodies"; at still one more site Russell saw workers dig up a pocketbook with a women's hand clutching the handle. All day long, Russell reported, "People found what they were looking for and fainted at the sight . . . afraid to look and afraid to go away." Sometimes Russell actually helped dig for the bodies.[18]

Russell's first-day writing output was impressive, especially considering the conditions under which he and the other reporters had to work. The *Herald* gave over three full pages to his stories. The main story, headlined "Death, Ruin, Plague," was remarkably similar to a modern news story—tight and crisply written, with a clean and comprehensive overview of the state of John-stown on Day Four of the disaster. Disease threatened the area if clean-up work did not proceed quickly, he told readers, perhaps hoping to put pressure on Pennsylvania officials to pour resources into the clean-up (which they quickly did). Russell explained the kind of cleanup that needed to take place, and observed that the *Herald* had suggested to officials what could be done to speed up the demolition of wrecked houses that clogged the riverway. Dyna-mite was Russell's solution. His story then provided a cogent background of what had happened to cause the dam burst and how the blaze that burned up so many houses had started. He wrote a chilling description of the fire, using the kind of refrain and repetition that would later find its way into many of his thirty-one books and his speeches when he ran for political office. He wrote: "Thousands of people stood upon the river bank and saw and heard it all and still were powerless to help. They saw people kneeling in the flames and pray-ing. They saw families gathered together with their arms around each other and waited for death. They saw people going and tearing their hair. . . . Some saw their friends and some their wives and children presiding before them . . . men laid down on the ground and wept."[19]

After Russell gathered his facts, he had to find a place to write, he needed a telegraph wire on which to transmit, and he needed a place to rest his aching and tired bones. In the wrecked city that was Johnstown, all of those needs pre-sented challenges. Most of the reporters took over an old brickworks near the stone bridge where houses had piled up, occupying two floors of one building and an adjacent woodshed. The place became known as the "Lime Kiln Club," and a comradeship grew among the reporters, many of whom became life-long friends. The writing conditions were less than ideal. The reporters crafted their copy using barrelheads, coffin lids, and shovel bottoms as writing desks. They were a motley-looking crew. "In a short time," one observer reported, "the faces of the hard-working writers became nearly black as if they were ne-groes [sic]." With stories in hand, the reporters had to get them quickly to a telegraph operator, no easy task since telegraph wires were limited and com-peting writers were many. By late Monday the number of telegraph opera-tors—of which Russell said were "painfully inadequate"—had been increased enough to allow for day and night shifts. Nonetheless, Russell lamented, "many good stories were written but few got into print."[20]

The competition between newspapers was fierce.[21] Through blind luck and sheer force of personality, Russell had an advantage. The Associated Press's general manager, William H. Smith, happened to be in Pennsylvania right be-fore the flood and, by coincidence, was on a hill overlooking the valley when the flood rolled over Johnstown. Writing steadily for two hours, he filed the first dispatches from the scene. He also established, in a remote and secret location, one telegraph line just for the AP. Once his main stories were filed after the first two days of the disaster, however, he inexplicably abandoned the site, leaving the telegraph operator with no work. The operator, "being of great goodness of heart," said Russell, confided in the *Herald* reporter and offered his services. "In response I gave him enough to do," Russell later wrote. As his copy flowed to the *Herald*, no one in New York—or Johnstown—could understand how Russell was getting so much through or why the *Herald* was able consistently to fill two and three pages with stories. The break helped make Russell a celebrity. One New York newspaper wrote a story called "How Russell Got the Wire," reporting that he had devised an elaborate system of relays and signals to dispatch his words. "This was pure fiction," Russell later wrote, but in order to protect the operator he never revealed this until his 1914 autobiography.[22]

While Russell had found a way to dispatch his stories, room and board was a different story. With food in short supply for thousands of people and long lines of survivors waiting for relief supplies, the reporters, like everyone else, had to beg for food. It consisted mostly of canned meat, stale bread, leftover cheese, hot coffee, and whiskey. When the dashing Richard Harding Davis, later to become America's most famous war correspondent, came to Johnstown from Philadelphia to report the disaster, he stepped off a carriage and asked where he could find a good steak and a freshly starched shirt. The reporters laughed. Since many of the relief organizations that had sprung up distrusted the press corps and refused to feed them, Russell and his New York colleagues made do with sandwiches they had brought from the last farmer who helped them. Eventually, the reporters hired their own cook, a German who was paid fifty cents by each reporter to cook meals at his house, which, oddly, had not been ruined.

The search for news provided more danger than the search for food. Russell reported in the *Herald* that he had to walk across swaying footbridges to reach news sites. Moreover, on more than one occasion, thieves and ruffians, who were looting the dead and drinking wildly from abandoned barrels of whiskey, threatened the reporters and anyone else who might stand in their way. "Human buzzards flocking to the scene of horrors" was how Russell described them.[23]

As for sleeping quarters, the four New York reporters found a great barn that had previously housed a steel company's horses. They convinced the owner, an austere foreigner who spoke little English, to let them sleep in the lofts, a "savage shelter," Russell admitted, with rats crawling around, but that nonetheless gave the reporters a place to plop, exhausted, each night. Russell feared that he and his colleagues would burn to death in the wood structure be-cause the owner insisted on locking the barn's single door from the outside every evening as they retired. But each morning, the proprietor of the Hotel Boheme, as Russell called it, would unlock the door at sunrise and the reporters would begin again begin searching for the stories that were easier to find than food in Johnstown.[24]

III. THE LESSONS OF JOHNSTOWN: POWER, POTENTIAL, PROFITS

What Russell found most of all in Johnstown was death. It hung in the air and it lay scattered on and under the muddy ground. On Day Five, June 4, as rescue crews continued to find ten bodies an hour, he wrote: "The town seems like a great tomb." Soon after the dam burst, the director of rescue efforts had told the press that between twelve thousand and fifteen thousand bodies might eventually be recovered, an estimate that turned out to be greatly exaggerated. In the end, the final count was more like twenty-two hundred, still enough to far surpass statistics of any other American flood. Wading through mud and water, Russell wandered over a twenty-three-mile region, from South Fork to New Florence. He described what he witnessed:

> I walked over this extraordinary mess this morning and saw the fragments of thousands of articles. In one place the roots of forty frame houses were packed in together just as you would place forty bended cards one on top of another. The iron rods of a bridge were twisted into a perfect spiral six times around one of the girders. Just beneath it was a women's trunk. . . . From under the trunk men were lifting the body of its owner, perhaps, so burned, so horribly mutilated, so torn limb from limb that even the workmen who have seen so many of these frightful sights that they have begun to get used to them turned away sick at heart. . . . In another place I saw a child's skull in a bed of ashes, but no sign of a body.

At another point, he added, "The place is deserted. Arms and legs are protruding from the mud and it makes the most sickening of pictures." Amidst the gloom and stench, he managed to coach some survivors into telling their stories. One man recalled riding twenty-three miles down the rampaging river on a log before he clutched on to a house, saving himself. A watchman told of climbing a hill to escape the onrushing river that he said seemed three stories high.[25]

Over the next days, Russell watched—and described—the gruesome rescue efforts: a charred body being speared with a pitchfork, for example. In clearing out a pile of lumber, he saw workers uncover a girl who was tightly clutching a baby. Russell graphically described the "pathetic incident," balancing sensational scenes of the disaster with more sober and constructive reporting, a juggling act he would follow throughout his journalism career. For example, he described the "overpowering . . . stench that assails one's sense," in order to warn authorities of possible diseases.[26] From the outset, the *Herald* called for greater relief efforts and began its own campaign to raise money, eventually turning over a large donation and considerable supplies to a children's aid society in Johnstown. In particular, he called on Pennsylvania to provide the workmen needed for the clean-up, writing, "Action cannot and must not be delayed." He began to poke his head into other areas, donning his watchdog's hat to wonder in one story why relief funds were not evident. "Some inquisitive people," Russell wrote, "are asking how and where the committee has spent" the half a million dollars that it had been sent.[27]

Newspapers across the country reported that their circulations soared as readers flocked to follow the Johnstown flood story. By midweek dozens of reporters, sketch artists, and photographers, some from as far away as San Francisco, had descended like locusts upon Johnstown, coming in on special trains, handcars, and on horseback. Despite the press's reputation that it consisted of nothing more than a collection of drunken louts and laggards, the reporters eventually won plaudits for their writing and conduct. Observer-turned-historian George T. Ferris cited their "courage and industry," adding, "There is no doubt that the health of most of them suffered." In fact, the four reporters from New York came to call themselves the "Johnstown Sufferers." Russell came down with rheumatism that never left him. The press's purity of purpose was summarized by Reverend C. N. Field of Philadelphia, who had hurried to Johnstown to offer his help. He observed: "If a few priests had been in Johnstown and had worked half as hard as these reporters, they might have done untold good. The reporters endured hardships of every kind—all for the sake of their papers and to give news to the world. . . . I was ashamed of myself when I compared myself to a reporter."[28]

By the middle of the second week, the sun began to shine again in Johnstown which, Russell concluded, "begins to look a little like the habituation of a civilized community." For the next two days the *Herald*'s coverage was optimistic and upbeat, and by June 12, when Russell personally delivered the *Her-*

ald's supplies and donations, it was clear that the story, like the river, had begun to ebb. On June 13, for the first time in twelve days, there were no stories in the *Herald* from Johnstown. Russell and the rest of what came to be called "The Big Four" from New York had returned to their home bases. It was time to turn to new stories.[29]

Russell, a lover of Shakespeare and Swinburne, as well as of political economy, was undoubtedly more thoughtful than the typical reporter of the 1880s. Although many young men who came to journalism after the Civil War saw it as a service to democracy or as a training ground for literature, an equal number or more tumbled into journalism with little training, no purpose, and few scruples. It was a profession for the young and the footloose—long hours, low pay, and lots of liquor, which perhaps the reporters needed as a balm to soothe themselves in the wake of the gruesome events they often had to chronicle. But Russell, who never favored liquor, likely because his grandfathers were both English-born temperance supporters, always had a ministerial and mature tone in his reportorial work. As early as 1881, when he graduated from a private preparatory boarding school in New England, he sketched out his purpose in life. He "who fixes his ambition upon a life devoted to Humanity," he wrote in the school's newspaper, "chooses the grandest, loftiest, highest aim that ever caused the human heart to warm." There is only one way to be "truly happy," Russell concluded, and that "is to make some one else happy."[30] This hardly sounded like a member of the Bohemian Brigade, as the press was sometimes called. It more resembled a man of the cloth.

Johnstown was a defining event for Russell as he came to understand that reporting incidents, beyond their pure narrative value, was full of meaning and consequence. Russell's coverage of the Johnstown Flood is useful for introducing and starting to understand him. It presents a snapshot of how he behaved under pressure and in a crisis. What is immediately evident is Russell's ambivalence about journalism and about private enterprise and capitalism. "As with travel," he wrote about reporting, "the charm lies in the changing perspective that constantly challenges the attention with a new object." If not for this variety, the "hardship and vicissitude, sometimes walked with risk" and the brutal "scenes of nature" could easily make a reporter "loathe his calling and forget his duties."[31] Much of the Johnstown assignment he did not loathe, however. It is clear that he loved the pursuit of the Johnstown story. Despite the life-threatening perils it presented, this was an adventure, akin to his youthful rafting trips down the Mississippi River. He spoke with glee about sliding down mud paths and outwitting the Philadelphia reporters. His memoir entitled "The Rocky Road to Johnstown" is, in fact, mostly devoted to retelling how he chased down this story; he devotes scant space to describing what he found when he arrived, probably a calculated decision to avoid sensational and gruesome details of the disaster scene.

Along with the chase, it is evident that Russell got a charge out of finding a clever, albeit fortuitous way to transmit the stories that enabled him to "scoop" the rest of the press corps—and make his name in journalism. After Johnstown he said, "I found myself elevated to a place in the Journalistic Academy." While he argued later that his good fortune was the result of mere luck, he also, in his typically self-effacing way, let the reader understand that his affable personality and conversational charm allowed him to disarm the telegraph operator and thus make the transmissions possible. Despite what he wrote, it was not luck that led to his success. His skill, in this case as a newsgatherer, certainly had something to do with his success. And that explains—in part, at least—why, soon after he returned to New York from Johnstown, he was called one of the ten best reporters in America, an honor he found important enough to mention in his memoirs.[32]

Russell also stressed his work in journalism because he felt it was important—that delivering information to people constituted a vital part of democracy, even if, as he later lamented, the people needed to hear a fact repeated twenty times before they would remember or understand it.[33] Journalism was always Russell's true calling, even though it led him logically down other career paths. It provided him with his true social education and led him to understand and identify what he saw as the worst parts of a society—poverty, unemployment, slums, racial tension, and the root of them all: the financial chicanery and manipulation of unrestrained, profit-seeking private corporations. It also led him to believe that none of that could be altered without the reporting of facts—without journalism. He clung to this belief always, even during the years when he despaired about the direction of America before World War I. In fact, throughout his career and life—even though it included political activism, government diplomacy, and the writing of poetry—he always considered himself, first, foremost, and primarily, a journalist, "an impartial observer of men and manners."[34]

In Russell's work in Johnstown, three aspects of a progressive and constructive journalism are glimpsed, if only fleetingly. As his stories began to hint at an emerging scandal in the use of relief money being sent to the beleaguered area, he acted as a check on government. Similarly, he put pressure on government when he sounded the alarm in his early stories, warning about the possible spread of disease if clean-up efforts weren't pursued with more vigor. Moreover, Russell was not content to sit idly by and merely watch the recovery effort. Despite his claims of being a neutral observer, he eschewed neutrality in a literal sense by actually helping to dig up bodies. In a more typically journalistic manner he chipped in with advice: form a commission, he suggested, to coordinate relief efforts; use dynamite to blow up the clogged logjam on the river. Russell was not content to observe, even at this early stage of his career.

Finally, Russell learned the power of the press as a catalyst in mobilizing the public. He was able to raise money and provide supplies to a private group that was coordinating disaster relief, in an era before either the government or insurance could help victims. When all newspaper relief efforts were completed, the press had helped raise nearly four million dollars—more than had ever been raised in America. About $516,000 came from New York City, including $2,000 from Joseph Pulitzer of the *New York World*, Russell's future employer. The press could not save mankind from disaster, Russell knew, but it sure could raise a lot of money to do some good.[35] For the generation of reporters who came to the profession of reporting after the Civil War believing that journalism was a noble profession, almost a higher calling, surely that belief was underscored by the success of the relief efforts in Johnstown. For Russell, the lesson of Johnstown also underscored his belief that good, not evil, lurked in the hearts of mankind. If evil was about, it was created by economic environment, not by the natural order of things.

In Johnstown, Russell found ample evidence that the natural order, "the system," as he later called it, had gone awry—in the causes of the disaster itself, as well as in his viewing of aspects of the press's behavior. Historians are quite clear on what caused the dam to break: negligence, plain and simple. The dam above Johnstown was originally built to create a reservoir that would fill a canal, which would in turn provide a road linking Johnstown to Pittsburgh. By the time it was completed in 1852, however, a rail line had made the roadway obsolete. Nearly thirty years later, a Pittsburgh realtor bought the dam, which was in serious disrepair. He then reconstructed the earthwork dam—the world's largest—and created Conemaugh Lake. One hundred wealthy Pittsburgh families, including Andrew Carnegie, Henry Clay Frick, and the Mellons, spent $2,000 each to become members of the South Fork Fishing and Hunting Club and have the privilege of spending two weeks in the rugged, isolated beauty of the valley. The wealthy club members failed to take care of their dam, however. It was patched with mud, rocks, hay, even horse manure. One spillway was covered with a screen so as to prevent the stock of fish from escaping. Once clogged with debris, that screen became a plug, blocking the rising water from escaping the reservoir. The result of the indifference of the stingy industrialists from Pittsburgh was the Johnstown Flood. The social lesson, which was a national disgrace, was not lost on Russell, although neither he nor any members of the press ever publicly assailed or even mentioned the affluent owners of the failed dam.[36]

Then there was the journalistic lesson. Even though Russell told with some glee his story of getting to Johnstown, he was harshly critical of what it all meant. "I was hired," he admitted, "to outwit my fellow-workers, to surpass them in cunning and adroitness, to secure something they did not secure." What he had to do to get the story was of no concern to Russell's employers. "By whatsoever means, I must do this," they believed, and while, two decades later, he publicly rebelled at the rules of the game, in 1891 he was content to play by those rules.[37] If his editors back in New York had argued that getting to the site and telling the story was necessary in order to prod authorities and protect the flood's victims, or if the true motive was to disseminate the disaster's facts so that the public could then share relief supplies with the poor homeless and helpless families, then the chase and the maneuvering could be rationalized and the ends might justify the means. But Russell came to disbelieve this, just as the public had known better about the press' real motivation.

The "Big Four" reporters from New York had to trick the other reporters so that "the proprietor of the newspaper might have the exclusive sale of a merchantable commodity and thereby increase his profits," Russell later concluded. Lincoln Steffens, who became Russell's colleague of sorts after the turn of the century as they were joined in the muckraking journalism movement, described Russell as "the most sensitive, sincere, imaginative of the whole tribe, and the most wounded, too."[38] When the Johnstown victims bled, Russell bled with them. His anguish was evident in his writing, in searing and empathic images such as a father stroking the heads of his dead family. Russell might have had fun getting to Johnstown, but when he got there he had work to do, serious work, and his goal was not to pad the profits of James Gordon Bennett Jr., the *Herald* owner who was off cavorting in Paris. Russell's coverage of the Johnstown flood was his first journalistic crusade, a crusade for which he had been preparing ever since the days when, as a teenager, he set foot inside his father's small-town newspaper in Davenport, Iowa, where he was schooled about the true purpose of journalism: to seek out evil and protect the people.

CHAPTER TWO

THE PIOUS AND THE POWERFUL ⸒

I. FROM THE THAMES TO THE MISSISSIPPI

ON A HOT, SUN-FLOODED DAY IN 1869, NINE-YEAR-OLD Charles Edward Russell was left alone with his grandfather, the Reverend William Rutledge, at his grandfather's Le Claire, Iowa, home near the banks of the Mississippi River. His mother and grandmother had gone bargain-hunting to a nearby town. Little Charles was in his grandfather's study reading a history of England, the mother country of his grandparents and his parents. He was not all that interested in the text, he admitted; he was looking at the photographs only as a way of avoiding going outside the house where a raft that had come down from Black River, Wisconsin, had just tied up. Young Charles, along with his friends and many local residents, was particularly fearful of anyone from Black River because, local legend had it, the Black River rafters "would as soon stab you as look at you." Everyone knew, Russell said, that "the real business of their souls was battle, murder, and sudden death."[1] Just the day before, Russell's fears had come true when Johnny Gordon, one of his buddies, had gone aboard a Black River raft to deliver foodstuffs for Waldo Parkhurst, the grocer. Johnny didn't notice that a man lay coiled up on the raft, who sprung to his feet with a howl when Johnny stepped on his toe. Dropping his baskets, Johnny ran, but the man trailed after in hot pursuit with a long-handled boat hook that he threw at Johnny, catching him in the leg. The alert Johnny, bloodied, dove from the raft, swam to the nearby shore, and then hobbled to the Russell household.

Thoughts of Johnny Gordon raced through Russell's mind as a knock came at the back door. Was the man with the boat hook looking for revenge on the Russells for harboring Johnny and mending his leg? Russell shuddered at the thought, but would never tell his grandfather—a bellowing, fearless Baptist preacher known as "the Elder"—that he was afraid. Grandpa Rutledge, young Russell knew, "feared nothing that walked, drunk or sober."[2] This man would climb on the roof of his house in a fierce rainstorm just to get a closer look at lightning bolts. Rather than face his grandfather, Russell answered the knock. With trembling hand, he pulled the door's bolt and there stood a group of raftsmen—Black River raftsmen.

The band of men at the door had big black slouch hats clutched in their hands, with red handkerchiefs tied around their necks. They looked scruffy but scared. "Sonny," one of them said, "kin you get us a sight of the Elder? We need him right bad—an' we ain't goin' to hurt nobody."[3] Once summoned, the Reverend Rutledge politely escorted the group to his parlor, gave them buttermilk—an act of kindness that astonished Russell—and inquired how he could help. One of the Black River rafters had, as Russell put it, "been taken powerful bad," and was near death. He wanted a parson. Reverend Rutledge and his grandson walked to the raft to comfort the dying man with a powerful passage from the Bible. When the reverend finished reading, one of the rafters, who had a great black beard, fouled with whiskey and tobacco, escorted the young Russell and his grandfather back to the house where, with the reverend's permission, he handed the boy a small pocket knife as a gift. Silently, he returned to the raft, never looking back. After that day, Russell said, he never again feared the Black River rafters, a fact that won him distinction in the eyes of his friends.

As an adult, Russell never made too much of the lessons that might have come from this incident. But later in his life, in fact nearly forty years later, when he entered the hard-boiled realm of American politics in New York, he was not unlike his grandfather, the preacher. Russell bellowed about injustice, nosed up to foul sights and people with compassion, and mixed it up—pleasantly, it might be said—with people from all political, social, and racial hues. He wandered the Lower East Side poverty districts, the Tenderloin vice region, and the fashionable Fifth Avenue area. He seemed comfortable in various milieus, although his sympathy rested always with the underclass, even if the rest of society wanted little to do with such lepers and outcasts as the Black River rafters. Writing a column of commentary for a newspaper, he often concluded his weekly advice with the word "Amen," as if ending a prayer or a sermon.[4] Although "the Elder" died when Russell was nine years old, the lessons his grandfather taught in his formative years stayed with Russell, as did his other most important early experience—the apprentice training in journalism he received from his father, Edward. Edward Russell had married Rutledge's daughter Lydia and moved the family from Le Claire to the bustling Midwest port city of Davenport, Iowa, where pioneer immigrants like the Russells and Rutledges mingled with older-stock Americans.

Charles Edward Russell was born to Lydia Rutledge and Edward Russell in Davenport on September 25, 1860. Located 182 miles west of Chicago, Davenport was at the confluence of three great influences on American life: steamboats, railroads, and farms. The steamboats, which young Russell learned to pilot quite well, plied the river in search of Davenport's mill products and its rich limestone as well as, eventually, its corn and hogs. Life along Davenport's five miles of Mississippi riverfront gave young Russell a storehouse of tales.

Soon after the Civil War, the railroads, which came in from St. Paul, Minnesota, Chicago, Milwaukee, and the Pacific, competed with and overtook the steamboat as the main way Davenport farmers and producers shipped out their goods. Understanding and explaining the might and power of these railroads eventually became an obsession for Russell when he began to write for mass circulation national magazines after the turn of the century. The corn, which fed Iowa's livestock, especially the hogs that were raised near Davenport, was an early and successful product in Iowa; two of Russell's brothers worked as young men on local farms. In Charles Russell's early years, however, the Mississippi River was the hub of most activities for both him and Davenport.[5]

Incorporated in 1851, Davenport had grown rapidly following the opening to traffic in 1856 of the first Mississippi River bridge and the establishment soon after of the United States arsenal at nearby Rock Island. Charles got an eyeful playing near the docks of the Mississippi where he often launched rafts with his friends. At one point, Russell managed to work on a steamboat as a pilot's "cub"—an errand boy for the captain—and he got the adventure of his life. The steamboat he was working on, the *Alec Scott*, was racing a competitor at top speed down the Mississippi from St. Louis to New Orleans. The captain, who wanted to speak with the boat's engineer, sent Russell to the engine room where he discovered that the engineer, for unknown reasons, had tied up a crewman assistant who was held up at gunpoint. Suddenly, the engineer turned the gun on young Russell, who fled. Russell remembers, "I don't think I ever moved quite so quick in my life." While the boat's captain and co-pilot went down to the engine room to disarm the engineer, cub Russell was left at the wheel of the steamboat running at top speed in one of the most treacherous sections of the river. It would be difficult to navigate for a veteran pilot, impossible for a neophyte. Russell tried his best to control the large wooden steering wheel. He sat on it. He stuck his feet in the spokes. Nothing worked. Finally, sensing disaster, he blew the steamboat's whistles, telling the passengers to get out lifeboats. "I put my foot on the wheel, I shut my eyes and waited for the crash," Russell later remembered. Miraculously, however, the steamer stopped. The boat reversed and the engines ceased. Down below, unbeknownst to Russell, the captain had gotten a water hose, cooled down the crazed engineer, and shut off the engines to avoid disaster. Said pilot cub Russell: "I was as badly scared as any tenderfoot. I would have given all the money I could make in a lifetime to be on dry ground."[6]

When he was back on land, Russell saw lots of drunken sailors frequenting the wharves and gin spots, and they provided him with a glimpse of seedy life that he would not see much of until he went to New York as a reporter in 1886. Russell, who liked to play baseball and a game called scrubs, was apparently a bit of a cutup. He told a Davenport friend: "I admit that I was about the orneriest kid in town and always playing pranks." If he had an ornery and irascible streak, it likely came from his father, who one history of Iowa pointed out, was known for the "steadfastness of his convictions . . . one of his strongest characteristics."[7]

Russell's father, like his mother, was born near London, England, one of five children who immigrated to America in September 1845 with Charles Russell's grandfather, Scotch-born William Russell. The Russell family had not fared well in England, partly because William had quit a good job in a whiskey distillery when the temperance movement burst onto London. "It was characteristic of him to put his convictions ahead of his material interests," Charles Russell recalled of his grandfather. After quitting his job, William worked earnestly for reform as secretary of a secret temperance society and then publicly as a temperance lecturer. However, he barely was able to keep his family fed. Edward Russell later told Charles and his sisters about those days of struggle in London. In particular, he recalled the harsh boarding school to which he was sent where life resembled conditions in a Charles Dickens novel, replete with painful whippings for the students. The boarding school experience, Charles Russell felt, planted in his father "a hatred for cruelty, a passionate love for justice and a sympathy with the oppressed that shaped all his after life."[8] And they shaped his son's life.

In England, William Russell and William Rutledge were acquaintances, probably because both were ardent reformers and teetotalers. Rutledge, an itinerant preacher and master tailor, met Russell, a blacksmith, on a trip to London. In 1842, Rutledge moved to America, going initially to Philadelphia, where he became an ordained Baptist minister and urged the Russells to join him. When a fire in the small coffee shop that William Russell operated near the Thames River burned the establishment to the ground, he decided to follow Rutledge's suggestion. The family sailed for New York, moving after a short time to the remote village of Callicoon in western New York, on the Delaware River. After a failed attempt at farming in the rugged woods of Sullivan County in the Catskill Mountains, the Russell family accepted the invitation—again—of their British friend. William Rutledge, who had gone from Philadelphia to Iowa, urged them to move closer to a real river in the Midwest. Russell, with his wife, daughter, and three of his sons in tow (Edward stayed behind to work), visited Le Claire, Iowa, where Reverend Rutledge was preaching for free to a Baptist congregation. To pay his bills, the reverend was working as a tailor, barely eking out a living. Souls on Sunday; trousers on weekdays.[9]

In New York, the harsh climate and rocky soil had not been kind to the Russells, but the fertile Upper Mississippi, where pioneers were flocking, seemed more hospitable. Iowa, in particular, was attracting European immigrants, especially Germans. Consequently, the Russells sold their New York property to relocate near the booming Mississippi, the nation's chief artery of traffic. In September 1848, Edward Russell, who had become a carpenter's apprentice after arriving in New York, joined his family in Le Claire. The Russell boys all found work—Edward as a carpenter, William and Josiah as farmhands, and Thomas at the sawmill.

Four years later, in April 1852, Edward married Rutledge's daughter Lydia, Charles Edward's mother who also bore three daughters. Lydia became a homemaker; she loved music and Shakespeare, two interests she passed on to her son, who would eventually write four volumes of poetry. Her collection of Shakespeare's works became one of her son's prized possessions. As for Edward, he worked by day and studied and read at night. He became particularly interested in political discussions and could not avoid, of course, the issue of slavery, which, probably at the urging of Reverend Rutledge, he grew to oppose fiercely. Using the pen name Agricola, he made his first contribution to a newspaper, the *Iowa True Democrat*, an antislavery journal then published in Mount Pleasant, Iowa. He become a frequent contributor to a minor abolitionist publication, the *National Era*. In the fall of 1858, at the urging of his friends, he became editor of the weekly *Le Claire Republic*, which he left in 1859 because it paid so little money—"about enough," his son reported, "to sustain a canary bird." He returned to carpentry, but soon after took a job in nearby Davenport in the county clerk's office. Two years later he became an assistant postmaster until, in 1862, when Charles Edward was two years old, he became part owner and editor of the *Davenport Gazette*. "A newspaper was his natural home,"

Charles Edward said. He "could never be happy without pen in hand and the rumble of a press near by."[10]

II. FROM IOWA TO VERMONT

The *Gazette*, in existence for twenty-one years when Edward Russell took over, grew steadily under his stewardship until it became an award-winning Republican paper, one of the largest dailies in Iowa. Journalistic objectivity was not even an ideal for the American press in the years before the Civil War, so it is no surprise that Russell's newspaper clearly identified itself with one political party. Edward Russell was a busy man, known for arriving at his newspaper at seven o'clock each morning and then not leaving until midnight, when the morning-published *Gazette* was finally put to bed and readied for printing. Nonetheless, Russell also found time to serve as postmaster of Davenport. He was appointed to the position by President Lincoln in 1864, undoubtedly a reward for his support of the president and for his founding in 1860 of the Scott County Republican Party. Such political patronage had been common for many years, and friendly newspaper editors, in particular, were often rewarded with positions as postmaster.[11] In October 1865, however, Russell was removed from office by President Andrew Johnson, who succeeded the slain president in April. Russell wrote that his father was removed from office by Johnson for political reasons, an allegation confirmed by three other historical sources.[12] The *Gazette* had been one of the first to criticize Johnson's Reconstruction policies after the Civil War as Russell quickly allied himself with the radical Republicans who were poised to thwart Johnson's Reconstruction ideas. Indeed, his criticism went beyond Johnson's views on Reconstruction; the *Gazette*, staunch opponent of slavery and its extension to the states bordering North and South, had earlier denounced Johnson when he was proposed as a running mate of Lincoln. Was Johnson aware of this? There is no way to tell, and it is possible that Johnson simply ousted Russell because he wanted to install his own man, not a Lincoln appointee, in the postmaster's position. Johnson had been a Democrat until the start of the Civil War; party loyalty might not have run deep. More likely, Russell's barbs, coming from one of the largest daily newspapers in Iowa, had stung the new president. In fact, if Russell had known the truth about Johnson's true feelings about African Americans, the barbs might have been even nastier. While the president had publicly stated that he wanted to be the black man's Moses, he also had told the governor of Missouri that America was "a country for white men, and by God, as long as I am President, it shall be a government for white men." To one of the top officials in his administration, he explained in 1865, "Everyone would and must admit that the white race was superior to the black." Edward Russell, on the contrary, always told his son that "God's children of a dark complexion are as much God's children as those of a light complexion."[13] Acting on this belief, Edward helped Iowa in 1865 enact an amendment to its constitution to allow blacks to vote in the state. Voting rights for blacks after the Civil War was one of the key issues at the crux of the great controversy over Reconstruction in which Johnson found himself embroiled soon after he assumed the presidency. He had a growing corps of enemies and critics in the Radical Republicans, who eventually sought his impeachment. It would make sense then, when he could, to rid himself of an enemy. Russell might still be able to criticize the president in his newspaper, but Johnson could make sure that the government would not pay part of his critic's salary. With Russell's ousting, Johnson got his revenge; not the last time an opponent struck back at the opinionated editor.[14] With the election of Ulysses S. Grant to the presidency, Russell got back his postmaster's job in 1868. Petitioned by Davenporters who supported Edward Russell, President Grant, probably looking quickly to undo Johnson's influence, installed Russell back in office where he wore his dual hat again, spreading the word in print and in the mails.

As for the young Charles Russell, he felt most comfortable in two places— around the waterfront and in the newspaper offices of the *Gazette* which shifted locales eight times between its founding in 1841 and 1872 when Edward Russell, still the editor and part owner, moved the newspaper into an impressive-looking three-story red-brick building. The *Gazette* occupied the entire corner of East Third and Perry Streets in Davenport and boasted three presses, including a large cylinder press. Edward Russell made clear to his son and his staff the purpose of journalism. The press, he lectured, must be "the guardian and nourisher of civic virtue." Its goal: "terrify evil-doers and arouse the communal conscience."[15]

Unfortunately, Charles might have taken this command too literally too early in his career. A disaster struck the newspaper near 4:00 A.M., when the printing press had begun to print page four, which was always reserved for local news. A compositor, playing tricks near the presses, dropped a glue brush into a press. It made unreadable an Edward Russell story, placed on that page, that accused a local company of trying to pay bribes to the Davenport fire department in order to secure a contract to install electrical fire alarms. The original handwritten copy of the story could not be found, and Edward Russell, who lived too far away to be reached by messenger, could not be reached since the newspaper had yet to install a telephone. The young Russell, fledgling crusader, decided he could re-create the story without his father's help. "I know what my father thinks about this business," he told himself. Russell proceeded to write a new version, had it set in type, and then ordered the presses to roll. The story by the young man who later became a fastidious researcher and fact checker was filled with epithets such as "thieves" and "scoundrels," and he had gotten the facts all wrong to boot. Two libel suits were threatened the next day, threats his father was able to forestall. Although the young Russell had much to learn, the newspaper apparently did not suffer too much disgrace. It won plaudits, for example, at one Iowa State Fair, when the *Gazette* was named the state's best daily newspaper and was cited also for producing the "best and greatest variety of work from a single office," albeit work that was at times a bit overzealous.[16]

In the summers, with no school to attend, the young Russell spent considerable time at the *Gazette* office, mostly pasting labels on newspapers to be mailed to customers. He was especially entranced by the tramp printers who would float into town and work for short periods in the composing room. One in particular—Russell called him Scotty—was held in high esteem because he was a wizard at typesetting lines of hot metal type that brought the news into print and because, having hopped freight trains across America, roaming from city to city, he seemed so worldly. Most of all, though, Scotty was held in awe because he had worked in New York, the place Russell the youngster called "the newspaper mecca of those that dared . . . the far away shrine of perfect printing, the wonderful metropolis, in the mists of imagination looming great and strange."[17] To Scotty, every place but New York City was second class.

While Russell and the *Gazette* staff took a break from office work by standing near a window on Perry Street, just outside Edward Russell's office, Scotty the philosopher held court. He regaled the others with tales of his newspaper life: of how Horace Greeley's handwriting was impossible to read; of how he had chatted with legendary editor Charles A. Dana of the *Sun;* and of how James Gordon Bennett, Jr. himself actually supervised the *Herald*'s composing room. Scotty had worked with Samuel Medill at the *Chicago Tribune* and he had actually been cursed by the fabled *Chicago Times* editor Wilbur Storey. "He has been everywhere and seen everything," Russell said of his first hero. Inevitably, however, all conversations turned back to New York, wherein Russell became a "rapt and joyous listener" as Scotty took his Midwestern naifs on a tour of Manhattan's underside, from the Bowery to Hell's Kitchen. And then they would return to newspaper work.

"Did you ever see a good head line written outside of New York?" he would ask. "Now tell me, did you? Well, neither did anybody else. And look at the way they dish up their stuff there; it isn't newspaper writing, it's literature. . . . Boston is nothing compared to New York."[18] Scotty was a "soiled and sorry ragamuffin," Russell knew, but he told tales more interesting than fiction, and he knew about life. Charles Edward Russell wanted to be able to tell such stories and know about life in New York. Before going to Broadway, however, Russell took a detour to New England. In 1880, after seeing an advertisement in a religious journal, his parents enrolled him in a private boarding school in St. Johnsbury, Vermont, a charming New England village located at the juncture of the Connecticut and Passumpsic rivers. The village, St. Johnsbury Academy proudly pointed out, was "widely known for the intelligence, public spirit and high-toned morality of its people." In fact, the academy boasted, St. Johnsbury was perfectly located: "Temptations are comparatively few, and incentives to culture are many and strong."[19]

Russell was brought up in a Christian Evangelical household; his grandfather was a Baptist preacher; his father the Sunday school superintendent and one of the leading officials in Iowa's Young Men's Christian Association. They were all temperance advocates, and his father was reputed to have never tasted alcohol in his life. But the piety of St. Johnsbury Academy—whose 1881 catalogue points out that "good manners and morals are as important as mere intellectual acquisition"[20]—was too much for the cutup from Davenport to take. After listening to the often ribald tales of the tramp printers at his father's newspaper, Russell, nineteen years old, was probably more than ready to leave the oppressive religiosity of his household, looking, as all young people do, to make his own way. In going to St. Johnsbury, however, he simply had gone from one pew to another.

Founded in 1842, St. Johnsbury Academy was a coeducational preparatory school, essentially a four-year high school to prepare students for college; it cost the Russells about $500—for room, board, and tuition—to send Charles Edward there for two years. Tuition was relatively low because, unknown to the Russells, the town's leading family, the Fairbankses, had just endowed the academy with a $100,000 gift. Russell was eventually impressed by the school's academic life. "All the instructors were experts," he wrote after studying Latin, Greek, French, and German, all indispensable tools for the correspondent who eventually traveled the world. He took lessons in English grammar, British literature and history, European history, and political economy—a thorough and well-rounded course of study that helped make Russell an erudite adult.[21]

One instructor, Wendell Phillips Stafford, who later became a federal judge, inspired in Russell a love of public speaking as he guided his student to many of the famous speeches of Wendell Phillips (no relation to the teacher), who, as a reformer and orator, was a prominent abolitionist and outspoken foe of Andrew Johnson. Russell especially admired a speech in which Phillips said that a man's possessions were of no value unless they were used for the common good. Russell never forgot Phillips; in 1914 he wrote an admiring biography of the man he called "the greatest of Americans."[22] So smitten was Russell with the idea of public speaking that he made his first appearance on a stage in Peacham, Vermont, on February 3, 1881, giving a talk on "Free Trade vs. Protection." He supported free trade because protection of American commerce with such things as an import tariff "is the very essence of all things unjust and wrong." He equated free trade with freedom of the press and freedom of conscience; protection, he argued, was akin to slavery. Luckily, Russell later wrote, no record was kept of his speech because "my private conviction is that it was fairly bad."[23]

Occasional excitement about ideas, however, could not make up for the insufferable discipline and rules of behavior that so rankled Russell. He disagreed with the maxims expressed in the academy's student guidebook which noted: "The rules of the school are not arbitrary or unnecessarily strict, but simply sufficient to protect pupils in the proper disposal of their time [and] to guard against temptations." All students were required to attend a church and Bible service each Sunday and then sign a card on Monday assuring the principal that they had indeed attended. Morning prayers in chapel were also compulsory. At eight o'clock each evening, the academy bell rang, signaling that students could not leave their rooms. The school's dormitory was coed, but alas, Russell recalled, the sexes were separated by a solid wall of masonry, with the principal living on one side and his assistant on the other. "Either or both would have been sure to detect any outbreak of levity" or, worse, "an attempt to tunnel the wall," observed Russell.[24]

At the occasional formal get-togethers for students, no dancing was allowed, nor was alcohol, tobacco, or card playing. At these affairs, however, the school's three hundred students would march past each other in what resembled a military review. Russell must have liked something he saw at one of these affairs because one Abby Osborne Rust, the editor of the newly established school newspaper, caught his eye. Her father was the chief engineer for the Portland and Ogdensburg Railroad; the family resided in St. Johnsbury. In 1882, a year after graduating, Russell returned to St. Johnsbury as a not-so-disinterested observer of commencement exercises at which Abby delivered the class essay. In March 1884, Russell and Miss Rust were married.

Despite finding a romantic interest, Russell was appalled by the atmosphere in St. Johnsbury. "The whole thing reeked with piety; aggressive, militant, grim, implacable," he commented. "It oozed from every pore of the buildings and projected through the crannies of doors and windows." Since he felt that he was receiving a good education, Russell did not want to flee St. Johnsbury. Nonetheless, he wrote, "smug religious formalism drove me into violent revolt" and "my soul longed for a protest."[25] His outlet was found in the discovery of Robert G. Ingersoll, lawyer, lecturer, and agnostic. One of the most popular lecturers in America in the late nineteenth century, Ingersoll had made a name for himself, not only as a defense attorney in some celebrated trials but as a public speaker who used seemingly scientific arguments to attack the "superstitions" of the Bible and the beliefs of Christianity, thus earning the nickname "the great agnostic." Reformers such as Brand Whitlock and Tom L. Johnson, along with Russell, later said that Ingersoll had inspired them also. An Ingersoll biographer points out, "In teaching men to question the dogmas of religious faith, he taught them to question other dogmas also," but especially the gospel of wealth which was, in part, the rationale behind the rise of nineteenth-century American capitalists.[26] Using clippings of articles from the *Chicago Tribune*, Russell began to follow—and embrace—Ingersoll's exhortations. On Sunday afternoons, in a room in a house at the top of Western Avenue, he gathered a few similarly dissatisfied and yearning souls, and read to them from Ingersoll. If only the Reverend Rutledge could see his grandson preaching such a contrary gospel.

This room on Western Avenue, where Russell was a boarder with two or three other students, enabled him to escape the piety of the St. Johnsbury campus for part of the day at least, but it did not free him from the other nettling part of life in St. Johnsbury. The house he lived in sat on a hill that overlooked the E & T Fairbanks factory, which employed hundreds of the town's residents. The Fairbankses were one of the most famous families in Vermont history, the family that started, paid the bills, and handsomely endowed St. Johnsbury Academy; the family that gave the town a library, an art gallery, a natural history museum, and two governors. In short, the Fairbankses were the patron saints and benefactors of St. Johnsbury. About the people of St. Johnsbury, Russell eventually concluded: "Under their frozen exterior no other people were more kindly, friendly, neighborly, and good to know." But regarding the Fairbanks family, Russell was filled with nothing but contempt. "In plain terms, the town was a barony, and so far as autocratic rule was concerned, reproduced neatly the status of a Rhine village in the Middle Ages," he charged.[27] The Fairbanks family were the barons and, to Russell, the enemy.

Russell was not far from the truth about who ran St. Johnsbury emy, for example, began in earnest when three brothers, Erastus, and Joseph P. Fairbanks, used money they had made in their scale purchase property and begin construction. For its first forty years, the Fairbanks paid all the bills of the academy; in 1881 they gave $100,000 for construction of a new building; and in 1881 they set up a permanent endowment of $100,000.[28] Consequently, one of their heirs always headed the board of directors. To some, it might seem, the Fairbanks boys were models of American progress. Thaddeus, who had begun a small iron foundry in 1823, patented a series of inventions—a plow, a parlor stove, a flax machine—that first attracted attention to the Fairbanks name. In 1831 he developed the idea for a scale, the first of its kind, that could be used to weigh carts loaded with hemp. Thereafter, the Fairbanks Company manufactured scales (it had thirty-two patents on scales alone), became known worldwide, and earned a considerable fortune for the brothers. Part of their success was due to the business acumen of Joseph, who had studied law and traveled widely to sell the Fairbanks scales. Erastus, the oldest of the three brothers, was the public man—the firm's chief executive, whose energetic management helped double sales volume every three years leading up to the Civil War, and then, as Vermont governor for two terms, until 1864, successfully pushed for a law that prohibited alcohol. He also helped found the national Republican Party. Ironically, he had much in common with Charles's father Edward, a teetotaler and founder of the Iowa GOP. Erastus died in 1864, after which he became revered and legendary around St. Johnsbury.[29] So why did the Fairbanks family so upset the upstart from the Midwest? Didn't he expect that the people of a company town would bow down to the benevolent owners of the company? Did he believe for a moment that, with hundreds of jobs at stake, they would bite the hand that was feeding them? Writing about his St. Johnsbury experience fifty years later, Russell explained his anger. It was simple: the Fairbanks family pointed out "the problem of Accumulated Wealth, the persistence of autocracy in a professed republic." Yes, Russell understood the arguments made about how the Fairbankses personified the American Dream. These were good, God-fearing, hardworking, creative men; the wealth they made would trickle down to the rest of the population; they deserved power because they owned the factory that gave work to so many local residents. But no, Russell couldn't embrace the "accepted theories about Trickle and Filter and the beneficent giving of work to men."[30]

He then used a tried-and-true journalistic formula for explaining how he had reached this conclusion—find a person whose situation is typical of others. This is known as a "feature" approach and is one way of giving a large, unmanageable story a focus by boiling it down and providing it with human interest. Russell became very good at this in his magazine writing after the turn of the century, and he had the journalistic instinct, even in 1881. His focus was one

Jim Dow, a man he had encountered in St. Johnsbury who challenged the myth of the Fairbankses' greatness. Dow, who lived with Russell in the Eastman boarding house, was a thoughtful, decent, and well-read worker at the Fairbanks factory. His craftsmanship, Russell said, was an indispensable link in the making of the Fairbankses' scales; Dow's labor—and that of all those like him—made him as important as any Fairbanks at the top of the pecking order. Without the skilled workers, there would be no lucrative scale business. And yet, Dow received a pittance for a wage, not enough even to clothe himself decently, not enough, he told Russell, to allow him to marry and support a family. To Russell's amazement, Dow was not bitter, just resigned to the way things were: Fairbanks at the top, workers at the bottom. "He gave his skill, knowledge, careful attention, labor, but nobody gave him anything," Russell wrote.[31] The "Accumulated Wealth and Power" of the Fairbanks family might have given St. Johnsbury a beautiful library, with wonderful paintings, but it did little for workers like Dow, Russell charged. The feature approach was convenient for Russell to use to justify his anger at the Fairbanks. Written in his 1933 autobiography, it was a typical rhetoric from a man who had harangued great wealth throughout his career and who had grown to believe that the government, not private persons, should own the means of production. Some historians had come to believe that the great industrialists of America were robber barons who, like Rockefeller, had bribed their way to monopoly and then held workers captive to keep their profits high. Yet there is no indication that the Fairbankses were of the same ilk, say, as Rockefeller or Vanderbilt. They paid decent wages, were never tarnished by any allegations about their business practices, and they gave much of their considerable wealth back to the town of St. Johnsbury. Paternal, perhaps; pious, certainly; but not corrupt.

Along with Robert Ingersoll, something else had gotten into Russell's rebellious young mind that inflamed his passions against the Fairbankses. One day in March 1881 Russell wandered into St. Johnsbury's public library—a gift to the town from the Fairbankses—and began to read the *Atlantic Monthly* magazine, which was then publishing Henry Demarest Lloyd's articles attacking the Standard Oil Corporation and exposing the methods used to build the great oil monopoly. As he began to read what became a best-selling book, *Wealth Against Commonwealth*, Russell said he was "swept by an increasing and irresistible interest." When he finished, Russell knew what he had only sensed before: "this industrial development of which we had been so proud was a source, not of strength, but of fatal weakness." What some called "great business enterprise" was "no more than greed preying upon need."[32] Lloyd, of course, was talking about John D. Rockefeller's company, but Russell substituted in his mind the

local captains of industry—the Fairbankses, those unelected rulers of St. Johnsbury who threatened true democracy. "In the West we knew that some men
were richer than others," Russell observed, "but had any one of the richer assumed dictatorial powers because of his wealth he would have been torn out of
his estate."[33] In St. Johnsbury, on the contrary, the Fairbankses were put on
pedestals and revered.

Graham Newell, who lived in St. Johnsbury most of his life, who graduated from and taught at the academy and who knew Russell in his later years,
conceded that "everyone in town always knew that most of what we had came
from the largesse of the Fairbanks family. But we never resented it. It seemed
good for us and the town." Newell, who became familiar with Russell's work,
said that he and others have tried to figure out why Russell bore such a grudge.
"It is hard to tell just what his big gripe with St. Johnsbury was," commented
Claire Johnson, who has written a history about the town. Newell may have hit
upon the answer, however. "Russell was what today we might call a hippie,"
Newell said. "He had this youthful antipathy to authority."[34] It could be seen in
his attraction to Ingersoll, whose preaching challenged the dogma of Russell's
parents and of the authority of the powers-that-be at the academy. Moreover,
Ingersoll's suggestion that accumulated wealth was not a natural by-product of
goodness and ingenuity fit perfectly into Russell's growing anger at the powerful Fairbankses who controlled St. Johnsbury. Add this to Lloyd's angry indictment of Rockefeller's monopoly, an indictment that roused an entire
generation, and it was logical and natural for Russell to resent the Fairbankses
as a power that would never be tolerated in the populist Midwest. After gradu-
ation, he couldn't wait to return to Iowa where old-fashioned democratic values prevailed. However, the naive prodigal son was in for a big surprise.

PART III: EDWARD RUSSELL IS DERAILED

Charles Edward Russell's return to Davenport must have been a mixed blessing. He had received a solid formal education at St. Johnsbury, but also, in
Wendell Phillips and Henry Demarest Lloyd, he had discovered lifelong heroes. Consequently, he returned home fired up but also considerably changed.
What must the household conversations have been like? Since, as Russell once
noted, there is "an eternal proneness of the Englishman to jaw about politics
and religion," things must have heated up considerably when Charles suggested that old Ingersoll might be on to something in criticizing the Bible. Politics more than likely found Charles and his father on similar wavelengths
since, as Russell pointed out, in his family "opposition to the corporations was

held to be the next great work after the destruction of slavery."[35] Initially Russell resumed his job as the *Gazette*'s telegraph editor, the position he held before leaving for Vermont. His mind was on other political matters, however, as he became consumed with the issue of foreign trade and its effect on American commerce, especially its effect on the farmers of Iowa. He looked around at his neighbors, including his mother's cousin, John W. Willis, who owned a farm south of Davenport, and saw that "for all their toil, skill, care, fortitude, and privations they had nothing to show except the bare fact of an existence kept by a hand-to-hand fight against adversity."[36]

Even though the Iowa soil was fertile, Russell knew the farmer's "grinding labor" produced less than that of a French peasant who tilled much less land. "Industry, sobriety, integrity, frugality, all the virtues be praised in song and story might work gloriously elsewhere but they broke down at the farm gate," Russell found. In 1882 the farmers of America were a dispirited and restless lot, not only in the Midwest, but in the South and the Far West where the strains of the Populist revolt were beginning to spread. Populists put the blame mostly on the currency, the "financial question," as it was called.[37] They wanted changes in how money was created and on what basis it was circulated, which would in turn determine who shared in the fruits of production. To Russell and a growing group of Iowans, another financial issue was more important—the protective tariff. Russell believed that tariffs set by the government to protect manufacturers of articles in iron, steel, wood, and textiles, for example, shielded them from foreign competition and constituted, in essence, a tax on the consumer for the benefit of the producer. Farmers had no such protection.

Needing a flag to fly and a cause to rally around, the young Russell jumped into his first crusade. Along with a banker and two newspaper editors, Russell formed and became vice president of the Iowa State Free Trade League, a group that, he said, "roared, shouted, and bellowed and for a time drove the forces of evil back to their trenches." Russell's strident, almost demagogic, and perhaps sophomoric position on the tariff can be seen in a pamphlet issued by the *Iowa State Leader*, a newspaper published by the president of the fledgling free-trade group. He wrote that only "ignorance and stupidity" supported the tariff. "Every man too lazy to think, and every man too ignorant to read is a 'protectionist.'" Once he got beyond the sharp rhetoric, however, Russell also used facts, figures, and logical argument to denounce what he said amounted to "a system of legalized robbery." For Russell it all boiled down to this: the tariff allowed the few to profit while the many suffered. This, he wrote, "is a system of slavery. And no system of slavery shall ever receive my support." He signed the pamphlet "CHAS. E. RUSSELL."[38] Russell's position, quite clearly, was a mirror of his St. Johnsbury political economy professor, Arthur Latham Perry, whose textbook labeled the tariff "public plunder . . . worthy only of the dark ages." Russell, in fact, repeated in the pamphlet, without attribution, Perry's assertion that only two or three economists in America still believe in the worth of a protective tariff.[39] Ingersoll, Lloyd, and now Professor Perry, all of whom Russell had encountered in the East, all attacking privilege and accumulated wealth, had followed him to the Mississippi. Since the Republican Party was the chief supporter of the tariff, Russell's arguments must have riled many of Iowa's Republicans. Nonetheless, his father's Republican newspaper, the *Gazette*, went along with young Russell's arguments and took a strong editorial stance against the tariff. Six years later the tariff question led Edward Russell to quit the Republican Party, which he had helped found in Iowa; in the presidential election of 1888 he voted for a Democrat for the first time, lamenting: "The fact is that Republican leaders . . . see only the interests of the speculative and money-getting crowd."[40]

In October 1882, the *Gazette* reorganized its staff and Charles was temporarily named managing editor, the top editorial position. His father was only fifty-three years old, but he was suffering from overwork. A few years earlier his physician had ordered rest and sent him on a three-month holiday to England, his first return abroad. It is likely that the father wanted the son to be more involved in managing the growing newspaper, although Charles continued to be active also in free trade politics. In December he was re-elected as the Free Trade League's vice president, and in June 1883 he helped organize the first national Free Trade Conference in Detroit where Professor Perry gave one of the main addresses. With the newspaper and the Free Trade League seemingly prospering, Russell observed: "We might well think we had the enemy on the run."[41]

The leading force behind the Free Trade League was its president, Henry J. Philpott, who edited the *Des Moines Leader*. After returning from Detroit, Philpott lost his job when the *Leader* changed ownership. Soon after, he started a weekly newspaper devoted to free trade principles, but Philpott contracted tuberculosis and died quickly. Dispirited, Russell turned his full attention back to the *Gazette*, where he was needed because his father had begun to engage with matters unrelated to newspapering.

After the Civil War, when the issue of slavery dissipated, Edward Russell turned to the large industrial combination as the next great oppressive force to be fought. "We are driven to choose between abject servitude to this monster of evil, or unequivocal resistance to its further spread," he declared. The protective tariff that Charles was fighting was one manifestation of this "monster";

the other was the railroad companies that, by 1870 or so, had become perhaps the dominant economic and political powers in America. As his son remembered it, the *Gazette* "thundered against railroad absolutism as probably the editor's ancestors had resisted Charles the First."[42] In editorials Edward Russell blasted what he saw as the lawless, arbitrary manipulation of freight rates by the railroads, a fact of life that every Iowan understood. Because of Edward Russell's criticisms, one rail line refused to ship coal that the *Gazette* needed to run its steam-fired printing press, forcing Russell to use his ingenuity. He hired workers to mine a local coal deposit, giving him enough fuel to run his engine until, some weeks later, the railroad lifted the embargo.[43]

Edward Russell believed that the answer to the problems presented by the railroads—rate discrimination, pooling of resources, and overcharges—was plain, old-fashioned competition. The solution that he and others sought was a competing water line, a canal, that would connect Lake Michigan to the Mississippi River and exit near Rock Island and Davenport. The 188-mile east - west line, which became known as the Hennepin Canal, would run parallel to and compete directly with the Chicago, Rock Island & Pacific Railroad line. Such a canal had been discussed for many years—a convention in 1845 endorsed the concept as did another in 1866. In 1870 a federal survey estimated that it would cost $12.5 million to build, and in 1872 President Grant asked Congress to investigate its construction. As far back as 1863, Russell's *Gazette* had begun to champion the canal cause as a cheap alternative to the railroads. Moreover, with Iowa's growing agricultural output, a secondary means of transportation was needed to supplement the railroads as well as to keep them honest.[44]

Edward Russell went beyond just writing editorials. In 1881, when his son was in Vermont, he traveled to Washington, D.C. to make the case for the Hennepin Canal to the House of Representatives' River and Harbor Committee. In May 1881 he served as secretary to and helped organize a convention in Davenport at which four hundred representatives from seven different states gathered to urge that Congress pass an appropriation for the canal. The convention made two things clear: the canal was of national, not just local, importance, and support for the canal was increasing. Russell became a member of the Hennepin Canal Commission, which sent him and others to urge editorial writers from eastern newspapers to support its construction. In 1882, after nearly seven years of intense lobbying, Congress came through with a million-dollar appropriation, which was later cut to a mere $30,000 for an official survey of a canal route. The appropriation did insure the future of the Hennepin Canal.[45]

"It was a victory that cost my father dear and in the end wrought a great change in his life," Charles Russell concluded, however. In 1882 the *Gazette*, which was not making a profit, was sold to M. M. Rutt, a lumber dealer from Atlantic, Iowa. Edward Russell left the editor's job, but was asked to return in a few months when Rutt found he could not handle the editorial side of the operation. When the company was reorganized, Edward Russell returned and took a minority block of shares in the newspaper.[46] Meanwhile, the fight for construction money for the Hennepin Canal continued, with the railroad interests, in particular, opposing an appropriation. Statistics compiled by the U.S. Army Corps of Engineers showed that when the rails had competition from a nearby water route, rail transportation costs for shippers were greatly reduced. Moreover, as a government agency pointed out, free waterways could "limit and restrain corporations." But that was exactly what the railroads did not want.[47]

In 1884, as Congress debated the Hennepin Canal, Edward Russell returned to Washington to lobby again for a final construction appropriation. While in the Capitol, he received a telegram with shocking news: the man he had left in charge of the *Gazette* had been removed as editor, Edward Russell's name had been removed from the masthead, and the newspaper had been taken over by a company that had bought out Rutt's majority shares. "The railroad and corporation interests [were] in full control of the property," his son explained. "The railroads wished to be rid of the *Gazette* and its editor as the strongest champion of the canal and took the sure way to achieve that end."[48] The Chicago, Rock Island & Pacific Railroad, through a dummy corporation, had taken over the newspaper. Edward Russell was out of a job . . . and so was his son.

Trying to determine whether the rail interests really did force out Edward Russell is difficult. Aside from the son's assertion, there is no corroboration. However, a number of factors make it believable. First, there is little doubt that 1884 was a key year in the fight against the Hennepin Canal. Lobbyists had gotten Congress to delete considerable money from the survey, but their next—and more important—challenge was to stifle money for construction. Edward Russell was loud in support of the canal, as well as a disquieting voice against growing railroad power. His obituary in the *Davenport Democrat* noted: "The name of no one man was more prominently identified with the movement known as the Hennepin canal." Describing him as the canal's key "agitator," the obituary said no one's "intensity of zeal" for the canal equaled Edward Russell's.[49] Just as Andrew Johnson found it convenient and useful to get rid of this pesky voice in 1865, so would the railroad interests in 1884. Second, the rail interests were known for pushing their weight around. Rail growth in Iowa had been phenomenal throughout the 1870s, but by the early 1880s complaints against railroad business practices—and their habit of intervening in political matters to push their own interests—had become common. As one historian of Iowa's railroads notes, they were known for their "definite and serious mischiefs." As commissions to regulate their power were emerging in Iowa, for example, the railroads began to strike back when they could. Charles Russell cited a typical railroad tactic: a hardware storeowner in Davenport who supported the canal found that his freight rates inexplicably doubled one month. When he withdrew his support of the canal his rates returned to normal.[50] When presented the opportunity to rid themselves of a vocal opponent, it is logical that the railroads would target Edward Russell.

Yet there are also reasons to question the story. One scholar believes that the canal would have actually helped the rails. Boats could more easily carry certain bulky parcels that were not profitable for the rails to transport, and the canal might actually bring more goods to points on the river where the rails would be the only available carrier. Beyond that, there were numerous other interests opposed to the canal, perhaps more so than the railroads. Finally, despite the crusading nature of his newspaper, it is possible that Edward Russell's *Gazette* was out of step with a new, emerging journalism, one less concerned with partisan politics. The *Gazette* had not been profitable under Russell, he had suffered some health setbacks, and he was stubborn and irascible. Would it not make sense to install a new editor? Whatever the answer to that question, the real point is that Charles Russell believed his father had been done in by a cabal of commercial power. Russell declared: "He had been sacrificed to the corporation interests that had attained to the arbitrary power he had long feared and tried to prevent."[51]

Once out of a job, Charles Russell wasted little time in relocating. His goal was to prepare himself a bit more before seeking a job in New York City. He headed north to Minnesota, where eventually his parents and two aunts went to live. First, in the winter of 1884, he became an editorial writer on the *St. Paul Pioneer Press;* then in early 1885 he became night editor for the *Minneapolis Tribune,* the city's leading political newspaper, which had just moved into a new eight-story building. Its owner, A. B. Nettleton, was a staunch Republican disciple who advocated a variety of reform causes. Russell's reporting caused some consternation for one source, who thanked Russell for an article he had written but complained, "I did not expect that you war [*sic*] going to publish remarks that I let drop while I was in your room."[52] He left the *Tribune* in 1886 to become managing editor of the *Minneapolis Journal* and then went to its sister publication, the *Detroit Tribune*. One observer noted that Russell was "quick to notice the pith and point of all matter coming before him, and a dull line very rarely escapes his critical eye." The editor of those newspapers, R. B. Gelatt, described Russell as "faithful, energetic, and able" and said that he was a "versatile and entertaining writer." In June 1886, as Russell prepared to leave the Midwest, Gelatt told Russell that he could understand why he would want to try the "wider field" offered in New York, adding, "Your management of our news departments has been sagacious, wide-awake, and economical, and the 'scoops' of our counterparts have been few." Gelatt concluded: "God bless you and good luck attend."[53] Charles Edward Russell was off to pursue his dream of becoming a newspaperman in New York City.

CHAPTER THREE

HAYMARKET SQUARE
TO LIZZIE BORDEN

I. EDUCATION ON MULBERRY STREET

WITH THIRTY-SEVEN DOLLARS IN HIS POCKET, the twenty-six-year-old Charles Edward Russell came to New York on June 17, 1886, finally reaching "the great city . . . the city of my dreams." Considering himself a "skilled practitioner of the art" of journalism, he fully expected to be welcomed with open arms into the New York journalism fraternity.[1] His father wrote a letter of introduction to one of the most famous editors in America, Charles A. Dana of the *New York Sun*, noting that his son was "trained to journalism from boyhood [and] he has by good use of his education, varied experience and solid abilities attained fair repute already as a newspaper man." But New York was not Iowa. The son had entered a world—and a profession—he knew little about. He mistook Governor's Island for Blackwell Island and he could not locate the entrance to the Brooklyn Bridge. New Yorkers seemed mean-spirited, the pace of life was grinding, the sights and smells were foreign, and the newspapers were different from what he knew in the Midwest. What began as a dream soon turned into "black despair." Later he recalled the "sense of isolation" that became "a stinging part of the sufferings laid upon me."[2] His friend Scotty, the tramp printer, never said how overwhelming New York could be.

Manhattan Island, then as now, was the hub of all activity. Even though the city's newspapers devoted considerable attention to Brooklyn and Queens, these outer boroughs didn't combine with New York until 1898. Manhattan was the city, and like the rest of America, it was truly a land of contrasts. The population was growing quickly as thousands of immigrants flooded neighborhoods, creating both opportunities and problems. While mansions lined Fifth Avenue and commerce flourished on Wall Street and on the bustling docks, filthy tenements and crime also dominated much of Manhattan. It was a tough, expensive city that had little in common with Davenport or Detroit. "A dollar in New York hardly seemed to last so long as a quarter in Detroit," he commented. As for the people, "Everybody with whom I came in contact seemed to take pains to be disagreeable," Russell said.[3]

Nonetheless, since Manhattan alone had fifteen dailies, Russell was confident a young reporter could easily find work. Did he want to work at one of the newspapers geared to a highbrow audience, to "gentlemen and scholars"? Or would he find more comfort in Joseph Pulitzer-style journalism wherein sensationalism and crusading sought to capture "the people?"

Russell knew the choices well. The New York newspapers, identified by their dynamic owners or editors, were famous throughout the country. James Gordon Bennett's *New York Herald*, his first choice, was the most famous—or infamous. Taking over the newspaper in the 1830s and lowering its price to one cent, Bennett created a new genre: the penny press, a newspaper whose reporters went places, covered things, and wrote in ways that no one else had. James Gordon Bennett Jr., who took over for his father by 1886, kept the paper lively, although certainly its quality was declining when Russell came to New York. The *Sun* was the place where many ambitious Midwest youths wanted to work under Dana, who was old and conservative but still formidable. For example, Indiana-born David Graham Phillips, who became Russell's good friend and eventual muckraking colleague, worked in Cincinnati and then came to the *Sun* because it was a writer's paper.

The *New York Tribune*, the *New York Post*, and the *New York Times* were similar newspapers—respectable organs of politics and refinement. Edited by E. L. Godkin, the *Post* was liberal but rather dull. Godkin, wanting little color, tried to keep crime news out of his paper. Equally dull was the *Tribune*, where Whitelaw Reid offered a Republican voice to counter Godkin. The *Times*, respected since Henry Raymond founded it in 1869, had helped smash "Boss" Tweed in the 1870s, but it was steadily going downhill, buffeted, as were all the newspapers, by the "personal journalism" of Pulitzer. Coming from St. Louis in 1883, he bought and revitalized the *New York World*. In the process, Joseph Pulitzer transformed the American press with journalism that combined sensation, reportage, political acumen, and marketing. Russell was fresh and eager, with five years of full-time newspapering behind him, but would anyone want him?

At the *Herald* he climbed three flights of stairs to reach a vestibule, rang a bell to get the attention of the newsroom, and gave his card to a young boy who asked him, "Well, whadda youse want?" The boy disappeared, then returned with a discomfiting answer: "City editor says he regrets t'say there's no vacancy." Undeterred, Russell journeyed, in succession, to the *World*, the *Sun*, the *Tribune*, all morning newspapers, only to get the same answer: there were no reporting jobs. Finally, the city editor of the *Commercial Advertiser*, a staid paper published in a ramshackle building, greeted Russell with bad news—in the summertime reporters only got fired, not hired. After failing to even get an interview at any of the city's daily newspapers, Russell was disconsolate. He concluded: "I was a failure."[4]

Broke and worried, Russell turned to freelance writing to survive, working each evening on sketches, stories, poems, and even—to his dismay—puns. His income was sparse, but his output was prodigious. Moreover, Russell began to get an education about life in New York. Its people, who at first seemed so foreign and cold, became more curious as, with a reporter's careful eye, he discovered the characters who lurked around, for example, the famous central Manhattan thoroughfare, Broadway. He labeled them "Broadway oddities"—the jolly old German who sold rubber birds, the disheveled peddler thrusting newspapers in people's faces, the Italian kids who hung around Trinity Church, the silver-haired little man with blue cape and queer hat, just returned from missionary work in India, and the detectives who watched them all, looking, he wrote, "to see what notorious criminals move in the swim."[5]

Hustling for stories forced Russell into some strange encounters. On the ferry to Hoboken, New Jersey, he ran into "a queer old colored man with a shuffling gait, [wearing] scanty white wool, [with] one eye bulged like a knot on a tree, [and] long skinny fingers." "Do you know who that is?" a ferry employee whispered to Russell. "That's a negro doctor . . . one of them things they call Voodoos." He cuts the heart out of black chickens, makes potions and powders, and then scares his patients into believing anything he wants, Russell reported. Then there was the old gravedigger from Queens, a "pleasant, companionable, philosophical fellow" who had dug 2,052 graves and could identify every one. Russell got the man to talk—"won my way to his heart," he bragged—by filling his pipe and offering a light. Digging graves was "simply a matter of business," he said. "We've got to be like doctors, coroners, policemen, and newspaper reporters."[6]

Since Manhattan was too expensive, Russell took an apartment in Brooklyn with his friend Nelson Hirsh, who had come with him from Detroit. The move was fortuitous: they found a sympathetic landlady who let the duo slide on rent payments until they could make ends meet; and Brooklyn proved to be fertile reporting ground. He found a group of garrulous women who raised birds, and another group which met weekly to play poker. The *Brooklyn Eagle* printed the stories. On a more serious note, he found dozens of households in Brooklyn where women, living alone and fearful of thieves, "huddled with terror if they hear a doorknob turned or a footstep." Russell interviewed a police sergeant, who, in a long tedious quotation, explained how the police investigate such burglaries. The *Eagle* again printed the story with a tagline at the end, "C. E. R."[7] For some reason, Russell instinctively relied on police detectives for many of his early stories. He liked to sit with the detectives—who a few years later would become his best sources—and induce them to spin yarns, which he then turned into feature articles. When a millionaire's wife was murdered, Russell used the homicide as an excuse to get veteran city detectives to talk about the "wonderful crimes" they did and didn't solve.[8] Readers must have wondered why Russell bothered with these stories. The answer was that he needed the money.

Detectives also led Russell into New York's mysterious underworld. One evening he followed a detective along a narrow street near the Brooklyn docks, through a dirty alley and down a flight of rickety stairs. "Did you ever see a 'barrel house'?" the detective asked. "Never? Come with me then, if you care to find out." In a technique Russell perfected in his muckraking magazine writing after the turn of the century, Russell led the reader on a fascinating tour of a dark and smoky tavern where drunken men smoked foul pipes, imbibed cheap liquor, and ended up clawing each other. The detail and dialogue gave New Yorkers an intimate look at one of the city's most horrid dives, far worse than what Russell had seen along the Mississippi River.[9] Equally frightening in a different way was a night Russell spent in deserted lower Manhattan in the wee hours of the morning as two men in white linens stood at the gates of Bellevue Hospital and greeted a cab that delivered a fashionably attired young man. As they opened the door, the man exited, fell to the ground, and then yelled, "Take it away! Don't you see it. It's going to bite me. There's two of them now." The man shivered on the ground as the men in white led him to the public hospital where he was a regular visitor, a victim of too much booze. The man was tied to a bed with handcuffs, after which a soothing dram was poured into his mouth. Finally, he stopped yelling and slept. "How many alcoholic patients have you had in here to-night?" he asked. "That makes thirteen . . . a fair night's work." Russell then pumped the attendants for detailed—much too detailed, in fact—information about the kinds of patients the hospital got, until suddenly an electric signal rang and they ran to the gates again to retrieve a bloodied man who had been run over by a beer wagon. The sun was rising as "another day of ghastly experience began at Bellevue Hospital," Russell concluded.[10]

Even though Russell was having some luck placing stories—including sending pieces about New York back to Detroit and Minneapolis—he was making barely enough money to get by, a fact which influenced his view of the world and his style of journalism. To earn enough money just to survive, Russell realized that he would need to find any excuse possible to come up with stories—potboilers, they were called—and he would need to write those stories at great length. A glimpse at the variety of stories he covered can be seen from an 1886 journal, which noted his paltry pay: January 2, dishonest clerks, $4; January 8, women marketing, Judge Poland, leprosy, labor ministry, $12.25; January 9, fountains, $5.50; January 16, poker players, $4.80; January 22, detectives, $5.44. For all of January he earned $32.79; in February he made $20.92.[11] In the 1880s, reporters were paid mostly on space rates—the more they wrote, the more they got paid. Consequently, some of his stories were long but downright foolish—a Brooklyn cat that danced to music; a family that chewed gum all day; a Bowery museum where snakes got baths; competitive beer drinking. He wrote forty inches (more than two columns) about how women behaved at the market, and he devoted twenty-six inches to describing stomachaches. And yet he proved himself remarkably nimble as a writer. Whether the source of his story was "the old landlady" or a "merry, round-faced, little old maid," he was consistently interesting as he let New Yorkers, in cracker-barrel fashion, tell their stories.[12] Russell also fancied himself a murder mystery writer—a fancy that served him well a few years later when he wrote about gruesome New York City killings. He churned out stories on a sensational homicide in Arkansas, on the famous Johnny Woods murder back in LeClaire, Iowa, and, inexplicably, on an 1816 killing in a small German university town.[13] He even wrote a ghost story, set in Canada, complete with a haunted house and wild tales of thievery, a piece that seemed more like fiction than journalism. In fact, it might have been fiction—at least partly. Critics of journalism were increasingly carping at the tendency of reporters in the 1880s to embrace "stories" over issues and facts. The Post's Godkin, for example, complained that the number of "honest, painstaking, scrupulous, and accurate men employed as reporters and correspondents" was lower than it should be because people were not encouraged to be honest and accurate. More important today, he lamented, is "spiciness and enterprise."[14]

Russell demonstrated both of those characteristics. His story about a doctor who fell in love with his leprosy-infected patient—"they lived in each other's arms"—befitted the sensationalism of an 1890s "yellow journal." So, too, did his story of a pretty woman with a "finely tuned form" who while having an affair discovered her husband in an adjacent room where he too was fooling around. And yet there is evidence also of an enterprise and responsibility in his work. He carefully documented with statistics the growth of drug and grocery stores, for example. In another story, showing how some things never change, he described how women abused by their husbands had their spouses arrested, then bailed them out, only to wind up again back in court, abused once more.[15] This alternating pattern—sensationalism and human interest balanced with enterprise and responsibility—would mark the rest of Russell's career in journalism. He could play to the crowd and he could deal with substance.

Being without a full-time job continued to haunt Russell. "I had often heard about men that were said to be 'out of work,' but until this experience," Russell said, "I had never sensed any part of the true meaning of the phrase." Describing himself as terrified and humiliated, Russell hung around in coffeehouses and free luncheon bars, observing a stream of idle men. Why, he asked himself, are there so many men who are idle when there is so much work to be done? He was actually reduced at one point to having twelve cents in his pocket when a check arrived from Detroit, allowing him and Hirsh to chow down their cheap but filling staple—beef and beans. One afternoon, sitting near the southern tip of Manhattan Island, Russell contemplated giving up his pursuit of work in New York. Hirsh, sour on journalism, had already done so, taking a job as a letter carrier. Russell thought he might just follow in Scotty's footsteps and ride the rails back out West. By chance, the next day, he met the one man he knew in New York newspaper circles who alerted him to a job at the *Commercial Advertiser*, an evening paper, started in 1793, a steadfast Republican organ with a circulation of only twenty-five hundred. Lincoln Steffens, who later became one of its editors, said the newspaper "looked like a wretched old street walker" and acted like a "used-up, ex-'good' governor."[16] Russell didn't care what kind of newspaper it was; he needed work, going the next day to the office at daybreak before the janitor even opened the building. He sat in the newsroom when the editor arrived; twenty minutes later he was hired, informed that the space rate was only $4.32. Even worse, he learned, if a *Commercial Advertiser* reporter went on an assignment and no story resulted, there would be no pay at all.

"Many a gallant spirit has gone down in a brave but futile attempt to fill those columns," Russell commented about the *Commercial Advertiser*'s pay scale. In the end, two things made the experience bearable for Russell—first, the editor was the estimable writer George Cary Eggleston, and, second, he was given a choice assignment to cover the Jefferson Market Courthouse.

Explaining why the forty-six-year-old Eggleston was at the *Commercial Advertiser* is difficult. After being reared on an aristocratic Virginia plantation, he had written critically acclaimed boys' stories, a novel, and his charming autobiography, *A Rebel's Recollections.* After a brief stint as a reporter, he was the literary editor of the *Post* before becoming editor-in-chief for the *Advertiser* at which he assembled a first-class staff and made the paper pay dividends by his third year. Said Eggleston: "I enjoyed my work as I suppose a man condemned to death enjoys the work of writing his confessions." What delighted him most though was in finding "cubs fresh from college" who he tutored, helping them "discover their untried abilities."[17]

Russell's chance for such discovery came on his first assignment—covering police court, which he thought meant sitting at a table, listening to dignified court proceedings, taking notes, and then writing lucid stories. Instead, he encountered the bedlam of New York's judiciary and the byproducts of its stinking slums. In most of the cases, a magistrate mumbled sotto voce and quickly as a line of miserables passed in front of his bench. Reporters crowded near the judge to hear if anything interesting might be occurring. Usually, he wrote, it went this way:

> Judge: S'lmnly swear aff'davit by you scribed 's true s' help y' God what about this case?
> Prosecutor: Solicitin' on the street.
> Judge: Officer says y' were soliciting what'v you got to say?
> Defendant: Nothing.
> Judge: Ten dollars.[18]

With the case dismissed, out on the street went the prostitute. Russell was puzzled that so many of these women reappeared each day in court. The punishment never deterred them, "and the whole thing seemed exceedingly futile and foolish." Day after day he watched as prostitutes, petty thieves, landlords, young toughs, vagrants, and saloonkeepers entered court. Their stories were rich commentary on the travails of life in New York City.[19]

Russell was putting in ten- to twelve-hour days producing stories for the paper's two editions. But he found time to further his education by wandering the Lower East Side of Manhattan, from Mulberry Street across the Bowery to the East River, and learning intimately about slum life. He was shocked, commenting, "I began to see that poverty was the condition of the majority of the people, with areas and depths of which I had never dreamed." He noted the filth, the smells, the lack of ventilation and sunlight, the numbers of people, speaking so many languages, crowded into so few rooms. The real surprise was that "not all the dwellers in that frightful region turned savage," Russell said. "It seemed glorious that any good survived."[20] The real lesson, however, was the effect the reporting had on his view of environment. Virtually all the people and cases that spilled into court were caused by the slums of New York, he came to believe. Society is so desperate to lock up people, but no one ever asks about the conditions that produce the problems. What did society expect from gang leader Danny Driscoll, whom Russell covered many times in court? He grew up in the tenements of tenement-bred parents, he lived by his guile on the streets, took a mistress when he was a teenager, went to the penitentiary, and then returned to the streets. Finally, on June 24, 1886, after making the rounds of the saloons, Driscoll got into a scrape at a bawdyhouse where his girl, Bezie, was in the midst of an argument. Driscoll shot her by mistake; she died. Two years later, Driscoll was hanged at the Tombs prison. "We had made him what he was," Russell wrote years later. "So we took our finished product and choked the life out of it and believed we had done a good job—some of us." What a "colossal irony," Russell complained. "Hanging the victims of that machinery instead of abolishing the machine."[21]

Adding to his frustrations were the limitations he began to see in reporting. The city editor assigned Russell to keep lookout for a potential train strike in Manhattan. As he sat watch, he observed a mother washing clothes in a tub of water at the top of a tenement stairway. She kept an eye on her children below, trying to ensure that they did not get hit by passing trains. "How can people live in this way?" Russell asked. Their life seemed so bleak, and when no strike materialized, Russell asked to write about the family. The city editor squelched the idea—no news in poverty. Russell wrote no story, received no pay, and lost forty cents from his train ride.[22]

When a train strike did occur in Manhattan, the editor asked Russell to produce the names and addresses of the leaders of the strike whom the paper intended to criticize. Russell visited with the wife of one of the men, a kindly and intelligent woman who explained about her husband's paltry wages. Russell sympathized, and he refused to produce the names the editor wanted. He identified with the strikers (although he did not say so) and not the owners, which was no surprise. He knew it was time to find another newspaper. Editor Eggleston had "personal magnetism, tact, good nature, and sympathy," but his newspaper, nonetheless, had served its purpose. "The only education I ever had that amounted to anything," Russell observed years later, "was when I was a police reporter on the East Side of New York. One could learn there more about life as it really was than in any formal school of cloisters and dons that ever existed." But he was ready to move on.[23]

II. A WITNESS TO EXECUTIONS

By 1887 New York journalism was headed in a new direction as a powerful force took the city by storm. That force was Joseph Pulitzer, a brilliant and eccentric Hungarian immigrant, hungry to influence politics and make a fortune. He made his mark in various ways—championing the causes of immigrants, unabashedly crusading for the underdog, muckraking the rich and famous, and leading public opinion with astute commentary on public policies. In order to do this, however, he needed the best and the brightest talent in New York.

Understanding his grace and intelligence, for example, Pulitzer stole Eggleston from the *Commercial Advertiser* and made him an editorial writer. Russell probably should have heeded Eggleston, who had found that daily journalism made him "worn, weary, and inexpressibly oppressed." Think of what it means, the sensitive Eggleston said, "to toil all day in the making of a newspaper, and to feel, when all is done that the result is utterly inadequate."[24] And to be broke at the same time, Eggleston should have noted. Pulitzer had the remedy, however: he offered Eggleston and Russell more money to join the *World*. The trade-off, of course, was anonymity. Virtually no one on the *World* was allowed to sign an article. It was Pulitzer's newspaper.

This anonymity makes tracing Russell's work difficult. He discusses only a few reporting incidents in his two years under Pulitzer, but one is worth exploring. He was a witness to the events that led up to the hanging of the four men, all political radicals, who were convicted of conspiracy in throwing a bomb in the famous Haymarket Square riot in Chicago on May 4, 1886. After the incident, Russell conducted his own careful investigation into what was one of the cataclysmic American events of the late 1800s that led to America's first "red scare."

Before the Haymarket affair, Russell had witnessed his first execution in Iowa, and he blamed himself for allowing it to happen. In the summer of 1883, Davenport was in the midst of its quietest time. News consisted of births, deaths, traveling salesmen arriving at hotels, and an occasional drunken sailor. "Nobody did anything except to eat and sleep," Russell complained. And then a murder occurred at the Heilwagner farm, eleven miles north of Davenport. When Otto Heilwagner's wife disappeared, her father-in-law, William, alone at the farm with her and known to dislike her wild ways, was accused. At his trial the Bavarian immigrant made no attempt to defend himself, answering in monosyllables, seemingly unaware of what was going on. He declared his innocence, but offered no evidence. He was convicted and sentenced to hang.

Russell, at first, looked at the case "with professional impartiality," but something about Heilwagner's demeanor convinced him of the man's innocence. He went to the Heilwagner's cell and tried to get details that might break the case. All the man would say was, "I just go weed my onions." The murder was committed in August; Heilwagner was hanged in March. His final words: "Gentlemen, I am innocent of this crime." Ten years later, the words rang true when the son, Otto, committed suicide and left a note confessing to his unfaithful wife's murder. The father had known all along and protected the son. "It was a rugged introduction for a novice to the business of crime detecting and legalized life-taking," Russell said after the first of eleven executions he witnessed in his career. The hanging "sickened" Russell and turned him into a lifelong opponent of capital punishment. Moreover, he felt, "If I had been expert at my trade I might have saved that man."[25] Russell's next experience with execution came four years later. The *World* sent him as its correspondent to Chicago, probably because as an Iowa native he was familiar with the Midwest city. Like New York, Chicago teemed with commerce and urban squalor. But while New York was a shipping center, the Lake City was a rail hub for farm products and livestock to be shipped to the rest of the nation. Chicago was also a city with thousands of industrial workers, who, treated poorly by the owners, were beginning both to rebel and organize. In fact, the decade of the 1880s was witness to one of great labor disturbances in America. The workers were upset by the growth of a small, immensely wealthy class, by the inadequacy of wages to pay for the cost of living, and by the owners' utter contempt for workers' rights, whether for an eight-hour day or for compensation for injuries or death on the job. To put it mildly, workers were restive and discontented; increasingly they listened when propagandists urged new forms of political organization—as well as methods other than the ballot box for achieving those ends.[26]

Russell encountered such a propagandist on the lakefront in Chicago one Sunday afternoon. A shabby, gaunt man with a mellow voice, Albert Parsons, the editor of a fiery labor journal, stood before a small and unenthusiastic crowd, denouncing the rich and advocating, in rather abstract terms, some sort of social revolution. Russell looked fondly at Parsons, not because of his rhetoric, but because on numerous occasions Parsons had protected reporters from angry crowds. "The reporters were often in great danger," Russell pointed out. "The feeling was bitter against the whole 'capitalistic press.'"[27] Chicago was a city awash in ideological conflict: labor versus management; workers versus police; capitalists versus an amalgam of socialists and anarchists.

It is no surprise that radicals saw Russell's newspaper, the *World*, as enemy. Even Russell later admitted that he and the rest of the press corps knew little about the differences between socialism, anarchism, and communism. He comically recalled that each time there was a threat of labor violence while he was a reporter in New York, he would be asked immediately to find dangerous socialists. Reporters always went to one German immigrant who lived in lower Manhattan. Asked about political violence, he responded with a rambling harangue, but argued forcefully for a society in which, as Russell understood it, "there would be no law, no government, no system and no work."

"And that is what you call Socialism?" asked Russell, naively.

"Socialismus? Sociliasmus? Ach, mein Gott, nein! Es ist die Anarchie!" the German exploded.

"Oh, well," replied the reporters, "same thing." Socialism and anarchism were "interchangeable terms" for reporters, Russell said.[28] Probably, in 1887, when he still considered himself a Republican, Russell didn't know the difference. He had read literature, history, and political economy, but there is no indication that he knew Marx or had studied anarchists such as Bakunin or Proudhon. "It was true," he admitted years later, "I had never read *Das Kapital* and could not have told Karl Marx from Frederick Engels if I had met them walking arm in arm up the street." Of course that was also typical of most American rebels of the time; their rebellion tended to be more homegrown than imported. But certain questions being raised in radical circles must have caught Russell's attention in Chicago. Was private property, as anarchists argued, truly the enemy? Was a social revolution to destroy the existing order necessary? Most importantly, would violence be needed in order to topple the capitalist system? Russell had no answers in 1887, and so he took more to observing the events and people who were framing the questions. He was, after all, just a reporter. "In this business," he noted, "you have very little call to determine why things happen. About all you can attend to competently is the happening."[29]

The Haymarket riot shocked the nation. As a crowd of about 1,500 listened on May 4 to speeches—including one from Parsons—in support of an eight-hour day, 180 policemen arrived and ordered the group to disband. With no warning, a dynamite bomb was hurled from the crowd toward the police and exploded. Seven policemen were killed and seventy were wounded. Russell, who was in New York when the incident occurred, recalled that "rage and blind passion seized a great part of the population." In a recap of the affair for the *World*, he wrote: "So all at once the city woke up to the danger that had been growing up in it for years. The people saw with terror that a dozen resolute men with dynamite bombs could blow up a dozen buildings and hundreds of persons in an instant. There was nothing too energetic that could be done for the protection of the city then. The police went to work with an ardor."[30] The press and public opinion quickly blamed the radical anarchists and socialists of Chicago. The police, in a fury, put out a dragnet, developed a theory of conspiracy, and arrested seven men, including Parsons. Four were eventually hanged.

It cannot be determined with certainty when Russell arrived in Chicago. In an autobiographical note, he said, simply, "covered the Anarchist troubles in Chicago for the *World.*" In a 1908 magazine article and in an identical chapter in a 1914 autobiography, he wrote in detail about the incident. A few things can be concluded from these accounts. First, he carefully studied the crime, investigation, and trial and reached conclusions that are very similar to historian Henry David, who in 1936, after an exhaustive investigation, decided that none of the alleged conspirators actually threw the bomb. David wrote, "On the basis of the reliable evidence, they must be considered innocent." After his investigation, Russell wrote: "The eight men were convicted, nominally by the jury, in reality by a misinformed public opinion resolutely bent upon having a hanging. Anything more like a lynching I have never known. . . . Blood was to have blood; I grieve to state there was but little consideration as to whose blood."[31] What is also clear, however, is that Russell never wrote anything at the time of the incident that showed his sympathies, which is odd. His memoirs paint a sympathetic portrait of some of the accused Haymarket bomb throwers who he visited regularly in prison as they awaited execution. About Parsons, he wrote, "I conceived a strong liking"; he was a "genial and attractive companion." Russell said he wasn't even sure Parsons believed in the violence he seemed to advocate. Yet, the day after his hanging, when he recapped the events, Russell painted Parsons as a wild-eyed terrorist whose "harangues" were bent on violence. Russell's reportage was caught up in the fervor of the times, and certainly matched the fever of the *World*, which said of the hangings: "Society cannot afford to let these men escape."[32] It didn't, of course.

On November 11, all of Chicago—and the nation—awaited the execution of the seven men. At 8:45 A.M. Louis Lingg avoided the noose by thrusting a bomb in his mouth and killing himself. Two others were given reprieves; the governor granted them life in prison. Four awaited death. Russell said the mood in Chicago "had become almost intolerable." As police with riot rifles swarmed all over the city, rumors circulated that some twenty-thousand anarchists were planning to assault the jail. At six in the morning two hundred reporters, including Russell, were admitted to the jail. Russell described the scene:

> From six until nigh about eleven we stood there, two hundred of us, cooped in the jailer's office, waiting with nerves played upon by more disquieting rumors than I have ever heard in a like period. So great was the nervous tension that two of the reporters, tired and experienced men, turned sick and faint. . . . In all my experience this was the only occasion on which any reporter flinched from duty, however trying; but it is hard now to understand the tremendous power of the infectional panic that had seized upon the city and had its storm center at that jail.

The men were duly executed—"four lives crushed out," Russell wrote, "according to the fashion of surviving barbarism."[33] The great question that was never asked, Russell realized years later, was: what had driven these men into an attack upon the social order? He also could have asked why neither he nor anyone else in the press asked the question. The answer is threefold: as a relatively new reporter, in fact, as one who was only writing "sidebar" or ancillary stories on the Haymarket saga, Russell didn't have the authority to speak with such a clear voice. Even editorial writers needed Pulitzer's approval. Moreover, despite his later opposition to capital punishment, Russell might have felt that the hangings had a palliative effect. A year after the executions, he returned to the various Chicago neighborhoods "where anarchy was wont to thrive. The drinking dives that used to echo every night with curses against capitalists . . . were as quiet as the grave," he found. The city, he concluded, "has been free from fear for the first time since 1877." Lastly, his timidity in voicing his own opinion in his reporting reflected what he had learned about professional comportment and journalistic expectations. "Be exactly like a doctor at a clinic," a veteran reporter had told him. "Interested in the dissection but not moved by it."[34] Could the son of a crusading editor and grandson of a fire-breathing preacher be content merely to observe? For a while he would have to be. He had a few more executions to watch before he could begin to protest.

Sing Sing prison was one of America's notorious penitentiaries. Sitting on 130 acres of land on the east bank of the Hudson River, thirty miles north of New York City, it was the repository for the city's worst criminals right from its opening in 1826. Russell knew it well from his time at the *Commercial Advertiser,* when he accompanied famous felons as they were carted off to Sing Sing. In March 1887, Russell methodically detailed the journey from Manhattan to Sing Sing of Alderman John O'Neill, who had accepted bribes in return for a his vote on a city franchise, and William J. Rourke, who was found guilty of murder. "Both took their first prison meal today. It consisted of bean soup, bread and coffee," he wrote in a story that ended with Rourke's father covering his son's face with kisses as they bade each other farewell. Given remarkable access to the inmates, Russell wrote intimate profiles of Sing Sing's prisoners.[35]

When he left the *World* in 1889 to join the *Herald* he was asked to venture once again to Sing Sing to observe an experimental new method of executing criminals: electrocution. The advent of electricity brought with it the notion that executions could be done more efficiently than hanging. "Instantaneous and painless" one magazine raved. The first New York electrocution came in 1890 at a prison in Auburn, New York, but it was controversial. The victim did not die very quickly, and his suffering may have been intense. Since part of New York's electrocution law barred reporters from observing the executions or even reporting them in detail, no one was quite sure what had happened. An editorial in the *Times* conceded that the new method had flaws, "but when the facts are sifted down it appears pretty clear that execution by electricity is altogether feasible and every way preferable to hanging." The real problem, the *Times* argued, is that by excluding the press, a misimpression develops about what really happens in the execution chamber.[36]

Nonetheless, the state stuck to the order barring reporters from the death scene. On July 8, 1891, four more men were executed by electrocution at Sing Sing. When the newspapers printed varying and critical accounts about how the deaths took place they were severely castigated. Some said the criticism was jeopardizing the electrocution experiment. On December 8, when wifemurderer Martin Loppy was electrocuted, the infuriated New York governor stationed state police on highways with orders to kill any newsman who even tried to get near Sing Sing. But again, the stories that followed the murder painted a horrid picture. Four times the electric current had to be applied before Loppy died.

Finally, in the winter of 1892, the "veil of stupid secrecy," as Russell called it, was lifted. A few reporters, including Russell, were chosen to join a group of nineteen witnesses, mostly doctors, as Charles McElvaine, a twenty-three-year-old Brooklyn man, was led to what the *Times* labeled as Sing Sing's "perfect execution plant." After a foiled robbery, McElvaine, then nineteen, had repeatedly stabbed a grocery store owner as the his horrified wife watched. His conviction and sentencing were swift. By 11:00 A.M. on February 9, the witnesses stood around the large oak execution chair. Russell described the scene. "The place was very still now . . . breathlessly still," he wrote. McElvaine entered. His sallow face had "a brutal, cruel look" and he appeared "half human" as he blew a kiss to the onlookers. "His gaze encountered the stony, unsympathetic stare of the witnesses," Russell said. With his hands shackled, McElvaine declared, "Forgive my sins. Let her go!" As the electrical charge surged, his body convulsed, his teeth shone, and his face contorted. After fifty seconds, he went limp. Then McElvaine startled all when he wheezed, coughed, and gasped. The switch went back on again for thirty-eight seconds, until purple spots appeared on the dead man's head. It was over. Russell looked at one of the other reporters, Arthur Brisbane, who became a famous editor for both Pulitzer and William Randolph Hearst, and saw that his usually ruddy face turned a greenish white. "He was visibly shaking," Russell saw. Brisbane stayed through the electrocution but left before the autopsy, sick to his stomach.[37] Russell seemed unmoved by what he had witnessed. The lead of his story was clinical:

> With the purely animal courage which had so long sustained him fast ebbing away and the innate coward in him struggling to his lips in a wavering cry, Murderer Charles McElvaine sat in the execution chair at Sing Sing yesterday morning. In the next breath, in a function of a second, his life as a conscious being had ceased. . . . The electrical shock had passed through him and robbed out his miserable existence with merciful and unerring swiftness.

Showing again no sign of opposition to capital punishment, Russell then praised the new method as a "success" and ended his story on a surprisingly personal note. "I have seen an electrocution. It is not as painful a thing to see as a hanging, even when it is as unfortunate in some of its features as this one was yesterday."[38]

Russell was even more unequivocal eight weeks later when he watched a second electrocution at Sing Sing, this time of Italian immigrant Joseph Cotto, whom he labeled "an abject coward." Cotto stabbed a companion twelve times in the back as they stole vegetables in Brooklyn, then tried to blame his girlfriend. His execution was particularly important for the electrocution experiment. If it failed, the legislature was threatening to return to hangings. Ten reporters witnessed the death which the *Herald* splashed across the top of its first news page ("Execution of Murderer Cotto") along side a four-column drawing of Cotto in the electric chair. Russell wrote a dramatic, detailed description of the death—the ashen gray face, the trembling lips, the saliva flying from Cotto's mouth at the moment of death. After interviewing many of the doctors present, Russell concluded: "The new method was humane, instantaneous and from the point of view of civilization immeasurably an advance over hanging." The following day he visited Cotto's mistress, who declared: "He was a bad man." Many years later, Russell would become a vice president of the

American League to Abolish Capital Punishment, calling it a "strange relic of darkness." But if he had any regrets about the executions he had witnessed, it could not be found in Russell's news coverage of executions.[39]

III. THE ACE DETECTIVE

As a teenager growing up in Davenport, Iowa, Russell was fond of reading the New York newspapers that came into town. He especially liked it when the reporters played detective and wrote murder-mystery stories. When a ghastly crime was committed in New York, both the police and the press would hunt for the murderer. "I was fond of imagining myself to be Amos Cummings or some other famous New York reporter," Russell said. Cummings was a well-known murder-mystery feature writer for the *Sun* in the 1870s. In the Heilwagner murder case, Russell tried his hand at sleuthing, searching fruitlessly for clues that might have vindicated the old German accused of murdering his daughter-in-law. "Here was a mystery ready . . . for the solving, and I did not know what to do with it," he lamented.[40] The city reporters undoubtedly would have known what to do. Oddly, when he came to New York the desire to make his name as a detective-writer burned in Russell more than a passion for social justice or reform issues. Of course, his detective work helped changed that perspective—and helped train him as an investigator. In short, the detective phase that was to come helped further his reportorial and social education.

His first chance came in 1887 when an unidentified woman was found murdered in Manhattan. Despite a tentative identification of one Ana Larsen, no clues could be found as to the woman's background. Russell doggedly pursued various sources until a trail led to Rahway, New Jersey, where he found the real Ana Larsen very much alive. "She was very reluctant to say anything for publication," Russell told the *World*'s readers, but Russell bragged that his "persistent questioning" retrieved facts that even the New York City police did not have. In an example of classic Pulitzer self-promotion, Russell and the *World* took full credit for their "unremitting" effort, for not sparing "labor or expense," and, of course, for breaking open the case. Russell's wish for detective fame was coming true.[41]

By 1889 the *Herald* was keeping him busy with various assignments, sometimes rather risky ones. Once he disguised himself as a coal heaver on a canal boat. The toughs he encountered were far worse than those of the Brooklyn "barrel house." The region was "so given over to savagery and abandoned by the forces of law and government," Russell recalled, "that a parallel for it can hardly be found in a civilized society." Working undercover, Russell listened to unrestrained conversations about various crimes. When he used those conversations to write about one particularly atrocious assault, the police followed with an arrest for murder.[42]

Russell was more comfortable and much safer when he played the reporting game undisguised. For example, he earned more plaudits for his personal enterprise—the characteristic that later distinguished the muckraking journalists—in tracking down the fate of the steamer *Danmark* which was lost at sea with seven hundred passengers. Trying to get information from a ship captain, he almost drowned in a rowboat in New York's harbor. Eventually he got the story in more detail than any other reporter. Of course, the *Danmark* story would seem a trifling matter when, two months later, he went to Johnstown to write about the great flood disaster.[43]

In the process of investigating puzzling and intricate mysteries, Russell became a famous New York newspaperman. By 1890 he was heralded as one of the ten best reporters in America. A magazine, writing about a murder Russell was investigating, referred to him and Jacob Riis as "brilliant New York newspaper men." Part of that fame came from his persistent detective work, which revealed the qualities that distinguished his later muckraking work: he was an extremely hard worker, constantly digging for new information; he was able to charm and beguile sources from all walks of life into talking to him; he was an astute observer of people, carefully watching their mannerisms and speech patterns, for example, to get their measure and determine their credibility; and he had a facile mind that was able to ask countless questions and pose all sorts of theories as facts emerged in an ongoing story. One more thing: he knew how to milk a story for all it was worth. "There was a chance to drag out a story from almost any event," he once commented.[44]

Aside from learning the ways of the police, Russell's reporting also introduced him to life in New York's dreariest and most dangerous neighborhoods. A murder in a dirty Lower East Side hotel, mostly known as a hangout for drunken sailors and prostitutes, particularly drew his attention. In a crime "far more shocking and more mysterious than all the rest," he told his New Yorker readers, a young woman had her throat cut and her intestines removed, with the murderer then taking away the entrails. Russell described "this horrible thing" in some detail, then cornered Chief Detective Byrnes, with whom he had worked in the Ruttinger case: "Do you think it is Jack the Ripper?" he asked, referring to the infamous London killer then on the loose. "I decline to say," Byrnes replied, heightening the drama.[45] Over the next few days, police focused instead on a mysterious Dutchman as the suspect. But what was most interesting about Russell's reportage was his writing about the neighborhood where the murder took place, an area he knew well from his days at the *Commercial Advertiser*. With little news available about the suspect, Russell suddenly became more of a sociologist than a newsman. He wrote: "The whole locality is suggestive of crime and fairly bristles with vice in its most hideous mien. Within a minute walk [of the crime scene] are scores of dives given up to deeds and scenes so foul that their description would be impossible, and even if narrated the narrative would be regarded as incredible." He proceeded to describe some of the "foul nests of iniquity" where women lay in wait for men, where in Blind Men's Alley men and women "flock together and live in horrible squalor." He seemed almost overcome by the sordid scene. "Their wretchedness is of a character which words cannot do justice, and the only curcease of misery that ever comes to them is when they become insensible from drinking stale beer."[46] No wonder, he wrote, the crime was committed here, in a district that has put more criminals in the state's prisons than any other in the state. One could almost sense that Russell the detective was seeing clues and patterns that were leading him to a larger field of study. The murders were part of a social pattern, or were, at the least, related to horrid social conditions. One person may have died from "Jack the Ripper"'s fiendish knife but every day thousands were dying slow deaths from ignored conditions. One more murder mystery—his last and one of America's most infamous—confirmed Russell's growing suspicions.

"The most remarkable murder New England has ever known." That was how Russell described what he found on August 6, 1892 in Fall River, Massachusetts. Two days before, Andrew J. Borden, a wealthy retired undertaker, and his second wife, Abbie, were hacked to death in their two-story clapboard house. Abbie was struck nineteen times with an ax, mostly on her head, which was chopped to pieces. Andrew Borden was killed with ax blows to the head while he slept in a downstairs room. Blood was splattered all over walls and doors of both rooms. All of New England was abuzz at this brutal slaying in a town that was the largest cotton-mill center in the United States. Reporters from nearby Boston and New York were rushed to the crime scene. The *Herald*, of course, turned to Russell, not only to cover the investigation but to solve the puzzle of who had committed the crime.[47]

Russell filled three full columns of the *Herald* on Sunday, August 7. He recounted how the police searched the Borden house for the murder weapon—which was never found—and for other clues as to how someone could have entered the house with a maid present, killed the elderly Bordens, and then fled without notice. Russell immediately sought a motive. "Who would profit by Borden's death?" he asked the family attorney. No one, he replied, since Andrew Borden had a will that left a natural distribution of his considerable estate. The attorney then shook his head and told Russell: "I have read many cases in the books, the newspapers, and in fiction . . . and I never heard of a case like this. A most outrageous, brutal crime, perpetrated in midday in an open house on a prominent thoroughfare and absolutely motiveless."[48]

On Day Two of his coverage, declaring that "the case is no doubt pretty dark," Russell carefully—and quite accurately—recreated the events around the murder. He began to question the story of the thirty-two-year-old Lizzie, who said she had gone to a barn to retrieve fishing tackle when the murder had taken place. Russell's final paragraph noted ominously, "There is every reason to believe that members of the family are directly accountable for the death of the two victims." The following day police mistakenly dropped a box filled with axes taken from the Borden house while reporters watched; but none had blood on them.

While Russell carefully reported various emerging theories and rumors, his most telling sentence further implicated Lizzie. "The Bordens are a hot-blooded race. To be 'as fiery as a Borden' is an old byword in Fall River." That was a legend, however, that historians did not confirm.[49] As police gathered evidence and as the local press urged the police to charge Lizzie, Russell watched her carefully and described a "grim and self-composed woman" who revealed little to the public. As she emerged from a closed-door coroner's inquest, Russell said she was drawn and anxious. As soon as she spotted a knot of waiting reporters, however, she changed. "You could see the very muscles move in her face as she composed her expression to read haughty indifference. . . . all traces of emotion disappeared." Was this the face of a cool, calculating murderer? Russell seemed to think so, as did the police who charged her with the murder.

The story of Lizzie Borden's trial (which Russell did not cover) and her eventual acquittal has become "a part of American folklore, a legend celebrated in verse, song, drama, ballet and literature." For Russell, however, the month he spent in this industrial city with eighty thousand residents was important because it considerably furthered his social education. When the coroner's inquest went behind closed doors and Russell had little to report, he began to wander about Fall River. "It was my first good opportunity to observe deliberately the inside of a mill town," he later recalled. He was startled. "The results seemed wholly at variance with my previous ideas as to the grandeur and glory of industrial development."[50]

Russell found that the mill workers lived in squalid quarters and poverty. Sanitation was poor; the rooms were dark and ill smelling. It was worse, in many ways, than what he had found in the tenements of the Lower East Side of

Manhattan; he called it "a kind of blackness. . . . a ghastly train of ruined lives."
A friend took him one Sunday to visit a mill worker and his family of six who
lived in two rooms. The man made $7 a week; his two oldest children made $1
and $2.50. Both had left school and were likely to spend the rest of their days in
the mills. One of the boys, thirteen years old, was "prematurely old, hopelessly
dull, obviously inert," Russell found. He chewed tobacco and had begun to
stoop like his father. There were hundreds of boys like him. "They had been
born in the mills; their world was circumscribed by the mills; they expected to
die in the mills."

Russell couldn't help contrasting the lovely homes of the mill owners he
had seen on the main streets with the tenements of the back streets. "Standing
that day in Fall River," he said, "I fell into a train of thought, obvious enough,
and yet, if I may make the confession, quite new to me." How could the disparity in lives be justified? Why should the mill owner, who barely works, live in
luxury while the worker suffers so? It was essentially the same question he had
first asked in St. Johnsbury about Jim Dow and the Fairbanks family. Increasingly, "it was impossible to avoid that question," Russell found.[51] The Lizzie
Borden murder had taken on a different meaning for him. Some years later he
wrote:

> I had been sent to Fall River to investigate a murder. It suddenly struck me as
> strange that nobody ever seemed to investigate this other kind of murder
> going slowly on before me. The murder I had been sent to investigate had
> been done with a hatchet; death had been instantaneous. It suddenly occurred
> to me that of the two methods slaughter with the hatchet was the more merci-
> ful. Many persons wished to hang the perpetrators of the murder with the
> hatchet. How did it happen that no one wanted to arrest or prosecute the per-
> petrators of the murders in these tenements?[52]

After the Borden murder episode, Russell spent two more years reporting before he became an editor. But by 1892 reporting had served its major purpose;
certain issues were coming clearly into focus. And what he had concluded was
that the best of what he saw, "for instruction and things to think about," was not
Fifth Avenue but Mulberry Street. His interest was in the mill workers' lives,
not in the mansions of the mill owners. The only question was, when would he
feel free to say or do something about what journalism had taught him.[53]

CHAPTER FOUR

CRUSADING AGAINST THE BOSSES

I. POLITICS UP CLOSE

THE EDUCATION OF CHARLES EDWARD RUSSELL was not confined to what he learned as he prowled the streets of New York City. While he made his name as an ace reporter-detective, he also began to get choice assignments to cover politics. His first big one came in the spring of 1892 when the *New York Herald* sent him to Minneapolis to cover the Republican National Convention as its chief correspondent. It was a bittersweet homecoming. "After the floods in the South and West, the heat in Washington, the mud in New York and the gloom and murkiness in Chicago," Russell said, " the clean streets and wide open hospitality [of Minneapolis] is most welcome."[1] But Minneapolis—where two aunts now lived—brought sad memories also. A year earlier he had he returned to the city sadly to attend the funeral of his father, who was only fifty-eight years old when he died. In his final days Edward Russell longed to be back in Davenport, fighting against the "interests" with his beloved *Davenport Gazette*. "At times," Edward Russell wrote a friend, "I have wished myself again in Iowa, and there so situated as to be able to devote labor and voice to continuous advocacy of . . . real reform."[2] But his spirit had likely been crushed over the battles he had fought and lost. As his son gazed at the casket, he recalled his father's victories but also the bitter losses and betrayals that had culminated in his father's newspaper being taken away.

One of Edward Russell's earlier losses, in fact, gave the son his first glimpse at the inner and grimy working of politics, which perhaps should have warned him to be wary. In 1876, when Charles was sixteen, his father was at the most active—and popular—stage of his career. The Scott County Republican Convention unanimously nominated him to be the district's choice for representative to Congress. He stood a good chance of winning in what was largely a Republican area. But at the last minute, after the nomination was his, the county Republican leader decided that he wanted the nomination, which Charles Russell labeled as a "betrayal." Edward Russell "felt the treachery deeply," his son said, but he did not fight the party leader's decision. In fact, he went along with the request and ceded the vote to his opponent. He then became the chairman of the new candidate's campaign, helping elect him to Congress. The son learned a lesson about politics, however: it was a dirty business that was ruled by money and the lust for personal power and prestige. Rarely, Russell sadly began to learn, was politics solely or even mostly about important issues.[3]

Ironically, William Russell and William Rutledge, Charles Russell's grandfathers, had come to the United States from England not only because they thought America offered opportunity but more importantly because they admired the democratic ideals for which America stood. Like so many immigrants of the 1830s, they envisioned egalitarianism, not caste; they saw political institutions that reflected the people's desires and needs, not those of royalty. Their grandson grew up believing in those same ideals. However, what Russell eventually observed first-hand—from his father's bitter experience with organizational politics to backroom vote buying and horse-trading at national political conventions—turned his idealism, at least about conventional politics, to cynicism. While he did spearhead a significant but momentary crusading triumph over "boss" rule in New York, Russell's early journalistic experience, as this chapter will show, also nurtured seeds of discontent and motivated him to explore ethical alternatives to the dirty politics that his reporting found.

Russell learned early on in his newspaper career that money was a dominant factor in politics. Both political parties, he believed, used campaign contributions from business interests to buy votes of delegates at nominating conventions and of voters on election day. "The whole thing was rotten and produced a huge crop of still worse rottenness," he declared.[4] His first clear view of this came in 1883 when, as a reporter for the *Gazette*, he covered the Iowa State Democratic Party convention.

Russell had become friendly with James Baird Weaver, an Iowan who had been the Greenback Party's presidential candidate in 1880, who served three terms in Congress, and who became the Populist Party's presidential candidate in 1892. Two things made Weaver attractive to Russell: he thought the railroads were the greatest menace to American democracy, and he felt that a small group of bankers were controlling the country's finances. It is no wonder that he became the Populist Party's presidential candidate, since its platform sought to nationalize the railroads and closely regulate the banks. Weaver seemed to cast a spell over Russell. "He never walked down the street or entered a public assembly anywhere without instantly drawing all eyes," Russell recalled admiringly years after he covered Weaver while he served in Congress. Russell liked the fact that Wall Street loathed Weaver, that respected publications called him vile names, and that Weaver denounced the governing class. He was Russell's kind of guy: a dissenter. They sat together at the 1883 Iowa convention and the fifty-three-year-old Weaver tutored the twenty-three-year-old Russell on the emerging ways of politics. Look at the convention floor, he said. The most active participants on the floor were the lobbyists from the railroad companies and the lawyers from the business interests. At one point he showed Russell fourteen railroad lobbyists as they worked the delegates; none of them had ever before taken any interest in conventions. But, Weaver pointed out, they had learned it was cheaper to manipulate a convention than to buy an election.[5]

Russell's growing cynicism about bourgeois politics can be glimpsed also in some of his reporting when he first came to New York in 1886. In an article he sent to the *Detroit Tribune* he reported that financier August Belmont had to pay more than $150,000 to re-elect his son to Congress. The people "got an idea that they would like to have a man in Congress instead of a manikin [*sic*]," he wrote. So Belmont had to buy the election. He told also of a clerk who was dismissed from his $15,000-a-year New York City Health Department job. Why? "He was lacking in one great essential to succeed in New York politics— dishonesty. So the machine men tossed him overboard." He cast a similar theme in a story on a clerk who stole money from his father's department store. "It nearly broke his father's heart," Russell reported. "What did he do with him, deprive him of pocket money for a year? Oh, no, he got him elected to the legislature."[6]

Russell covered his first national political convention in 1888 when the Republicans met in Chicago where Russell played a minor role as one of the *New York World*'s correspondent. "You will see a grand and impressive sight," he was told by a friend, "representatives of the nation assembled to select the nation's ruler." However, Russell only saw political machinations that were unconnected to any issues. All that mattered, in the end, was what the manufacturing interests wanted. Russell acted mostly as a legman for Ballard Smith, a dashing and arrogant Dartmouth graduate who ran the show for the *World*, which commandeered a suite of rooms in the swanky Richeleu Hotel. In the adjacent suite was Chauncey Depew, the New York senator who was friendly with the *World* and close with Smith. The doors between the suites were always open. Russell was surprised. "The operations of the machine that are rarely seen were performed before our eyes," he found.[7]

Russell had two tasks at the convention—to run errands for Smith and to keep tabs on the Iowa delegation. Since he was from Iowa, he knew the leaders of that state's delegation. In fact, Iowa's Senator Allison was one of his father's friends and one of the six contenders for the nomination. Russell stuck close to the Iowa leaders as jockeying over whether to choose Allison, James G. Blaine, John Sherman, Benjamin Harrison, or Chauncey Depew took place behind the scenes. The party's leaders did not impress Russell. "I have never seen a more pliable exhibition of fumbling indecision and backing and filling. I think it is a safe assertion," he concluded, "that all great men look wonderfully small at close range."[8]

While the leaders huddled, a movement began to draft the reluctant Blaine, a former U.S. Senator and Secretary of State who had narrowly lost the nomination in 1876 but who was the nominee in 1884. "The Plumed Knight," as he was called, lost the 1884 election when the "rum, Romanism and rebellion" epithet used to characterize the Democrats backfired. In the spring of 1888 Blaine had sent a letter to the party leaders, saying he was not a candidate under any circumstances. Nonetheless, many at the convention continued to work for him. Russell received a tip that Blaine's two sons were secretly working against their father. He told Smith, who was astonished. Russell sought out Walker Blaine, whom he knew well. The son was clearly uncomfortable discussing his father's nomination. Finally, Russell confronted Walker with what he had heard; the son was embarrassed. Russell talked off the record with him and they decided what parts of the conversation could be used. Walker Blaine admitted that the family was opposed to the father's nomination because it would hurt his health. Russell did not believe him. Only after the convention did Smith tell Russell the real reason for the family's opposition was Mrs. Blaine's fear of a repeat of 1884, when newspapers alleged that Blaine's eldest son was fathered before his parents were married. That turned out to be false. "Other matters were debated still more personal and private," Russell recalled.[9] Russell was surprised—and offended—that politics was in the gutter.

Russell found the convention eye-opening in other ways. The leaders and the business interests made any decision that mattered at the convention behind the scenes, Russell found. "Every reporter that has followed politics must know all about it." And yet no one wrote about it. A look at the *World*'s coverage of the convention confirms this. Ballard Smith's stories follow the public shifts of the convention and the nomination of Harrison, but none of the back-room jockeying that he and Russell were privy to was included in their reporting.[10] But in these, his early years of reporting, Russell played the game without rocking the boat.

II. THE BUYING OF THE PRESIDENCY

Russell got his chance to use all that he had thus far learned about politics when he returned to Minneapolis in 1892.[11] By all rights, it should have been a quiet convention. Benjamin Harrison had defeated President Grover Cleveland for the presidency in 1888 and was likely to be the GOP nominee again. But Russell and the press corps found intrigue—and more than a bit of political and financial mischief. After losing the nomination to Harrison in 1888, James G. Blaine was named Secretary of State; at the age of fifty eight his days as a presidential aspirant seemingly over. But his four years in the Harrison cabinet were disquieting, marked by personal tragedy and strained relations with the president. Soon after joining the cabinet, Blaine asked the president to appoint his son, Walker, who was his father's most trusted aide, as Assistant Secretary of State. Harrison refused, apparently fearing that a Blaine faction might form to oppose his policies.[12] Two years later, Walker Blaine died of pneumonia. A month later, after coming to Washington for her older brother's funeral, Alice Blaine also died, devastating the family. But Blaine continued his work as Secretary of State, even though his health had suffered greatly. Mrs. Blaine, for her part, grew more and more angry with the president, her pique increased by Harrison's refusal to give a government job to her son-in-law. Despite his public disavowals, whispers began that Blaine might oppose Harrison for the nomination of 1892.[13]

Thus, when Blaine came to New York, ostensibly to visit a doctor just two weeks before the Republican convention, Russell was waiting for him at the train station. Blaine exited his train, "slowly and carefully like a man conscious of an infirmity," Russell told the *Herald*'s readers. He seemed in "excellent spirits," but Russell observed that "he had lost the old imperiousness of manner." Russell asked for an interview and Blaine declined, saying he was tired from the long journey. But Russell cajoled him into answering a few gentle questions. All he would concede about his trip, despite rumors that he had come to New York to consult with party leaders opposed to Harrison, was, "It has no connection with any public affair—not with politics, either." No one believed Blaine, however. In the column next to Russell's story the *Herald* printed a headline declaring, "Blaine Gets Nearer to the Nomination." The story called his nomination in Minneapolis "inevitable."[14]

The following day Russell and nearly two dozen other correspondents met with Blaine. He stood on one side of a table, facing the reporters who were shocked at his appearance. His "death-like pallor," Russell found, made the room "depressing and funereal." Yet Blaine swore that his health was "very good indeed." And, he said, he had come to New York with no thought about seeking the nomination for the presidency. Both statements were complete lies and Russell knew it. "His health had been bad and growing worse. His malady was incurable and he knew it," Russell recalled years later. As for seeking the nomination, Russell knew Blaine was "infected with the presidential fever . . . [it] never leaves the victim while the victim lives."[15] Russell wrote little about the true nature of Blaine's health, however, going so far as to quote sources that declared, "There will be no trouble about his health." Eight months after the convention, Blaine died. But Russell did debunk Blaine's declaration that he wasn't interested in the presidency. After leaving the group interview with Blaine, Russell met an acquaintance from his days as a reporter in Chicago. The source, whom he did not identify, had just met with the powerful former New York Senator Thomas C. Platt, who had become an implacable foe of Harrison and a leader of what Russell labeled the "Blaine boom." The source divulged what had occurred at the meeting and Russell was able to write the next day: "James G. Blaine will accept the republican [sic] nomination for the President if it is offered to him." Citing a source "very close to Mr. Blaine himself," Russell declared, "The Blaine blood is up."[16] He then detailed the antagonisms that had developed between Blaine and Harrison and painted an optimistic picture of his chances at the upcoming convention.

The following day Platt gave Russell a rare and candid interview in which he extolled some of President Harrison's policies but concluded, nonetheless, that he could not hold the Republican Party together in the upcoming election and that another man was needed. The office was not his "private property," Platt declared. What Russell apparently didn't know—and didn't write—when he gave Platt so much space in the *Herald* was that Platt and Pennsylvania boss Matthew Quay were working behind the scenes to oust Harrison. They were angry at his administration because they felt Harrison had snubbed them in giving out patronage jobs. Platt thus was using Russell to grind his political ax, although it gave Russell a juicy story for the *Herald*'s front page.[17]

So off Russell went to Minneapolis to cover a convention that he predicted would be "the bitterest fight that has been seen in a national convention since 1880 and the days of the 'Old Guard.'"[18] Russell's ten days of coverage displayed again his strength as a writer and a reporter: he spun a dramatic story about the Secretary of State challenging the President of the

United States, while at the same time getting behind the scenes to reveal the inner dirty workings of the political machines behind the candidates. Unlike 1888, when Russell was a cub reporter, he had the authority to muckrake a bit at this convention.

As soon as he arrived in Minneapolis on June 3, Russell sounded out all the leaders of the Republican Party and began his first day's story with: "Black clouds will hover over the convention. All eyes are watching the gathering storm. It is coming." The cloud burst the next day when Blaine formally announced his resignation from the cabinet. It was unclear if it had been forced or voluntary, although a Blaine biographer concluded that Blaine, not Harrison, had made the choice. For his part, Russell simply reported that the Blaine resignation let loose a "magical" force in Minneapolis. "Every Blaine man in the city was swinging his hat and thanking God," Russell wrote. From that point on, the race was on between Harrison and Blaine. "It is now Blaine and chaos, with Harrison doubly confounded," Russell wrote as he observed how the two sides began their maneuvering to round up votes.[19]

Russell straddled two lines in his reporting, lines that mirrored his mixed emotions about the political process then unfolding. On the one hand, he took it seriously as an important democratic process. He stayed in close touch with the party leaders of various state delegations, he made careful head counts to determine which candidate seemed to be ahead in the balloting, and he offered sage political commentary on the strengths and weaknesses of Harrison and Blaine. But he also seemed angry at the methods that were being used to garner the nomination. Having covered the 1888 convention, Russell had a basis for comparison. "Many of the actors were the same," Russell found, "but the situation was now very different." In 1888 Russell found that manufacturers—what he called the "Protected Interests"—controlled the convention. By 1892 Russell concluded that many of those interests had combined into the "trusts" that he and the other muckrakers would attack so thoroughly after the turn of the century. And the combinations had largely decided that Grover Cleveland, the Democrat and former president, would be their candidate. Thus, they had little interest in the Republican convention, which, Russell found, simply became "a battleground of jealous and warring leaders."[20]

Those leaders had money to spend, however, and they used it to bribe delegates. By the fourth day of the convention, Russell told the *Herald*'s readers that "plotting, persuasion, intrigue, bull dozing and supplication" were dominating the nomination process. The Southern delegates, in particular, Russell found, were the ones being wooed, "pulled and hauled from one camp to another."[21] The black delegates from the South were the focus of the most attention. "I cannot say that any of the downtrodden colored brethren of the South have been bribed to-day," Russell reported on June 7, but he did find that they were being paid $400 by both sides for tickets that allowed them entry to the convention floor.

A day later Russell became even bolder in making his bribery charges. "Both sides are openly engaged in buying up these votes," he alleged. As much as $1,200 was being paid certain black Southern delegates, he wrote in a passage in a June 8 story.[22] Russell then used some of his own enterprise to confirm the bribery by going undercover. He put on the badge of a New York alternate and went one afternoon among the black delegates. Believing that he was closely affiliated with Platt of New York, the delegates offered Russell their votes for anywhere from $100 to $300. "The thing was done on the street corners as if it were as legitimate as buying apples," he recalled later in a memoir. In his memoir, Russell cited only Harrison's forces as guilty of bribery. Writing for the *Herald* in 1892, however, he blamed both sides. He wrote that it was "humiliating" that Harrison and Blaine "felt obliged to resort to bribery and all sorts of political expediencies." In fact, he charged that the Blaine forces "far outclass their adversaries" in the bribery game. A Blaine biographer, writing one year after the convention, concurred with Russell's reporting, saying that the Blaine forces used "all the arts and machinery within their control to carry their object."[23]

On the day before Harrison finally won the nomination, Russell expressed his disappointment with the convention. "The white plumes still flaunt," he wrote about Blaine, "but their feathers are bedraggled. The big hat is still waved, but its fur is ruffled and its crown indented." With the "scandalous use of money" so prevalent, Russell wondered, might it not make sense for the Republicans to turn to a third candidate, perhaps William McKinley of Ohio, who had been untainted by the corruption? If not, he predicted, "the great party of moral ideas will be defeated at the polls," which it was.[24] But Russell was a voice in the wilderness; McKinley's time would not come for four more years. Harrison was nominated easily on June 10. Russell left Minneapolis having learned another bitter lesson about conventional politics; it was dirty indeed. He turned next to the Democratic Party convention that would assemble in ten days in Chicago.

No liquor was served at the Minneapolis convention, irking Russell and his staff. But in Chicago the liquor was plentiful, and the reporters needed it to cope with the convention's problems. Unexpected construction forced the *Herald*'s reporting team out of its planned quarters and into an unfinished hotel. Then, one of Russell's top reporters fell ill and left him short-staffed. And the temporary building that had been constructed just for the convention, nicknamed the "wigwam," was so flimsy that it leaked and shook in the wind. Russell blamed "a gang of greedy speculators" for the shoddy construction. All they wanted, he said, was to get twenty-two thousand paying spectators into the building in order "to establish a new record in quick fortune making." Complicating matters, the summer weather in Chicago was violent. "The rain fell in a way I have never witnessed outside the tropics, the lightning was sharp, the thunder terrific . . . the air hot, heavy and depressing," Russell said.[25]

As for the political situation, Russell found it "exciting and puzzling," but in reality there was little of the personal drama of the kind that pitted a president against a cabinet member. Grover Cleveland was clearly the front runner for the nomination, with the largest number of delegates by far, but he seemed not to have enough votes to win on the first ballot. His managers feared that if he failed on the first ballot, another candidate could emerge. The only viable challenger was former New York Governor David B. Hill, whose alliance with New York City's Tammany Hall Democrats had the potential to thwart his fellow New Yorker, Cleveland. If the Hill-Tammany block could combine with the free silverites who opposed Cleveland, the convention might yet provide some sizzle for the press.

Perhaps the most exciting—and perilous—moment of the convention came not from political intrigue, but from the "wigwam." On June 21, as the Cleveland forces sought their margin of victory, a fierce storm struck Chicago. Rain leaked into the building, and the press corps actually sat in its seats with umbrellas. "The chances of a terrible disaster were too plain for the most careless to ignore," Russell remarked. At about four o'clock, just as New York's governor moved from his seat to consult a delegate, a huge electric light fell on the spot where he was sitting. It would have killed him instantly. The loud crash sent the already nervous audience of twenty-two thousand into a panic. Thousands sprang for the exits, which became choked and impassable. The reporters' tables were overrun, and Russell found himself lying on the floor "crushed beneath the heels of a frantic mob." He thought he would die: "To tell the truth, I gave myself up for lost," Russell said. But mysteriously the panic subsided when the crowd realized there was no real danger. All Russell saw around him were ashen faces. "My own, no doubt, [was] as white as any," he recalled.[26]

The rest of the convention was largely a bore. "Nobody wanted to hear most of the tiresome splutterers" who gave speeches, Russell said. The only interesting occurrence was behind the scenes, where Cleveland's chief lieutenant, William C. Whitney, a former Secretary of the Navy who had made his fortune by assembling a railroad empire in New York City, was cajoling delegates to join the former president's bandwagon. Russell was greatly impressed by Whitney's magnetism. Russell watched as, day after day, state delegation after delegation was escorted in to see Whitney. He talked to the delegates "plainly, man-to-man and on the level. No political hyprocisy . . . no political cunning."[27] Then, each evening, Whitney met with the reporters and spoke openly about his meetings. When Russell sought to confirm what Whitney had told the reporters, he always found he was telling the truth. All the newspapermen, Russell included, grew to respect Whitney, who soon piled up the votes Cleveland needed to lock up the nomination on the first ballot.[28]

Still, Russell wondered—but not in print—how delegations that were so firmly opposed to Cleveland were magically transformed by Whitney. "As to the logic that had persuaded them of their previous errors I may say that some of us entertained suspicions, but we never could verify them," Russell said. His suspicion was that Whitney was using money to win over delegates. Not the kind of bribery he had seen in Minneapolis, however, but the backroom brand of money that the "gigantic and overshadowing influence" of financiers who supported Cleveland could promise. Russell felt that Tammany Hall, for example, was promised contracts and jobs that were at Whitney's disposal in New York City. "To this day I know not what passed between [Whitney] and the boss of the Promiseland delegation," Russell commented. Maybe, he said sarcastically, they were discussing dried prunes. His implication, of course, was that Whitney was giving away the company store in order to win the presidency for Cleveland. "Back of Mr. Whitney, supporting him and even going behind him, was the great Financial Interest that ruled absolutely the second Cleveland administration," Russell charged.[29]

Russell drew these conclusions in his 1914 memoir of his reporting career, but in 1892, as he explained, "none of us ever wrote or suggested the conclusions we had formed in our own minds." His convention coverage never hinted that Whitney might have been making backroom deals that could compromise a soon-to-be President Cleveland. "If my service as a political reporter taught me anything," Russell reflects, "it was this vast and irreconcilable difference between things as they really are and things as they are prepared for representation to the general public."[30]

In writing this, Russell was reflecting on and criticizing his own reporting, as well as that of the rest of the press corps. Why would Russell, so schooled by his father to be the community's conscience and brimming with anger at injustice, not write what he knew to be true? A few possibilities emerge. The first is that his newspaper would not let him. In the 1880s and 1890s editors and publishers had clear political agendas for their newspapers. The ideal of objectivity was only emerging and was hardly defined. Stories were more likely to be loaded in the direction of a newspaper's political beliefs. While newspapers were no longer the partisan mouthpieces they had been in the early 1800s, they did still identify with political parties. Editors might have denied this was so, but news values clearly reflected political passions. Yet there is no evidence in anything Russell wrote about his experience that suggests that James Gordon Bennett, Jr., an absentee publisher to begin with, was meddling in his paper's political coverage. Joseph Pulitzer, whose staff Russell would soon join again, was involved in all his newspaper's political decisions. But the *Herald* had no such interfering publisher.

Another factor that increasingly effected news coverage was commerce, which had become so dominant in all phases of American life. Did advertising buyouts or promises of purchased advertisements manipulate the press? This was an idea that Russell embraced later in his career and one he learned about especially when he became an editor. In fact, Russell told of an incident, later in his career, when Whitney used his considerable power as a prominent New York businessman to kill a news story he did not want printed. But there is no evidence that commerce interfered with or stopped Russell from writing the reality of what he saw at the conventions. Perhaps Russell was reflecting another possibility: maybe it was the candidates and their handlers who carefully nurtured false impressions among the press, manipulating reporters and "spinning" accounts in ways that gullible reporters were accepting. Certainly Whitney had charmed Russell, as did New York Senator Chauncey Depew, who often took Russell aside to feed him the political tidbits of the day. The close relationships between the press and the politicos can be seen in the fact that they shared hotel suites at the conventions, mingling as equals more than adversaries. Thus, the working habits of reporters—the access to sources, the high-level political circles they ran in—mitigated against the kind of unvarnished truth that Russell longed for and reveled in when he became a muckraker after the turn of the century. Finally and perhaps most importantly was the fact that Russell was still not ready to reject conventional politics. He still clung to the hope that the two major parties could deal with the issues that the excesses of industrialism were posing. Powerful and decisive Republican leaders such as William Whitney, despite his apparent backroom antics, were attractive to Russell. As a thirty-two-year-old newsman from a Republican family, perhaps still a bit starry-eyed as he sidled up to nationally known political figures, Russell had not yet seen or learned enough to reject conventional politics. But contradictions in what he was encountering were emerging for him—that is certain. He knew that what he witnessed often in politics was not what he or his newspapers were writing. And this constituted part of his education about the grimy nature of political discourse and about the freedom he did not yet have in journalism.

III. OUSTING THE BOSS OF BROOKLYN

After seven years as a reporter, Russell was ready for new challenges. He made the move that most reporters inevitably make: he became an editor. The *Herald* asked him to take charge of its Brooklyn edition as both an editor and a writer. Having been an editor in four Midwestern newspapers, Russell was certainly back on familiar turf. He wasted little time in making use of his new authority.

Traveling from his Brooklyn apartment to Manhattan one morning, Russell ran into a source, Bob Kelly, a knowledgeable informant about Brooklyn politics. While standing in front of an ornate mansion that Brooklyn's former reform mayor, Seth Low, had lived in, Kelly filled Russell's ear with behind-the-scenes tales of Brooklyn's political machine. Russell listened as Kelly complained about the absolute power of the ruddy-faced sixty-seven-year-old "boss" of Brooklyn, Hugh McLaughlin, who for more than twenty years had controlled the city's politics.[31] Operating from the front room of an auction house on Willoughby Street, while whittling on pieces of wood, "Boss" McLaughlin was known to give orders about every aspect of Brooklyn's political life. As one of the first and longest reigning bosses in America, McLaughlin came to power in the 1850s at the same time as "Boss" William Marcy Tweed was running his Tammany Hall machine across the river. These unelected power brokers maintained control by doling out jobs and contracts and putting their puppets into elected office.[32] When the conversation with Kelly was over, Russell took a ferry across the East River and tossed over in his mind what Kelly told him. By the time the *Herald*'s city editor William C. Reick came in to his office, Russell had readied a proposal. "I believe it is about time for an open revolt [against the Brooklyn machine]," he said. "There hasn't been one for some years and it must be about due. I think we could make a hit if we started on it." Reick asked if the McLaughlin forces could be beaten. Russell said he thought they could, and he outlined the grievances against McLaughlin and his hand-picked mayor, David Boody. In short, he said, McLaughlin's ring was guilty of fraud, corruption, squandering of public money, plundering of the taxpayers, and the amassing of private fortunes at the people's expense. He told Reick: "I think that since Tweed's day there had not been an equal of the

combined power and arrogance of the group that managed Brooklyn."[33]
Reick gave Russell the go-ahead to mount an attack.

With a population of nearly one million people, Brooklyn was the third
largest city in America in 1893. Situated a stone's throw across the East River
from New York City, but not yet a part of the booming metropolis, this City of
Churches, as Brooklyn was known, had grown dramatically in size and population since the end of the Civil War. The construction of the engineering marvel,
the Brooklyn Bridge, had connected it physically to Manhattan in 1883. But if
the newspapers and a growing band of angry citizens were to be believed, what a
visitor encountered in crossing that bridge was indeed less than marvelous.

Here's how the New York *Herald*, in a story written by Russell, described
Brooklyn in 1893: A traveler crossing over from Manhattan might think he had
entered a prairie village, he reported. The streets were "wretchedly paved, un-
cared for, full of dreadful odors, and deep with mud and accumulated nasti-
ness." Vast open spaces were filled with rubbish and refuse. The public
buildings were "small and poor," and the city's main thoroughfare was dominated by a deafening and dismal elevated trolley system. The few policemen
who could be found on its streets looked "spiritless and ineffectual."[34]

Basic municipal necessities were of the "crudest kind." Although Brooklyn's population had grown by 400,000 in twelve years, its water supply had remained the same for twenty years. Three times in 1893, in fact, the city had
been completely without water after a main aqueduct ruptured. Four Brooklyn
residents died because of the lack of water, which, even when available, was
foul. The sewer system was so inadequate that, after heavy rains, raw sewage
bubbled into the streets, threatening to spread disease. In certain outlying areas
of Brooklyn, closer to Long Island, where new house construction had taken
place, no sewers or running water were available. The city government had
piled up huge amounts of debt and was in bankruptcy. Thus, it couldn't afford
to make improvements, even while the tax burden on citizens had increased
dramatically in the two years since Mayor Boody had been elected.

The reason why Brooklyn was such a mess and "the worst governed city in
the United States," the *Herald* declared, was easy to explain. It had nothing to
do with the boom in population, with the hordes of job-seeking immigrants
and the consequent increased demand for municipal services, or even with the
complexities of delivering those services in a time of rapid change. The reason,
pure and simple, was the rotten nature of Brooklyn politics. Running the government were six men "who hold no office, are not in any way chosen by the
people to govern, and have no responsibility except to themselves and their
pocketbooks." And those pocketbooks, the *Herald* indicated, were considerably

full of ill-gotten money. "It makes not the slightest difference in the world who is called Mayor of Brooklyn," the *Herald* said. "Mr. McLaughlin and his company are the real rulers."[35]

As Russell saw it, "the situation created by the Bad Men of Brooklyn was not essentially different from that created by the Good Men of St. Johnsbury." But when he encountered unelected and absolute power in the form of the Fairbanks family in Vermont, back in 1880, he was in no position to challenge it; he simply knew it was anti-democratic and unacceptable. As an editor at the *Herald*, however, Russell knew he had an opportunity. Years later, reflecting on his days in daily journalism, he wrote that "the newspaper does not employ reporters to create stories." Reporters and editors "have very little call to determine why things happen," he added.[36] But that was certainly not the attitude he took in the summer of 1893 when Russell decided to mount his first major reportorial crusade—against "Boss" McLaughlin and the Brooklyn Democratic machine.

Showing how little attention the Gilded Age newspaper paid to the concept of neutrality, Russell set out immediately to form alliances with various reformers and good government groups, as well as, surprisingly, the Brooklyn correspondent of the *New York Times*. He was "most sympathetic with our purpose," Russell noted, and so the two newspapers dispensed with the "newspaper rivalry that has spoiled so many good enterprises" and worked together.[37] It is impossible to tell if the newspapers' desire to oust Mayor Boody prompted a citizens' revolt or if the citizens' restlessness pushed the newspapers into action. Most likely, the relationship was symbiotic. In the months leading up to the election of November 1893, the newspapers not only outlined on their own the corrupt activities and misgovernment of McLaughlin's forces, they also reported in detail on the activities of the emerging reform forces.

The focus and fury of the press and public was on "Old Man" Hugh McLaughlin, a simple churchgoing man who doted on his family and loved to grow flowers in his garden. He delighted more in hunting, fishing, and fine dogs than in public policy or governmental issues. Each summer he spent at least a month on sporting expeditions to fishing paradises scattered from Maine to Florida; at times he hunted in the Adirondack Mountains. Normally, when he went away, McLaughlin had little to worry about. His nephew, Hugh "Bub" McLaughlin, second in command, ran the political end of the organization, while the loyal W. C. Kingsley, who McLaughlin had taken care of with street-paving contracts, acted as the brains of the machine.[38] But in 1893, with McLaughlin on vacation, both the citizens of Brooklyn and the press became restless.

By midsummer the *Herald* signaled its attitude toward the upcoming November election. In an article written by Russell, a citizen was prominently quoted as saying that Mayor Boody was "an excellent gentleman and able man but as a mayor he has been a total failure." Said the article's author, "I have not seen the truth about the mayor stated more exactly." Boody, in fact, was lucky not to be in jail. In July a grand jury almost indicted him. Boody had vetoed legislation that gave a railway franchise to a company that was willing to pay the city $30,000. He then transferred the franchise to a company that paid the city nothing but was made up of McLaughlin's friends. In unsealing grand jury testimony, a judge suggested that the investigation of Boody continue.[39] As for McLaughlin, he too was having problems. The *Times* reported his leisure activities while on vacation, but also suggested that he was quite ill, that his power was lessening, and that successors were waiting in the wings. McLaughlin had heard all this before, of course. Exposure of corruption in the 1870s had caused him much embarrassment. After the machine candidate lost in the election of 1877, the New York *Tribune* said of the McLaughlin organization, "now it has been finally broken—in fact it has burst."[40] But it was not so as McLaughlin, by controlling the nominations, continued to elect his candidates to most major positions in Brooklyn's government, including Boody as mayor in 1891. Would 1893 be different?

IV. THE PRESS GANGS UP

In early September McLaughlin returned to Brooklyn. The *Times* declared: "The Boss is back," brought home unexpectedly by "courtiers from the front laden with news of evil." The news came first from reform groups that were sprouting up in opposition to Boody and from the *Herald*, which was laying out in enterprising fashion the scandals that beset Boody's administration.[41] Although Boody was a Democrat, organizations such as the Brooklyn Democratic Club and the Kings County Democratic Citizens Union, composed of leading business and professional men, were condemning his administration. When he was elected in 1891, the club said in a September report, it was expected that Boody would clean up city government. Instead, he "succumbed at once to the evil influences" that had beset the previous administration. From the awarding of city franchises to the operation of the schools, "sinister influences" pervade this administration, the club charged.[42] Good-government groups arose also on the Republican side. One composed of one hundred citizens pledged to find an independent candidate—either Democrat or Republican—who could unite voters "to overthrow the ring," as one of its promoters

told the *Times*. The leading candidate was William J. Gaynor, a lawyer and former police commissioner whose fight against a private water company and corrupt railway franchise owners had made him a Brooklyn reform legend.
Eventually he became mayor of New York City. In pushing for Gaynor's nomination, one citizen told the *Times*, "one man, single-handed has stood out
against the corrupt acts" of McLaughlin. That man was Gaynor, who was flat-
tered but wanted a judgeship, not the mayoralty.[43]

While the citizens were forming alliances and discussing candidates, Russell marshaled evidence against Boody and McLaughlin. On October 8, in a
story that covered nearly two full pages of the *Herald* and included large
sketches of Boody and McLaughlin, Russell wrote in biting terms about how a
"cleverly managed machine" was responsible for "a long series of steals and dis-
graceful scandals." This impressive article mixed strong rhetoric typical of a
righteous crusade with a heavy dose of facts. Russell harped on the fact that
McLaughlin, "the dictator of the local democratic party," along with a group of
six associates—the ring—were in complete control of Brooklyn's government.
"Their power is as absolute in Brooklyn as the power of the Czar in Russia,"
wrote Russell. As troubling to Russell was the fact that the ring had not "the
slightest responsibility to its electors."[44]

Russell's indictment of the McLaughlin ring was threefold: they gave away
city contracts to friends; they let cronies control franchises for municipal services such as the rails and electricity; and they pushed through legislation that
swindled the public out of thousands of dollars. Anthony Barrett, a lawyer and
one of the six ring rulers who also controlled a key Brooklyn railway franchise,
was typical of the ring's largesse. "He is rich," Russell wrote, because he lives
off the taxpayer. But he was not as rich as McLaughlin, whose wealth, mostly in
real estate, was said to be $1.5 million. In typical sarcastic fashion, Russell
wrote: "Possibly [Mclaughlin's fortune] is the result of strict economy; possibly
he has found legitimate sources of income of which the rest of us have not been
informed."[45] Others didn't give Brooklyn's rulers such benefit of the doubt. A
Brooklyn minister in his Sunday sermon laid it on the line: "The fact is that our
Municipal Government is honeycombed with corruption," he declared. Citizens were equally frank. "I want a man (for mayor) without a boss," said one at
a public meeting reported by the *Times*. "I am tired of the corrupt machine that
rules things in Brooklyn," screamed another.[46]

Meanwhile, Russell kept giving the angry citizens more reason to be outraged with their government. For example, on October 22 he wrote a carefully
documented history of the company that controlled the city's electricity. Its
president was "Bub" McLaughlin, while its owners, Russell found, were re-

markably similar to "the gentlemen who rule Brooklyn from the auction room in Willoughby Street." Using the formula that would work for him in his future muckraking exposés, Russell combed thorough city contracts, read court documents, and interviewed reformers who had battled the company. He then showed how the company charged citizens more money, provided inferior service, and paid the city less than what other companies had offered. "One of the most glaring outrages that mark the maladministration of government in Brooklyn under the rule of McLaughlin and the auction room ring," Russell concluded.[47]

With both the press and citizens squealing, McLaughlin seemed on the run. "They are saying this is a Republican year," the *Times* reported. "Political prediction is an exceedingly unsafe thing," Russell wrote on October 29, but he added, "revolt against ring rule is deeper and further reaching . . . than anybody suspected."[48] When Gaynor refused the nomination, the Republicans chose Charles Schieren, a fifty-one-year-old German-born merchant who had made a fortune by patenting durable leather belts that could withstand the strain of high-speed electrical machinery. Schieren's greatest attributes were that he was considered an independent—no ties to the ring or political parties—and that he was independently wealthy. Facing a cheering crowd in late October, Schieren declared: "It is high time for the citizens to throw off this yoke and have a change of Government."[49]

McLaughlin was not prepared to go down without a fight, however, and he turned to his fellow "boss," John Y. McKane, who was also Brooklyn's chief of police, to get out the vote for Boody—with legal and illegal efforts. The *Times*, the *Herald*, and the reformers moved into the last stage of their crusade: fighting the ring's attempt to bring in "floaters"—illegal voters from outside Brooklyn—to cast their votes for Boody. McKane had already been touched by Russell's pen in a particularly nasty October 1 commentary. McKane was a prominent member of a Brooklyn Methodist church, "a phase of character very laudable indeed," Russell wrote. "If only his life outside his church was more consistent with such professions there would be no cause for criticism . . . and no occasion for this article."[50] This was the same refrain that the muckrakers would later apply to capitalists like Rockefeller and Andrew Carnegie. Russell blamed McKane for all the evils of his neighborhood. Asked Russell: Since he controls virtually "every movement and undertaking, public or private" in the Coney Island and Gravesend sections of Brooklyn ("a little state by the sea"), how does one explain that they are the "home and haven of every species of vice and degradation"? While the schoolchildren meet in church on Sunday mornings, McKane protects saloons, prostitutes, fakirs—and takes kickbacks

from them all. What an "odd genius," Russell wrote: Sunday school superintendent and "king" of Brooklyn's dives. Ironically, Russell felt differently about
McLaughlin. "Under his rule the social evil, which raged in its most repulsive
forms [in Manhattan], never dared to cross the Bridge." Russell's only problem
with McLaughlin: nobody chose him to govern Brooklyn.[51]

A few days before the election, Russell used the *Herald*'s pages to charge
McKane with registering voters who were not residents of Brooklyn. "The
gang in Brooklyn has no shame," Russell wrote. The *Times* added that the
McLaughlin machine is involved in "a great deal of direct bribery, a still larger
amount of indirect bribery, a good deal of bulldozing, and all the fraudulent
voting that can safely be arranged for."[52] Luckily for the forces of reform,
Gaynor jumped into the fray, went into court, and accused McKane of illegally
registering 6,218 voters. The judge demanded that McKane appear before him
to explain. Meanwhile, Russell, a veteran of wandering through Manhattan's
seedy East Side hotels, went to Brooklyn's flophouses to prove that suddenly on
the eve of the election, they were being filled with illegal voters, mostly vagrants brought over from Manhattan's Bowery. Russell approached one clerk
and asked why his hotel was so crowded. "With a twinkle in his eye," he told
Russell that it must be the quality of service. The point was clear: the "ring"
was stacking the deck for Election Day. Gaynor, who was portrayed by Russell
as a hero, thanked the *Herald* for its efforts. "It is not partisan work but a telling
battle for good government," he said.[53]

As Election Day neared, Russell was all but gloating. "Never before in its
history was the reigning family of Brooklyn so discredited in the public mind as
it is to-day," he wrote on November 3. If Schieren was elected, Russell added,
he would open up the Boody administration's records, and surely Sing Sing
Prison would beckon for the McLaughlin gang. For Russell, the election was
clearly a case of truth and justice versus hypocrisy and corruption. "On the one
side are the people—republicans and democrats—and on the other the reigning family and its thousands of hangers-on and would-be hangers on," he
wrote. Russell's rhetoric was typical for his time. Two authors point out that
"the struggle between 'bossism' and 'reform' usually appeared as a direct clash
between the forces of good and evil, between corruption and purity."[54]

The reigning family battled the reformers until the very end. The day before the election, McKane had fourteen allies of Gaynor thrown into jail without any charges against them and without the possibility of bail. The men had
gone to Coney Island to copy the names of illegally registered voters when
McKane, in defiance of a court order, had them arrested. "Not since the lawless
era of the Tweed regime have the people . . . had such an illustration of utter

disregard . . . for the courts," wrote the *Times*. After spending a night in jail, the men were ordered released by a state judge. The *Herald* and *Times* both head-lined McKane's brazen contempt for the law.[55]

Despite the antics of McKane and the considerable money the machine was spending in the final moments of the campaign, Russell was optimistic about victory. He spent the last days before the election talking with voters—"the plain people," he wrote. He went to Brooklyn's docks, to its sugar refiner-ies, to its construction sites, and to the drivers and conductors of the elevated railroads. "They are aroused," he wrote. "They have a chance to topple over the throne upon which McLaughlin sits, and they are going to do it." The *Times*'s story read more like an editorial than news. "If Brooklyn's honest men will only perform . . . the task which rests upon them the reign of the rogues will . . . reach a violent and immediate end," it declared. "If the voters of the city do their duty," the ring will disappear "like a poisonous cloud."[56]

On election night, the *Herald* signaled the results of the election with a great search light from Manhattan's famous Madison Square Garden. The light told Brooklynites that Mayor Boody had been beaten by Schieren by nearly 30,000 votes. William Gaynor was elected as a state judge by 25,000 votes. "The Ring is shattered," declared the *Times*. Commented Mayor-elect Schieren, "I feel I owe a great debt of gratitude to the Herald." Gaynor added: "The Herald has done grand work during this campaign."[57]

The defeat of McLaughlin's candidate was undoubtedly a victory for Brooklyn's citizens. During his two years in office, Schieren succeeded in bring-ing the city out of bankruptcy, the Williamsburg Bridge was planned, and a number of parks were laid out. For Russell, the victory was an affirmation that sleeping citizens could be aroused to bring about progress even when banks, sa-loons, and public utility companies allied against them. The great strength of the McLaughlin machine, Russell believed, had been "the chronic indifference of the average citizen." But the alliance of reformers and the press had awakened the people from their slumber. Of course, Russell was not naive enough to be-lieve that suddenly politics had been made clean. "Only school boys and the half-witted believed that politics could ever be purified," he wrote. However, he was naive enough to believe that "the reign of King Hugh was broken that night."[58] In this he was mistaken—or perhaps he was simply in reformer's de-nial. Even though McLaughlin announced his retirement after the defeat of 1893, he returned to the scene a year later—just as Russell left the *Herald* and moved to Joseph Pulitzer's *World*. In fact, McLaughlin was so much still a force in Brooklyn politics that one member of the board of education remarked that Democrats on the board did not dare to so much as vote for a janitor without

McLaughlin's consent. In 1895 McLaughlin's handpicked candidate was elected as the last mayor of the city of Brooklyn. After Brooklyn merged with the rest of New York in 1897, McLaughlin's influence persisted. He essentially chose the city's chief financial officer and the Brooklyn borough president. He remained the boss of Brooklyn until 1903 when he retired from politics after forty years. One year later McLaughlin died.[59]

The resurrection of Boss McLaughlin was not lost on Russell. Reform victories, while useful and exhilarating, were shortlived. Recalling in his autobiography the momentary win over the machine, Russell noted that some of the men elected to office under the banner of reform were soon under indictment. "The man in the street," Russell wrote forty years after the fact, "began to feel that we had exchanged a gang of crooks for a band of chumps, a state of mind all to the good for grafting, which had only retired to cover and was waiting."[60] Nevertheless, in 1893 the fleeting nature of reform had not yet dawned on Russell; more crusades were on the horizon.

CHAPTER FIVE

THE BEST JOB AT THE *WORLD*

I. THE PULSE OF THE CITY

MANAGING THE CITY NEWS IN DAVENPORT, Detroit, or Minneapolis did not prepare Charles Edward Russell for what awaited him when he moved, in December 1894, from the *New York Herald* to the largest circulation newspaper in
America, the *New York World*. He took over the third most important position
at the newspaper, the city editor's job, replacing his old friend, Richard Farrelly, one of the "Big Four" reporters who had covered the Johnstown flood
with him five years earlier. Thus Russell began a three-year stint under Joseph
Pulitzer, the eccentric and demanding genius publisher who controlled every
detail of his newsroom and his newspaper but who also provided important and
lifelong social lessons for Russell.

At the *Herald*, Russell supervised a small staff covering Brooklyn. Now,
suddenly he was in charge of a staff of dozens of reporters covering all of met-
ropolitan New York, an area with a population of more than three million,
larger than Paris. The events and news that emerged from a city that was
wealthier than any state in America, with more people on its payroll than the
U.S. Army, began anew Russell's education about America's ills—and about
corporate maneuverings. He entered Pulitzer's twenty-three-story domed
newsroom to find a cutthroat atmosphere, a feverish pace, and a dichotomous
city. It is difficult to say which was more demanding, Pulitzer or the city.

The *World* was perhaps the best in the nation at covering the political
scene; its inside news pages were chock full of international stories; and the

editorial page was of a particularly high quality with immense influence over the governing elites. Nonetheless, city news usually dominated the *World*'s eight-column jumbled first page. Russell was working at a newspaper that was both popular—1896 circulation: 732,579—and important. The explanation, in part, was that the *World*'s city news always traveled the high and low roads of journalism at the same time, socially conscious one moment and sensational and juicy the next, a Pulitzer formula for success and a tack that Russell often followed in his own writing. On April 23, for example, the *World* showed its typical enterprise by protecting the interests of its readers with a detailed story on the newly emerged "ice trust" that was jacking up prices to consumers. "Competition is dead," it declared about the new monopoly, a constant theme not only of Pulitzer but also of the Gilded Age, during which the Sherman Anti-Trust Act was passed.[1] On a nearby page the *World* told how the state legislature, bowing to popular demand, was reducing the price of rail fares in Manhattan. On the same pages, however, it reported in grisly detail how a twelve-year-old boy was mangled, his limbs severed, in a trolley crash, and how an unknown woman was found murdered under a stairway. For a laugh, readers could peruse stories like "Corpse in a Rum Cask." The *World* reported that a ship captain had brought into port a man who died at sea and was pre-served in a barrel of rum. Should the barrel be considered an import or a cas-ket? the newspaper asked.[2]

The pace and energy of the city was both exhilarating and exhausting for Russell. Typical was May 5, 1896, a Tuesday, when "Iron-faced Charley," as he was known to his reporters, came to work and had to face the following news: in Brooklyn a woman died when she was hit by lightning while four others were dead in an apartment fire. In Manhattan horses rampaged through Central Park when their carriages collided. Further downtown three people were seriously hurt when a streetcar ran them over. Uptown, a baby ate rat poison and was near death. On the West Side of town a man killed his partner by ac-cident at a rifle range, while at the nearby Hudson River one fisherman was dead and another lost when their boat capsized.[3] Over on Staten Island a woman was buried alive, while in Queens two bodies were found—one muti-lated and the other burned to death. Lastly was a sensitive race story. A watch-man on Thirty-fifth Street and Fifth Avenue taunted a group of black men. "Only dead niggers are good ones," he reportedly said. The blacks threw bricks at him, and he fired his gun at them. The blacks then drew razors and almost lynched him until the police arrived and intervened. The watchman and one black man were hospitalized, but no one was arrested. The *World* put it on page one.[4]

Quickly, after many such days, Russell began to understand: Davenport, Iowa this was not. To make matters worse, he had to deal with Pulitzer, the Hungarian immigrant who believed in pitting his editors against each other to raise their competitive creativity—and their blood pressures. As a Pulitzer biographer notes: "One formula that seems to stand the test of time is to assemble a group of first-class newspaper men and let them fight it out."[5] The result, of course, was back-stabbing and in-house competition. "You have to keep a sharp watch on your desk and chair," the biographer reported. "If you go out to lunch, some other editor is apt to be sitting in your place when you return." About the job of city editor Russell consequently concluded, in his understated way, "It is a task likely to keep [one] from falling asleep at his desk."[6]

When his day was ended, usually after twelve or more hours, Russell, usually very tired, went out to eat with his best friend in the newsroom, David Graham Phillips, who, like Russell, was from the Midwest (Indiana), reared in a Protestant household, educated in the East (Princeton), and schooled in the ways of journalism in the Heartland (Cincinnati) before coming to New York as a reporter. The two met when Phillips was a reporter at the *New York Sun*. Both were dandy dressers with similar political instincts and were lovers of literature. Russell wanted to become a poet; Phillips a novelist.[7] At times, with the day behind them, they sat at the Mouquin Restaurant in downtown Manhattan and clashed in a friendly way over literature: Russell, the idealist, saw uplifting possibilities in the world around him. Phillips, who would write twenty-six novels and become one of America's most popular writers, was a realist, and what he saw often made him despair. What they agreed on, however, was that journalism was only a stepping stone—a way to get enough money to be free to write.[8]

II. MURDER, MAYHEM, LITERATURE

Russell had worked the streets of New York City long enough to know that it was a fertile ground for fascinating stories, the kind that the masses loved to read. "Whether truth is stranger than fiction I do not pretend to say," Russell commented about the news coming his way in his years as city editor, "but I know it is better than fiction."[9] So, to Pulitzer's delight, Russell pushed his staff to find bizarre and interesting man-bites-dog stories that abound in every big city.

In April 1896, for example, the *World* reported in detail the story of a seventeen-year-old who, while being chased by the police, was apparently killed by a trolley. When his father arrived to identify the boy at the morgue he held the boy's head; it was warm. He opened his eyes and said, "Pop, oh pop."

Screaming, the father called for a doctor, but it was too late. The boy died in his arms. Why, the *World* asked, had the police declared the boy dead when he wasn't?[10] A few weeks later, the *World* returned to the morgue to ask readers for help: a finger found on a sidewalk in Manhattan was in the morgue, awaiting an owner. "Who Wants a Finger?" a headline asked.[11] Russell's reporters found a millionaire merchant who hired a hypnotist in hopes that he could be cured of blindness, a story that surely interested the nearly blind Pulitzer, who had the newspaper read to him each and every day by his secretary. No hypnotist, however, could help the man who smoked ten packs of cigarettes a day and ended up in an insane asylum in Brooklyn. And no hospital could help a Boston lawyer who, drunk, fell into the Harlem River. When the tide came in at 5:00 A.M., the man drowned.[12]

Domestic disputes and suicides were common on Russell's cityside pages. Some of them were comical. A woman stumbled into a Brooklyn police station with a knife in her skull. Her husband confessed, sort of. "I—I cut her a little on the head," he said, after accusing his wife of being a drunkard and a bad mother. At least the woman was better off than the four wives of the German barber who, in order to collect life insurance, killed them all. Police were exhuming the body of Wife Number Four, the *World* reported in an exclusive story that was typical in its self-promotion.[13]

The *World* liked juicy divorces, too. In "Mrs. Frank Peeped In," Russell's staff reported how the mother of a young bride trapped her husband, a doctor, while he made love to his patients. Climbing a ladder, she peeped in on him while females visited. Then, while he was in the act, she barged into the office with a neighbor. A story with a good old-fashioned sex angle always interested Pulitzer and Russell— and readers. Russell made sure, however, that his stories, juicy as they might be, never went too far. As historian George Juergens points out, "The evidence is overwhelming that the World did not achieve its great circulation by defying contemporary convention, but by going only so far as convention allowed."[14]

Pulitzer had no qualms about printing stories that dealt with sex and scandal because he felt they could be purposeful and they drew the audience he needed. "Of course, newspapers are 'made to sell,'" Pulitzer once wrote, "and in that respect they resemble the highest work of art and intellect as well as the sermons preached in pulpits."[15] That was a lesson that Russell, grandson of a preacher and son of crusading editor, found attractive—the newspaper as a moral force, even when it exposed sordid personal scandal. "Sinners do not shrink from vice," Pulitzer wrote at another point, "but they are awfully afraid of exposure in the newspapers. No pulpit orator can reach the evil-doer like a . . . newspaper with a quarter of a million of readers."[16]

Politicians would come in for their share of exposure on the pages assembled by Russell and Pulitzer, but so too would the unelected power brokers. The *World* was downright preachy about the extramarital relationship of a prominent realtor who was a pillar of a Manhattan Baptist church. Just as Russell had attacked a churchgoing but corrupt Brooklyn politico while at the *Herald*, the *World* went after the realtor as a way to reveal character—or the lack of it.

Since Russell left no diaries and wrote little of his days managing the *World* newsroom, it is difficult to determine how much of the city pages were truly his creations.[17] Nonetheless, Russell took credit for much of what appeared on the city pages. The city editor, he declared, "is the real captain of the ship, the only person in the establishment that has any real power." Editorial writers—at the *World* these included his old boss George Cary Eggleston and eventually Phillips—"emit great thoughts," but only the proofreader is interested in what they write, Russell said, mockingly. The managing editor, a job he took eventually with Pulitzer's archenemy, William Randolph Hearst, "is largely a figure of ornament." And forget the business manager: he "consorts with the powers of evil" (the advertisers), said Russell. That meant for Russell that the city editor was most important, but only "if he knows his business and has the others properly cowed."[18]

He could not cow Pulitzer, however. One fall, when a steamship arrived in New York and reported that passengers had contracted cholera, the *World* was ready to tell New York that the ship was under quarantine to prevent an epidemic. A city health officer told Russell that printing the news would be bad for the city's business; Russell rebuked him. But forty-five minutes later he backed off, carrying an order from Pulitzer: kill the story. Compliantly, Russell recalled, "we forgot it," as did every other New York City newspaper.[19] Russell was tougher with his own reporters than with the business staff, however. Ivy Lee, who later became famous as a public relations counsel to John D. Rockefeller, worked for Russell at the *World* and recalled him as "very strict and sometimes forbidding."[20]

In most newsrooms, the editor who assigns stories, as Russell did, determines much of what readers see on a daily basis. But reporters who are more closely in touch with events than editors also regularly bring story ideas to editors. Consequently the creativity and social sense of reporters are vital. Russell wanted his reporters to be "artistic craftsmen." He believed that "far more surely than the dramatist or the novelist the reporter can hold the mirror up to nature." Surely he echoed Pulitzer, who wrote in the *World*, "The daily journal is like the mirror—it reflects that which is before it."[21] Russell

put together a staff that he felt was the best ever assembled, a distinct possi-
bility since Pulitzer had been raiding other newsrooms for a decade and pay-
ing hefty salaries to lure reporters. Joining Phillips on the staff was
Maximillian Foster, later a widely read short-story writer and novelist;
Rudolph Block, writer of popular ghetto stories under the pseudonym Bruno
Lessing; famous short-story writers Marie Manning, Anne O'Hagan, Jacob
Dreyfus, and Hartley Davis; Arthur Greaves, who became city editor of the
New York Times, and Alexander Kennealey, later editor of the *London Mirror;*
playwright Bayard Veiller; and highly regarded critics Charles H. Meltzer,
E. F. Coward, and Oliver Howard Dunbar. Arthur Brisbane, who had cov-
ered the state's electrocutions with Russell three years earlier, was also on the
city staff, the only reporter under Pulitzer who was allowed to sign his articles. Brisbane wandered the city on special assignments.

Russell was a keen judge of talent, an important quality for a general in de-
ploying his troops. His first official act as city editor, in fact, was to take
Phillips, who became his inseparable companion, away from the "key-hole"
type of reporting that he so despised. Although Phillips had some notable
scoops as a news reporter, he was better suited to crafting fine, descriptive stories—human interest features—that showed off his emerging literary skill.[22]
Russell had Phillips rewrite news gathered by other reporters—a common task
for the "rewrite" editor—and his stories produced a sensation in New York. On
Thanksgiving Day in 1895 he assigned Phillips to write a moving portrait of
seventy-six men, women, and children who awaited death in a Bronx hospice.
"Death, We Salute Thee!" won raves for Phillips.

Russell felt, and rightly so, that editors were the guiding forces behind not
only what became news, but for how stories were written. "As a painter before
his easel so sits every day the city editor before the paper he is to make," Russell said. The city editor, he declared, "is an artist." In his early years at the
job—before yellow became the paper's dominant color—he blended a variety
of news into what he felt was "the highest type of literature."[23] Indeed, many
stories on Russell's pages are written in a compelling storylike style. Like any
good story, they lead the reader to reach a particular conclusion at the story's
climax. A debonair swindler who duped women into marriage was really a notorious criminal, and the *World* told the tale like a short story, leading up the
swindler's confession. A short heart-wrenching story of five-year-old girl living
in a Queens mansion was typical. When the girl's nightgown caught fire while
she played near a coal stove, she was badly burned. A nurse found her "en-
veloped in the most cruel embrace that a mortal ever knew," screaming, "the
cruel fire licking her limbs." When the fire was put out, her body was rubbed

with oil and wrapped in softest down. "Save her life!" cried her wealthy father, "and take all I have." But, the *World* reported as the reader reached the story's final paragraph, "at a late hour last night the message came that Little Joyce was dying." Not an eye was dry in New York City.[24]

In similar heart-wrenching style, the *World* told of the Ryers, an old and feeble couple on Staten Island, who had their only pennies—$3.35, to be exact—stolen from them one evening by thieves who ignored the fact that they were crippled and poor. Replete with detailed dialogue—"Be quick about it," one thief yelled, "or you'll soon be smoking in hell"—the story ends with police inspecting a bloodstained shutter where the thieves escaped the house. Instead of using the modern technique of a summary lead, which gives away the ending as the story begins, the *World* used a more traditional storytelling fashion. This was not something that was invented at the *World*, certainly, but its reporters were quite good at building drama, and Russell encouraged this. As a historian who has studied the *World*'s news pages commented, "The emphasis on crime and tragedy was not in itself a unique way of attracting readers. The World's triumph is that it did it so well."[25]

III. FIGHTING FOR THE PEOPLE

New York City gave Russell the artist a marvelous easel on which to paint, and with the staff that he and Pulitzer had assembled Russell had a vast storehouse of color combinations at his fingertips. He used them often to coax the kinds of stories that pulled in readers, but he used them also to crusade and fight for the immigrants, the poor and the plain folk who were the *World*'s special parishioners.

In an editorial in the *World*, Joseph Pulitzer wrote: "The World attributes its success not only to its news and conceded ability but to its principles and conviction."[26] That being the case, Russell was the perfect man for Pulitzer's newspaper. His disdain for excess wealth and unelected power and his belief in holding elected officials accountable were developed before he took over as city editor. But as city editor he got the chance to put these principles into practice. The Pulitzer-Russell pages embraced the poor, mocked the blue-blooded wealthy, and crusaded especially against the emerging plutocratic monopolies that many felt were threatening democracy.

What's clear from looking at a sample of the city pages over the three-year period that Russell was city editor is that one issue, above all, dominated Pulitzer and Russell's minds—and the American consciousness as well. That issue was the "trusts," the monopolies that had begun to control commerce ever since the Civil War. Between 1867 and 1897, eighty-six new industrial combinations were formed with an amassed capital of $1.4 billion. Names that typified the American Dream and Nightmare—Rockefeller, Carnegie, Gould, Harriman, Armour—were etched into the public consciousness. The new captains of industry wielded economic power that not only threatened entry into the marketplace but loomed large over the political landscape as well. The government, however, was neither ready nor able to combat the likes of the big companies. The federal Sherman Antitrust Act (1890) was the government's official albeit feeble attempt to thwart monopoly. But the law lacked teeth and enforcement personnel, and the government's lawyers were hardly a match for the capital and resources of, for example, John D. Rockefeller's Standard Oil.

As for a public that had been schooled in the ways of an open marketplace and decentralized power (whether in government or commerce), the economic changes brought on by monopoly were alarming. The large industrial combination was an anomaly in nineteenth-century America.[27] Thus, Pulitzer and the press jumped into the vacuum to help frame the public's view—and to sell newspapers. Pulitzer and Russell must have known that this seeming threat to middle-class security—on both local and national levels—would pique the reading public.

While Russell was still working for the rival *Herald*, Pulitzer began his assault on the trusts. Russell's best friend, David Graham Phillips, was assigned in April 1893 to investigate, as Phillips wrote, "the unholy alliances of bandits who prey unmolested upon the people . . . poisoning the whole atmosphere" of trade and commerce. The Lead Trust. The Whiskey Trust. The Copper Trust. The Rubber Trust. It is, Phillips wrote, "an amazing story of unscrupulousness" by "bands of robber barons." For twelve days and with 35,000 words Phillips pleaded for government action, ending his articles each day with a demand to the U.S. Attorney General Richard Olney to enforce the Sherman Anti-Trust Act: "Such, Mr. Olney, are the facts. And here, sir, is the law."[28]

By 1895, with little movement taking place toward controlling the trusts on a national level, Pulitzer turned his pages to the urban scene where Russell's city pages went after the "telephone octopus," the ice trust, and then the rail and trolley magnates who were monopolizing the city's commuting lines. Using language and approaches that were remarkably similar to what Russell would employ when he became a magazine muckraker a decade later, the *World* employed a bit of history to show how the trusts had developed, some plain language (often without facts) to show how bribes were used to influence regulatory legislation, and outright editorial conclusions (even in news stories) to demand changes.

In short, the *World* under Russell continued what Pulitzer had been doing successfully in both St. Louis, where he had his first newspaper, and New York—crusading for change. For both social and readership reasons, JP, as he was called, insisted on always having a crusade in his newspaper. "It is Mr. Pulitzer's wish to have constantly on hand and waged vigorously a campaign, crusade or battle directed on proper lines; this is a fixed principle," an undated memo in the Pulitzer Papers notes.[29]

The need for unified and reasonably priced municipal utility services—water, gas, electric, transportation—had become evident in urban areas such as New York and Chicago where services had grown in fragmented and confusing ways. A patchwork of different companies often controlled different parts of the cities. Water, gas, and trolley service—all could be supplied by a half-dozen or more companies in the same city. Even though consolidation was a logical development, logic and efficiency often did not dictate changes. The lust for monopoly that would, in turn, lead to big money and big profit did.

In the winter of 1895 a bill was pending in the New York State legislature, supported heartily by the *World*, that would strictly control telephone prices and the profits that the "telephone octopus" could make. As it covered legislative hearings and pointed out discrepancies in testimony by American Bell Telephone Company officials, the *World* was urging its passage. At the same time, its reporting warned that "boodle" from the lobbyists for American Bell was resulting in "wholesale bribery" of lawmakers, threatening the people's interests. "There is more money at Albany this year than ever before," the *World* reported, and the capital is "reeking with corruption."[30] In the next week, the *World* attacked two more trusts. Headlines warned of the "Electric Trust Now" (March 23) and the "Whiskey Trust's Crimes" (March 27).

Although no names were mentioned, "an honest member" of the state assembly from Brooklyn told the *World* how behind the scenes money was moving all around to influence voting. Could the assemblyman have been one of Russell's old Brooklyn sources from his *Herald* days and the crusade against "Boss" McLaughlin? The "bosses," after all, were in the center of the corruption, the *World* reported, adding, "A corporation which wants legislation or wants to be protected against legislation makes his bargain with the bosses of the political parties."[31] "Boss" Richard Croker of New York was the main benefactor of the trust's largesse, the *World* charged. The real issue, however, as Russell and Pulitzer saw it, in a harbinger of what reformers would argue consistently after the turn of the century, was that monopoly was not only corrupting politics but was forcing higher costs on the people. "It is because of its absolute ownership of the subways and of its control of all subways that will be built for the next two years that the monopoly exists," the *World* pointed out. "Competition is impossible."

The same theme ran through a crusade that Russell's city pages mounted in the spring of 1896 against the Ice Trust, a group of companies that joined together to control delivery of an essential ice-box ingredient. When the price of ice rose, just as the warm season was upon the city, the *World* investigated rumors that local companies had consolidated. Russell sent a reporter to track down company presidents, who, miffed at the spotlight, rebuffed the reporter. Two were too busy to talk, one denied mergers were taking place, and another told the reporter to get lost: "That is a private matter. I decline to make my private matters public."[32]

The hand of Russell the editor is all over this story. Much as Russell would do later in his muckraking work, the story detailed the companies' stock histories and the various mergers that had come close to creating a loose but clear common ownership. "The law," the *World* concluded, "is very easy of evasion." Pulitzer and Russell wanted their parishioners to know: "Competition is dead." And the result? "Everyone will pay the piper." The *World* had a simple solution—enforce the existing law, and then the only question will be, "How soon will it be broken up?"[33]

In late April 1895, the thinking of Pulitzer and Russell was evident in a page one cartoon. A steer, representing the beef trust, was goring a person carrying a sword embazoned "U.S." Leering in the bullfighting ring were the steel, gas, coffee, fish, cordage, oil, lead, telephone, sugar, and whiskey trusts. "If the beef trust escapes unpunished," a headline blared, "then we shall see the other giant monopolies in the arena."[34] The next day in a page-one story on the leather trust, the *World* warned: The "iron grip" of the trusts is upon us![35]

The trust problem defied an easy solution and in fact it would not be until nearly a decade later that the federal government—in part because of Russell's magazine exposés—would move aggressively into court to block trust abuses. But on a local level, Pulitzer-Russell and the *World* were able to exert more influence, with an activism that would shock even contemporary advocates of "civic" journalism. At the same time that Russell's reporters were exposing various activities in the city, Pulitzer's lawyers were going into court seeking injunctions to block the activities that were being exposed. The Pulitzer press was an independent force, protecting the people's interests when government failed to do so. "Oh, damn the World," declared Alderman Charles A. Parker. "That cursed paper is always investigating something or somebody."[36]

Stuntgirl Nellie Bly, for example, famous for her exposé of prison conditions in New York City and her seventy-two-day trip around the world, spiced the *World's* city pages with a visit to Abdullah, the mind reader. "I hate frauds as much as I hate death," declared Bly (real name Elizabeth Cochrane), who in a long and comical tale showed the mind reader to be a fraud.[37] More serious were frauds the *World* uncovered in the office of the Manhattan district attorney. A detailed story showed how private agents who received large amounts of cash—"ready money," the *World* called it—negotiated bail for the accused. No charge of dishonesty or graft was made, but "questionable practices" in the DA's office made clear that "reform is needed."[38]

Pulitzer, known as the schoolmaster in the newsroom, was undoubtedly tutoring Russell in a basic lesson of his version of how democracy can work. "There is not a crime, there is not a dodge, there is not a trick, there is not a swindle, there is not a vice which does not live by secrecy," Pulitzer advised. "Get these things out in the open, describe them, ridicule them in the press, and sooner or later public opinion will sweep them away."[39] It was a credo that the muckrakers would adopt in just a few years.

When the mere rousing of public opinion was not enough, the *World* took matters in its own hands, becoming activist in ways that defied neutrality. The *World's* lawyers went so far as to go into court seeking injunctions against those whom they saw as the bad guys. In Russell's final few months as city editor, the *World* mounted two vigorous new crusades, the first against companies it saw as "grabbing" the trolley and rail franchises, and the second against the city government for its inept upkeep of the city's streets. And it made some enemies in the process. When it investigated Alderman Parker, who it claimed was giving away the city's rail franchises for bribe money, he told a *World* reporter: "If I knew the man who has written some things about me for that paper I would break his neck. Yes, I would break every bone in his body."[40]

No wonder Parker was angry. The *World's* cityside reporters had uncovered a juicy story. The owners of a Manhattan rail line wanted not only to renew their franchise agreement—its contract and license—with the city. The company wanted the contract in perpetuity: a monopoly forever. Tammany Hall, which controlled local politics, had told the city's alderman to vote in favor of the franchise renewal because the *World* learned the company had secretly offered to give big contributions to the Republicans in the upcoming election. Enter the *World's* lawyers, who sued in court and received an injunction. Throughout the fall months, the *World* kept up the pressure.[41] Citizens lauded the *World's* efforts (September 29: "Whole World Praises the World") while the alderman grumbled about the publicity. The president of the Third Avenue rail syndicate, which was exposed and halted in its bid, gave a *World* reporter a remarkably candid interview, outlining what the targets of muckraking often said about their enemy, the press.

Reporter: "Well, Mr. [P. H.] Flynn, what do you think about the World's in-
    junction against this franchise grab?"
Flynn: "Oh, yes, 'grab' you call it, and I must take all the blame, I suppose.
    What do I think? Why I think it is a————outrage. What business has
    the World to mix up in this matter?"
Reporter: "All the newspapers agree a perpetuity would be wrong."
Flynn: "This is all very well, but I tell you all the newspapers are alike. They
    are always poking their way into matters that do not concern them.
    There is altogether too much of this business. All the newspapers are
    alike. They are no good. It is not the newspaper's business to mix up in
    such things."

Then Flynn let loose with a series of profanities.[42]

There was no Pulitzer-Russell response to Flynn in that day's *World*, just
an unceasing attack on the franchise grab and an even fiercer attack on how the
city was or was not maintaining its streets. "The World lays bare the secret of
torn-up streets," it blared one day, following up with a look at how the city
fumbled and stumbled in repairing street surfaces. Showing the paper's enterprise and activism, Russell then hired the chief engineer of Philadelphia to in-
spect New York's streets. He was "astonished and surprised" at the
"inexplicable" poor condition of New York streets. The *World* laid the blame
squarely at the feet of the man in charge. No mincing words for the *World*.[43]

Pulitzer knew and taught Russell that "the success of a journal must depend on its character . . . an earnest, vigorous advocacy of the public welfare, a
sincere devotion to the cause of good government and public virtue and a fearless and unceasing warfare against all fraud, sham, dishonesty."[44] Of course,
Pulitzer also must have known that as 1897 was drawing to a close an entry into
New York, a rival who would try to top every crusade and exposé his paper
mounted, would make it increasingly difficult to maintain his high journalistic
ideals. A dark cloud was gathering over New York journalism, over all of journalism in fact; and Russell, a coveted and talented editor, and a man of principle, like Pulitzer, would get caught in the storm that was bursting and would
drag everyone down into the gutter.

Nonetheless, for Russell, the excitement of overseeing coverage of New
York City was the noblest and most exciting time of his newspaper years. "The
best job on earth," he declared, "is that of city editor of a New York daily.
Other employments are but rubbish in comparison."[45] And yet, with money
and a greater opportunity dangling in front of him, Russell would soon leave
the best job he ever had.

CHAPTER SIX

HEARST,
YELLOW JOURNALISM,
CHICAGO

I. PARTING WITH PULITZER

JOSEPH PULITZER WAS NO STRANGER TO NEWSPAPER RAIDS. After all, in 1893 he had raided Charles A. Dana's *New York Sun* to steal the promising writer and young dandy David Graham Phillips, who became a famous feature writer for Pulitzer. In fact, stealing Phillips for the *New York World's* staff must have given Pulitzer great pleasure. When Pulitzer entered New York journalism, Dana had publicly mocked him, poking fun at his big nose and his Jewish heritage. The old master Dana and the upstart Pulitzer clearly did not like each other as they engaged in a nasty and very public feud. But Pulitzer did not confine his raids just to Dana's paper. He went after talent wherever he saw it.[1] In 1888 he had turned to James Gordon Bennett Jr.'s *New York Herald* to steal away Charles Edward Russell and make him the *World's* city editor. Over the long haul neither the *Herald* nor the *Sun*, the one-time circulation leaders of New York City journalism, could withstand the Pulitzer raids. Pulitzer's innovative and aggressive brand of journalism, his appeals to the poor and the city's burgeoning immigrant population, his consistent crusading for the underdog, his newspaper's lucid and easy-to-read writing, and his uncanny knack for promoting his paper's scoops, coupled with his aggressive stealing of talent, all combined to make the *World* the new king of New York City journalism. By the end of 1895, the techniques that Pulitzer had perfected, which became known as the "new journalism," had enabled him to outpace all competition.[2] The *World* was reaching 450,000 people, an unheard of number. But what goes around comes around, as Pulitzer was soon to learn.

The first real indication that the bubble was soon to burst for Pulitzer, Russell, and the *World* came in January 1896. A new kid in town, William Randolph Hearst, had invaded New York and was doing everything he possibly could to imitate Joseph Pulitzer's success—including stealing his staff. "There was every expectation in New York's newspaper community that Hearst would fail . . . miserably," writes Hearst biographer David Nasaw.[3] Hearst, who had a stockpile of money behind him from his father's mining fortune, first entered the news business in San Francisco, where he turned the *Examiner* into a success with a Pulitzer-like crusading and sensational newspaper. But like Russell and other eager journalists, the thirty-two-year-old wunderkind decided he needed to do better to make his mark on the world stage, increase his fortune, and enhance his political credentials. The only way to do that was to go to New York. Hearst bought the lowly *New York Journal* in the fall of 1895. Then, from across the continent, he dragged his stalwart staff—among others, the acerbic reporter Alfred Henry Lewis, the sob sister Annie Laurie, and his brilliant genius managing editor Sam Chamberlain—and installed them in the *Journal's* Park Row offices, just opposite the *World's* gilt-domed building that towered over newspaper row in lower Manhattan. As a Pulitzer biographer put it, "There was about Hearst the air of a precocious, unpredictable, slightly raffish adolescent taking the measure of an aging and ailing rival."[4]

Hearst was ready to begin the war that soon turned into the famous "yellow journalism" phase of American newspapers—and plunged Charles Edward Russell into the thick of an experience that surely had his father, the principled editor, turning over in his grave. Hearst struck the first blow with the Sunday supplement to his newspaper. Publishing a Sunday newspaper was a relatively new phenomenon in journalism, and it quickly proved to be a big moneymaker. Advertisers from the new urban department stores flocked to the various supplements, as did readers. With time on their hands on leisurely weekend days, they pored over the features that became a part of the sections devoted to murder mysteries, pseudo-science, sports, and women's issues. Readers especially liked the comic strips, another innovation and regular feature in Pulitzer's paper since 1889. R. F. Outcault's "Yellow Kid," a toothless, grinning tenement urchin living in "Hogan's Alley," was the most popular of the comic characters. The "funnies" section was the innovation of Sunday editor Morrill Goddard, a Dartmouth graduate who had been with Pulitzer for nine years. Under the direction of the thirty-year-old Goddard, the Sunday edition had soared from a circulation of 266,000 in 1893 to 450,000 in 1895. Hearst wanted Goddard for the *Journal*, but Goddard did not want to leave behind his loyal and talented staff. So Hearst, in one of his lavish spending sprees, told Goddard to bring over his entire staff, which he did. Pulitzer, not to be outdone, had his business manager and trusted aide S. S. Carvalho make a counteroffer. Goddard took the offer, and he and his Sunday staff returned to the *World* . . . but only for twenty-four hours. Hearst opened his checkbook once again and stole Goddard back. No surprise there, of course, since Hearst's largesse is estimated to have increased salaries by twenty five percent in New York City. As Hearst business manger Charles Palmer said to a visitor, "Oh, we don't bother about money around here. Open any closet and you'll smell . . . [it] burning."[5]

Pulitzer was furious. He vowed to sink the newcomer in the same way he had overtaken Bennett and Dana. But Hearst was different from Pulitzer's previous rivals: for one thing his pocketbook had no bottom. Eventually he spent $8 million of the Hearst fortune before he turned a profit. He was also good at imitating and even outdoing Pulitzer in the innovative journalism that Pulitzer had pioneered. Moreover, Hearst had a keen sense of what the people of fin-de-siecle America seemed to want. Nasaw points out that "the Hearst papers articulated [America's] 'vulnerability, unease, and anger' more powerfully and persistently than any other public medium in the 1890s." In February 1896, Pulitzer upped the ante by dropping the price of his newspaper to one cent, a move that Hearst felt played into his hands. "Smelling blood, Hearst moved in for the kill," comments Nasaw.[6]

Both Hearst and Pulitzer were millionaires, but Pulitzer was self-made while Hearst's fortune was inherited (actually on loan from his mother) and his pockets deeper than Pulitzer's. At some point, Hearst felt that Pulitzer would not be able to withstand the money—or the staff—losses. A second telling blow came in the winter of 1896. Pulitzer, who paid good salaries and was thoughtful in honoring valued personnel, decided to hold a birthday banquet in honor of Richard Farrelly, his managing editor. Russell had replaced Farrelly as city editor when Farrelly took over as the *World's* top editor. But the night before the banquet, Farrelly received an offer from Hearst to join the *Journal* staff. To Pulitzer's shock, Farrelly took the offer. "Farrelly has gone over to the enemy," an aide told Pulitzer. "To Gush?" he asked using his secret code name for Hearst. Pulitzer canceled the dinner party.[7]

Since no letters or diaries from Russell's years working for either Pulitzer or Hearst are available, it's difficult to know what he was thinking as this battle of titans took place. He commented in one memoir written in 1914 that he viewed Pulitzer as "the unequaled wizard and wonder worker" of journalism.[8] In that same memoir he wrote how his time as city editor under Pulitzer was special, during which he learned to appreciate the craft of journalism. But it was also a time that gave him pause as he watched unfold what a top Pulitzer aide called "the most extraordinary dollar-matching contest in the history of journalism." The *World* newsroom was never a calm or easy place to work in. Activity was always feverish, perhaps reflecting the feverish conditions of New York City. Pulitzer believed in creative tension in his newsroom, and he was increasingly a very difficult man to work for. His eyesight had largely failed, and aides had to read him the newspaper. His sensitive hearing made him recoil at even the sound of slurping soup. He changed top editors at the drop of a hat. As Russell recalled it, the *World* "was conducted for a time by a procession of managing editors that walked in at the front door, got out an issue or two, disappeared in the rear, and were seen no more."[9] Even more problematic, however, was the condition of unrest bred by the "yellow journalism" fever brought on by the Pulitzer-Hearst rivalry.

First and foremost, of course, was what the competition did to the content of the *World*. Competition normally has a positive effect on the quality and price of products. But in the news business, it often drives journalists into the gutter in search of titillating news that will lure readers. "Your yellow journalist," commented Willis J. Abbot, an editor for Hearst, "can work himself into quite a fiery fever of enthusiasm over a Christmas fund or a squalid murder, as over a presidential campaign. He sees everything through a magnifying glass and can make a first-page sensation out of a story which a more sober paper would dismiss with a paragraph inside." Russell called it a "species of blackmail."[10] Nonetheless, this fiery fever overtook the *World's* newsroom and brought with it espionage and secrecy more befitting an intelligence agency. After Pulitzer dropped the price of his paper to one cent, he put into place an elaborate system of codes so that he could communicate with his staff without Hearst intercepting his messages. Thus, Pulitzer (nickname: Andes) could send a note to top editor Arthur Brisbane (Horace) asking whether the circulation (Curate) of his morning edition (Genuine) had increased. More importantly, he wanted to know, was the Sunday *World* (Genuine) making a profit (Mental)? To top editor Don Seitz (Gulch), he wondered, was there any chance that Hearst (Medusa or Gush or Magnetic) would try next to steal his city editor (Grandam)? Weren't Russell (Gabion), David Graham Phillips (Gumboil) and "Horace" all close friends who would remain loyal? The answer, unfortunately for Pulitzer, was no. In the fall of 1897 Medusa struck again; this time he went after "Gabion" and Horace. The prevailing story on Park Row, where all the newspapers were housed, was that newsmen awaited the day that they would receive a business card with the enclosed statement: "Mr. Hearst would be pleased to have you call." This meant that Hearst was about to offer a job. The card came to Russell in the summer of 1897.[11]

Russell accepted the offer, leaving the *World* and joining the *Journal* in October ostensibly as a managing editor, a term that was applied to any number of editors. It was unclear exactly what his duties would be. Fellow Pulitzer editor Brisbane, whom Russell had met many years before when both were reporters covering electrocutions in New York, tried to talk Russell out of jumping ship. The two huddled at Brisbane's Hempstead, Long Island, estate that summer.

"Charlie, don't be a fool," said Brisbane.

"What makes you think I'm a fool? Hearst is giving me more than Pulitzer did."

"It's not the question of money alone," said Arthur. "You've got to take a long view on this matter. Both of us are young. We've gone far but we can't afford to spoil our future."

They argued hour after hour. Brisbane was eloquent and logical and had Russell almost convinced that he had made a mistake. Russell recalled: "At one point he tried to clinch the argument by stating 'Such an unknown upstart can never succeed here in New York. Why, just look at the difference in the heads of Pulitzer and Hearst. Jo Pulitzer has a head as long as that of a horse. Compare it with Hearst's! Then you'll realize how obvious it is that Pulitzer will lick Hearst in short order. Quit your job as soon as possible and return to your position with us. Remaining for any length of time with that California millionaire is plainly a case of journalistic suicide.'"[12] But Russell could not be convinced to stay with Pulitzer. Ironically, six weeks later, Brisbane joined Russell at the *Journal* and became a lifelong confidante of Hearst and one of the most famous and highly paid newsmen in America. Russell's buddy Phillips did not believe that the move would be permanent. "You'll be back here," he told Russell. "You are a *World* man and can not keep way."[13] Phillips was wrong. Russell stayed in the Hearst camp for many years.

Why would Russell jump ship to Hearst's *Journal* when, after all, Pulitzer, the schoolmaster of journalism, was such a champion of the people's causes, a man who believed in so many of the same progressive causes as did Russell? There are various possible explanations. Certainly the lure of larger salary must have been part of the reason. Hearst was offering the kind of money that was unheard of in journalism circles, even in New York. He was also offering journalists something that no one before had offered—security. He gave editors long-term contracts. With a wife and a now twelve-year-old son, Russell had to be interested in the possibility of secure employment. The move to Hearst was also a step up. He was an ambitious thirty-seven-year-old and his job as city editor was grinding and not as prestigious as that of managing editor. Thus, the move was not only for a raise in pay but a step up the journalistic ladder.

More important, however, were the working conditions under Pulitzer. He was a cranky eccentric, albeit one with progressive instincts. He gave his staff little freedom; no bylines or signed articles were allowed. Pulitzer insisted that no one's name but his be on the newspaper's masthead. Hearst offered the potential of creative freedom, as well as something else that was attractive to Russell: if Pulitzer was for the underdog, Hearst was for the under-underdog, and he had the money to back up his affection for the masses. Hearst's style of journalism—typified by the slogan "While Others Talk the *Journal* Acts"—appealed to the activist Russell. He worked for Hearst for six years because he had a sense that Hearst was for the people. Yes, his newspaper was sensational, yes, it was interested in suicides, sex, and scandals. But it was also enterprising, crusading, and in tune with the people's issues. How odd, of course, that Charles Edward Russell, dignified and private, so passionate about democracy, a man who loved Shakespeare and wrote poetry, an aficionado of highbrow arts, would in his professional life want to work at the most populist and sensational newspaper ever printed!

II. ENTER THE WHIRLWIND

The *Journal* under William Randolph Hearst is difficult to describe. Hearst editor Willis J. Abbot wrote to a friend soon after he became an editor at the *Journal*. "I had secured very remunerative employment in a lunatic asylum," he observed. Frantic, chaotic, hard-driving, unpredictable—those words best describe the *Journal's* newspages and its newsroom as it sought to overtake Pulitzer's *World*. Hearst's newspapers, Russell once wrote, "seem always to be shouting or roaring about something, always to be in a state of ferment and tension."[14] Russell recalled vividly the first time he ever saw the tall, blue-eyed thirty-three-year-old Hearst. It was a sweltering summer afternoon in 1896; Russell was walking to his Brooklyn home when a good-looking young man, carrying a straw hat and a newspaper, came running by "at fierce speed." The man was Hearst, who had spotted an error in his newspaper and was returning to his newsroom on Park Row to make a correction. "It was typical of the man's true absorption," Russell observed. Indeed Hearst, the "mad" overseer of the asylum, was no absentee or hands-off publisher. On the contrary, he did everything but carry the lines of hot type. After dinner and the theater,

Hearst, often in formal attire, would enter the newsroom. "At the sound of his well-known step on the stairs the night editor groans in spirit," Russell remembered. Hearst would roll up his shirtsleeves and take out his editor's blue pencil, reshuffling and editing the pages and putting new headlines on certain stories. "Take that out of the first page and put it on the third page. Drop the first-page cut. Reset your seven-column line in forty-eight-point Howland—it's too big."[15] While Hearst made changes in a calm and methodical style, his editors would stand around, playing games and practical jokes, while they awaited "the chief's" final instructions. Day in and day out, in his early years as a publisher Hearst was directly involved in the production of his newspaper. He handpicked his staff and he assigned stories. "Despite a liberal conferring of titles," Abbot recalled, "Mr. Hearst was the only editor-in-chief of any of his papers."[16]

The newspaper that Hearst produced, like the man, was a daily contradiction, a schizoid spray of printer's ink. On one hand, it played up every suicide, robbery, and assault that occurred in the city. Every bizarre man-bites-dog story that came along—and some that were made up—hit the front pages. News accounts were often exaggerated to fit a story line. Readers were told of a man with a sliver of steel in his head. "Brain Pierced but then Lives," blared the headline. Near it was a gruesome story of a man whose head was decapitated. The story described the head tumbling away after a trolley accident. "His Head Severed by Trolley." A few days later the big news was about a woman "Stripped Naked in the Court Room." Crime and underwear, one editor said, was the formula for success.[17] By April 1898, as the "yellow journalism war" with Pulitzer heated up, especially over the Spanish-American War, the sensationalism only worsened.[18] The headlines on page five on April 6, 1898 capture the *Journal* at the height of what Russell referred to as "the depths to which we had fallen." "Parboiled alive in bathtub" blared one. Read the others: "Demented woman's dance on roof," "Leap from hospital window," "Stabbed with scissors by barber." Hearst biographer Procter analyzed Hearst's formula: "First and foremost, stories had to be well written, the subject matter embellishing a certain shock value or appealing to baser human emotions or eliciting mystery and intrigue almost beyond human comprehension. To attract even more attention—and induce further reader inquiry—huge black headlines depicted the crux of the story together with graphic illustrations or cartoons and fantastic emotion."[19]

If readers were looking for a steady diet of high-minded writing about public policy, the *Journal* was not the place to go. But if they wanted grisly crime stories, Hearst's newspaper was their home; it was obsessed with cops and robbers. As far back as the 1830s, in the "penny press" era of journalism, newspapers had discovered that crime stories were popular with readers and a key to building circulation. Russell, who had been a famous police-detective reporter at the *Herald*, fit in well with this aspect of the *Journal*. He was a veteran at hunting down clues on murder stories, and he was a perfect match for the special team of reporters Hearst had assembled to solve murder mysteries in New York. If it was a particularly big case, even Hearst joined the marauding band of reporters known as "the wrecking crew." Some of the crew would actually pose as city detectives as they interviewed witnesses and used Hearst's cash to talk reluctant sources into confiding in *Journal* reporters.[20] Sometimes Hearst would hire private detectives to help solve a case or use a "reformed" murderer to write an "expert" account. Always, lurking everywhere, of course, was the dogfight with Pulitzer. If the *World* had ten men on a story, Hearst would assign twenty.

If it was a slow news day, the Hearst men then had to "create" news. This did not necessarily mean that they would make up stories; "yellow journalism" was more known for embellishing than fictionalizing. Sometimes Hearst's reporters found clues in murders that the police missed; at times they ballyhooed a Hearst fundraising effort. When the *Journal* sent urban youths off to Long Island for a summer vacation, when it raised money for victims of a fire or helped pay the heating bills of the poor in the particularly cold winter of 1896–1897, it made sure its readers knew. Part of the formula for successful "yellow journalism" was to self-promote whenever possible. After a New Year's celebration sponsored by the *Journal*, the paper boasted: observers "can scarcely find adjectives strong enough to express their admiration."[21]

The activism and enterprise of Hearst's staff often took on a serious tone, and this is the side of Hearst that was most attractive to Russell, the one he fondly recalled in a 1904 magazine article he wrote about Hearst. In August 1897 a great flood hit Galveston, Texas, killings hundreds and threatening thousands. "The news reached us on one of the few nights Mr. Hearst did not come to the office," Russell remembered. "I awakened him at his house with a telephone call about three o'clock and told of the appalling magnitude of the disaster." Russell the editor was worried about getting news from a town cut off from communication. Hearst the publisher was most concerned about providing relief to the victims. Russell worried that it was too late to rouse the public and raise money for relief. "Why do you want to wait for the public? We will do it ourselves," Hearst said. Russell objected that the cost would be enormous and that the results for the newspaper would be minimal. "Never mind about the cost; never mind about the results," Hearst replied. Russell was ordered to fill trains with relief supplies sent from New York, Chicago, and San Francisco, where Hearst had newspapers. Of course, his newspapers publicized the efforts extensively. The trains reached Galveston and helped the victims. "It was magnificent," Russell declared, "but it was not journalism."[22]

Hearst, however, was in the process of redefining journalism. Russell seemed to understand this. "The Hearst innovations in newspaper-making may be said to have revolutionized the business," he wrote. Another enterprising tactic that Russell admired was that Hearst actually hired lawyers to go into court to block New York City from pursuing certain policies or from issuing contracts that he felt were inimical to the people's interests. At a time when businesses were often in cahoots with elected officials, buying lucrative franchise contracts for transportation and other utilities, Hearst's newspaper stepped into a void as a kind of public advocate, a watchdog with bite. During Russell's first winter under Hearst, for example, the newspaper's lawyers thwarted the owners of a Brooklyn trolley company that was trying to run a track loop through Manhattan. A court had issued an injunction, but the trolley owners continued construction. Hearst's lawyer sued to enforce the injunction. "The *Journal* was on guard," the newspaper bragged. A few days later, the newspaper demanded that the "death loop," a dangerous curved rail line, be permanently halted. The city's bridge commissioner had the legal—and moral—power to stop construction, the newspaper insisted.[23] But if he wouldn't act, the *Journal* would, Hearst promised his readers. The trolley line was halted.

The *Journal*'s crusading in 1896 also helped prevent the installation of unneeded gas lines in the city. In the spring of 1899 Hearst's crusades continued against New York's "water trust," a monopolistic coalition that controlled citizens' water supply. What Hearst and other progressives wanted was for the city's government to manage public utilities—gas, power, coal, ice, milk, even water, all of which were controlled by the private companies. When Hearst took over the *Journal*, the trusts were consolidating their control over the economy. Citizens needed a voice to protect themselves from the monopolies. Enter the *Journal*, along with Hearst's genius for marketing and for sensing the mood of the American public. Procter points this out, writing, "Hearst was determined to identify the *Journal* with the people of New York. He wanted them to consider it a voice against injustice, the protector of the poor and downtrodden, the defender of the average citizen against public corruption and corporate greed."[24] And that is where Russell fit in with William Randolph Hearst. "Rightly or wrongly," Russell said about Hearst, "he was convinced that he had a mission to fight for the weak, to represent the unrepresented, to better conditions, to protect the unprotected." Russell shared many of Hearst's progressive views, although eventually he would become more radical than his boss. More-over, Russell was learning from "the chief," ("Mr. Hearst," as Russell called him) about how enterprising journalism could protect the people.[25]

For Russell, the time with Hearst in New York was step three in his jour-nalism education. His first lesson had come on the streets as a reporter, when the kid from the Midwest was introduced to poverty and crime that he had nei-ther seen nor imagined. Russell's second lesson came at the feet of the master crusader-storyteller Pulitzer, who first compelled him to pay attention to the issue of monopoly control and from whom he first learned to muckrake. Rus-sell then learned to take journalistic activism to a new level by watching the promotional and journalistic genius Hearst bring the *Journal* to new heights— and journalism to new depths. Russell learned his lessons well enough so that, in 1900, Hearst installed him as the publisher and overseer of his third newspa-per in Chicago.

III. Triumphs in the Chicago Madhouse

Historians are still trying to figure out William Randolph Hearst, who cre-ated the first chain of newspapers in America and then moved logically into magazine publishing and newsreel production. Hearst inherited and earned a fortune in his lifetime. His fabulous mansion, San Simeon, in California, typ-ifies the extravagant wealth that was always at Hearst's fingertips; his assets at one point totaled between $200 and $400 million. His news empire presaged today's media chains and syndicates. His gluing together of entertainment and news values also foreshadowed a trend that continues to this day in the American media. The film *Citizen Kane*, roughly based on Hearst's life, firmly stamped an impression on the American psyche. He is undoubtedly an Amer-ican legend, but he is a confusing legend, a bundle of contradictory impulses. Was he a profit-inspired scoundrel or a champion of the masses? Was he a politically ambitious media mogul or a man who worked tirelessly for pro-gressive causes? Was he a self-important publicity hound or a quiet philan-thropist? A philandering husband or public advocate of moral values? In truth, he was all of these, as much as they contradict each other. After work-ing many years as a Hearst editor, Willis J. Abbot saw the dichotomy, con-cluding that his boss embodied "a bunch of contradictions." He observed, "Hearst was to me a puzzle." Russell also saw two sides to the man. "An odd sense of duality," was how he described Hearst in his flattering 1904 maga-zine profile. The man's newspapers were so wild, yet the man "is so quiet and modest of manner, so low of voice, of such an impeccable calm and grave, deferential courtesy, that, fresh from reading of a howling extra, the patent incongruity of maker and product" is shocking.[26]

Russell was impressed by Hearst's intellect. "He knows men, knows affairs, knows history, and on questions of national policy he has positive opinions that he does not hesitate to declare," he said. He admired Hearst's "insatiable appetite for hard work." Unlike Hearst's detractors, Russell did not feel that either personal ambition or lust for money drove "the chief." "No man ever does anything from one motive," Russell said. Hearst's motives included "the excitement of contest, the naked joy of success, the sheer love of the business, and the allurement of the hazard." What drove Hearst most, however, was what Russell called "his idealistic notion of the mission of journalism," their shared belief that the newspaper could and should be an important and progressive force.[27]

If journalism was in the end a noble calling, how could Russell explain away the excesses of yellow journalism for which Hearst is largely responsible? Russell simply felt that Hearst was doing what was logical and necessary in the increasingly urban-centered world of 1890s journalism: making money in order to give his newspaper influence. "A newspaper without profits is a newspaper without influence, position, standing or use in the world," Russell wrote in a magazine.[28] This statement shows how much Russell had accepted the need to sensationalize, when necessary, in order to succeed in a competitive newspaper market.

The notion that making a newspaper is different than other businesses is "a mere fantasy," Russell wrote. If a newspaper cannot make money, "its proper place is the junk heap, like any other hopelessly unprofitable venture."[29] Russell was surprisingly cynical about the function of a newspaper. "Why," he asked, "are profits from newspaper-making less honorable than profits from shoe-making or rail-making?" Why does the newspaper have to take responsibility in "leading, reforming and guiding of mankind? There is nothing about a newspaper that compels its publisher to be a guardian of the public welfare." Nobody, he said, tells book publishers that they have to conduct their business for any other purpose than to make profits. A strange stance indeed for one who would soon concentrate his journalism on the sole purpose of bringing about reforms. But Russell's argument was based on reality of newspaper economics: large audiences, which are attractive to advertisers, insure profit. "From the editor-in-chief to the driver of the delivery wagon, there is and can be but one aim, one effort, one activity"—the building of a reading audience. "Circulation is success; the want of it is failure," he wrote, summing up why the plunge to yellow journalism and the sensationalism of the late 1890s had to be made.[30] Reach a lot of people or succumb.

With that settled, Russell turned to what was necessary to build an audience. "The only way to dispose of the newspaper product is to know intimately the minds, tastes, preferences, habits, ideas and ideals of the people that consume the product," he wrote. "To sympathize with them and to understand them. What do they like?" Hearst's answer—and Russell's, seemingly—was that they like crime, scandal, and sensation mixed in with a tolerable dose of crusading and exposé journalism. But they like and need a dose of facts also, Russell added, repeating a refrain that was embraced by reformers after the turn of the century. "The average American is an exceedingly intelligent, well-informed person. Give him the facts and he can make his own opinions; and, as a rule, his thinking will be just as good as that of any self-appointed leader or editorial guide."[31] Russell's thoughts may have been nobler than his boss's, however. Hearst was eyeing a new newspaper in Chicago, but he wanted to establish it less to give people the facts than to give the Democratic Party a partisan organ of opinion in the Midwest and to enhance his own credentials in the party.

Hearst's politics were always transparent. In his early years he was a Democrat who yearned for a place on the national stage. He got his wish eventually when he was elected twice to Congress; in 1904 he came in second for the Democratic nomination for the presidency. His two newspapers unabashedly supported William Jennings Bryan in his unsuccessful 1896 bid to defeat the Republican William McKinley. Soon after the 1898 election Hearst declared that the *Journal* was the national voice of the Democratic Party. Before objectivity became the profession's ideal, taking such a partisan stance was not a journalistic sin, since in 1898 newspapers still made their political preferences quite clear. But most newspapers had begun to separate their editorial and news voices; Hearst's had not.[32]

In April 1899 the Democratic Party, seeking a strong Democratic voice in the Midwest where Republican newspapers dominated, asked Hearst to start up a new newspaper in Chicago in order to give Bryan and the Democrats a platform. Hearst turned to his mother, Phoebe, who held the purse strings to his father's fortune. She was not pleased at his request for start-up money for another newspaper. "I have been feeling greatly depressed and did not feel like writing," she confided to her financial adviser Orrin Peck as she was traveling in Europe in May 1899. "Will is insisting upon buying a paper in Chicago. Says he will come over to see me if I do not go home very soon . . . it is madness. I never know when or how we will break out into some additional expensive scheme. I cannot tell you how distressed I feel about the heavy monthly loss on the *Journal* and then to contemplate starting another nightmare is a hopeless situation. I have written and telegraphed that no argument can induce me to

commit such a folly as that of starting another newspaper." Peck agreed. "As
you say it is madness," he replied. "He doubtless wishes to control the press of
the U.S. . . . It's like dashing along a mad road with runaway horses and trying
to harness in another. I see the situation is most desperate and makes one simply ill."[33]

Hearst persisted despite his mother's reservations, telling her that the *Journal* was soon to make a profit. He sent a telegram to Bryan about how he
wanted to help the cause: "The undertaking is big and the prospect of another
period of work and strain is not pleasant to contemplate. Still I am most anxious to please you and to be of service to the party. If the good accomplished
would compensate for effort and expense, etc. I suppose the satisfaction of
being of some value would lead me to disregard all other considerations."
Hearst had only once request. He wanted the party to realize that he was starting this newspaper "for the party's sake, not for money."[34]

Hearst sent S. S. Carvalho, Pulitzer's former trusted top aide, whom he
had stolen, out to Chicago to lay the groundwork for the *Chicago American*, in-
tending to publish in six weeks. The goal was to be on the streets before the
Democratic National Convention in St. Louis in July. Carvalho rented an old
wine-company building in a run-down neighborhood and recruited eight hundred men to work around the clock in three shifts. A huge newspaper printing
press was sent by rail to Chicago. Hearst and Brisbane arrived soon after, along
with a host of faithful Hearst staffers, Russell included. He installed Brisbane as
his first editor, but Russell would be particularly useful. He was from the Midwest and he had covered Chicago in his early years as a freelancer for Pulitzer.
For Russell, it was a bit like returning home, although his wife, Abby, continued to live at their Brooklyn apartment with their son. Hearst then carried out
his normal practice of raiding the other Chicago newspapers, at times doubling
and tripling the salaries of reporters, pressman, and printers. When Hearst arrived, Chicago had eight newspapers. "When the smoke cleared a few years
later," one biographer noted, "some were dying, others dead, and only the im-
perturbable *Tribune* and the *Daily News* emerged relatively unscathed and un-
changed." And true to his promise to the Democrats, Hearst had the *American*
up and running well before the convention. The first edition hit the streets on
July 4, 1900, when William Jennings Bryan sent a telegram to Chicago, giving
the word to "Start the Press." He wrote to Hearst, "I am confident that a large
circulation awaits the *Chicago American*."[35]

Brisbane edited the *American* for a short while but then turned over the
reins to Russell, who became the *American's* publisher. Finally, Russell could
run his own newspaper—at least as much as any editor could run a William

Randolph Hearst publication. And he had that freedom in a place that, while not quite New York, offered both a prairie sensibility and urban excitement. As the agricultural clearinghouse of the nation, with wheat packers and pork packers mingling with hordes of immigrant workers, Chicago was a great town to find news. The "queen and guttersnipe" of cities, "the cynosure and cesspool of the world," one foreign visitor called it. Loud, dirty, chaotic, growing furiously with a population of 1.7 million—a hotbed of growing industrialism.[36] In short, it was a perfect place to find scandals, readers, and Democratic voters as well as to crusade for civic betterment, even if a bigger circulation, more profit, and political advantages were the motives.

What did a Charles Edward Russell newspaper look like? It looked much like a William Randolph Hearst newspaper—both enlightening and "yellow." The *American's* goal, stated an editorial written by Russell, is "to interest, to instruct, and above all to stimulate thoughtful lines of human progress."[37] To do so, editions hit the streets all day long, in the morning, at noon, at four and five P.M. and then at ten o'clock at night. Sometimes "extras" were printed when calamities occurred. The headlines were always bold and sensational. The news pages focused on crime, natural disasters, and the bizarre. When none of those was available—and that was rare—the newspaper was sure to have gimmicks and promotions for Chicagoans. Its editorials were well-argued and generally progressive. Mix in a steady diet of crusades against local ignominies and a drumbeat of positive news about the Democratic Party and you have the *American* under Russell. The *American* office, a high-ceilinged forty-by-sixty-foot room where fifty reporters at a time usually worked, was commonly referred to as "the madhouse." Noise and confusion ruled in the newsroom. "Mingled with the clutter of telegraph instruments and typewriters, and the sounds of humming feet, were voices talking, shouting, sometimes cursing," recalled one of Russell's reporters, William Salisbury. Some of the cursing might have come from reporters who were fired at the *American.* "Changes in the staff took place so often that it was hard to keep track of them all," said Salisbury.[38]

A typical news day at the *American* came in September when the flood hit Galveston, Texas. "Texas Death Horror May Reach 10,000" was the page one headline. All of pages two and three were devoted to the disaster. Page four featured an *American* crusade that was urging the city's "gas trust" to cut its prices. Other sidebar stories editorialized for municipal ownership of the gas utility, a constant theme in Hearst newspapers, whether in San Francisco, New York, or Chicago. Page six was all about labor disturbances all over the nation, with a decidedly pro-worker slant. No surprise in that; Hearst was always for the unions. Salisbury said that reporters were instructed: "If the facts don't warrant your favoring the unions, at least be neutral."[39] Page seven had an eight-column head-line about the upcoming convention of the Democrats. A story about William McKinley was buried on page ten, even though he had just given his acceptance speech for the Republican presidential nomination the previous day.

If anything was outstanding or different about Russell's *American*, it was the persistence of its crusades. Two were successful during Russell's months as publisher of the *American*. The first came about after a reporter received complaints about problems that citizens were having with their water pressure. Something was wrong with the underground pipes. James O'Shaugnessy—a "bright and young reporter," Russell said—decided with Hearstian bravado to undertake his own investigation. He hired some laborers and at a street intersection late one night and gave new meaning to the journalistic tactic of "digging up dirt." The reporter and crew dug up the roadway until they found the water pipes. Once underground, O'Shaugnessy discovered that a nearby meat-packing company that needed a heavy water supply had illegally diverted water by tapping into the pipe. On September 7, 1900, the *American*, in eighty-point type, filled page one with the boldfaced headline: "Water Thieves Caught!" In the following weeks the newspaper wrote ten other stories on the matter.[40] Only one news story reported something new—that two more diversionary pipes had been found. The other stories simply repeated the previous exposé news. On November 9, the *American* identified Armour, the largest of the city's meat packers, as the culprit. The story appeared in the first three editions of the newspaper, but then mysteriously disappeared in the final two editions. Could the meat packers have pressured the *American* to quash the story? Given the paper's hostile attitude toward monopoly power, this seems unlikely. Two Hearst historians allege that his newspaper regularly gave favorable news coverage for placement of advertisements, but this seems unlikely in the water story, which was an *American* exclusive. The paper was relatively quiet in the next few weeks. It did not report again on the water thieves until January 14, when one of the accused confessed, and once more on January 18, when there was a conviction of one of the alleged water thieves. The *American* took full credit for the conviction. Frustration followed, however, because no penalties were levied against the meat packers, although the water diversion stopped.[41] For Russell, the exposé was simply Round One against the meat packers. In a little more than three years he would return to attack the meat-packing monopoly for a national magazine.

A similar if somewhat more extensive pattern of exposé leading to crusade came in a second major series of articles, also during September and October, when Russell's *American* attacked the private company that was providing heating and cooking gas for Chicagoans. This crusade differed from the first: no exposé started it. Instead, the *American* simply declared one day that gas prices were too high and pledged to help citizens. On September 8, the newspaper offered a coupon for residents to send in to protest the high gas prices. On September 9 an exposé story reported how one company was monopolizing the gas trade in the city. Result: high prices. This was a common refrain for the *American* and for other reformers in American cities as they championed the cause of municipal ownership of utilities. Water, gas, ice, electricity, the rails—all should be "directed by public authority [and] ought to belong to the public," it declared in a typical editorial.[42] In essence, the *American's* stance on municipal ownership was what Russell adopted on a larger scale as he began to turn toward socialism: government ownership of key industries. The *American's* crusade paid quick dividends. The gas company immediately announced a lowering of prices, but the *American* was only partly satisfied. It announced its real intention: "Municipal Ownership A Good Thing." The public, the newspaper asserted, "should own or be owned." Chicago needs municipal ownership, "and the sooner the better."[43]

While the *American* was crusading for the people's issues and building its circulation in the process, its reporters were earning reputations in other ways—as the sleaziest and trickiest in the Windy City. The ways in which the *American* gathered the news were, to say the least, controversial. This should come as no surprise. Chicago journalism is fabled for its reportorial "monkey shines." The *American* often got the story first by signing up coroners, hotel clerks, hospital supervisors, and telephone operators to leak tidbits to *American* reporters.[44] Sometimes its news was sensationalized greatly. William Salisbury recalled one typical episode. Two Polish immigrants who were lovers conspired to murder the husband who was interfering with their affair. The wife pushed him off a pier into the icy winter water; a tugboat crew fished him out. A reporter telephoned the details to Salisbury. The lovers confessed. Then Salisbury asked if the wife was good-looking. "No. She's a homely bat," Salisbury was told: "The lover must have been off his trolley." But the next day the *American's* art department had drawn a gorgeous woman to go alongside the story.[45]

Life at the *American* soured Salisbury on journalism, even though he began there full of enthusiasm and believing in Hearst. After a few months on the paper, he had begun to see another side to Hearst's brand of journalism—the manipulation of sources, the exaggeration, the outright lies, the snuggling with advertisers. Salisbury finally clashed with Russell. He and three other staffers, apparently under orders from an editor, took names of clergy from the telephone book and quoted them in a story praising the *American's* Easter Sunday supplement without even talking to them. Indignant, many of the clergy wrote letters threatening to sue the newspaper. The interview comments were retracted, and Hearst ordered the four staffers and the night city editor fired. Salisbury pleaded his case to Russell. "If he had been chief judge of the National Supreme Court, he couldn't have looked more grave and august," Salisbury recalled. Salisbury explained to Russell how he had been ordered to concoct the interviews.

> "Do you mean to tell me," Russell cried, "that you would write anything for the columns of Mr. Hearst's newspaper that was not absolutely true?"
> "Well—yes—I have—sometimes."
> "Terrible," Russell replied.
> "I—er—I supposed a little exaggeration was expected once in a while."
> "Monstrous!" said Russell.
> "I—er—uh—I thought this was—er—understood in headquarters—"
> "Preposterous!"
> "In fact, I have often heard orders issued to—er—uh—'doctor up' a story a little to make it interesting, you know."
> "Outrageous!"

And so the conversation went, with Russell denying any knowledge of the inner workings of yellow journalism as practiced at the *American*. When Salisbury confronted Russell with the fact that the *American* had hired snitches to steal news from the early editions of other Chicago newspapers, Russell stammered and declined to discuss the allegation. The meeting was ended; Salisbury was fired. But Salisbury says he learned a clear lesson, one that likely was becoming clear to Russell as well as he managed the "Madison Avenue madhouse" under the watchful eye of William Randolph Hearst: "Journalism in America is but a business to newspaper owners and managers," Salisbury concluded. "Editors, reporters and correspondents are but puppets on strings." Soon enough the great treadmill of journalism "grinds out the lives of its workers . . . and then throws them aside."[46]

After eight years on the streets as a reporter; after three years directing Joseph Pulitzer's New York City news coverage; after five years in the maelstrom of yellow journalism under Hearst—Russell was coming close to the point of being used up and broken down. And then in January of 1901 his world came crashing down. His wife, Abby, contracted typhoid fever. He rushed back to New York to be with her. It seemed only yesterday that she had accompanied Russell on the piano as he recited poetry. Their now sixteen-year-old son, John Edward, was with his parents. At first, Abby improved and seemed on the road to recovery. Then, on January 12, Abby Osborn Rust Russell died at the age of thirty five.[47] Her father had died just two years before back in St. Johnsbury, Vermont. Charles and John made the trek back to wintry Vermont to bury Abby and ponder the future. Soon after, Russell's health broke and he suffered what can only be described as a nervous breakdown. Hearst gave Russell, who was forty one, unlimited leave with pay.

CHAPTER SEVEN

EXPOSING THE
WORLD'S GREATEST TRUST

PART I: FROM POETRY TO SAVAGERY

BATTERED BY THE DEATH OF HIS WIFE AND BRUISED from the grinding lifestyle of the daily newspaper, Charles Edward Russell gave in to his doctor's wishes. He took a year off from work. On March 1, 1902, at the age of forty two, Russell boarded the steamship *Lahn* in New York, bound for Italy and Germany in search, as a newspaper reported, of "repose and recuperation." Because of problems with his eyes, he spent much of his time wearing black goggles.[1] "It is especially miserable being ill in Hotel beds, and foreign at that," he wrote as he trooped across Europe in search of what a lifelong friend, the actress Julia Marlowe, described as "the cure," a regimen of hot baths and Spartan food. "What an existence," he complained. "Up at 6 A.M.! and all morning filling inside with water and all afternoon soaking. . . ."[2]

After recuperating in various spas, a waterlogged Russell returned to America, firmly convinced that his days in journalism were over. He had lived the frenzied life of reporter and editor for nearly twenty years, reaching the pinnacle of his profession as one of the great reporters in the nation's media capital, New York City. He had edited two of the most powerful crusading newspapers in the world, publications that had profound influence not only on the shape of journalism but also on the shape of the nation. And he topped it all off by publishing his own newspaper—albeit on behalf of the ambitious William Randolph Hearst—in what was America's second greatest city. But the pace of the newsroom, even for a healthy man, was torturous. There was the overseeing of dozens of reporters, fielding requests and complaints from both the public and the merchant community, trying to keep pace with a world in constant turmoil in cities that were growing tremendously and were havens for the wretched poor, thieving politicians, and the corrupt rich. All the while he was trying to satisfy two demanding, eccentric, brilliant, and politically irascible publishers. No wonder that when his wife died unexpectedly his world tumbled down—and his health broke. "No more of that kind of work for this poor old man," he wrote his friend Wallace Rice. "He knows when he has had enough."[3]

To continue his recuperation, Russell moved to Evanston, Illinois, a small town north of Chicago. His son, John, had just enrolled in Northwestern University, situated on the shore of Lake Michigan, in the area where the wealthy Chicago industrialists had built the lavish homes that Russell would later criticize. Russell's son was in a liberal arts program, and he told school officials that he wanted to be an artist. His father the journalist was also turning to the arts to continue his recovery. Russell felt there would be respite in the writing of poetry and the study of music, an odd choice for a man so engaged by the harshness of domestic politics and squalor of urban poverty as well. Yet for many years he had embraced simultaneously the beauty of highbrow lyricism and the tumultuous world of social struggle. His first book of poems, *Such Stuff as Dreams*, was published soon after his wife's death. Some of it was a melancholy remembrance of Abby, who had now become a "tear-touched memory." In "Dead Music" he wrote: "I shall not hear again the notes/ that once beneath her fingers grew." In another poem, he recalled walks along the river with Abby when, "rapt with vain dreams we crept from haunts of men." But now, "the river's shore is barren grown, harsh all the tuneful roar of streams, and now a darkness comes to pen the shadows of the hill."[4] He told a friend, "I have been ill and am still far from well."[5]

Despite his desolation, Russell was nonetheless purposeful. "For the first time in my life," he wrote, "a little leisure" was possible, and yet he wanted to use it to "carry out a purpose long cherished." Russell had concluded that "the separate arts of music and poetry are really but one."[6] To demonstrate this, he turned to analyzing the work of the British poet, Charles Algernon Swinburne, Russell was interested in the exquisite political melodies he found in Swinburne's "A Song of Italy" (1867), in which the poet passionately embraces liberty. He wanted to put Swinburne's lyrics to music. This allowed him to use his knowledge of the work of Theodore Thomas, the founder of the American orchestra, whom he had discovered first at the age of fifteen when Thomas stayed at the Russell household in Davenport. After this visit, Russell became a "humble follower and disciple."[7] With newspapering behind him, Russell figured: "I now conceived that with a piano, my Swinburne, and some sheets of music paper I could demonstrate" the unity of music and poetry.[8]

But Russell was abruptly and fortuitously taken away from his work in the fall of 1904. "One day, as I was making some musical analyses of the amphibrach foot, there was brought to me a telegram from my friend." The friend was Erman Ridgway, editor of *Everybody's* magazine, which had been publishing since that summer a spectacular series of exposés of Wall Street by financier Thomas Lawson. Along with *McClure's*, *Everybody's* was one of the newly emerging popular mass-circulation magazines that were muckraking corporate and political life in America. Ridgway asked a favor: Would Russell contact J. W. Midgley, a noted railroad expert who had just finished testifying in Chicago before the Interstate Commerce Commission, to see if his "extraordinary testimony" was worth an article?[9]

Russell agreed to help his friend, but the newsman in him—the years of working the streets that made his nose for news twitch when a story beckoned—first led to a detour; he bought a newspaper to learn about Midgley's testimony. "What I read gave me a new sensation," he recalled. Was it possible that the news accounts accurately portrayed this "huge commercial tyranny" that was to be seen from the testimony of Midgley and others?[10] The witnesses outlined what Russell would soon label "The Greatest Trust in the World"— the organization of the nation's meat packers, with headquarters in Chicago, into a giant cartel, one that dwarfed even John D. Rockefeller's Standard Oil and threatened to turn democracy into plutocracy.

So intrigued was Russell that he headed for Chicago. "I thought I would stroll over to the Interstate Commerce Commission," he wrote.[11] Although the Elkins Act of 1903 had strengthened the regulatory powers of this federal agency, it was still no match for the beef industry's battery of lawyers and lobbyists with their devious and nefarious methods. No one thought that it would be. Public support for central authority to control private capital was only beginning to emerge in Gilded Age America. Begun in April 1887, the ICC was an agency in search of a mandate—and some teeth. The law that created the ICC was ambiguous, as was the public and government's support for it. What was needed—and what was coming—was an onslaught of publicity about why the government needed more power to intervene in the affairs of private enterprises that could no longer be trusted.[12]

The testimony Russell heard in October 1904 was from two Midwesterners— not unlike the hard-working Iowans with whom he had grown up. They told sad tales: one witness testified that he opposed the meat packers and then they ruined him; the other, a farmer, showed how the trust's monopolistic control of markets devalued his crop so much that it was hardly worth his summer's labor by the time he got to market. Listening to those witnesses was enough "to start boiling blood in the veins of any American," Russell concluded.[13] This was also a story to speed up the heart rate of any true Pulitzer-Hearst man: David against Goliath, underdog against top dog, workers against owners. To put it in the terms of the political movement then energizing America—Progressivism—it was a story of "the people" being overwhelmed by "the interests."[14]

With Midgley too busy to write an article for *Everybody's*, Ridgway turned to Russell. A part of Russell was reluctant, the part that had "not the least disposition" to disrupt his newfound "real employment." But the temptation to rejoin the battle—and an emerging exposé movement—was too much for Russell to resist. "I popped back, 'Yes' before I knew it," Russell said. "The next thing I knew a muck-rake was put into my hand and I was plunged into the midst of the game."[15]

PART II: "ON THE TRACK OF THE MONSTER. . . ."

Having worked on and off as a reporter in the 1880s in Chicago and having published the *Chicago American* at the turn of the century, Russell probably knew what was common knowledge in the Windy City: the meat packers had great influence over everything from the railroads to local elections. Indeed, the *American's* exposure of the city's water thieves had led the newspaper and city authorities directly to the meat packers, as Russell noted in one of his autobiographies, concluding: "I was aware of the virtually absolute power of these companies and knew that any one attacking them would have an unpleasant time."[16]

Russell was also keenly aware that the time was ripe for an attack on monopolies. Agitation against concentrated corporate power, jangling in the American political landscape since the 1890s, was beginning to reach new heights. In the South and in the West farmers had long complained that Eastern financiers and railroad moguls manipulated them unfairly. In the East, those who had risen in status—both workers and middle-class professionals—feared that the "trusts" had them at their mercy. In Chicago, as Russell knew from covering the Haymarket incident, workers were particularly active—and were the focus of attention from the growing socialist movement and the trade unions.[17]

Nevertheless, Russell was optimistic as 1904 began, speculating in a book review that perhaps America had seen "the turning of the reactionary tide" against the excesses of industrialism. Certainly, journalists were beginning to do their part and were indeed a key force in the revolt.[18] The public's awakening began in 1902, when Ida Tarbell and Lincoln Steffens began their muckraking in *McClure's* magazine, and the American public, in monthly installments, was handed a steady diet of exposure to corporate and political abuses. Although recuperating, Russell nonetheless followed closely the political and journalistic developments. He read and reviewed Tarbell's work, calling her history of Standard Oil "as interesting as a novel," and citing it as "the best piece of historical writing ever done by a woman." When her "unquestionable fact" was coupled with Steffens's "extraordinary series" on political graft in urban America and with Thomas Lawson's "disclosures of reckless viciousness" on Wall Street, Russell saw a pattern; a "nightmare of savagery," he called it.[19]

When Russell began to write about the beef trust in February 1905, he said he was a neutral observer—"It is not my business here to be an advocate." But the lessons he learned at the feet of Pulitzer and Hearst and what he was seeing all around him in monopoly power had turned Russell into a passionate researcher. He knew after the ICC hearings in Chicago that something was terribly wrong with the might wielded by a few packers—Armour and Swift, in particular—who were able to control prices for both consumers and producers. "One man's voice in a telephone determines how much a million farmers shall lose on their cattle," he told to his readers. "A whole vast industry from the Rio Grande to North Dakota can hang on the voice of the man in a telephone."[20] It was easy for Russell to see the problem and even to identify its causes.

Russell's graying hair and piercing blue eyes made him a distinguished and distinguishable figure as he began to split his time between Packingtown, where the animals were slaughtered, and the produce houses in Chicago, where the packers' bureaucracy was housed. "I had not been at work for ten days before I was an object of marked suspicion in the Stock Yards region," Russell wrote.[21] For one thing, Russell was identified as a Hearst man (he still received mail at the *American*) and since Hearst's newspapers in Chicago had battled with the packers since that paper began, the packers figured Russell must be an enemy. Secondly, the ICC hearings had targeted and tarnished the packers. Why else would a reporter be making the rounds, asking all sorts of questions, unless he was out to follow these telling blows and expose more dirty deeds? Lastly, Russell admitted he "had not been at pains to conceal a connection" to *Everybody's* magazine, which was running serially Lawson's attacking articles. And after all, as Russell wrote, the entire nation "gasped and wondered and gasped again" while reading Lawson's articles. Because of Lawson, Russell concluded, "My appearance was construed as foreshadowing an attack."[22] The meat packers began to visit and warn Russell's sources, not the last time Russell would be threatened. Tarbell had been told, in blunt language, that her reporting on Rockefeller had put her life in jeopardy a few years earlier, and muckraker Mark Sullivan was shadowed by goons when he went about investigating patent medicine frauds some years later. For his part, Russell noted, "It was well understood about the yards that I was a visitor of evil intent and not to be talked with."[23]

Perhaps Russell would have been wiser to use the tactic that Upton Sinclair had recently undertaken—go undercover and live and work in Packingtown to get the inside facts. But secrecy was not Russell's style; in fact, he argued in all his work for less secrecy from government and private corporations. Secrecy and covert reporting were just too undignified—and unnecessary—for this formal and scholarly man. It's also possible that Russell merely underestimated the wrath of the packers. As he noted later, "I figured I had about three months for unimpeded investigation."[24] He was wrong. The trust blocked his investigation after less than two weeks. As luck would have it, other events bailed him out when the packers moved to cut off his sources.

Russell's eight-part series of articles began in February 1905, running alongside a profile of Lawson by famous reporter James Creelman. While Lawson gave *Everybody's* 500,000 readers the inside scoop on how he beat "the system," Russell spoke in an intimate way to his readers, much less bombastic than the swaggering Lawson. He warned about "a power greater than the government . . . a greater power than in the history of men has been exercised by king, emperor or irresponsible oligarchy." Using the delayed identification technique so common in a feature story he might have written for Pulitzer, Russell wrote for five pages in a highly dramatic way before finally naming his target: the meat packers, "a commercial force without precedent in Trust history," a force that even government investigators, in disbelief, conceded raked in $700 million in 1904. To hear Russell tell the story—and he was as much a storyteller as a reporter—the beef trust had a stranglehold on every aspect of American commerce, from meat and melons to railroads and finance, from growers in California and Georgia to laborers in Chicago and New York, "from every farmer to every dinner-table." He wrote: "It [is] able to control the price of every loaf of bread." Moreover, "It controls or influences the prices of one-half the food consumed by the nation." So powerful is this combine that "multi-millionaires, railroad magnates and captains of industry quail before it."[25] The theme of Russell's articles typified what Progressives were arguing. The system of private capital was out of control; wealthy industry leaders, "driven along by an economic evolution beyond their knowledge or control," were snuffing out competition and killing what Russell labeled "the American idea—the idea of equal opportunity."[26]

Russell's first article established that the huge and profitable meat-packing industry—in 1903 alone the Swift Company made $200 million in profits and brought nearly 8 million steers, pigs, chickens and sheep to market—was controlled by four major companies. The first three, Armour, Swift, and Morris, owned the fourth, the National Packing Company, which wiped out "the least vestige of competition." He declared: "One market was all markets." The major figure in this alliance of "agreeing gentleman" was Jonathan Ogden Armour, "young, cool, ambitious, resourceful, probably the ablest, certainly the most daring manipulator." Armour, who had inherited his father's meat-packing business in 1901, had been on the stockyard scene for only three years. Nevertheless, Russell concluded, "No more extraordinary figure has ever appeared in the world's commercial affairs, no man, not even Mr. Rockefeller, has conceived a commercial empire so dazzling."

Armour was the kind of robber baron who logically could have been the central character in Russell's exposé. If Tarbell had Rockefeller, Russell had Armour, a name every beef-eating American could identify with. After inheriting his father's sprawling packing industry, the son dropped out of Yale and turned a $200 million fortune into a $1 billion gold mine as well as the largest and most powerful meat empire in the world. He could have been the bad guy of the story. Russell chose not to portray him this way, however, because, he concluded, "the system—not the individual—is essentially at fault," a theme Russell clung to as he muckraked right up until the onset of World War I.[27]

Russell insisted that the conspiracies in restraint of trade used by Armour and Swift to compile their fortunes were wrong; for their lawlessness they deserved to be in prison. But the fabulous wealth of men like Armour was also the perfectly logical outcome of a system "that holds it laudable to pile up great fortunes by whatsoever means acquired." Their behavior came not from their hearts or character, but from the logical incentives of capitalism. Although the beef trust overlords were motivated by greed, not service, that was what America wanted—no, demanded—from these capitalists: to make money at any cost. None of that took away from the grisly fact, Russell felt, that these "bandit gentlemen" represented "the highest and most dangerous achievement in corporation management" and posed a serious risk to a free and democratic government.[28] Not until the Germans engaged the Allies in a world war did Russell again use such forceful language about a threat to democracy.

Russell's research led him to believe that a secret cartel of meat packers existed. "It is as intangible as the air, as mysterious as destiny, as certain as a perfect machine," he wrote. A government inquiry eventually agreed with Russell that four major packing companies did the bulk of the meat business, but the government disagreed that the group acted in concert to thwart competition. Russell said their success in throttling competition was largely the result of illegal rebates made to the railroad operators. Since such kickbacks allowed the big packers to pay less than competitors for shipping dressed meat, they could greatly reduce their costs. With the rail lines in their pocket, they could in turn demand favorable prices from farmers and ranchers who wanted to sell their meat or produce to the packers.

A typical trick, Russell found, was for the packers to raise greatly their asking price, which would cause them a short-run loss in profit. Seeing higher prices, however, the growers would subsequently flood the market with more products, and the cartel would in turn drop its asking price. Thus, the packers would buy cheaply in a flooded market, but sell at a high price to consumers. This "controlled and manipulated market," Russell repeated in his articles, is a "curse . . . utterly wrong . . . a violation of natural laws." The packers' price control affected two groups—producers, of course, who were at the mercy of the beef trust manipulations, and consumers, who were forced daily to pay higher prices on everything from bakery to meat products. The result, he argued, was that consumers were being gouged while the packers made exorbitant profits. Meanwhile, the producers—and their underwriters, such as the banks—were barely able to survive; in fact, many didn't. As Russell wrote of the beef trust, "It racked the producer and it racked the consumer."[29]

In the thousands of words Russell wrote about the beef trust, there was nothing about those who labored in the stockyards, the workers who slaughtered Armour's 3.5 million hogs in 1904, for example. In fact, although Russell would turn to socialism as the cure for private monopolies in 1908, he wrote very little in any of his magazine or book-length works about the plight of workers. That left the whole field of the incivility of labor conditions to one interested observer, Upton Sinclair. This square-jawed young man from Baltimore, an avowed socialist, had gone to live in Packingtown in 1904. There he saw the horrible living conditions that so angered readers when his novel, *The Jungle*, was published in 1906. He saw realtors take advantage of the immigrant laborers; he saw long hours that even the strongest of the men could not withstand; he saw women harassed and raped by supervisors; he saw little children who worked in the factories and were chewed up by an industrial system that was essentially unregulated—and that exploited both children and adults. All of this he indignantly seared into the pages of his novel. By creating composite characters in Jurgis Rudkus and his family, he showed how workers in Packingtown were abused by a factory system that made profits so easy to come by for Armour, Swift, and others.

When *Everybody's* hit the newsstands in late January, Sinclair read Russell's first installment with fascination. He wrote to Russell, whom he did not know: "I have just seen your Everybody's articles. Apparently you & I have been on the track of the monster at the same time." He said that "the Macmillans" would publish his book in the springtime, which did not occur since his material was considered too controversial (and suspect). It was eventually published by an independent publisher. Sinclair did not think Russell's exposé would hurt his upcoming fictive attack on "the monster." It's good, he wrote that "the public will have your facts in the meantime."[30]

After Russell's first article appeared, the beef trust's executives ordered his sources to avoid him. "I lacked innumerable and indispensable details that I could see no way of getting," he said. But luck overcame skill. Just as a telegraph operator miraculously became available to Russell at the Johnstown flood fifteen years earlier, a secret source appeared to help him out in this investigation. Typically, when a reporter writes once on a topic, sources come out of the woodwork. Many times they are disgruntled company or bureaucratic insiders who have a stake in the outcome of an investigation or are seeking a measure of revenge. Ida Tarbell learned this fact of reportorial life in her investigation of Rockefeller. After her articles began to appear, a source came forward with documented proof of bribes being paid to railroad officials (proof that actually came from a rail depot garbage pail). This gave Tarbell a key piece of evidence against Rockefeller.

Russell had similar good luck with two different sources. The first was an unidentified friend who worked in Packingtown, probably someone he had met during his days as the *American's* publisher. This friend, who collected considerable information for Russell and put himself in danger in the process, may be the "informant" Russell referred to on occasion in the beef trust articles. The finding of the third source involved blind luck. After his February article appeared, Russell began to receive a tremendous amount of mail, much of it critical of his article. But the mail also brought an unsigned letter from a writer who told Russell about the movements of a man who each day visited the packers' top officials. Apparently the man was carrying messages between the trust's leaders and aiding their conspiracy. Russell used a confidante of his own to confirm the contents of each letter. "Invariably, after most careful investigation, I found [each letter] perfectly correct," Russell wrote. The outcome was that eventually the letters led Russell to "a mass of information far beyond my requirements." One of the areas the informant led Russell to concerned rebates, involving the same kind of preferential treatment and lawbreaking that Tarbell had found at Standard Oil. "The traffic of the country is rotten with forbidden rebates and scandalous discriminations," Russell concluded, "and behind it all is the Bandit of Commerce, taking toll."[31]

Rebates were extensive in the early years of the twentieth century and were based on the power of large shippers to exploit a competitive railroad situation.[32] A packer with hundreds of tons of beef to ship could tell the operator of a freight line that it would take its considerable business (the trust was the largest shipper in the world!) elsewhere unless the rail kicked back—or rebated—part of the published shipping cost. Federal law had declared that rails, as common carriers, had to charge equal amounts to competing shippers. The Elkins Anti-Rebating Act of 1903 made both corporations and individuals liable for a $20,000 fine for either giving or receiving a rebate. Thus, the rebates were clearly illegal, but of course they were also hidden, disguised by such practices as false classifications and underbilling of weights. Rebates took about 10 percent of the gross revenue of the railroads. "Wherever we turn in this story," Russell charged, "there is but one prospect, and that is graft."[33]

PART III: PLUTOCRACY OR DEMOCRACY?

Before Russell began to snoop about the stockyards, the manipulations of the beef packers had drawn attention. Both the *New York Herald* and the *Chicago Tribune* published exposés about collusion by the meat packers in 1902. In 1903 a federal judge granted an injunction against the five major packers, agreeing that they had conspired to restrain trade. Then in 1904 Congress held hearings about rising prices. Russell gave an example of the kind of story that congressmen were hearing. A Nebraska farmer mortgaged his farm to the hilt and borrowed all that banks would loan; he tasted seven years of profits from selling his livestock to the Chicago packers. In 1901, the year J. Ogden Armour took over his father's company, the farmer found that when he went to market "the buyers had strangely disappeared. There was no more bidding." All buyers offered the same low price. "One man bought for all," Russell wrote, and the result was a loss of $8 on every head of cattle for every Midwestern farmer for the years 1901 to 1904. In Iowa alone the loss was $12.5 million; forty banks closed and seven bank officers committed suicide.[34]

Howls of protest reached the floor of the Fifth-eighth Congress at which a 1904 resolution asked the federal Department of Commerce to conduct a "thorough investigation" into what had caused meat prices to be higher for consumers and lower for sellers than at any time in the past five years. Has "any contract, combination, or conspiracy in restraint of commerce" caused these "unusual conditions," the resolution asked?[35] Russell had the answer: the beef trust was the culprit! Russell's conclusion, of course, cannot be viewed as startling since the public had been concerned about monopolies for more than two decades. In 1890 Congress passed the Sherman Anti-Trust Act as a way of starting to control the growth of monopolies, although enforcement of the act was haphazard, sporadic, and half-hearted. In 1899 a congressional committee's inquiry into the "trusts" found that one of the primary reasons for the new combines was to avoid competition (not such a surprise either). The committee also discovered that fantastic salaries and fees were going to those connected with the monopoly corporations. Theodore Roosevelt, acutely aware of the intense public interest in the trust problem, knew that the appearance of government scrutiny was good politics—and might also brake the continued growth of monopoly without direct government intervention, a typically moderate Rooseveltian approach.[36]

The investigation of the beef trust ordered by Congress was conducted by James R. Garfield, a nephew of the former president who was Roosevelt's commissioner of corporations and one of his close advisers. While Russell's articles were appearing, Garfield issued a statistic-laden, chart-filled report that in essence cleared the industry of the two major charges against it: that it was a monopoly and that it made exorbitant profits. He concluded that there was no conspiracy, no common ownership, no illegal combination, and no trust. Yes, there was a "Big Six" of meat packers, but "even if they were acting in combination they could not habitually depress the price of cattle and increase their profits to an abnormal degree without bringing into the field powerful competitors," Garfield found. As for the profits that came from slaughtering 5.5 million head of cattle and 15 million hogs a year, they were "very reasonable." In fact, the report concluded, at times the profits could be "extraordinarily small."

The government cited testimony of Armour, the man whose company was making $200 million a year but who sounded more like the owner of a mom-and-pop corner store. He said, "There are good years and bad years," a contention he repeated in articles written for the conservative *Saturday Evening Post*.[37] Whatever profits were made, Garfield said, were the result not of packers gouging consumers but rather simply the demand for the packers' products. Garfield knew his conclusion would irk the public. "Now will come the storm," he wrote in a diary, "but it is the truth and I care not for popular clamor."[38]Russell was indignant. He interrupted his articles in June 1905 to respond, asking, "Have we heard before of a government department palpably and openly seeking to defend a lawless combination, and misstating, coloring and distorting the facts about it?" He then directed his most biting words against Garfield, referring to his "gross inaccuracies, amazing misstatements, and half-truths." But blame him not, Russell opined sarcastically, for when Garfield went to Chicago to investigate the trust, he spent his time being wined and dined by the city's best families who were only too glad to welcome the inquisitor. The implication was that Garfield had been bought off by the city's business elite, a contention with which a Garfield biographer agreed.[39] Russell proceeded to rebut the Garfield report, using more detail than in any other section of his articles.

Garfield was able to conclude that there was no monopoly because he looked only at the packers' Illinois companies, a "manifestly deceptive" approach, Russell charged. "We should have had all the story or none." Using statistics from a variety of published sources, Russell then attacked the government's logic—and facts—on the profit issue. "Mr. Garfield's estimates [are] worthless," Russell wrote. His response was impressive, impassioned, and well-documented, although one scholar who studied the meat-packing industry feels Russell "overstated" the extent of the packers' control.[40] The fact-driven approach in this part is in contrast to the more anecdotal and rhetorical style of the other parts. Russell probably changed his style to argue against the government findings on the government's level—the level of numbers and fact. He showed that he could combat a battery of government investigators, alone. Later developments confirmed Russell's allegations more than Garfield's. In 1906 packers were indicted by a federal grand jury and charged with the two crimes Russell said they were guilty of: illegal rebating and violating the antitrust statutes. At the trial on the rebating charges, Garfield admitted that he met privately and secretly with the trust's representatives and that he agreed not to use certain incriminating evidence. He denied that he did this to cover up the truth. Garfield told the court that when he visited the packers he was merely fact-finding, as requested by Congress, and not seeking evidence of criminal behavior. The packers said Garfield told them specifically that evidence he uncovered would not be used for a prosecution. Garfield denied he ever made such a pledge, but the packers produced contrary evidence, based on a transcript from a secret stenographer who recorded Garfield's words. The attorney general of the United States then took the witness stand to back up Garfield, saying that his incriminating evidence should be allowed as evidence for the government. The federal judge, however, did not believe Garfield's testimony and refused to accept the damning evidence he provided against both Armour and Swift. The judge ruled that the 161 individual leaders of the meat-packing companies would be immune from prosecution. The corporations, however, could be prosecuted.[41]

This case, which was appearing on the front pages of newspapers across America at a time when the public was closely watching to see if the government could put a leash on the runaway power of the monopolies, was important to President Roosevelt. He reacted angrily to the judge's decision to protect Armour and Swift, calling the ruling a "farce" and promising to press on with prosecutions and to propose new legislation to change court rules on immunity. Russell's words, written only months before, predicted this victory by the meat-packing executives. The trust, he said, would "withstand almost any investigation" and would proceed "with utter indifference to any kind of legal restraint." Perhaps someday, Russell speculated, "there will come along a tribunal or an investigator" powerful enough to get the trust. "When that happens look out for your Beef Trust, Mr. Armour; it will not last long thereafter." But in 1906 Roosevelt didn't have either the power or the inclination to be that authority; Russell and the public had to content themselves with a conviction on the rebating charges—a mere $15,000 fine each for Armour & Company, Swift & Company, Cudahy & Company, and the Nelson Morris Packing Company. This was barely a slap on the wrist; a few hours of profits would absorb such a fine. On the more serious charge of anti-trust violations, the packers were able to delay a trial until 1911.[42]

Although the court victory was minimal, Russell's exposé had the packers on the ropes: they were under fire in a national magazine, under investigation by the government, and under indictment for violating a variety of laws. Exactly what Russell wanted to see happen next is unclear from his articles. "I am not arguing for nor against anything," he wrote, which was a statement not to believed; he simply wasn't sure what he wanted to argue for in 1905.

On the one hand, Russell's implied solutions seemed almost Jeffersonian as he longed to turn back the clock to an old-fashioned, unfettered marketplace free of "arbitrary interference with natural conditions of supply and demand." If America could get rid of this "curse of a manipulated market," then perhaps all would be well again. Did he merely want a free and open marketplace, with real competition, unfettered by giantism and bribery? Or did this mean he wanted no market at all, but state ownership of property? Russell's thinking is unclear. He was sure that the development of a beef trust—or any trust—was the logical result of "the idea of the survival of the fittest, the right of the strong to annihilate the weak, the theory that in business any advantage is fair." Perhaps if the government or the people owned the beef industry—the means of production, if you will—then the best of the trust (its efficiency) would be preserved, and the worst (the price fixing) would be eliminated. Russell did not say this, and he wouldn't reach this conclusion, at least not publicly, for three more years. For now, he asserted more moderately that regulations might work—"if they're enforced." But he did not say either what kind of regulations he might want. Would it be price controls? Anti-price fixing laws? Uniform rates on the rails? More power for the Interstate Commerce Commission?

Sounding like his grandfather the minister, Russell looked instead into the human soul. "There is no remedy," he wrote, as his articles concluded in September, "unless we are willing to look upon the issue as essentially an issue of morals and not of business." Russell's solution mirrored, in part, that reached by Tarbell, who also sought a return to the days before industrial combines had crushed the small oil refineries. She too thought that morality, fair play, and Christian principle in business could stop the menacing hand of the Rockefellers and the Armours. Unless there were changes, Russell predicted, there would be "no more republic but only an irresponsible and arbitrary oligarchy against which, logically, no citizen can have protection." Will it be, he asked, "The life of the Trusts or the life of the republic—which?"[43] Russell's question went unanswered, and his writing about the beef trust was soon overshadowed by the spectacular success of *The Jungle*.

IV. THE SHADOW OF *THE JUNGLE*

Charles Edward Russell loved poetry and music, but he never seriously tried his hand at fiction even though he knew that "people would at any time rather take their exposé stuff in fiction."[44] Given this, one wonders why he didn't try a more stylized version of the facts that he had culled about the beef trust. Certainly some of his articles could have included consumers to bring the stories alive. In the end, the beef trust articles had two flaws: they lacked the human interest that would sear a message into readers' minds, and they lacked a clear statement of how a trust might be controlled.

In contrast, Upton Sinclair chose to use fictional characters—the unforgettable Lithuanian immigrants who were so real that readers cried with anger and pity when they were mistreated by profit-driven owners. Sinclair had an enormous impact on the public. His novel appeared first in the weekly socialist magazine, *The Appeal to Reason*, in March 1905, a month after Russell's exposé began. *The Appeal* reached an audience of socialists already convinced that a corporate cabal was oppressing workers and gouging consumers. Sinclair desperately wanted to reach a larger audience. Five publishers had turned him down before Doubleday, Page & Company, after corroborating his facts, brought out *The Jungle* in February 1906. That was soon after Ridgway-Thayer published Russell's articles in book form and five months after Russell's magazine articles ended. Sinclair, like Russell, spent much time in the Packing-town stockyards, living there for seven weeks and getting workers to tell him their heart-wrenching stories. Sinclair relied mostly on undercover work, dis-guising himself as a worker in the twelve to fourteen months of his research. It took him a year to write *The Jungle.* When it appeared, the response was over-whelming. Twenty-five thousand copies were sold in the first forty-five days after publication. Sickened by the prospect that diseased carcasses were landing on their tables, the public clamored for change. The eventual result was the creation of the federal Food and Drug Administration.[45]

The clamor for change and federal intervention that emerged after the publication of *The Jungle,* however, would not have been possible without the groundwork laid by Russell's articles. The public and government response to Sinclair's work had been building for some time. It came first because of Rus-sell's national exposé of the beef trust's very existence, of its price gouging and illegal rebating and of its mounting political influence. Second, it came because of the work of Samuel Hopkins Adams, who boldly lampooned the makers of patent medicines at the very time that *The Jungle* and the beef trust articles were appearing. Adams's explicit call for a federal agency to regulate food and drugs not only complemented Russell's and Sinclair's but matched a chorus of similar demands coming from within the government.[46]

Thus, the coupling of the Russell and Adams articles with Sinclair's book became part of a complex social process whereby change resulted when pressure was exerted at two levels—with heightened public opinion and a mobilized gov-ernment. Initially the public needed to be aroused. While there were no public opinion polls in 1904, it did not take a genius to understand what was occurring: when thousands of readers forced *Everybody's* to increase its press run as Russell's articles appeared and when Sinclair's book became a runaway bestseller, it was clear that the public was interested and indignant. That indignation, in fact, is what led President Roosevelt to worry privately that the magazine writers were "building up a revolutionary feeling." He knew the country was in a fury.[47] On another level, however, there needed to be interest from policymakers for change to occur. Sinclair's "fiction" roused the public, but Russell's "facts" piqued the policymakers. Sinclair tacitly acknowledged this in his correspon-dence with Russell. Your facts, he told Russell, can only help the cause. Govern-ment officials responded directly and immediately to Russell's articles. They were reading and they were nervous. And while they denied that the "Big Four" controlled the meat business, they first of all launched a congressional investiga-tion, directly in response to his work. Second, Roosevelt had the government at-torneys pursue the meat packers in court for anti-trust violations. There was no cataclysmic onslaught against monopoly power after Russell's work appeared (although undoubtedly the growing number of socialists saw it as evidence of the need for state ownership). But it helped lay the groundwork and create a climate of acceptability for two important subsequent legislative developments—the creation of the federal Food and Drug Administration and strengthened railroad regulations. The creation of the FDA, in fact, may be the most significant and longest lasting of the reforms that came out of the Progressive Era. As one scholar who has carefully studied the beef trust episode concluded, "There can be no doubt that Sinclair and Russell heavily influenced public opinion."[48] While the greatest achievement of Russell's muckraking work was yet to come, his opening salvo—the attack on the most powerful trust in America—had made a considerable ripple. The beef trust articles mobilized the reformers in their battle against the forces of monopoly. But reform would be far from enough for Russell.

CHAPTER EIGHT

"SOLDIER FOR THE COMMON GOOD"

I. PURSUING THE "HIDEOUS DEMONS"

DESPITE THE TRIUMPH OF CHARLES EDWARD RUSSELL'S "beef trust" articles, which ended in September 1905, his health remained frail. At times, his son John had to write letters for him. His "best time," he told a friend, was being with "good fellows" and discussing "poetry and the things that are worthwhile." Poetry, in fact, gave Russell as much joy as journalism. His second book of poems, *The Twin Immortalities.* came out in 1904 but did not garner much praise or attention. It did include somber remembrances of his wife. About Abby, he wrote: "She has gone and left my day all night, / How dear are memories of the vanished light. / How sad the haunts her face withdrawn leaves bare."[1] The wounded poet, however, soon took a backseat to the angry muckraker as Russell began to search for another project. The exposés coming steadily from the pens of his muckraking colleagues made the focus of his attention clear: the evils emanating from the excesses of industrial competition.

Russell knew that Americans were always in hot pursuit of some "hideous demon of destruction." At times it was the rum fiend or the tobacco habit; at other times it was Tammany Hall, Anarchism, the Red Flag, or the Hordes of Europe. "There has always been something horned and horrible to disturb our slumbers with its stealthy approach," he commented. In 1905 monopoly was the demon. "Monopoly, of course, sought to strangle Competition. Blessed

Competition," he noted in typical sarcastic fashion, "must be rescued from the claws of Monopoly."[2] Although the journalistic warrior was soon fully roused to join the crusade, for Russell, monopoly was not the *real* demon; it was simply his excuse to delve into competing political philosophies. He wanted to know if "the jungle" of capitalism and competition that his friend Upton Sinclair was then describing to a national audience in magazine articles was inevitable and the natural result of human nature.[3] Was man a beast who would fight for survival, eliminating whoever and whatever got in his way? Was monopoly the natural product of struggle? Were Rockefeller, Carnegie, and Vanderbilt the best of mankind—the beasts emerging supreme in the jungle? Could Darwin, reduced to his basest philosophy, be correct about both the animal kingdom and human nature? Or was a more harmonious world possible in which the creatures actually helped each other, cooperating and not competing? Was that the real natural order? Russell needed to answer those questions, although journalistic exposé hardly afforded him the chance to do that.

Although Russell's "beef trust" articles had established him as a writer to be reckoned with, he still looked to his newspaper connections for a platform, walking a line between continuing to work for William Randolph Hearst and asserting his independence. He still turned up occasionally at the offices of the *Chicago American*, but it was unclear what title—if any—he held. In 1904 Hearst had steamrolled across the nation in pursuit of Democratic electoral votes, unsuccessfully pursuing the party's presidential nomination. As his advocates fanned out across the country to help, Russell returned to Iowa, trying to bring his native state into the Hearst column. "I thought Mr. Hearst a sincere radical," Russell told an Iowa newsman years later. Eventually, Hearst won the support of the Iowa delegation, despite much opposition from the party machine, but he never got the presidential nomination.[4] Despite his work for "the chief," however, Russell did not consider himself part of the Hearst crowd.

Nonetheless, his thoughts turned to Hearst when, in early 1905, Russell sat in the press gallery of the U.S. Senate, watching a debate. "I was struck with the patent fact that almost nobody in that chamber had any other reason to be there than his skill in valeting for some powerful Interest," Russell said. These "well-fed and portly gentlemen" were the people's enemies, not their advocates. Returning to New York, Russell met with Hearst, offering to write a series of articles on the predatory senators for Hearst's recently acquired *Cosmopolitan* magazine "He liked it," Russell found. Not that there was anything particularly novel in such a story idea. Reformers had long eyed the Senate as the bastion of the wealthy and sought to bring about direct election by the people, instead of the method then used whereby state legislatures, often notoriously corrupt, chose senators.[5] As Russell began to collect facts for the articles, however, Erman J. Ridgway of *Everybody's* magazine approached him with an intriguing proposal. While Americans were scrutinizing the results of industrial competition at home, why not see how the rest of the industrialized world was handling problems arising out of competition and industrial growth? How do other countries differ from America? He asked Russell to travel around the world to find out—a dream assignment.

Russell had traveled often to Europe as correspondent and vacationer. His scholarly mien, philosophical bent, intellectual curiosity, and skill as a researcher served him well. And at forty four, he was still trying to sort out a personal philosophy. The U.S. Senate assignment was passed along, at Russell's suggestion, to his good friend David Graham Phillips, whose "Treason of the Senate" articles eventually published in 1906 represented the most vitriolic attack on the political establishment of the muckraking era.[6] Russell, however, had bigger fish to fry—he was looking to indict the "system" and not just its key players. He accepted Ridgway's offer.

II. THE TRIP AROUND THE WORLD

As he boarded a steamship to Australia in December 1905 to begin a yearlong, nine-country tour, Russell hardly seemed an open-minded investigator. "We have been slow to admit the evil conditions that we face: we are driven to admit them now," he observed. As Russell saw it, "money madness and organized greed" in America were leading to a "moneyed autocracy, wealth in the hands of a few, lawless corporations, trusts that control food and energies" and "the imminent ruin of democratic ideals." Good men had been "transformed into mad devils by the opportunity of unlimited money-making and the craze for power," he argued. "They will stop at no crime and balk at no mean and dirty device to augment their fortunes." Russell asked, "What cure? What shall we do" to end this "perversion of all things good by the money power"?[7] Russell hoped to find answers in England, Germany, France, Switzerland, India, Japan, China, Australia, and New Zealand.

Russell, accompanied by son John, seemed cranky as his steamship, the *Moldavia*, began the trip to England. "The English are the most disagreeable of all traveling companions," he noted in his diary. "I have never seen a nastier lot of slobs and snobs than most of the Moldavia's passengers." They think it their "duty to annoy every American—perhaps to get even for the Revolution." He described one "large rotten fat lady who must be English for she has the English Buttinsky traits and the same old frantic English passion for patronizing and interfering with Americans."[8] Offended by the Brits' personal hygiene, he muttered, "Reminds me of the old assertion that Englishmen take a bath by looking at the tub." The food aboard ship made him angrier. About Christmas dinner, he wrote: "I have never seen a more dreadful thing." His complaint brought "stony silence" from the British passengers who respond only, he said, if you praise their country. "Intense disgust" filled Russell when the British passengers clamored to sit next to the few English aristocrats aboard. "I don't want to have anything to do with the English and always try to avoid them but they will butt in and jeer and make offensive remarks," he observed. The Midwestern egalitarianism that had been nurtured by his British immigrant parents was offended.[9] Russell's lone pleasure on the trip was poetry. On Christmas Day he and John read aloud from Swinburne's "Before a Crucifix."

When his ship landed, Russell was greeted by reporters who wondered about his mission. "I shall not try to establish either side of a question with which I have here nothing to do," he said, but "privilege, caste, class, corruption, great wealth in the hands of a few"—certainly these were problems that deserved attention. "We need not be Radicals, nor extremists, nor effected in the slightest degree by any doctrine of alleged remedy, to see very clearly that present conditions cannot go on." He then focused on the condition that most obsessed him: poverty. In London on a Sunday afternoon he visited a small park near the Thames River. He watched a family—a young man, his wife, a baby and a little boy—stumble through the park. The family was in tattered clothes, emaciated, dirty, stooping. The father sang a Charles Wesley hymn. "I have never known a thing more grotesque and horrible," Russell observed.[10] As the beggar wailed his song, people threw coins at the family, mostly, Russell thought, to get them out of sight and mind. The Pulitzer-Hearst disciple knew that the scene of the wretched family was rich material for his articles. "The paupers abound, the millionaires thrive," he noted. "Some men have too much of the fruits of the earth, some men have too little." The reason lay with the British class system—hunting preserves for the nobles, unproductive estates for the aristocracy, money wasted on nobility. "There is no where in England any recognition that the slum inhabitant is a human being of equal rights with the fortunate," he insisted. "Dwarfed bodies, twisted minds, joyless lives, misshapen children"—all were the products of "England's system of snobbery."[11]

Russell's bitterness toward the British ruling class increased when he traveled to India, the English colony where 300 million people lived in a way he described as "unfit for beasts, intolerable for swine, in filth unutterable." He donned a white linen suit and sat atop an elephant to watch a "spectacle that can hardly be matched," a country in which temples of splendor coexisted with famine and disease. He was aghast at all that he encountered. Ants and spiders crawled the walls of his hotel while station platforms crawled with dirty people. He saw people drinking sewage. Nothing on the Lower East Side of Manhattan had prepared him for India. The Indian people, he confided in his diary, are "ill fed, filthy, ignorant" and "represent the lowest type of humanity I have ever seen." But the British cared little for these "most hopeless of human creatures." Russell's anger boiled over. When he did not stand one day for the playing of "God Save the King," a shouting match ensued with a British citizen.[12]

Russell conceded in his diary that his anger was part of a "smoldering hostility" between the British and the Americans, but it was also reinforced by his observations of English behavior in India. The Prince of Wales had just visited India for three months of celebration when Russell arrived there. In Bombay and Delhi one pageant followed another; jewels and carpets of flowers were laid out for the prince; forty thousand troops were assembled as the prince was ushered to balls and banquets. The prince was moved by the reception, Russell was told, but did he not wonder: Where were all of India's poor people? Where were the teeming hordes infected with disease and beset by epidemic? Did he not wonder about a civilization that tolerated "fantastic pomp and perennial famine, illuminations and plague, waste and want"? He noted in his diary that the Brits had spent nearly $1 million for the prince. "When famine darkens the greater part of surrounding country never was [there a] stranger comment on civilization." No matter what progress the British had made in improving India in their 150 years of rule, Russell felt the disparities of this "huge evil" was inexplicable. The system of caste, "the most deplorable affliction that ever befell any people" he concluded, "has no more place in civilization than voodoism or witchcraft would have."[13]

The only good thing Russell found in England was a nascent cooperative movement. A group of workers who had been displaced after a strike in 1843—the Toad Lane Weavers of Rochdale—caught his attention. As a result of the strike, the weavers started a "peaceful revolution," cooperating with other workers in producing and exchanging goods and becoming relatively self-sufficient. In 1904 they baked 4.4 million loaves of bread for 24,120 members of a cooperative that earned $2.3 million. Russell lived with the workers, much like Upton Sinclair had in Packingtown outside of Chicago, but he did not find a "jungle." On the contrary, he found a "very strange people [who] believe that Cooperation will work to destroy race prejudice, break down national barriers, obliterate armaments, and bring about universal peace." Not coincidentally, American Socialists would use that same rhetoric a short time later. But the Weavers insisted that when not compelled by the "Competitive Idea," people become "decent, kindly, tolerant, and unselfish" instead of "the cruel devils of the money mart." Yes, Russell repeated, a strange people indeed who regard competition as "immoral and the great source of the world's evil." In England the growing forces of concentrated capital and cooperation, Russell predicted, "are like two fast trains trying to pass on a single track. One or the other seems certain to be smashed." The only other glimmer of hope Russell found in England was in the work of the London County Council, which he said was socialistic in its goals of operating and owning municipal services.[14]

Russell's diaries for his year abroad are largely an unreadable jumble, unlike his later diaries that made careful observations and that were undoubtedly written in hopes of publication. One notable entry is that he bought lots of cigars in various countries. But like a good newsman and researcher, he was too busy doing interviews, collecting facts, and scurrying around to meet various officials to keep a detailed log. Certainly the articles he wrote, replete with charts, statistics, and graphs, reveal impressive research bordering on sociology. Aside from the rich–poor gap, he wanted to learn how other countries regulated industries. In Germany he found a transportation system that he both admired and critiqued. The German trains, owned by the state, were the "most remarkable" in the world, with the "precision of a perfect machine." But he found signs posted everywhere reminding riders about government rules, a reproachful authoritarianism that made him nervous. Nonetheless, service was so good that Russell said his "democratic and American soul" was tempted to ignore—for now, at least—the heavy-handed state presence. In fact, he welcomed state takeover of insurance, which occurred, he said, after the Germans studied American insurance scandals. Russell especially applauded the German old-age insurance system, a form of Social Security hardly discussed in America. Despite these positives, however, Russell saw the same class distinctions in Germany as in England. The "palace and the slum lie side by side," he found.[15]

France was always Russell's favorite country to visit, and the gaiety of Paris endlessly charmed him. He limited his talk of France, however, to a meticulously detailed observation of how the government ruled the privately owned railroads with an iron fist. "It is the absolute master," he found, and can "do as it pleases" with the rails. In America, the railroad owners rob the people. "Not in France. The French people do not care to have the taxes they pay diverted to the pockets of money-grabbers." Was tough government regulation then the solution? Russell did not know, but "our lady of hope," as he once called France in a poem, was an encouraging model. Not so Italy, however, where the railroads were dismal and depressing. Riding one day in a filthy, unventilated, and very tardy train coming from Florence, he overheard two Americans.

Commented one man from Indiana, "We may not know a heap about art, but we can railroad" better than the Italians. In three months of riding the Italian rails, Russell found only one that left or arrived on time. He did not blame the Italian people, whom he found "honest, capable, and desirous of good as any of the rest of mankind." The fault was with the corporations, with "money mania . . .the monstrous cruelty, rapacity, and savagery of unfettered and organized Greed," a condition that was worldwide, he insisted.[16]

III. RUSSELL BECOMES A "COMRADE"

When Russell was ill in the years after his wife's death, he went to Carlsbad in Germany and other European spas seeking a cure for his ailments. Now, five years later, as he traveled in Europe on assignment, he sought a different kind of cure—a cure for what he perceived as the ills of democracy. He began to find it when he made his way to Switzerland, and then sailed to Australia and New Zealand. While traveling by automobile one afternoon in the Swiss country-side, Russell spotted a farmer eyeing him from his chalet, a man not unlike his uncles from Iowa. Russell pitied the poor man whose wheat and potato crop seemed so meager, his life so "painfully narrow and unfortunate." But when Russell stopped to inquire and speak with the man, he found that the farmer was actually quite learned, that he read newspapers and books, knew much about current events, and was even well aware of American political scandals and its rule by unelected bosses. The farmer, in fact, pitied Russell—or at least that is the story that Russell told. The farmer observed that Americans were too caught up in making money and accumulating wealth. Russell commented, "To be in harmony with one's surroundings, to work and to thrive a little and to rear children, to have liberty and security and be tolerant and self-respecting," that is what is important. And by this measure, Russell concluded, the Swiss were the "happiest people in Europe."[17]

Russell's reason was simple and simplistic: Switzerland was a "pure democracy . . .the most democratic government in the world." The Swiss voted often, more than any other industrialized nation; elections were no big deal. "Voting seems to them much like eating their breakfast," he said. And the 3.4 million people in the country did not turn their elected officials into superheroes. The only great Swiss men were scientists or writers. "All are great men in Switzerland, and one is as great and as divinely gifted as another," asserted Russell. Even more attractive was the Swiss progressive income tax that discouraged the building of great fortunes. The poor were not very poor and the rich not very rich. The government operated the rails, telephones, and telegraphs and owned all the slaughterhouses. "Everything done by their government is done out in the daylight."[18] Switzerland, he concluded, is "worth careful attention."

In New Zealand, a colony that had long been more independent from Britain than India, democracy again seemed triumphant to Russell, who saw its progressive experience as a direct refutation of American Social Darwinism. For one thing, women had voted there since 1893. Democracy couldn't flourish in a country in which one-half the population had no share in government, Russell observed. "Women are not idiots, nor children, nor dolls, nor dress-pattern exhibits," he said. On the contrary, in New Zealand they were progressive forces. Political life was "cleaner and purer because of them," he found. And the New Zealand household did not suffer either; it seemed as well ordered as any Russell had seen. Perhaps it was the inclusion of women that drove New Zealand's reform impulses. The country had an old-age pension system since 1898, slum conditions were unheard of, and wealth was distributed evenly. Part of the reason was that government carefully controlled the growth of private industries. "Let us have no trusts here such as exist in America," one man told Russell. No beef trusts, no Morgans, no Rockefellers, no Armours and "no government afraid to enforce the law upon the rich and the powerful." In New Zealand, as in Australia, Russell found the theme that would hold together not only his articles but his ideology as well. The search for aggrandizement and wealth are not the driving forces of human behavior. "I know we have always been so taught, but I am not quite sure of it," he said. People will work just as hard for a common cause as for their own fortunes. "There is no doubt left for me," he concluded," of the genuine blessing of Cooperation."[19]

As Russell prepared to sail home, he mused that his growing passion for Cooperation over Competition was indeed "strange and idealistic," but he had learned—or at least convinced himself—that in some countries it was "the normal state of man." Not in America, however, as he was reminded at various stops during his tour abroad. "The very boatmen on the Wanganui River and the Maori schoolboys [in New Zealand] will tell you that America is dominated by its rich men and corporations," he wrote. In India he was bluntly told that America's caste system was no different from that of the Hindus who have only done it better than the Westerners. "Wherever there is much power in the hands of a few men there is caste and always was and always will be. And if what I hear about America is true," the Indian told Russell, "you are finding that out for yourselves."[20] Russell agreed. He returned home believing firmly that the struggle in the world was "between those that uphold and draw profit from . . . the existing conditions of grab and gain, and those that protest against or attack present conditions as immoral, injurious, unnecessary, and perilous to progress." He was ready to join the protesters.

Russell's articles in *Everybody's* began appearing in April 1906 while he was on tour, the same month that Theodore Roosevelt, no friend of cooperative schemes, made his famous attack on the "man with the muckrake." In a speech in Washington, D.C., Roosevelt warned against the writers who looked at the muck of society and not at the genuine blessings of a competitive and free society. Roosevelt was aiming at Upton Sinclair, David Graham Phillips, and William Randolph Hearst, a potential presidential opponent.[21] Given his feelings about socialism, which was catching fire in America, he might have had Russell in mind also. Roosevelt once wrote that socialism was "hostile to the intellectual, the religious, the domestic and moral life; it is a form of communism with no moral foundation . . . based on the immediate annihilation of personal ownership of capital . . . the annihilation of the family, and ultimately the annihilation of civilization."[22] Russell was not surprised at the hostility socialism faced in the United States, but he felt it was based on misunderstanding—which the press had created.[23]

Much had happened on the reform front while Russell was gone. As he set foot back on American soil in September 1906, Edwin Markham, usually a poet, was revealing to the nation in Hearst's *Cosmopolitan* how children were used and abused in the workplace. Hearst, meanwhile, was in a tough fight for the New York governor's race, which he lost by only 60,000 votes. Sinclair's *The Jungle* had appeared in February, and regulations to clean up the meat industry were being debated in Congress. Tougher federal railroad regulations had passed the Congress in May. Phillips's nine-month-long "Treason" articles, ending in November, had stirred both the president and the nation. And the core of the muckraking movement, which was centered about *McClure's*, had just shifted as Lincoln Steffens, Ray Stannard Baker, and Ida Tarbell jumped ship to start the *American* magazine—and to argue over whether to present solutions or continue to muckrake problems. Russell wanted to do both as he sat down to finish his articles.[24]

In fact, the urge to reject the palliative measures that Progressives were suggesting had been stirring in Russell for some time. His first hero was Henry Demarest Lloyd, whom Russell discovered while studying in Vermont in 1881. Lloyd's muckraking classic, *Wealth Against Commonwealth*, attacking Standard Oil, suggested that common ownership made more sense than competition. Later, working as a newspaper reporter, Lloyd wrote about and admired Henry George, the "Red Game Cock," who ran unsuccessfully for New York mayor after his book, *Progress and Poverty*, captured the imagination of idealists with talk of socializing land ownership and equalizing taxes. "A most extraordinary man," Russell called him.[25] When Russell worked for Hearst, he took up the notion—endorsed by his populist boss—of municipal ownership of key utilities. Moreover, he began to believe that large monopolies were actually an efficient and logical development but that eventually they should be owned by the people and run by the state. In short, he began to embrace the tenets of socialism.

When he left Chicago and returned to New York, Russell was more formally introduced to socialism, which had been around in various guises since the 1870s but became the U.S. Socialist Party in 1901. Toward the end of 1903 William J. Ghent, author of two books critical of capitalism, invited Russell and a dozen reformers to join the Collectivist Society, sometimes also called the X Club.[26] The group met informally every few weeks in a midtown Manhattan Italian restaurant to exchange ideas. Joining the confab was Lincoln Steffens, *Collier's Weekly* editor Norman Hapgood, *Independent* editor Hamilton Holt, psychologist John Dewey, and philosopher Charles A. Beard. Ardent socialists like Algernon Lee, William English Walling, and J. G. Phelps Stokes attended also. English novelist H. G. Wells, traveling in the United States, addressed the club once and called it one of the few worthwhile things in America. The group had no mission; the members simply talked, sometimes late into the night. As the founder of the U.S. Socialist Party, Morris Hillquit noted, more often than not, socialism was the "favorite topic" of the gathered intelligentsia.[27]

A key moment in Russell's conversion came in late 1906, when he settled in Manhattan soon after returning from his worldwide tour. Robert Hunter, author of a 1904 book on poverty in America, invited twenty five reformers to Noroton, Connecticut, where his in-laws, the Stokeses, millionaire philanthropists with leftist leanings, entertained the group. Hunter was at the center of Progressive thought, as were many of the guests—David Graham Phillips; Finley Peter Dunne, best known for his "Mr. Dooley" character; Tom Watson, who became a U.S. Senator from Georgia; and Arthur Brisbane, Hearst's top editor, whose father, Albert, was a famous socialist. Hillquit recalled Russell as "an eloquent speaker" who "disguised a tender heart under the gruff appearance and manner of a bear." For three days and nights only meals interrupted the debate. "All phases of the Socialist philosophy and methods were expounded, analyzed, attacked, and defended," Hillquit recalled.[28]

Meanwhile, Russell's *Everybody's* articles on worldwide industrialism did not cause as much of a stir as had Steffens's exposés of municipal corruption or Tarbell's revelations about Rockefeller or even Russell's own beef trust articles. The reason was that they were neither startling nor exposé. In fact, one observer who was bothered by the articles' obvious bias told readers to take "great critical caution" in perusing Russell's articles. He was joined by a critic who complained of the "superficial character of his survey." Another commented that Russell failed to see "fairly obvious defects" in the communal system he advocated. But others called the series "comprehensive" and "rich in instructive detail." Nonetheless, they lacked the readability of either his beef trust articles or the muckraking that was soon to follow. Russell likely learned a lesson from the muted public reaction. If he wanted to have an impact, he needed fewer charts and statistics, fewer opinions, and more anecdotes and fictionlike storytelling; the kind that had, for example, made Samuel Hopkins Adams's look at medicinal frauds such a celebrated success a year earlier.[29]

Russell's trip around the world produced a series of articles that were sober, earnest, factual—and dry.[30] Nonetheless the articles reached a large audience; *Everybody's* circulated to more than a quarter-million people, and dozens of newspapers across the country, as was the fashion then, excerpted installments as they appeared. And the articles appeared at a propitious time: the American soil was fertile and ready to be planted with the seeds of change. Asserted Hillquit: "The ground was prepared by the crusade of political and economic reform of the first years of our century, which found expression in the 'literature of exposure.'" Russell and company had zeroed in on the excesses of industrialism and on the conflict between large-scale private economic power and the needs of the people. Remedies were needed. Unhappy with the pace of change in America and sensing intractable flaws in the competitive system, journalists, labor leaders, lawyers, educators, and even millionaires began to cast their lot with the Socialist Party. Party membership doubled between 1904 and 1908, from 20,750 to 41,750. The "golden years" of socialism had begun.[31]

Russell formally joined the party in the winter of 1908 because, he told the press, "I have become convinced of the utter futility of any other remedy for existing national evils except the remedy proposed by socialism." Russell said that the "dream of brotherhood and the end of greed" were his goals. "The socialist party is the most promising agency to bring about these ends." Russell's declaration made headlines in the Socialist press and back in his hometown in Davenport, Iowa. All of the major New York dailies devoted one or two paragraphs to the announcement. But after his declaration, Russell quickly wondered if he had made a mistake. When Robert Hunter ran as a Socialist for the New York State Assembly, Russell wrote a strong letter of support to a newspaper. But when Russell went to his first meeting of a local chapter of the party, he was publicly berated for writing it. "A lady member of the branch fitted with a prehensile tongue and a flow of oratory seldom surpassed even among her charming sex, arose and began to pour out upon my head the vials of an apparently inappeasable wrath," Russell later recalled.[32]

Russell's error was in writing a letter that supported only one candidate, not all Socialists. "I had violated some fundamental law of the Socialist state . . .and apparently was deemed to have incurred eternal damnation," Russell wrote. Thus, Russell was introduced to the world of squabbling socialists and internecine warfare—a harbinger of things to come. Nonetheless, like many Progressives, he believed that Socialism offered the best chance to end the conditions that most troubled him—and America: wealth in the hands of a few, poverty for too many, slum housing, monopoly companies that made true democracy unreachable, and children and workers abused by wealthy monopoly capitalists. Observed Russell, "The palaces rise, the steam yachts sail, the figures of the great fortunes mount, and in every city the slums spread, the bread lines grow, and the number of the poor increase. The only effective treatment is to remove the cause." Russell was not giving up on exposé journalism; on the contrary, he was about to enter his most prolific period of investigative reporting. "The truth about muck-raking," he commented, "is that it is a wholesome and necessary influence and no republic can afford to be without it." But exposé, he felt, does "nothing against the fundamental system that is the source" of America's ills.[33] A more radical remedy must be found. And a democratic socialism was it. "What we propose," Russell said in a speech soon after he declared for socialism, "is that . . . in the place of competition—steadily drawing resources away from the masses and into the hands of a few—which has been proved to be the curse of humanity, we shall substitute co-operative methods."[34]

Many years later, writing in his famous autobiography, Lincoln Steffens came closer to locating the reason why Russell, whom he described as earnest, emotional and gifted, turned to socialism. Steffens recalled that Russell's face often "looked as if he had suffered from the facts he saw and reported." After meeting Russell in a chance encounter, Steffens recounted that Russell told him: "I couldn't keep it up. It was too fierce, the conditions, the facts, and what was worse, I couldn't understand them. I'd form a theory, then go out and find that the theory was all wrong. I'd set up another theory, see it blow up, and so think again and again, till I couldn't stand it. I joined the socialist party. I had to have something to believe."[35]

In searching for a belief system, Russell was actually reaching back to his childhood and the sermons preached by his Baptist grandfather. He compared joining the party to entering the church and proving he had repented from the evil ways of capitalism. "Socialism is, after all," Russell noted, "nothing in the world but the practical application of the doctrines of Jesus." He added, "Every good Christian is a Socialist at heart." In fact, viewing Socialism as a religion was not uncommon for its believers, as Russell noted in a 1912 magazine article. "Socialism does not mean a political party organized to win elections and to secure offices. Socialism is . . . a religion."[36] If this was so, Russell asked himself, what would Jesus think—and do—if the world's richest church was also America's biggest slum landlord?

CHAPTER NINE

THE SHAME OF THE
WORLD'S RICHEST CHURCH

I. POVERTY AND PROGRESS

THE LOWER EAST SIDE OF MANHATTAN—an area more densely populated than Calcutta—both fascinated and repelled Charles Edward Russell when he prowled the city's neighborhood as a newspaper reporter in the 1880s and '90s. He had never seen such squalor and poverty growing up in the agrarian Midwest. "It is of a nature that one might expect to see in Chinese cities, but never in the foremost city of America," Russell commented. No Iowa farmer, he noted, "would house hogs in the way 100,000 people are housed in New York City." At times, Russell thought he had "crossed a frontier into a foreign land." In many ways, of course, New York resembled a foreign enclave. As the city's population soared from 1.5 million in 1870 to 5 million by 1910, thousands of immigrants—Germans, Italians, Jews—swarmed into unheated, unlit, waterless, and litter-filled tenements that made for horrible places to live but often brought a handsome profit for their owners. And the owner that especially caught Russell's eye was New York City's Trinity Church, "the mother of all churches." Trinity was not only the richest church in America, but it was also one of the biggest slum landlords (some said *the* biggest) in New York City.[1]

For Russell, newly converted to socialism in 1908, Trinity was a sensational symbolic target. The church towered over Wall Street; from its bronze front door one could see the offices of Rockefeller's Standard Oil Company, as well as the nation's mightiest banks and insurance companies. An attack on

Trinity, the church of J. Pierpont Morgan, the financier who headed the nation's "banking trust," was an attack on corporate America. Russell had worked long enough for Pulitzer and Hearst, the masters of sensationalist journalism, to know a great story when he saw one. Newspapers, in fact, had for years criticized the church, pointing out the delicious irony that one of the great moral institutions in New York City owned a slew of uninhabitable buildings. How could this pillar of the community, with one of the largest charitable outreaches in New York, reap a financial windfall from what Russell called "drunken, disreputable, decayed, topsy-turvy old houses"? Trinity had withstood these assaults for years, but Russell was determined to ask the questions again; this time in two national magazines for which he wrote three exposé articles in 1908 and 1909. The result would be his greatest achievement as a journalist and reformer as he applied the final blow to a forty-year effort to expose and eliminate the wretched tenements owned by Trinity. Eventually, Russell's attack forced the church to tear down its slums in favor of model housing, to open its financial ledgers to the public, and to radically alter its conception of the responsibilities of a Christian landlord.[2]

Russell's assault on Trinity Church was more than symbolic, however. It raised questions about both poverty and housing, issues dear to reformers and socialists alike. Although he would not admit it, in 1908 Russell could still be counted as both. As a reformer he knew that his exposé would exert public pressure on Trinity to clean up an environment that was ruining the lives of thousands. Because reformers placed great faith in the potency of a changed physical environment, the slum cause was as important as the regulation of the "trusts" and the control of municipal corruption. "There is such a thing as a criminal mind," Russell once wrote, "but in every instance it can be traced back to environment and living conditions."[3] Urban problems stemmed from rotten housing, not rotten hearts.

Russell saw Trinity as a wonderful example of systemic failure—capitalism had forced even a beneficent institution such as Trinity to "divide responsibility between church and Wall Street."[4] The "system" forced even the good men of Trinity into following bad policies. While reform and regulation might ease some of the tenement's worst excesses (Russell praised the work of tenement reformers), it did not go far enough to suit Russell's increasingly radical beliefs.[5] Thus, Russell's Trinity exposé could kill two birds with one stone: lending a hand to the forces of tenement reform that had been making slow progress in improving housing conditions while also condemning the profiteering that was—as Russell now saw it—at the root of the problem.

When Russell decided to go after Trinity, the magazine writers who had become known as the "muckrakers" had been going strong for nearly six years, ever since Ida Tarbell and Lincoln Steffens began it all in *McClure's* magazine with their startling exposés.[6] Mass circulation magazines, like *McClure's*, *Collier's*, and *Everybody's*, each reaching upwards of a half-million people, were akin to today's television newsmagazines, such as "60 Minutes" and "20/20." They entered thousands of homes all over the country, had no competition, and had a much greater impact than newspapers, which circulated only locally. The magazines in which the muckrakers made their homes were the turn-of-the-century's town forums, the place where industrialism's excesses were being revealed, where political shenanigans were unfurled in monthly installments, and where the connection between politics and business was becoming clearer with each exposé. Most importantly, the establishment was being forced to respond to the rising public indignation and demand for reform.[7]

The climax of it all came when Russell's best friend David Graham Phillips wrote a blistering indictment of the U.S. Senate in 1906. The articles appeared in *Cosmopolitan*, which had been purchased a year earlier by Russell's old boss, William Randolph Hearst, as he expanded his media empire from newspapers into magazines. "The Treason of Senate" articles accused seventeen U.S. Senators of being slaves and well-paid butlers for various corporate interests.[8] Phillips's "Treason" articles were a wild success. *Cosmopolitan* could not print enough copies to keep up with demand. The public and the forces of reform were roused, but so was President Theodore Roosevelt who, in April 1906, launched his famous counterattack. Fearful that these "muck-rakers"—Roosevelt was the first to use the word publicly—were building a revolutionary fervor in the nation, Roosevelt implored the writers and the nation to remember all that was good in capitalist America. Look at the sky, not at the muck, he urged, slyly unleashing a torrent of criticism of exposé journalism.[9] Russell understood what Roosevelt was trying to accomplish. He explained: "Whenever a depraved reformer suggests any change in this holy and perfectly authenticated order, there is first laughter, then contempt, then alarm, then a rapid banding together of the forces of righteousness [until there results] a glorious victory for the right and the total defeat of the forces of unrest[10]

Phillips was wounded by the attacks on his articles. "I had an anxious time with him [one] Sunday, walking him around the streets while I tried to comfort him under the blow," Russell remembered. "He was terribly cut up." After the "Treason" articles, Phillips never again wrote nonfiction, sticking only to the novels that made him one of the bestselling writers in America.[11] Russell feared the damage that Roosevelt's attack had brought. "Many of the magazine editors," he noted, "took fright at the presidential command and abandoned expose stuff." Louis Filler, the preeminent historian of the muck-raking movement, concurs. After Roosevelt's 1906 speech, the legend grew that "muckraking was dead. . . . that the public was thoroughly 'tired' of muckraking, and that the few remaining muckrakers were mere outlaws with no following."[12] But Russell was one of the outlaws who, at forty eight, was just beginning to hit his stride. Needing an outlet, he turned to Benjamin Hampton's *New Broadway Magazine*, which was a listless and dry little maga-zine with 12,000 readers when Hampton bought it in 1904. By 1908, with per-sistent muckraking articles, *Hampton's* circulation had soared to 480,000. Russell would have an audience.[13]

II. "HORRIBLE THINGS . . . UNSPEAKABLE TERROR"

Russell first heard about Trinity Church from his father. When the family ar-rived in America, they were briefly housed in a ramshackle Trinity tenement. The experience led the family to leave New York. Then, when he came to New York as a reporter Russell observed and wrote about the poor victims who lived in Trinity's properties.[14] Although it operated admirable schools and shelters, Trinity Church was also the owner of "the worst tenements in New York," Russell concluded. This, he declared, "was a disgrace to civilization and to the city of New York." The angry Russell set out to expose the Trinity-slum con-nection to a national audience and to pressure the church into revealing, for the first time since 1814, the extent of its wealth and income. This was no easy task. Reformers had been looking into Trinity's tenements on and off for nearly two decades and Trinity was the church of the establishment—wealthy, power-ful, well connected. Its board of directors was made up of Wall Street types who ran New York City, part of the "invisible government" that Steffens had written about in his 1902 "Shame of the Cities."[15]

As Russell and two researchers began to dig into Lower Manhattan's "pangs of poverty," finding "dirt, darkness and squalor," it was not Trinity's rulers who motivated them. It was the victims—"respectable and industrious Americans," as he called them, many of whom were to his surprise second- and third-generation citizens, victims he had seen for years but about whom he now had a reason to write. In November 1907, Russell visited dozens of the properties owned by Trinity and found "horrible things." He knocked at a door and a silver-haired, seventy-year-old woman answered. "She looked respectable and decent despite her surroundings, but the last vestige of the human spirit had long been crushed out of her," Russell found. Dressed in rags, gaunt and bent, with "unspeakable terror in her eyes," she cringed at Russell's questions. "The utter dreariness of her surroundings had shriveled away the soul of humanity," he wrote.[16]

And then there were the children—"chalk-faced" and "growing up in terrible places" owned by Trinity, Russell wrote. One little girl in particular struck him. Her family lived behind a tiny and scantily stocked store. The girl was sick, lying on a filthy old mattress in a wooden shed that was her bedroom. Russell wrote: "The floor was filthy, the walls were bare, the room was a cold, cheerless hole." The child lay against a wall, beyond which was a backyard, "reeking of things I must not speak about," Russell said. The child was dying, as were so many of the children who "had been stupefied by the crushing misery in which they lived."[17]

Russell speculated that the child had tuberculosis. Thus, he argued in the three articles he wrote about Trinity Church, the public had a vital self-interest in forcing a cleanup of the slums. When a reader complained that Russell had no right to attack a private church because it was "none of his business," Russell responded angrily. On the contrary, he wrote, "Such tenements as Trinity maintains are a very grave and incessant menace to the public health," the worst of all breeding places for tuberculosis. "Don't clean them up because your heart bleeds for the dying and suffering children," he observed with a note of sarcasm, clean them because if you don't "the germs of the rag-picker's child" would inevitably be "communicated to our own children or to ourselves."[18]

Beyond the threat of disease was the matter of taxes. Since Trinity made few improvements on its properties, the area where its properties abounded lagged far behind all others in Manhattan in producing tax revenue. Self-interest, not humanity, was the issue. Arguing for change for practical over humanitarian reasons became one of Russell's themes. He was hoping that the pragmatic American business spirit was more likely to respond to appeals to self-interest. So, for example, in 1911 he implored businessmen to combat poverty and poor urban housing because if they did not, he argued they would have no market for their goods and no workers for their factories. "You cannot achieve national success with a race of tenement house scarecrows," Russell wrote. Simply put, Russell said, "to tolerate slums does not pay. It is not good for business."[19]

It is unlikely that Russell had all that much enthusiasm for his own self-interest arguments—or that public health and tax revenue were the real motivating factors for the preacher's grandson. He was angry at the conditions of Trinity's tenements and his heart bled at the sight of suffering children. "Every protest against them [the tenements] is a service to our children," he wrote. When Trinity's defenders attacked his articles, Russell said he had no objection to the criticism. "I am glad to be called 'a muck-raker,'" he said. "The only thing I object to is living in a world full of needless horrors and suffering without uttering one word of protest, however feeble and unheard."[20] Russell's articles did not go unheard.

All through the winter and spring of 1908, Russell and two assistants visited scores of Trinity properties in Lower Manhattan—138 on Hudson Street alone; 66 on Varick Street; 26 on Charlton Street; another 26 on Canal Street; and a dozen on Clarkson Street. "Wherever you walk in this dreadful region, you find something that Trinity owns," Russell said. Usually, he said with a sneer, it was a simple matter to discover which tenements were Trinity's. "Whenever I saw a house that looked as if it were about to fall down, one that looked in every way rotten and weary and dirty and disreputable, I found that it was owned by Trinity," he wrote.[21] Beyond pounding the pavements, Russell pored over whatever documents he could get his hands on, although he got little help from Trinity. Slowly, he pieced together the history, finances, and tenement records of the church.

Trinity's growth into the most powerful church in America was closely intertwined with the city's growth. The church built its first chapel in 1696 when the Dutch and British controlled New York. Then, in 1704, England's Queen Anne gave Trinity possession of two large farms. As the city's population soared, the church parceled out its land for the building of houses. But the church did not build; it simply leased the land while others built housing, a pattern it maintained up to the time Russell wrote his exposé. When leases on property expired, Trinity would often take control of the buildings; in this way it inherited buildings but was never saddled with the cost of construction—or the burden or maintaining the property. Trinity soon became a wealthy landlord, receiving, as Russell wrote, "a steadily waxing tide of gold," profits that "made the church rich."

The church became richer in 1814 when New York State passed legislation—for reasons that were never understood—that allowed Trinity to take possession of all the property in New York City that had previously been held by a number of Presbyterian churches. The parishioners of these churches objected strenuously and New York's governor refused to sign the new legislation, even though it became law when the governor did not veto it. But the 1814 law marked a significant turning point for Trinity Church: first, it was the beginning of many years of public criticism of the church that dogged it up until Russell's articles. "From 1814 to this day the history of Trinity has been a story of conflict," Russell concluded, with Trinity "accused of almost every conceivable offense."[22]

Second, the 1814 law relieved Trinity of any obligation of reporting to the public or its parishioners anything about its finances. "From this time on," Russell found, "it has never been possible for any person outside of the [church's] vestry to gather any information as to the business of Trinity." Russell's sarcastic rhetoric, so characteristic of his writing, was applied without temperance. "Impenetrable secrecy; rule of absolute silence; more secret than any mystic order; an unlifted curtain; an appendage to medievalism." Russell applied these phrases to Trinity, which he labeled a "Church of Mystery." This phrase particularly galled the church's officials who rebuked the press for invoking this damning slogan. For ninety-three years, Russell declared, no one "has been able to learn the simplest facts" about Trinity Church. How does it spend its money? How much money does it have? How much property does it own? Those were the questions Russell began asking. He found "very able lawyers, skilled cross examiners, [and] famous ferrets of the bar, have taken in hand the task of discovering at least the form and shape and extent of the Mystery: universally they have failed to discover anything."[23]

By working in much the same way as a modern investigative reporter, however, Russell discovered more about the church than most had. He utilized at least one secret source, combed every available public document (records compiled by state investigators, the church's annual reports, city tax records), interviewed many residents of Trinity's properties, and spoke with church officials in a fruitless effort to get the church to respond to the allegations he was about to make. His best hope for information was the Reverend Morgan Dix, who at eighty-one years of age had been rector of Trinity for forty-six years. Although suffering from asthma, Dix was still firmly in charge, preaching in slow, measured cadences each Sunday to his wealthy congregation. For years he had defended Trinity against criticism, but much like a skillful attorney he was always careful not to reveal too much. Instead, he took the public relations tack of attacking the "organs of public opinion" which "go beyond their proper province."

When Russell came to visit—with a considerable reputation of his own as a powerful New York City newsman—Dix had at least to grant him an interview, but he didn't have much to say. Russell was a man of dignity; he did not drink, nor did he like to frequent the taverns so popular with other newsmen. He was comfortable visiting with a minister, but he was clearly uncomfortable with the minister's policies. Dix told Russell that souls were his concern, not profits, and that he did not know much about the business of the Trinity Corporation. What he did know was that the leaders of the church, all prominent businessmen, names well known in New York City—Chauncey and Delafield,

Fish and Parsons, Schermerhorn and Swords—had been unfairly accused. "The high standing of these gentlemen is a sufficient refutation of any such innuendoes," said Dr. Dix. Russell agreed but added, tongue in cheek, "I cannot help a lingering wish that some of them were of standing not so high and had ways of life that did not lead so straight to Wall Street, where the great money hunger is."[24]

When Dix proved little help, Russell turned to Trinity's chief financial officer, comptroller Henry Cammann, a fifty-year-old, bearded, gray-haired, soft-spoken man, "a good man of integrity and ability," Russell concluded. But like Dix, he had little to say. Russell told Cammann that his research indicated that Trinity had spent $152,139 in 1906 but that $401,157 was unaccounted for.

> "Your figures for the parish are not correct," Cammann replied.
>
> "What are the correct figures?" Russell asked.
>
> "It does not seem best to the vestry to take the public into our confidence concerning that matter," Cammann answered.
>
> "Not," Russell responded, "when there has been so much controversy about this very point, so many bitter attacks against Trinity have been based upon it, and a word from you would make everything clear, putting an end to misrepresentation that must be both painful and harmful to the church?"
>
> "No," Cammann told Russell, "not even on those grounds. We have found that everything we make public only invites further criticism, and it seems best, therefore, to say nothing."
>
> "But you have made nothing public since 1814, have you?"
>
> "No, not since 1814," Cammann replied.[25]

And so Russell was left to speculate on the wealth of Trinity Church. His series began in April 1908 with "Trinity: Church of Mystery" as the lead article in *Hampton's New Broadway Magazine,* It was accompanied by photographs of the church's towering spire overlooking Broadway at the foot of Wall Street. "This is not a muck-raking article," Hampton declared in an editor's note, an odd statement since, sentences later, he said that Russell was about to "lift the veil" behind which Trinity had hidden for so many years. Despite Hampton's statement, what followed *was* classic muckraking, an effective combination of rhetorical flourishes, dramatic narrative, and facts. Hampton knew he had a winner with Russell's articles. After a career in advertising, Hampton had a shrewd marketing feel and good judgment on what would interest the public. No wonder he had taken his magazine to a half-million circulation in 1907. In Russell's first article, he wrote, "I have no quarrel with Trinity." This was somewhat disingenuous since all Russell did for the next four months was quarrel with a church that was hiding, he wrote with some hyperbole, "the most re-markable business secret in the country."[26]

Russell's first attack on Trinity was part moral tale, part sermon, and con-siderable history. Relying heavily on documents compiled by a New York State Senate investigation of the church's finances, Russell wrote as much about what couldn't be found—that is, details of the church's finances—as he did about what could. His concluding point: this church has done "things impossible to reconcile with Christian character." A month later Russell lifted the curtain a bit more on the mystery, using statistics printed in various New York newspa-pers over nearly a decade, to speculate on the church's income and expenses.

In July, Russell climaxed his exposé with his most biting article. He guided an imaginary group of "inquiring and well-fed tourists"—and the readers of *Everybody's* magazine, which published the third article—on a tour of Trinity's tenements. "Come inside and see how you like it," Russell implored. He took them first to Lower Manhattan, not far from Hudson Park where a few chalk-faced children played. Behind the children, Russell pointed to the "frowsy, scaly, slatternly, bleary, decayed, and crumbling old houses, leering from dirty windows like old drunkards through bloodshot eyes." Russell told the tourists, "All about is the hell of the East Side tenement-house region." But Russell was not asking his audience to simply lament the bad housing conditions found in so much of New York. He asked: "Drunken, disreputable, decayed, topsy-turvy old houses, the homes of thousands of families and the breeding-places for so many children that are to carry on the world's work – who owns these terrible places? Who draws the wretched profit of their existence?" The answer was obvious: "Trinity Church, holder of one of the greatest estates in New York or in the country, owns many of them. This is the heart of her possessions: street after street is lined with her properties." "Wherever you walk in this dreadful region," Russell commented, "you find something that Trinity owns, and, as a rule, it is something that you know she ought not to own."[27]

Russell led the tourists further on their tour. He took them up the bro-ken stairs of one tenement on Hudson Street. "The halls are narrow, dark, dirty, and smell abominably," he wrote. No natural light was found, no ven-tilation, a horrible odor – "a prolific breeding place for the germs of tuber-culosis." One tap of running water had to suffice for several families. Leaving the tenement, Russell brought the tourists to a backyard where garbage was strewn all over, "a horror into which you set your foot with an uncontrollable physical revulsion against the loathsome contamination." To his shocked tourists, Russell commented: "Human beings actually live in these places; many human beings; and pay for the privilege." But listing properties and describing them was not enough for Russell—he needed to show the people living in the Trinity tenements.

The children always came first. Russell wrote, "I have now in mind some pictures that stand out above the others of the horrible things I saw in my wanderings here." Once, he spotted five young children leaving a Trinity tenement. One had a running sore on her ear; all of them looked sickly. They were dirty, pale, dull, "stupefied by the crushing misery in which they lived." No wonder, he added, so many turned to crime. "If you wished to rear a criminal, do you think you could devise a better training place?" In an aside, Russell told his tourists that one would think the residents of the Trinity tenements must be from Naples or Palermo. "So you think," he said. "But these are not foreigners. These are Americans; respectable and industrious Americans . . . old-time residents of the Eighth Ward."

Why, Russell asked the tourists, would a Christian church, that had so many wonderful charitable outreaches, treat people this way? It must be, he said, sarcastically, that the church's elders simply believed that "tenement house dwellers do not have feelings like ours. They are differently constituted, their fibers are different . . . they do not feel the pangs of poverty or mind the dirt, darkness, squalor." It must be so, Russell continued, because "I have heard it urged by very learned and wise persons." Still, he wondered, what was it like on the night of March 29, 1896, when two men and two women were killed in a fire in a Trinity tenement on Hudson Street. Wrote Russell, "While the fiber of the people that live in tenements is different from the fiber of the rest of us, it is not sufficiently different to prevent such people from being burned, nor from having their bones broken if they fall far enough."

How could Trinity Church draw an income from these tenements? "You would want to have the money disinfected before it touched your hand, would you not?" he asked. But he knew indeed that the church was making great profits. "Much profit, very great profit," was how he characterized it. Russell ended as he had begun, addressing his audience about the "extraordinary story" that he had just told. No one knew the extent of Trinity's holdings, the extent of its wealth or revenue, nor what it did with its money. "Strange conditions," Russell said. "But stranger than all is this: that a Christian church should be willing to take money from such tenements as Trinity owns in the old Eighth Ward."[28]

III. A MUCKRAKING TRIUMPH

Despite years of agitation against Trinity's secrecy and its slum tenements, nothing struck such a responsive chord with the public as did Russell's articles.

To make matters worse, after Russell's first two articles appeared, the Reverend Dix died on April 30 after an asthma attack; some blamed the pressure from Russell's articles for Dix's death. "It was poignantly suggested that grief and chagrin over the attacks upon his corporation had caused his death," Russell recalled. "Muck-raking had become murder." Meanwhile, newspapers throughout the nation, from Seattle to Boston, published summaries of Russell's allegations. The Socialist *New York Call* labeled Trinity "hell's chief recruiting station" and called her tenements "the worst in the world." Hearst's *New York Journal* ran a full-page cartoon showing Trinity's pulpit hovering over slum tenements.[29]

Other publications came to the church's defense, however, echoing sentiments expressed by muckraker Ray Stannard Baker, who was a bit perplexed that this "most notable church in America" was "curiously under attack during recent months." Baker agreed with Russell that Trinity had a long and somewhat disreputable history, that its finances had remained closed for too long, that even churches needed to be accountable to the citizenry, and that it was good that "democracy stands knocking at last at the closed doors of Old Trinity." But his investigative reporting found different facts about Trinity's tenements, which, he wrote, "are not as bad as I expected to find."[30] Surprisingly, Baker repeated the arguments Trinity made in its defense: its buildings were no worse than others in the area; its rents were very low; none of the properties supported saloons or prostitution; and the church did not own many of the buildings, just the land, and thus had no control over their condition. These were the exact arguments found in the church-related publications that apologized also for Trinity's behavior—and criticized Russell. "Some of the buildings may be old. Their condition may be run down," church comptroller Cammann told one New York newspaper, "but it all depends upon the vigilance of the authorities. The city and the lessees are responsible; not the Trinity Corporation."[31] To Russell, however, those weren't excuses for misery. He held the church responsible for the properties from which it profited. In fact, Russell had anticipated that Trinity's defenders would claim they had no jurisdiction over buildings the church did not own. "I know that well enough," Russell repeated three times in his final article on the church. "To rent property and permit it to become a breeding-place for tuberculosis is exactly as bad as to rent it for immoral purposes," Russell declared. Trinity's defense was based on a technicality but not morality.

Aside from reaching different conclusions about Trinity, the differences between the ideologies and journalism styles of Russell and Baker are evident in their approaches to Trinity. Those differences, in fact, reflect a split that was developing in the muckraking movement and in journalism. Furthermore, they reveal how Russell was veering away from the establishment pack and moving beyond the Progressive ideal that a bit of tinkering with the existing social system would cure the ailments the muckrakers were revealing. Russell was too angry to be so optimistic, and his heart was telling him that something deeper was at stake here. His belief that a changed environment was a key element in shaping behavior put him comfortably in the progressive-liberal camp. But his insistence that the never-ending lust for profit and private accumulation of wealth was the cause put him in the camp of the radicals—those radicals whom Roosevelt had attempted to slow down. Only Russell and Upton Sinclair ever publicly embraced Socialism and sought to rebuke capitalism. Steffens flirted with communism many years later but the dozen of so writers in the muckraking tribe generally were moderates.[32] At the very least, however, Russell's Trinity articles showed him to be angrier than the rest of the muckrakers.

Baker, on the other hand, known for his fastidious reporting, factuality, and balance, was more typical. His reporting mirrored a growing concern in journalism about fairness and neutrality. The *American* magazine, where Baker, Tarbell, and Steffens went after leaving *McClure's* in a controversial 1908 split, was engaged in a debate about the direction of journalism. Steffens wanted to offer solutions; Tarbell and Baker insisted that more facts were needed. Russell agreed with Steffens. He was working more in the crusading tradition that he had learned working under Pulitzer and Hearst. Facts were important, but they needed to point to solutions. Baker wanted balance. For example, he not only gave Trinity's defense of its tenement holdings; he also documented its missionary and philanthropic activities. His writing was far less rhetorical and sarcastic than Russell's. "I shall here set down the facts," Baker wrote. And while he too indicted Trinity ("The plain fact is that Trinity did not care for the people"), he did so in a tone of moderation, writing caustically but cautiously. Baker was professorial, more in the "information" mode typified by the *New York Times;* Russell was a fire-and-brimstone preacher, more an outraged advocate than educator. While Baker was bent on educating, Russell was campaigning. "The price of a battle-ship would build sanitary, airy, and spacious homes for 20,000 persons; such assets as the great insurance companies possess would turn all the slums of New York into civilized habitations," Russell wrote. Baker would never make such connections.[33]

Who was correct in the end on the condition of Trinity's tenements? Were they as bad as Russell depicted or were they typical of what existed in New York but no worse than many others tenements, as Baker indicated? "Facts" might seem to support Baker, but results supported Russell. One of the first results of Russell's exposé was that Trinity Church hired Emily Wayland Dinwiddie, an inspector with New York's Tenement House Department, to investigate its housing. Dinwiddie was supervised by a respected former city official, and the investigation was said to be independent of church officials, conducted by a private organization. No one questioned its integrity. "No effort has been spared to get at the real conditions," Dinwiddie said.[34]

Dinwiddie gave Trinity virtually a clean bill of health, but one must read her report carefully to learn the reasons why. After a house-to-house inspection, she concluded that "sensationally bad conditions were not found in the tenements and smaller dwelling houses owned and controlled by Trinity Church." In fact, 96 percent of the 810 apartments and 334 buildings were in relatively good condition. Only 12 buildings were in bad condition. Dinwiddie saw little overcrowding, with two families per house, which was better than the average for the rest of the city. Sanitation was a problem in only 2 percent of the buildings, while 85 percent of the families had their own water supply and 60 percent had their own toilets. The Trinity buildings, Dinwiddie found, were in "marked contrast" to others in the area. "Whether the result of contentment or of apathy, the length of residence common among the tenants does not indicate active dissatisfaction," she wrote.[35]

Dinwiddie's report was flawed, however. The problems were threefold. First, she constantly compared Trinity's buildings to others in the region. Lower Manhattan was notorious at the turn of the century for its horrid tenement conditions. It was hardly comforting to know that Trinity's buildings were better than the awful ones surrounding them. Second, it is difficult to know what standards Dinwiddie was using to measure cleanliness and safety. If the standards were those allowed by the laws of 1909, then her high marks for Trinity might be understandable. Those standards left much to be desired and, even if met, they would still make for conditions that were wholly inadequate. Even the Reverend William T. Manning, who took over when Reverend Dix died, conceded that "there is some of the property the condition of which is far from being what it ought to be."[36]

But the third and most serious flaw in Dinwiddie's report was in what she didn't discuss—the tenements that Trinity did not own but that sat on its property. Dinwiddie said she wanted to include these properties (there may have been as many as three hundred) but that the owners refused to allow her access to make an inspection, saying that Trinity had no legal control over them. What this meant, of course, was that the worst of Trinity's buildings—albeit ones the church didn't own—were left out of Dinwiddie's report. While Trinity's defense—that it could not force changes over property it did not control—was technically valid, everyone knew that it had for years done little to gain control over the buildings, that it had simply ignored the horrible conditions and collected rents. Its position was legally justifiable but morally indefensible. These were the buildings that Russell had focused on, not unfairly, and they were the ones that desperately needed attention. Russell knew it, Baker knew it, and Trinity's overlords knew it also.

One other fact made Dinwiddie's investigation especially suspect. Soon after she completed her investigation, she was hired by the church to supervise the improvement of Trinity's properties. Did her favorable findings get her the job with Trinity? Did she alter any conclusions in order to please the powerful and rich Trinity administrators? Although it is common enough today for regulators to take jobs with those they regulate, certainly questions are raised by her joining forces with Trinity so soon after her "independent" investigation.

Trinity Church had warded off attacks on its character and properties for nearly one hundred years. However, the combination of the surging tide of Progressive reform, an unrelated action by the church to disassociate itself from one of its nearby parish churches, and the appointment of a new rector, Reverend Manning, made change in response to Russell's articles inevitable.

Three months after Russell's last article, Trinity announced plans to close St. John's Chapel, one of the ten churches it controlled, and consolidate its operation with the nearby St. Luke's Church. The church cited financial concerns but moreover asserted that the two churches had overlapping congregations; efficiency of operation made the change necessary. Whatever the reason, the announcement caused a furor, just what a church already under fire didn't need. "The floodgates of criticism opened wide," one historian asserted. And the critics' easiest point of attack was the slum tenements owned by the church. Reverend Manning had responded privately to the Russell articles by appointing a committee to make a personal study of the church's holdings. "I say unhesitatingly," Manning declared, "that as property owners . . . we are bound to do everything in our power" to improve conditions. "We ought to set not only a high standard, but the very highest. Far better, if necessary, that all our charities should be given up . . . than that we should maintain any of them by revenue derived from properties in an unsanitary or questionable condition."[37]

Manning knew also that aside from tackling the tenement issue, he needed to rid the church of its air of mystery. Thus, the church began the year 1909 by slipping into the pews of its parishioners one Sunday morning a detailed financial statement—the first since 1814—for the Trinity Corporation. This was a clear victory for Russell. The *Times* put the story on page one, and as far west as St. Louis, newspapers applauded the action, declaring "a tremendous victory for publicity . . . a recognition of the people's right to know what a big corporation does with the money it handles." Russell had estimated that Trinity had assets totaling $39 million, but the church said its assets were only $14 million. This still made it the wealthiest church in the world. The church said it made only $732,741 on rents from its properties. "This property is not, as has been often asserted, a source of large revenue to the parish. It is quite the reverse," the report asserted.[38] Furthermore, the report said that the properties were not in the terrible condition that some had charged; nevertheless, the church was planning large-scale improvements to many properties.

The extent of those changes became clear a month later when the church, to everyone's shock, announced that it would no longer continue as a landlord and that it would sell all of its real estate, except for that housing its churches and offices. As long as the church had any tenements, an unnamed source told the *Times*, it would be criticized. The source then repeated what had become Trinity's frequent refrain: the properties were not as bad as had been charged. Citing Russell's articles on Trinity's tenements, the church said the pictures accompanying the text were of buildings not owned by the church—but of course the church did own the land.[39] Despite moving forward to change the practices that had drawn criticism, the church was also carefully plotting a public-relations defense strategy: hit back at the critics who were overstepping their journalistic limits; emphasize the positive by citing the church's charitable work; and obfuscate and confuse the issues by reiterating how its hands were tied on properties it did not own.

In April Reverend Manning spoke publicly for the first time in defense of the church he had headed for nearly a year. "The air has been full of the most astonishing statements . . . which no serious person could have been expected to believe," Manning said. "Honest difference of judgment" was one thing, "but the recent discussion can hardly be said to have been conducted in the spirit of generous and helpful criticism." Manning then responded to Russell. Since the church had opened its books to the public—an act, he said, that had been planned before the criticism—"it can never be said again that Trinity pursues a policy of secrecy or of mystery." As to the conditions of Trinity's tenements, the charges were "grossly untrue." Years later, still stinging from Manning's denial, Russell said he always asked one question of his critics: "You say these tenement houses are not really bad. Would you like to live in one of them? Take the best of them all. Would you like to live in it?"[40]

The answer from Manning was no, he would not. While he continued to offer the standard Trinity arguments about low rents and tolerable conditions, he maintained the church's new position: it would do whatever it took to clean up all the tenements, those the church owned and those that sat on its property. Such a decision did not come easily, because inside the church many opposed Manning's decision to spend considerable sums to make improvements. Dinwiddie forced the church to acquire houses as leases expired, as Russell suggested the church could. She made sure also that the church kept rents low for large families. By 1910, however, 225 tenements had been taken down by the church as not worth reconditioning. By 1916, the 367 houses owned by Trinity were in good condition and a credit to the parish. The city's newspapers actually began to feature stories about Trinity's model tenements.[41]

Charles Edward Russell and the forces of tenement house reform that had been building in New York City for two decades had forced America's wealthiest church to do the right thing—finally. Many years after the victory, Russell was exultant, recalling how his family had been forced to live in a terrible Trinity tenement. He commented, "The grandson of the émigré of that day had the pleasure of seeing that old rookery destroyed as a result of a campaign he had instigated." Unfortunately for the residents of Trinity's tenements, Russell added, "It was a work of grace sixty years delayed."[42]

Chapter Ten

Evil Prisons, Race Riots, Justice Denied

I. The "Abominable" Prisons of Georgia

AMERICA WAS IN THE THROES OF GREAT POLITICAL and social change in 1908, and keeping the status quo was not an option for a society suffering from the excesses of industrialism. The explosion of its urban immigrant populations, a rise in labor-capital tension, and a growing gap between rich and poor led to problems America could not afford to ignore, at least not without running the risk of serious upheaval. The unregulated capitalism that had grown exponentially since the Civil War needed to be restrained. Republican President Theodore Roosevelt, fearful that a social revolution might brew without change, had moved forcefully but carefully after taking over when William McKinley was assassinated in 1901. To meet some of the problems brought into the open by the muckrakers' exposés—notably the threat of monopolies, the poisoning of food, consumer rip-offs in insurance, and big money influence on politics—Roosevelt began to enlarge the federal government's role in regulating commerce.[1] Laissez-faire was out; moderate government intervention was in. Reform would do the trick, the Progressives argued, to the chagrin of many radicals who felt that reform was a bandage that would not cure the disease of the profit-making machine. Socialism had become a particularly attractive alternate in the early years of the century. Why not allow the government to own and operate some key industries?

This blasphemy, of course, particularly irked the Social Darwinists and even the moderates. The search for a cure to America's new-century ills was on.

At the heart of awakening the public to America's problems and to the variety of both reform and radical options faced by a maturing industrial society were the muckraking journalists—Ida Tarbell, Lincoln Steffens, Ray Stannard Baker, Samuel Hopkins Adams, and Charles Edward Russell. Writing in mass-circulation magazines that were reaching millions of Americans, this band of exposé journalists wrote nearly two thousand articles and a handful of books describing the excesses of industrialism and the impact those excesses were having on a public that increasingly felt anxious about its future. Progressivism was in fact largely a journalistic mentality. In other words, it was the journalists who were feeding the public with the facts that were fueling both their anger and anxiety. But the journalists who were at the brink of suggesting the solutions to the problems that they were exposing were feuding among themselves about the direction their work should take in 1908, and about whether it was even their responsibility to propose solutions.

Steffens, considered the prototypical muckraker, was not so sure it was a good thing to even be considered one. In a letter to Upton Sinclair on the occasion of Edmund Wilson's criticism of the muckrakers, he commented: "The fact that he lumps us is a bad sign."[2] Russell, on the other hand, gloried in the appellation; he saw it as a badge of honor. Soon after his articles on the beef trust were published in 1905, Russell commented, "I have been muck-raking ever since. I hope to keep on muck-raking. I like to muck-rake."[3] But not all the muckrakers sided with Russell. Many of the famous exposé journalists were actually befuddled in 1908 about the direction of journalism—and of America. They wondered whether enough facts had been placed on the table for Americans to see the problems and solutions clearly enough. In 1904 Steffens had warned his colleagues at *McClure's* magazine: "Look out for editorializing. That's easy and it doesn't count for much without the facts." When he wrote a series of articles on race in America in 1906 Baker declared that only "facts" would fill his articles.[4] But Steffens, a few scant years after his warning to his colleagues, changed his tune when the staff of *McClure's* moved over to the *American* magazine. By 1908 he was declaring, "We have the facts. The time has come to discuss the cause of our American corruption—and cures."[5] At the beginning of 1908, Russell seemed to be listening to both Baker and Steffens.

The year 1908 was momentous for the nation and for Russell. Roosevelt decided not to run for the presidency again, and he turned over the mantel of leadership to William Howard Taft, a conservative man who was elected but not able to stem either the rising tide of Progressivism that was sweeping all levels of government or the growing fervor for Socialism. Russell for his part began pounding away at America's obsession with profit-making while at the same time he moved to expose new ills that had been largely ignored by the muckrakers. He published sixteen articles in national magazines—including his attack on Trinity Church—as well as a book about lawless American corporations. In that year he also mounted his next big crusade, this time against cruelty and injustice in American prisons. He began the year and set the tone for how he was viewing the world by telling a national audience in *Human Life* magazine about John D. Rockefeller, the Standard Oil magnate who epitomized the best and worst of American capitalism. Russell had observed Rockefeller since his reporting days in New York. He covered Rockefeller at a trial in 1891, watching him in the courtroom, "that long, firm jaw, the cold, thin lips drawn over the death-like face of a corpse, the pallid skin, the face as cold as death, as hard as steel." Russell concluded, "all he wants is possession, accumulation." Those lips seemed to say, "Get money. Get money." What a sad example Rockefeller was for America's youth, he wrote. "How do we benefit by teaching young men to sneer at reform, scoff at democracy, and view gain as the chief end of man"?[6] Russell was no less critical of J. Pierpont Morgan, the other archetypal capitalist who, rumor had it, was the man behind the banking trust that had a stranglehold on the American economy. "At the lifting of the Morgan finger," he noted, "the financial heart is elated or depressed" by this man who had spent "fifty years of money grubbing." Why did Americans admire the "wholly barren and bitter existence" of a man "whose sole pursuit is gain"?[7] Expressing both disgust and anger, Russell pleaded to a national audience: "Let us have some one blessed thing done in this country on some other basis than that of dollars." America needed to "deal with causes," he declared, seemingly ready to plunge into offering solutions. But many hidden facts were still to be revealed, and muckraking of conditions was still needed. "The best way to abolish the muckraker is to abolish the muck," he said.[8] And so he turned his attention to the deep muck that surrounded America's prisons.

Sometime in 1907 *Everybody's* magazine received a letter from a young man, an ex-prisoner who told of his experience in the Georgia prison system. It's unclear why he wrote to *Everybody's*, but not surprising. A national magazine with a monthly circulation near 500,000, it had consistently muckraked on a wide range of issues, publishing fiction and nonfiction by the likes of Owen Wister, David Graham Phillips, Frank Norris, Alfred Henry Lewis, O. Henry, Booth Tarkington, and Booker T. Washington. Begun originally as the house organ of department store owner John Wanamaker, the magazine was sold to Erman J. Ridgway in 1903. Ridgway enlisted Russell to write his beef trust articles in 1905 and sent him on an around-the-world trip to investigate social conditions in other countries in 1906. But his magazine especially made its mark in 1904–5 when it published the revelations of Wall Street insider Thomas Lawson, whose "frenzied finance" exposé shocked the nation and sent the magazine's circulation soaring. Ridgway turned the letter over to Russell, who was already investigating Trinity Church. He assigned him a researcher, little-known journalist Hugh C. Weir, and the two unfolded the story of a fresh-faced boy who entered a Georgia prison for a minor burglary and came out a brutalized victim—and a criminal. *Everybody's* editors labeled it "the terrible story of life in a Georgia convicts' camp" that symbolized "conditions existing in every part of the United States."[9]

In storylike fashion that did not stop to give statistics or background on Georgia's prison system, Russell dramatically told the youth's shocking tale in narrative fashion. The tale of woe began in an Atlanta courtroom where the young man—whose identity was "carefully guarded"—pleaded guilty to stealing $300 from his employer's cash drawer. "He was no familiar and hardened criminal," yet he was sentenced to four years. The next day, shaved and shorn and wearing the stripes of a convict, he was placed on exhibition in front of agents for private contractors. Georgia had no prisons in 1908; in fact had not had any since the Civil War. With an upsurge in prisoners after the war— mostly black men—Georgia simply abolished its penitentiaries in 1879 and began to lease its prisoners to companies which paid the state $500,000 in twenty annual installments. "A very strange device," Russell said, selling people into the "the hands of private and irresponsible persons. . . ." He compared it to slavery. "Fifty years before . . . another man had gone similarly up and down another line, making similar selections for service. But the service of fifty years ago had been called slavery," he told the nation. In fact, this same argument had been made by W. E. B. Du Bois, the articulate black scholar and a friend of Russell's. "The convict lease system," Du Bois had declared, is "slavery in private hands . . . a direct child of slavery." And after all, Russell added, sarcastically, "Convicts and Negroes, we have decided, are outside the pale of humanity, having no souls, nor rights nor feelings."[10]

At first the young convict was hopeful he would survive prison. But, Russell noted, "the battered old hulks of professional criminals" drifted by him and they "shook the spirit of bravado. He did not want to end up like these men." One old bank robber was convinced that the kid was a professional criminal. "You're in the bank-sneak line, ain't you?" he asked, as Russell used dialect to re-create conversations. The kid answers, "I was thinking what I can do to keep straight when I get out of here." The man laughs. "Do you suppose anybody ever came in here and kept straight afterward . . . a crook you'll stay till the end of your days." This was Russell's first point: the prison system ruined rather than reformed people. "We are engaged in our favorite national pursuit of dosing the symptoms of an evil instead of cutting out its source," Russell wrote. It was a theme he would trumpet for the next decade. "It is the system, not the individual, that is as fault."[11]

The system in this case was convict leasing, which allowed the state to make money off prisoners, elected officials to receive contributions from the companies leasing the prisoners, and prisoners to be brutalized without oversight. "The whole thing is utterly and incurably and hopelessly evil," Russell declared, "probably the most atrocious thing of the kind on this earth and the foulest blot on our civilization." Eventually, the young convict, George, was taken to a remote camp to make bricks. "Nobody knew what went on there, and nobody cared," said Russell.[12] His first breakfast consisted of greasy corn bread and salt pork, which he had to eat with his hands. Worms crawled in the pork, which another prisoner ate when George couldn't. While a man with a rifle stood watch, the prisoners—men and women—filled 300-pound wheelbarrows with 50 to 70 bricks; 105 loads a day were required. When a prisoner failed to meet the minimum, he was strapped to a barrel in front of the other prisoners as two men held him down and a guard with a leather belt three feet long whipped him. Through it all, the man on the barrel "screams a horrible shrill scream of unutterable pain," Russell wrote. The whippings were supposed to be reported but only one in twenty was.

The narrative, written in a seamless fashion with little commentary, gets only more gruesome as one prisoner, rheumatic and unable to meet the daily workload, is whipped and left to die. Others, working in cold swampy water, contract pneumonia. And, despite state rules about conditions, the young convict realizes that no one heeds or enforces any regulations. "All these rules were as if they had never existed," offers Russell. George realizes he is of no concern to Georgia or the company to which he has been sold. "Between the two he is the lost and forgotten outcast and pariah . . . nobody cares. Why, then, should the convict care what war he makes upon the society that has thrust him into a pit and left him there?"[13]

Finally George's time came to be released. A guard says to him when he leaves. "Well, I suppose you are going to yegg it," meaning that he was going back to a life of crime. And George said, "By god, I am." He went back to Atlanta and turned burglar. Asked Russell: "And was he the only man that went forth from those gates resolved to prey upon the society that had preyed upon him? I think not." Self-interest alone should make Georgia eliminate the prison-leasing system. Otherwise, "the world at large must pay too dearly." One would think, Russell reasoned, that "our common humanity" would force an end to "this abominable system . . . this cancer." But dollars interfere with sense. Russell documented the profit made by the state, which, when relieved of a prison system, did nothing but make money from the labor of its prisoners. "These profits are the sole returns from a system that multiplies criminals, breeds brutality, encourages crime, and puts upon one of the fairest states in the Union a hideous blot. If the profits were a thousand times as great, they would be dear at that price." The Georgia lease system gave Russell his chance to make a frontal attack on the never-ending urge to make profits as the cause of the prisoner abuse, but instead his attack was muted. Certainly, he didn't blame the people of Georgia, who "abhor the system . . . never chose it nor wanted it nor approved of it. They have always loathed it. . . . And yet this hateful thing continues." Why? The people "have no direct control of their own affairs; and, second, the system is profitable to very powerful interests."[14] It was classic Progressive reasoning: the "people" have no power over the "interests."

The response to Russell's revelations, not unlike his Trinity articles, was immediate and considerable, more than perhaps he or *Everybody's* editors could have imagined. "The people of Georgia have been intensely aroused over this record of incompetence and brutality and greed," one writer noted. Mass meetings occurred in a number of cities. One Sunday in Atlanta there was a monster meeting in the city's opera house. The members of the state legislature were inundated with letters, telegrams, and petitions. One Georgia citizen commented that Russell's article was "the spark that set off the powder that is now exploding in the legislative halls of Georgia." A doctor testifying at a public hearing said he had just returned from England where even the British knew of the conditions and were attacking Georgia. The exposé "has made us stink in the nostrils of civilized people the world over."[15] One legislator, demanding an investigation, called the scandal "a stain upon our civilization and an insult to humanity." The newspapers, long silent on the prison lease system, now began to pick up Russell's trail of evidence and scandal. "Georgia's fair name has been trailed in the dirt in magazines and elsewhere for too long," declared the *Americus Times Recorder.* Added the *Cordele Rambler,* "We have been advertised to the world as allowing all kinds of cruelty, graft and corruption, and nothing short of an investigation will place us in good standing again."[16]

The squeals of indignation forced the Georgia legislature to take up the issue, albeit reluctantly, as some legislators tried to argue that the system should be investigated and perhaps reformed but not yet repealed. But as hearings got under way in July, it became impossible for the legislature not to act.

First it was revealed that, in violation of law, misdemeanor convicts were farmed out along with felony offenders. Then testimony confirmed the poor food, filthy living conditions, and the brutal overwork. Three brick companies were found to be the worst offenders. "Some of the convicts are being worked harder than beasts," one legislator declared. Russell's story of one convict, as headlines throughout Georgia trumpeted, was just the tip of the iceberg as the legislature pored over 18,000 prison reports from a six-year period.[17] Then the final blow to the existing lease system was applied when an eyewitness testified that he had seen convicts beaten to death. Day after day the evidence mounted—convicts being lined up and sold like slaves; cruelty and beatings in various camps; wardens taking money for leasing to favorite companies; a contractor who made $300,000 in a five-year deal with the state; state commissioners who knew of the graft money. One former warden admitted publicly that he took bribes. Perhaps the most pitiful case was that of a white sixteen-year-old who threw coffee on a warden's hog and then was beaten so brutally by guards that he died, allegedly of "tuberculosis." Some of the testimony was "unprintable," one writer commented. By early August the prison commission was defending its actions—but no one was buying it. The *Atlanta Constitution* in an editorial printed in bold face capital letters declared: "The people of Georgia are unalterably opposed to the continuation of the convict lease system. They wish to get as far away as possible from the system." End the convict lease system, the editorial pleaded.[18]

The legislature adjourned in early August, however, without taking action. The Senate wanted to continue the system for one more year while it investigated further; the Assembly wanted an immediate end. After a three-week hiatus, the public clamor forced the first special session of the Georgia legislature in twenty-five years. A compromise was finally reached on September 19, 1908. Prisoners were to be transferred to the state's counties to work on public roads, and they could only be leased to private contractors if the counties did not have work for them. This did not happen. More than two thousand prisoners were put to work on roads by the counties, and prison leasing was ended forever. *Everybody's* gloated. "Georgia didn't waste any time finding fault with us for calling attention to the spot on her pretty gown. Georgia cleaned the spot off quicker 'n scat—that's Georgia's. We are proud to have had a little share in the good work."[19]

While Russell was silent publicly about the reaction and never wrote about it, he was not content to stop with his exposé of Georgia's prisons. He used a three-part series of articles in *Hampton's* magazine, which was then publishing his Trinity church articles, to further examine prisons. Entitled "Beating Men

to Make them Good," the articles appeared in September, October and November of 1909 and they did what the narrative Georgia articles didn't—they
analyzed and offered opinion. Russell and his research assistant Weir produced
a meticulous survey of fourteen American prisons, replete with charts, tables,
and statistics. Russell was both gloomy and optimistic. On the gloomy side, he
wagged his finger at American communities, "filled with intelligent, extremely
self-satisfied, and highly moral people that survey with joy the cleanliness of
their town, their noble churches, handsome parks, admirable schools, and their
own incomparable virtues as model citizens." And yet, when it comes to their
jails, they are "murdering men's souls and bodies, and never once give the matter a thought." Nonetheless, Russell concluded, despite the "hellish horrors"
and a "long trail of manifold horrors, cruelties, and barbarisms, burnings, man-
glings, and beatings," reforms were taking place. He pointed especially to the
federal prison at Leavenworth, Kansas, and contrasted it with the "grimy old
dungeon," the Columbus (Ohio) Penitentiary. "Not very swift, but still—
progress," he wrote. "They are not enough to make us all sing for joy, not because we have actually gained much so far for decency, but because of the
shining promise that at some time hereafter we are to be decent." Russell's key
point: prison is a place to salvage those who have gone wrong, not to punish or
brutalize them for their mistakes. "Good will, decency, and kindness seem
much more effective in keeping men in order." Help the convict "straighten his
walk," he wrote.[20]

Like most Progressives, Russell believed that environment was primarily
responsible for shaping people's character. There were no bad men, only bad
conditions that made men go bad. "I have known criminals of every shade, kind
and degree," Russell said, "and I have yet to find one in whom there was not
plenty of good." Moreover, Russell had the Progressives' faith that institutions
could help reshape character. "It is not the character of the convicts that determines; it is the degree of enlightenment possessed by the authorities," he argued. "Men that have wholesome occupation in the fresh air, good food, good
treatment, and adequate rest turn naturally not toward evil, but away from it."
Russell pointed to young boys from New York City who were in trouble with
the law. "How little chance has the tenement-house boy, how little of inspiration and how much of evil are in his environment." What they needed, he argued, "was not punishment but opportunity."[21] Thus, the prison could—and
should—be a tool for saving those who had gone astray, a position that was at
odds with American prison history. The two major models of prison structure,
the Cherry Hill prison in Philadelphia and the Auburn prison in New York,
were both founded in 1830 using punishment, isolation, and hard work by pris-

oners as their tenets. Regeneration might come about for prisoners, but not because they were to be treated with kindness or self-respect or even decency.[22]

Russell used the example of notorious inmate Ira Marlatt to make his point. Imprisoned in the Columbus penitentiary for manslaughter, Marlatt was Ohio's most feared convict, a brute who complained to guards that he was not being paid his fair share for his prison work, a complaint that was apparently true. But the guards nonetheless had Marlatt "paddled" for insolence. "They paddled him until . . . there was no place left to paddle," Russell wrote. "They had torn the skin from him. Then they hung him up in the bull rings. He fought like a tiger; he could be subdued only by making him unconscious." When the brutal water treatment punishment did not work, the guards beat him until he nearly died. Eventually, Marlatt was put in a special lockup called the "Demon's Cage." He lived there for years, a legend in the Ohio prison system. One day a state senator came to visit, and asked to go into Marlatt's cage. "He'll kill you if you go near him," a guard told the senator. But he insisted and entered the cage. They sat side by side for thirty minutes. When he came out, the senator announced that Marlatt wanted to go back to work in the prison. He became a model prisoner. For Russell, Marlatt typified the "new spirit" that was beginning to enter American prisons. "Ingenious punishments" fail while "fresh air, good food, good treatment, and adequate rest turn [men] naturally not toward evil, but away from it."[23]

Russell had a final point to make, however, one that also fit into his growing belief that above all it was the lust for profit that most effected how America's prisons were run. Punishment of prisoners, Russell found, was used only in prisons where contract labor was in place. In Ohio, for example, one of the worst offending states, private companies ran the prison industry. "Corporal punishment and brutality," Russell pointed out, "are at the worst where the contract system is most absolute." He cited Alabama as a flagrant offender. What was illogical about punishment, he argued, was that discipline could be easily maintained without harsh punishment. Why then the punishment? "*To extract from the prisoners the profits of speculators in misfortune*," wrote Russell, using italics to emphasize his point: "Greed" of the contractors is the problem, he wrote. "Long ago I suspected this to be the fact; now I am sure of it." Russell ended his prison series by becoming, once again, the grandson of a preacher, standing on his journalistic pulpit, preaching to a national congregation. Somberly he concluded: "The hearts of men are not naturally cruel; cruelty is the offspring of greed, and greed is born of the social system that enables the strong to prey upon the weak and one man to live upon another's toil."[24] But Russell was ready to leap beyond the constraints of Progressivism, which argued continually that the system could be reshaped and reformed. "It is the system, not the individual, that is at fault, and nothing is so pathetically hopeless as the various movements for better government that go fumbling around the edges of the questions. Deal with causes and not results."[25] Russell was primed to take two steps: the first was to reject reform in favor of more radical solutions. And the second was to go beyond journalistic observation and for the first time take direct action as a participant in another social justice cause, the plight of African Americans.

II. THE FOUNDING OF THE NAACP

The National Association for the Advancement of Colored People, the oldest and most effective voice of black advocacy in America, got its start indirectly and inauspiciously on the night of June 1, 1908, in Springfield, Illinois. Joe James, a young black drifter from Alabama, arrived by train to this city of 47,000 people, the birthplace of Abraham Lincoln. Springfield was a logical place for the nineteen-year-old to seek a job. It had a modest black population of 2,500 and its coal mines and brickyards offered Jones a reasonable chance of finding work. James got waylaid on his first day in Springfield, however, for he ended up in the Levee, a small neighborhood that housed saloons, gambling dives, and houses of prostitution. Many of the saloons were black owned; with no friends or relatives in Springfield, James ended up in the Levee.

One evening, soon after his arrival, James got arrested, apparently because he beat some locals in a poker game; to get even, they told the police that James was a vagrant. He was arrested and went to the city jail, where he was a model prisoner. In fact, so trusted was James that he was sent from the jail one night in July to pick up food for the guards. He got waylaid again at a saloon. In return for drinks and food, he played the piano, after which he began drinking heavily and gambling. By 11:00 P.M., drunk, he stumbled out of the tavern.

That same night, a sixteen-year-old girl, the daughter of a white engineer, awoke to find a black man lying at the foot of her bed. She screamed, and the intruder fled, but her father, Clergy Ballard, followed him. They grappled in the front yard and the intruder stabbed Ballard several times. No one could identify the assailant, but before he died Ballard told his family that the man was black. Early the next morning, Joe James was spotted by the side of the road several blocks from the Ballard house; he was sound asleep. Ballard's relatives arrived shortly before the police and beat him severely. James was arrested and taken to jail, where he awaited trial for many weeks, even though there was little, if any, evidence to link him to the murder.

A second incident that inflamed Springfield, even if unjustifiably, came in August when Mabel Hallam, the wife of a city streetcar driver, was allegedly sexually assaulted in her home while her husband was working. She said a black man committed the assault while she was preparing to go to bed. Black workmen employed at a nearby house were considered suspects. From a police lineup Mrs. Hallam identified one of them as her attacker. He too was taken to the city jail. News of the arrest was displayed prominently in the city's newspapers, and many of Springfield's residents began to talk of seizing Joe James and George Richardson, who was accused of the Hallam assault.

By early evening of the Friday that Richardson was arrested small crowds of angry whites began to gather in Springfield outside the city jail. Cries of "Lynch the nigger!" and "Break down the jail!" could be heard. But the police chief, fearing mob violence and a lynching, had secretly whisked away the two prisoners outside the city. William Hallam, Mabel's husband, was allowed to search the jail and report to the crowd that it was indeed empty. When the crowd learned that the prisoners were gone, they became angry and began to throw bricks. But police held them at bay and they were forced to direct their growing anger elsewhere.

The crowd moved en masse to a nearby restaurant owned by a white man whose car had been used to take the black suspects out of town. The mob broke the restaurant's windows, chasing the employees, including the owner, into a basement where he was forced to fire warning shots to the menacing crowd. "Curse the day that Lincoln freed the nigger!" shouted one attacker. The restaurant was demolished and the restaurateur's car was set ablaze while the angry crowd danced with glee. Now the mob, which began to take on a life of its own, headed to the black commercial district. Random assaults on innocent blacks started occurring. City authorities had seriously underestimated the seriousness of the situation, and there were not enough police to control the mob's growing hunger for revenge against the city's black population—and against some whites who were considered friendly to blacks. The black business district was gutted. Blocks of black homes were burned. After several hours of looting and burning of businesses, black and white alike, the mob sought out human victims and this led to the most gruesome incident of the evening.[26]

At two in the morning, the rioters reached the house of Scott Burton, a fifty-six-year-old barber who had sent his wife and children out of town while he remained at his house, shotgun in hand. But the mob was more than he could handle; he tried to escape out a side door. The mob caught him, beat him unconscious, and dragged him to a street. They then hanged Burton from a dead tree in front of a saloon. While flames roared in the background, the rioters riddled the corpse with bullets, gashed it with knives, and tore off his clothing. Finally, at 2:30 in the morning, state militia troops arrived and dispersed the crowd, firing warning shots before the crazed rioters began to return to their homes.[27]

But the white Springfield rioters were not finished. They moved next to the house of William Donnegan, eighty, a retired shoemaker with severe rheumatism who owned a home near the governor's mansion and the state arsenal. Donegan met the crowd at his door. They dragged him outside, beat him with bricks, and slit his throat with a razor. The white rioters then hanged him from a tree from a clothesline. When the militia finally arrived to cut him down, it was too late. He died in a hospital the next day.

By Sunday morning the rioting was over. After state police finally imposed an uneasy peace, two innocent black men had been lynched, four white men were dead and scores more were injured. Nearly two thousand blacks had to flee their own hometown. But the nation—or at least the portion of the nation that cared—did not yet know much about Springfield riot. Nevertheless, the riot made clear that racial violence was not limited to the South—it was a national problem.[28] Both the North and the South were infected. It would take a tall radical but courtly Southerner, William English Walling, an old friend of Charles Edward Russell's, to get out the message about the riot's devastating effect—and to make a clarion call for action to prevent more lynchings from taking place.[29]

Russell knew little of the Springfield riots. The year 1908 was a busy one; he was enmeshed in various projects, including his campaign against Trinity Church, as well as the writing of feature profiles on John D. Rockefeller, labor leader Samuel Gompers, and Wisconsin Senator Robert La Follette.[30] But like so many of the muckrakers, he was virtually silent on the question of racial injustice.[31] Privately, however, he made his feelings clear. Quietly he sent a $1,000 contribution to Fisk University in 1904, becoming the first white man to donate to the black university. But in none of his major writings in the national magazines that he wrote for is there any reference to racial conditions. He was publicly indignant about poverty and slum housing; about prison conditions and corporate manipulations of the free marketplace; and about the endless attempts by the business community to buy political influence. But he expressed nary a word on racism.[32] Part of the explanation for that might have been that muckraking or exposé was an uncertain vehicle for dealing with an issue around which there was no popular indignation or even a consensus on how to structure the facts. Exposé usually meant revealing something that was hidden beneath the surface. Racism was out front for all to see. It needed to be explained, analyzed, and publicized, but muckraking journalism, as many commentators have pointed out, was often not very good at providing solutions for the problems it exposed. A second possibility was that for reform journalism to work, it needed active partners in order to mount a crusade. Powerful groups advocating Negro rights did not yet exist. The muckrakers could hardly look to the White House of the conservative William Howard Taft for help. When Russell attacked prison conditions, he consulted various reform groups. And as he exposed Trinity Church, he worked with housing reformers who were desperately trying to get New York City to improve its regulations. Maybe, when it came to race, Russell felt that advocates were more needed than writers. The third possibility—a glum one—is that writing about race was not a popular cause, not a story that would bring readers flocking into the circulation base. As Ray Stannard Baker wrote in 1906: "The people one ordinarily meets don't know anything about the Negro, don't discuss him, and don't care about him." Would they wish to read about their plight?[33]

Some magazines, however, were at the forefront in getting at least some information on race to the public. *McClure's, Cosmopolitan,* and the *American* joined older journals like the *Independent,* the *Nation,* and *Outlook* to denounce racial discrimination and violence. Baker, who had differed with Russell over his Trinity Church conclusions, led the way in 1906 with groundbreaking articles in the *American* magazine about racial conditions. His articles came after a vicious race riot occurred in Atlanta in 1906, one that was remarkably similar to Springfield's. Like most of the magazine editorial writers, Baker argued for enforcement of existing law. He also seemed to embrace a position of benign neglect that many Progressives had taken, similar to Booker T. Washington who stressed that blacks needed to improve their lot through hard work and industrial education. This was much easier said than done: while shiftless and irresponsible blacks were the constant targets of violence, blacks who had prospered and achieved success were equally resented and discriminated against by working-class whites. Whether foundering or succeeding, the black American was often under attack.

Russell summarized where America stood in the wake of the Springfield riots. The South, he said, "was virtually a unit in support of hatred and the ethics of the jungle. The Civil War raged there still, with hardly abated passions." But the North was little better, despite public impression. It was "utterly indifferent where it was not covertly or sneakingly applausive of helotry," he declared. Blacks, Russell pointed out, were disenfranchised by the millions, "denied their constitutional rights, denied the protection of the courts, denied the shield of justice, denied the opportunities of which other men boast, denied the bare right to economic welfare, persecuted, hounded with an inexplicable but insatiable hatred, exposed to the fury of maddened mobs, lynched, [and] burned alive."[34] With "the whole of society . . . crystallized" against the Negro, Russell knew something had to be done.

Enter Walling, who arrived in Springfield the morning after the eighty-year-old William Donnegan was lynched, as smoke still billowed from burned buildings. Walling was an odd character, even for the Progressive Era, when so many conflicting political winds were blowing in America. His mother's family had been Kentucky slaveholders, but the thirty-one-year-old Walling, a million-aire, was a passionate reformer and a member of the American Socialist Party. He and his wife, Anna Strunsky, had just returned from Russia where he had gone to write about riots in St. Petersburg. While visiting relatives in Chicago, they learned of the Springfield disturbance. He and Strunsky took a night train and reached Lincoln's birthplace Sunday morning. A police force of 3,700 had stopped the violence. "We at once discovered, to our amazement, that Spring-field had no shame. She stood for the action of the mob," Walling later wrote. To his shock, Walling found Springfield's residents unabashed. "Why, niggers came to think they were as good as we are!" they repeatedly told him.[35] Little by little, he pieced together the stories of the lynchings and the beatings.

Walling's article, "The Race War in the North," appeared in the weekly *Independent* magazine, which had been the Negro's steadiest champion among national journals. Walling pointed the finger of blame at the white Springfield residents whose "fanatical, blind and almost insane hatred" had initiated "a permanent warfare with the negro race." If this riot had happened thirty years ago, with the memory of Lincoln still fresh, Walling pointed out, "the whole country would have been aflame," demanding to know why Springfield's peo-ple could be allowed to act this way.[36] Walling concluded with a demand for ac-tion. "Either the spirit of the abolitionists . . . must be revived," he said, or the Southern racists will have "transferred the race war to the North." Springfield was a threat to the American democracy, prompting Walling to ask: "who real-izes the seriousness of the situation, and what large and powerful body of citi-zens is ready to come to their aid?"[37] Unfortunately, no body of citizens had yet been mobilized. But Walling, Russell, and a social worker from New York City were soon to change that.

III. "BARE HANDS, BRUISES, DERISION"

Mary White Ovington, a social worker who had studied Manhattan's black community, was stirred by Walling's article. She wrote immediately to Walling, who put her off until the new year, though it was clear that he was interested. They met in New York when he returned. After giving a lecture in Manhattan, Walling and Strunsky spent an evening of intense discussion with Ovington. She learned that Walling and his close friend, Russell, had already spent much time discussing the race question in conversations at New York's Liberal Club. Walling had told Russell that he was considering calling a meeting of interested citizens. Russell poured out to Walling his anger and dismay at racial conditions. Walling took his hand and said, "If you feel like that, and I feel like that, let us see if we cannot find some others, no matter how few, that feel the same way and see if we cannot take a stand somewhere against this monstrous flood of injustice that is sweeping us down hill." Walling convened a meeting in his New York apartment on West Thirty-ninth Street during the first week of 1909. Russell could not attend the initial meeting, but he became a regular after that as the group, ranging from four to a dozen people, began to flesh out the problem and a possible solution. "We talked informally about the possibilities of creating some society or or-ganization that might contend against the racial madness that possessed the North only a little less than the South," Russell recalled. "The whole thing seemed comically futile."[38] For his part, Russell was especially angry about the lynching of blacks. The reason was a personal one—Russell's father was nearly lynched by an angry mob in the years before the Civil War when he edited the *Davenport Gazette*.

As Russell recalled it for the group, Edward Russell was a prominent and indefatigable foe of slavery. Both his family and his mother's, the Rutledges, had secretly helped slaves escape from the South through the Underground Railroad. Edward Russell became known as the "nigger stealer" editor. It was common for the Russell family to have ruffians knock at their door in the wee hours of the morning and yell insults and curses at the father. "These condi-tions disturbed him not; he knew well enough," Russell said of his father, "that no man with impunity attacks a vested evil." But when "the mobsters began to gather around his house and terrify his family," Edward became concerned for their safety. Friends gave him a cane and a revolver, but he refused to carry them. After a summer of "horrors and sufferings," Edward Russell was forced to move the family to a house on the outskirts of town, more than a mile away from his newspaper office. This quieted things for a while, although once he was shot at while walking home one evening. The family moved again, even though Edward Russell kept up his antislavery editorials in what became known as the "nigger loving *Gazette*." The son believed that the town's support for slavery was based not on race prejudice, but on fear of losing profits from the bustling river trade from the South.

Russell's mother was sick with worry that terrible harm would come to Edward Russell, and it almost did on a Saturday night, the one night her husband was home with his family, since there was no Sunday newspaper to produce. The family heard noises outside the house as a drunken mob assembled. "My father looked out of a front window and the situation seemed really serious," Charles recalled. One man conspicuously held a rope in hand, as the group stood next to an inviting maple tree. Edward Russell walked out on the roof of the house's porch and with "winged words" began to convince the crowd that a lynching was not deserved. "The crowd listened," the son recalled, and then quietly "slipped away."[39] But Edward Russell, despite his ardent belief in the abolition of slavery, had less to fear than, say, William Donnegan. Russell was a prominent white man. The white mob opted to let him go, but nonetheless they needed someone to oppress, someone to step on. Charles Edward Russell, perhaps naively, never believed that race prejudice was at the heart of America's racial problems. Blacks were not the objects of white venom because of their color, but because of class and caste. "It persists solely—and most significantly—because of the survival of old, fetid, nauseous caveman Snobbery here in free America, democratic America, enlightened America," declared Russell. "It is the survival of the brutish instinct of primitive man that he could not feel comfortable unless he could deem himself better than somebody else; that he could not stand unless he had his foot on some other man's neck."[40] Edward Russell was spared, in part, because the whites still had blacks to subordinate.

Charles Russell's view of interracial relations began to form in his days growing up in Davenport. His father, a strong influence, told the son that it was a "sacred duty" to help the slaves find freedom. Moreover, Edward Russell taught him, it was "utterly preposterous" to believe that one race was superior to another. Yet, as the young Russell learned, that was the accepted creed around Davenport. To the natives of Davenport, the German immigrants were "damn foreigners." When young Charles crossed the river to nearby Moline, Illinois, it was the Swedes who were considered inferior. When Russell went to school in St. Johnsbury, he observed Vermonters sitting around, chewing tobacco and condemning the French Canadians. Later, as a reporter, he took a train ride and saw the "white" folks push the Italians out of seats. "This is a white man's country," one passenger declared. "There ain't no room here for damn dagos."[41] To Russell, this was no different from the way blacks were treated. (Although commonly applied just to Italian immigrants, Russell said that he heard the word "dago" applied to all foreigners.) Russell concluded that all non-natives, not just blacks, were victims of discrimination. "There is no race problem," Russell declared. "The only problem is the problem of snobbery." Despite Russell's belief that class was at the heart of the race problem, he still had to know that conditions for blacks—in terms of income and protection from white violence—were clearly worse than for immigrants. Walling, for example, stressed that blacks in America were treated even worse than Jews in Russia. While Russell was slowly becoming more radical in his economic views, he still clung to Progressive values. His abolitionist heritage called to him to join with others to seek a "shield between the Negro and his oppressor."[42] Despite the overarching problem of class-based social values in America, progress to Russell was still possible without a social upheaval.

What Walling wanted was an organization for the "advancement" of colored people that would take the lead in advocating for equal rights and opportunities for black Americans. Walling and Russell, however, were adamant that the Booker T. Washington approach of appeasement and more job opportunities was not enough. Something more radical was called for, more along the lines of the 1905 Niagara Movement that was led by Dr. W. E. B. Du Bois. Litigation, new laws, mass meetings, annual conventions, publicity—these were the things that an organization comprised of "fair-minded whites and intelligent blacks" must pursue, Russell felt.[43] Walling and Russell needed now to convince people to join. And they did, bringing in what one historian called the "cream of progressive reform"—Lillian Wald, Rabbi Stephen Wise, Reverend John Haynes Holmes, and Oswald Garrison Villard, the editor of the *New York Evening Post* and the *Nation* magazine. Villard's grandfather was the famous abolitionist, William Lloyd Garrison. Villard was a key figure, a wealthy, powerful, albeit somewhat conservative voice. Walling enlisted him to write a call to action that was to appear nationwide on February 12, 1909, Lincoln's birthday. Villard wrote of how "disheartened and discouraged" Lincoln would be to see America today, to see the "revolting brutalities" against blacks. "This government," he insisted, indignantly, "cannot exist half slave and half free any better today than it could in 1861." While Villard is given credit for writing the call, Russell likely had a hand in it too. In one speech, Russell used words much like those in the call. "The nation cannot endure half with rights and half with none any more than it could endure half slave and half free."[44] The powerful and impressive call was signed by fifty-three people, both black and white, including Russell and his muckraking colleague Lincoln Steffens. It implored citizens to attend the first National Negro Conference on May 31, 1909. Charles Edward Russell was chosen to chair the meeting.

The choice of Russell was logical. The "chief of the muckrakers" had a reputation as fair and even-handed among both blacks and whites. He was not recognized as too radical, yet his fury and passion for good causes would certainly lend prestige to the conference. The New York and national press would have to take this conference seriously with Russell, among the most famous journalists in America, chairing the event. Plus, he had first-hand knowledge of the conditions of blacks in America. In 1891 the *New York Herald* had sent him through the South—Virginia, North and South Carolina, and Georgia—to observe social conditions. Then again in 1906 he took another extensive tour of the South, retracing his earlier steps. He knew intimately conditions in Boston, New York, Chicago, and Washington, D.C. But writing stories was easier than chairing a conference with competing factions from different races. The fledgling organization faced many problems: How could it placate the Booker T. Washington forces without letting them derail the new and militant reform effort? "Some of the colored people," Mary Ovington recalled, "evidently were distrustful of us." How could they get blacks and whites to agree to cooperate, without either side seeming to dominate? Explained Walling, "We were determined not to become a little sect but to leave our doors open to all colored people who would stand by their race and to all white people who would take their stand with them."[45] Finally, could they agree on an agenda for change? For Russell, the agenda was simple: America needed an organization that would "stay the overwhelming reactionary flood" and go to battle for "tolerance, opportunity, and equality . . . an efficient instrument for racial justice."[46]

About three hundred people—including liberal reformers and black activists—gathered in New York City for the first National Negro Conference. The organizers, including Russell, were nervous. They knew that history was about to be made, but they had decided that the fullest discussion possible should take place. That was a risky strategy. Would the forces of Booker T. Washington try to disrupt the meeting? Washington received a late invitation from Villard, but he politely declined. Nonetheless, his emissaries were at the meeting and their interference would not bode well; if this organization got started it would need money from organizations and individuals supporting Washington. "If you wanted to raise money in New York for anything relating to the Negro, you must have Washington's endorsement," Ovington recalled.[47] Nerve-racking also was the mingling of the races at a very public meeting that was being closely watched by the national press. A lunch with blacks and whites seated together was planned on the first day, which was unusual even by the more relaxed standards of New York. As Russell sat on the stage, he looked out over a packed auditorium in the Charity Organization Society in lower Manhattan. Reformers, academics, social workers, journalists—all, as Walling put it, had heeded the call to "enlighten the public opinion of the whole country."

The keynote speaker was William Ward, editor of the *Independent*, which had printed Walling's Springfield riot article. Ward's stirring words called the audience to battle.

What followed was less enthralling, and perhaps even a bit uncomfortable. Russell introduced the morning's speakers who, often in scholarly fashion, laid out scientific data to show that blacks and whites were mentally and biologically equal. In fact, the official theme of the proceeding was the scientific evidence of human equality, much in dispute in 1909. Burt G. Wilder, a professor of neurology at Cornell University, discussed the brain weight of Negroes, all to prove that it was the same as that of whites. Of course, Russell never had any doubt about that. "Men are the same regardless of complexion or shape of nose or curl of hair," Russell believed. "The only real differences among them are differences of opportunity. Theories of the superior and the inferior race are mere fictions, convenient for the purposes of imperialistic exploitation or to excuse savagery, but otherwise footless."[48] But Russell did not express his beliefs; he simply ran the conference.

The morning went well, and the group went off to the interracial lunch at a nearby hotel. The press followed closely, wondering if some spats or awkward moments might emerge. Du Bois noted: "The curiosity of the spectators was toward the darker and less known portion of the audience," but the luncheon was convivial and pleasant. Russell commented, "I never was so interested in meeting people before."[49]

After lunch the meeting moved to the cavernous auditorium of Cooper Union for the Advancement of Science and Art. The afternoon session was highlighted by the speech of the highly regarded scholar Du Bois, who eventually became the most important figure in the NAACP. "Here was a man of manifestly unusual mind and equipment," Russell said of Du Bois. "He astonished and charmed all that heard him." Russell first heard Du Bois speak a year earlier at the Republican Club in Manhattan. Other distinguished speakers came before Du Bois that day, but Russell remembered that no one was as impressive as Du Bois. "In the logical and coherent arrangement of his matter . . . in research and knowledge, in the polished and carefully chosen cameos of his language, in the polished fluency of his utterance—unequaled." And yet, Russell knew that this man—because he was black—met "unprovoked hostility" wherever he went. He could not join a labor union or a social club, would be refused entry to many churches, most restaurants and hotels, and received the worst accommodations on trains. Only menial jobs would be available to him, despite his brilliance. If he protested his condition, he might be lynched. "If he were lynched, no effort would be made to punish his murderers," Russell knew. Why? "Because of his complexion," which, Russell noted, ironically, was only a few shades darker than his own. Wherever he goes in America, the Negro is "hated and spat upon," Russell said.[50] And that was why the National Negro Conference was so important. Something had to be done.

Nearly fifteen hundred people listened as Du Bois, in essence, refuted the approach of Booker T. Washington, the "Wizard of Tuskegee," who wanted blacks to accumulate wealth patiently as a means of gaining more freedom. Du Bois argued that wealth would follow when blacks had political power. Du Bois's speech may have energized and empowered the black participants at the conference. He later commented that in the afternoon session "the black mass moved forward and stretched out their hands to take charge. It was their problem. They must name the condition."[51] Some of the organizers' fears were realized as tension between blacks and whites mounted. In particular, Ida Wells Barnett, a crusading black journalist who had documented lynching murders in the South, and Monroe Trotter, the editor of the *Guardian* and a key member of the Niagara Movement, raised strident objections to various proposals. But Russell, Ovington said, "was the personification of courtesy. He let each talk, and yet guided the debate which went on and on."

The evening closed with Walling, whose speech was as stirring as Ward's morning talk. "If justice is to be done to the Negro in this democratic country, it must be done through the enlightened and active interest of some important . . . elements of the population," he told the crowd. Walling, a Southerner, lambasted the prejudice that typified the South. Although silent on stage, Russell must have been thinking of the times he traveled in the South, observing conditions as a reporter. Once he conversed with three lawyers in Atlanta. "They were talking about the race problem," he recalled. They each had a solution: one wanted to deport blacks back to Africa, although it might be too costly. The other two felt the problem would soon lessen because so many blacks were dying of tuberculosis or alcohol consumption and would soon be extinct. On another occasion he overheard men on a train applauding the fact that black looters had been shot in Galveston, Texas. "It was too good a chance to kill niggers and the boys couldn't let it go by," he heard them say. Russell could only see "a vast white population whose controlling thought at all times is hatred."[52]

The next day, June 1, was the trickiest—and most important—as the group tried to agree on resolutions. What would they stand for? What would their strategy be? And who would steer the new organization; the white liberals, the conservative Washingtonians, or the more radical faction from the Niagara Movement? Some points were easy to settle. Blacks and whites were equal; agreed. As Russell put it, "A Negro . . . is just like a white man, entitled to exactly the same rights and the same treatment—always, everywhere and under all conditions."[53] Both the North and South were guilty of utter discrimination; agreed. An organization had to be formed to mount a campaign that would insist on laws being enforced; agreed. The end of lynching must be a foremost goal; agreed. The way to achieve some of these goals would be with publicity; agreed. But no agreement was evident on who should serve on the steering committee of forty people. A coalition of blacks and whites would work best, but which ones? The fear was that too many people in favor of Booker T. Washington's ideas would comprise the committee. Mrs. Barnett was fearful that Villard, a Washington supporter, would exercise too much influence. And in fact, behind the scenes Villard was calling the shots. But Mrs. Barnett assured her friends that she had seen the list and that she was indeed on it. As the meeting approached midnight, with all the participants exhausted and edgy, Villard offered various resolutions, which, Du Bois's biographer noted, "were received like live bait tossed to piranhas, mangled, chewed, and regurgitated." J. Milton Waldron, another veteran of the Niagara Movement, urged Russell to force the conference into a third day. "God almighty was a million years in making the world—why not go another day," he said.[54] But Russell refused. He recognized Du Bois who read the names of the so-called Committee of Forty, an interracial group that leaned much more toward Du Bois than Washington, even though Mrs. Barnett and Trotter were left off. Russell was, of course, one of the members. Russell now quickly gaveled the meeting to a close, thinking all had been settled.

But, as Mrs. Barnett recalled, "bedlam broke loose." Mrs. Barnett's supporters, including Russell's newspaper friend John Milholland, were angry. Villard, Walling, Russell, and Du Bois quickly huddled, and Russell called Mrs. Barnett back to meet with them. Du Bois explained that her name had been left off so that others opposed to Washington could be placed on the committee. Mrs. Barnett felt that she was omitted because Mary Ovington, jealous of her, had insisted on it. In her recollection of the events, Ovington conceded only that the "powerful personalities" of Barnett and Trotter might not be "fitted to accept the restraint of organization." Nonetheless, she applauded what she said was Russell's initiative. "Quite illegally," Ovington said, Russell tried to put Barnett back on the committee. She refused, although later she admitted, "I did a foolish thing." Barnett wished she could have joined the fledgling group; it was soon to become the nation's most powerful weapon of black advancement. A new era in black-white relations had begun. Wrote Du Bois: "The problem of the twentieth century was about to be attacked, vigorously and collectively."[55]

The Committee of Forty met off and on in 1910, planning for another national conference. Some things were settled before the second conference: the group would be called the National Association for the Advancement of Colored People. A committee of thirty people would act as a board of directors. Russell was on the board. Then, in May, when the committee met for the first time, with Russell chairing again, W. E. B. Du Bois was appointed ostensibly as director of publicity. But in reality he was asked to run the new organization. A man of charisma and vision, Du Bois, whom Russell so admired, would for the next twenty-five years try with "bare hands to lift the earth" and make the NAACP a key force for black emancipation.[56] Russell used remarkably similar words in remembering how it all had begun. "Four or five men and women—what could their bare hands achieve except bruises and derision?" He answered his own question many years after the NAACP had become a powerful force for reform. At a memorial service when Walling died, he recalled "the victims it has snatched from an unmerited gallows, the persecution it had thwarted, the pursuing hatred it had frustrated, the lives it had brightened, the millions of consciences it had awakened to the most glaring of our social transgressions, the slow but steady emancipation of people that had suffered an ineffable wrong, the slow approach toward the reality of equality."

Russell's impatience with those who persisted in opposing improved conditions for black Americans came through in a weekly column he wrote in 1910–11 for *The Coming Nation*. All victims "look alike to us," he wrote. "If there be among the congregation those to whom race prejudice is an essential of being—well, parting is sweet sorrow." The grandson of the Baptist preacher ended his sermon sarcastically, as he often did, noting: "The organ will now play . . . [and] those that conscientiously believe in race hatred and cannot live without it will have an opportunity to move towards the door."[57]

CHAPTER ELEVEN

OUT FROM BEHIND THE PEN

I. "AGITATION, PROPAGANDA, EDUCATION"

WHEN CHARLES EDWARD RUSSELL WAS CHOSEN by the Socialist Party in 1910 to run for governor of New York State in what would be his first of four runs for political office, the *New York Times* accorded him unusual defer-ence. Given that socialism had always been mixed up in the public mind with bomb-throwing anarchists, one would expect the *Times*, always a voice of the establishment, to largely ignore fringe candidates. As Russell observed about Socialism, "No other movement in our times has been so fiercely de-nounced." Socialists, he noted, were viewed as "dangerous and detestable wild beasts." And yet the *Times* treated Russell as one of the three legitimate choices for Governor. The other two candidates were John Alden Dix, the Democrat who was a rough-and-tumble political fighter, and Henry L. Stim-son, a Republican and longtime advocate of clean and open government who later became famous as Secretary of State. On three Sundays leading up to the election, the *Times* devoted full cover-page articles in its fledgling maga-zine to the three men. Stimson was depicted as a "strong personality," fond of books and the outdoor life. Dix came across as a political insider, with a suc-cessful career as the owner of lumber mills in the Adirondack Mountains. And then there was Russell, the magazine writer, whom the *Times* labeled "an intellectual," a man whose only manual labor "has been done mostly at the typewriter," which was odd, the newspaper said, for someone who ostensibly represented workers. Highlighting the feature profile of Russell was a large sketch showing his chiseled chin and bright eyes. "An old newspaper man, his name is familiar to every reader of magazines," the *Times* noted.[1]

Although he would not fare so well in terms of news coverage in his three later bids for political office, perhaps it was not surprising that Russell and Socialism were treated so prominently in 1910. This was, after all, the age of "muscularity and vigor" for socialism, its Golden Years[2]—and Russell, one of the most famous writers in America, was at the peak of his productivity and at the height of his muckraking triumphs. His attack on the Georgia prisons had just caused a national furor that led to the scrapping of the state's prisoner lease system. New York's Trinity Church was still reeling from his exposé and was now making startling changes in its tenement operations. Less public was Russell's involvement in the founding of the NAACP, but in progressive and socialist circles it was clear that Russell the magazine writer had come out from behind the pen. He now was engaging in direct action to change social conditions. The line between Russell the muckraking reporter and Russell the socialist advocate became increasingly difficult to separate. Beyond the changes that his writing was promoting was the fact that it was impossible to escape Russell's name—he was everywhere in the national magazines.

Between the time Russell's beef trust articles ended in September 1905 and the New York governor's race took place in November 1910, Russell wrote more than one hundred magazine articles and had three books and two collections of poetry published. He had nine articles in five magazines in the first four months of 1909 alone. And his work often put him in the eye of the storm. The beef trust articles had firmly put Russell on the national stage, but just as they ended he captured the public fancy again with a five-part series of articles in *Everybody's* magazine, then circulating to 550,000 people. Russell asked a simple question about how the fortunes of some of America's greatest industrialists and financiers were accumulated: "Where did you get it, gentlemen?" His answer: "Their profits were utterly illegal." How could the public applaud these men because of the "piles of dollars" they had gathered? "Have we ever stopped to bother very much about the means [by] which the piles were gathered?" Focusing on New York rail magnate Thomas Fortune Ryan, who consolidated many of New York City's trolley systems, he painted a picture of capitalists who bribed legislators, watered stock, and duped the public to accumulate huge fortunes. And, in the end, the service provided by the trolleys Ryan took over was worse than before. The capitalists that Russell profiled had no redeeming qualities, unlike the John D. Rockefeller whom Ida Tarbell drew, who was ruthless but brilliant. When Russell's articles were turned into a book in 1908, it was titled "Lawless Wealth," an apt description of how he saw fortunes being made in America. Russell knew that his history would cause a controversy. "To question in any way the ability, energy, and foresight of men [who] accumulate great fortunes is fraught with some danger," he wrote. "It is attacking the most sacred doctrine of that commercial religion of which they are the high priests." But Russell did not blame the capitalists, who were not evil men; he blamed the public. If you leave a pile of silver dollars on the doorstep, he said, someone will steal it. His main point: "So long as we give over public utilities to private greed we should expect to have them used for the piling up of great fortunes at our expense."[3] Russell did not say it so clearly in these articles, but his goal was becoming obvious: public ownership of key industries.

As Russell predicted, *Lawless Wealth*'s harsh view of the esteemed capitalists caused a stir. One newspaper praised Russell as the "prince of the muckrakers" but noted how he seemed to find "keenest enjoyment in telling how bad the American richmen are." The *Times* commented that Russell did muckraking "perhaps better than anybody else. His style is vivid, his explanation of intricate finance clear, his convictions sincere." And yet his "denunciatory sermons" showed no "reserve, moderation, no mixture of motives." His capitalists were "bad through and through," which made this book a "source of error rather than instruction." The *Times* added, "Mr. Russell may easily enough like muckraking, since it gave him his opportunity, but the taste is fading."[3]

In fact, the *Times* was not far off the mark. Most of the muckrakers were backing off their exposé writing. Some of their reforms had come to fruition and the public seemed to be tiring of the onslaught against industrialism's ills. As Lincoln Steffens recalled about 1910, "Most of all I wanted to stop muckraking. . . . [It] looked useless. Society moved like a glacier; if it progressed it grew like an oak tree—slowly. One might water and manure the soils about it, but it was no use shouting at it." Russell, on the other hand, was shouting louder than he ever had before, plunging deeper into his attack on American capitalism and moving well past the perimeters of progressivism. He was more and more convinced that reform was a futile folly that would do nothing to alter the growing influence of J. P. Morgan and John D. Rockefeller, the corporate behemoths that Russell saw lurking everywhere. "The corner of Wall and Broad Streets," the headquarters of the Standard Oil Co., Russell said, that is "where sit the real rulers of America."[4]

At fifty, Russell was busier than ever, pressing his case as an editor for Benjamin Hampton's radical but still establishment *Broadway* magazine along with writing a weekly column for *The Coming Nation*, a new Socialist publication that allowed him more freedom to comment than ever before. His life began to revolve more and more around a swirl of Socialist activities. Morris Hillquit, a key figure in New York in the advocacy and organization of socialism, commented that "the life of the socialist propagandist is the continuous feast of speaking and writing." Running for office "is an almost inescapable part of the work," even though there was little expectation that Socialists, despite the tremendous gains they had made since 1900, stood any chance of winning a major election.[5] It was simply duty—spread the gospel, proselytize, and push capitalism in a constructive direction while waiting and hoping for the promised land—the cooperative commonwealth—to become reality. "Agitation, propaganda, education, literature, campaigns, meetings, a party press"—those would be the tools, Russell declared. As 1910 unfolded, Russell combined preaching, writing, muckraking, and running for political office, roles that were increasingly difficult if not impossible to separate. He did it, however, out of anger at what he continued to see, and out of a continued conviction—much like that of other Progressives—that he really could move the glacier. "Guns roar and armies march and generals maneuver in the center of all men's attention, but the real force that moves the world and is always mightier than all of these is the force of moral conviction," he wrote. Indeed, Russell did not lack conviction as he laid out his criticism of capitalism in magazines, books, and on the stump. The system, he said, simply, is "wrong, rotten, cruel and fatal."[6] And the way to move it, the greatest power, he observed, is "the power of a protest against a fundamental wrong." What, then, according to the man who was alternately called the "chief" or the "prince" of the muckrakers" was fundamentally wrong with America?

II. POVERTY AND PROSTITUTION

"It seems to me now that the abolition of poverty is the only thing at present that is worth thinking about," Russell told a reporter who was writing a long and flattering profile of him in 1908. What angered him especially was the gap between those at the bottom and the top of the economic ladder, a fact that first confronted Russell in the 1890s. Using a storehouse of anecdotes from his reporting days, he emphasized the injustice of this discrepancy repeatedly in speeches and writing. While working as a reporter for the *New York Herald* in 1892, he told audiences, heating prices inexplicably went up in the city; Russell was sent to Pennsylvania to see if a coal shortage was the cause. It was not; the owners were simply holding back on production while keeping the miners unemployed. He saw shivering and starving coal workers' families, while in the background stood the palatial houses of the well-fed coal barons. "For this con-

1. Downtown Davenport, Iowa, around 1870, when Charles Edward Russell was growing up in the Mississippi River town and learned the newspaper business at his father's nearby office. (Courtesy of Davenport Public Library)

left   2. Logs and debris from wrecked houses piled up at a stone arch bridge in Johnstown, Pennsylvania, soon after a dam broke and flooded the Conemaugh Valley. A fire from spilled oil eventually broke out at the logjam, adding to the turmoil at the site of America's worst flood in 1889. (Courtesy of Johnstown Area Heritage Association)

above   3. Russell (right, standing) poses with the "Big Four" reporters who arrived from New York. They are William J. Kenney of the *Times*, Richard A. Farrelly of the *World*, and Ervin Wardman of the *Tribune*. (Courtesy of Library of Congress)

above   4. The electric chair at Sing Sing prison in Ossining, New York, was the scene of 614 legal executions. Russell, who would later become a staunch opponent of capital punishment, was one of the first reporters allowed to witness and write about legal executions in the early 1890s while working as a reporter for the *New York Herald*. (Courtesy of Ossining Historical Society Museum)

right   5. The domed Pulitzer Building on Park Row in downtown Manhattan was Russell's workplace from 1894 to 1897, when he was the city editor of Joseph Pulitzer's *New York World*, the largest circulation newspaper in the nation. (Collection of the New York Historical Society)

6. David Graham Phillips, Russell's best friend, stands writing at his "black pulpit" where he would write his popular novels up until when he was shot and killed in 1911. (Courtesy of Library of Congress)

7. William Randolph Hearst, who Russell worked for in New York when he left Pulitzer's *New York World*. He is pictured here around 1900, about the time he sent Russell to Chicago to begin publishing his third newspaper. (Courtesy of Bison Archives)

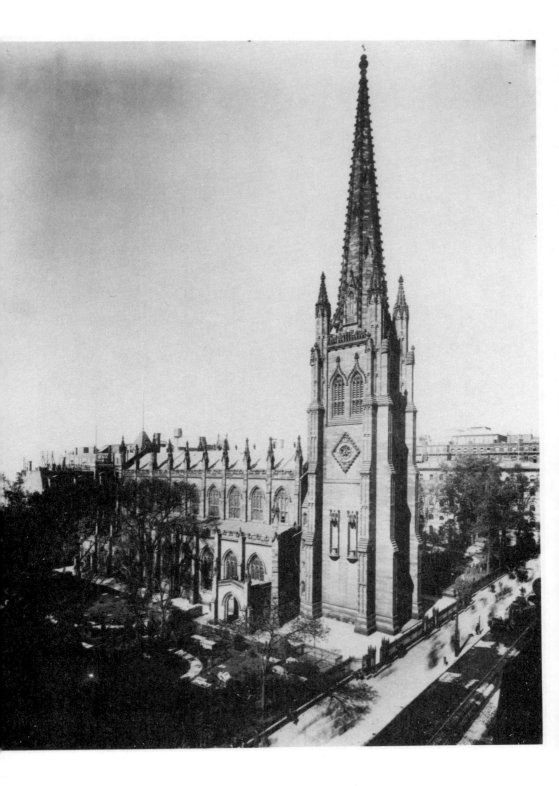

left   8. New York City's Trinity Church, which Russell attacked as a slum landlord in 1909, towers over downtown Manhattan. (Courtesy of the Collection of the New York Historical Society)

above   9. Eugene V. Debs, who defeated Russell for the 1912 Socialist Party presidential nomination and ran for president five times, is shown here giving one of his spellbinding orations in Ohio. This particular speech landed him in a federal prison for opposing World War I. (Courtesy of Library of Congress)

"The Russell Brothers"
celebrated pedestrians, oarsmen, ball-players, musicians, art-critics, and travellers."

left 10. In rare moment of levity, Russell poses with his son, John, whom he often traveled with and who later became a highly regarded short-story writer. The photo was taken around 1915. The caption says: "The Russell Brothers, celebrated pedestrians, oarsmen, ballplayers, musicians, art-critics, and travellers [*sic*]." (Courtesy of Library of Congress)

above 11. Edward Sothern and Julia Marlowe, America's most famous acting couple and also the regular companions in Europe of Russell and his wife, Theresa. (Courtesy of Library of Congress)

12. The members of the Root Mission pose in the U.S. Embassy in Russia in 1917. U.S. Ambassador David Francis and Elihu Root are seated in the center, and Russell is seated at the far right. (Courtesy of Library of Congress)

13. Russell, wearing white pants in the center of the photo, tried to dress more casually in order to fit in with Russian workers, with whom he visited in June 1918. (Courtesy of Library of Congress)

left 14. Russell, hands in pocket and wearing a bow tie, poses with the delegation of socialists sent to Europe by Woodrow Wilson during the waning days of World War I in an effort to lend support to various labor groups in Europe. (Courtesy of Library of Congress)

above 15. Russell peers out of a trench in France in the spring of 1918 under the watchful eye of a French military officer. During this visit, Russell and his fellow Socialists had to scurry to safety as bullets whizzed by them. (Courtesy of Library of Congress)

16. Charles Edward Russell in the late 1930s. (Courtesy of Library of Congress)

dition I could find no defense, excuse, nor even palliation, and I have been able to find none since." Why should 1 percent of the people own 55 percent of the wealth, he asked, a question he repeated to himself after returning from Fall River, Massachusetts, where he covered the Lizzie Borden ax murders that same year. The palaces of the mill owners towered over the shacks of the workers. Why the disparity? "It was impossible to avoid that question; it was thrust too persistently in my face."[7]

How could one explain or justify the contrast, for example, between the fabulous mansions that lined New York City's Fifth Avenue and the grinding poverty on the Lower East Side? Moreover, Russell could find nothing admirable about those who had accumulated great fortunes. Why were the rich held up as models of American greatness? "The life spent in the pursuit of gain is a very pitiable life," he observed. Businessmen "cringe and crawl and wallow and wade through filth, but they get the money. The beautiful dough, the long green, the grand old Mazume, that's the stuff. Get it. No matter how you get it."[8] And when businessmen did accumulate great riches, Russell pointed out, scornfully, they bought yachts, entertain French actresses, and built mansions with gold doorknobs. As "the palaces rise, the steam yachts sail [and] the figures of the great fortunes mount," Russell observed, "in every city the slums spread, the bread lines grow, and the numbers of the poor increase." J. P. Morgan, the archetypal banking mogul, took three Episcopal bishops to Chicago on a trip that cost $30,000. Meanwhile, "Worn-out William," a fictitious urban dweller, lives on the edge. "We give poor old William no chance. For him the Poorhouse or the river," Russell wrote.[9] If the tycoons of American wealth angered Russell, the poor thoroughly depressed him. Take a family he had known since his reporting days, the Bernsteins of Manhattan, who lived in poverty in a disease-plagued tenement. Visit them, he urged his listeners.

> Go into some of the courtyards . . . the filthy and vile overcrowded dwellings, the poisoned air, the moldy dampness of ancient and dark passageways, the reeking halls, the ragged crowds, the toiling men, the tired women, the ill-developed, half-nourished children, the jostling mass on the sidewalks, the forlorn and unkempt appearances of the streets, the painful evidence of a daily and grim struggle, hand to hand eye to eye for bare life and breath. . . .

When one of the Bernstein children died, the father turned to Russell and said, "I did my best." Russell could not hide his anger. "Why, yes, I am bitter. God send me more bitterness . . . with what voice we have we utter bitter protest and utter it without ceasing," he wrote in his weekly *Coming Nation* column, a series of strident and sarcastic editorials. As Thanksgiving Day approached, Russell wished that the poor would creep up from the slums to the houses of the rich and peer in their windows. "Why do these creatures come to bother me?" the rich would ask. "Because you and your kind have made us what we are and we want you to see on this day of feasting the results of your work."[10]

Russell's views on poverty made headlines after one speech he gave in Philadelphia. He criticized the clergy who talked too much of the "curse of drink" and not enough about the cause of poverty. "Although I am a total abstainer," he declared, "I would keep drunk all the time were I obliged to live under the same horrible conditions that these people do." Conditions in the world's great cities "make hollow mockery of civilization," he added, while urging reformers to send rum to the poor, not flowers and fruit. When Russell repeated his remarks in a speech in New York City, two Protestant ministers, saying nothing about poverty, told the *New York World* they were astonished at Russell's comments."[11]

Russell's reply was to point to New York City where he counted 10,000 rich and 32.5 million poor. "Instead of being a country of general prosperity it is evidently a country of general poverty. There is something radically wrong in this situation." Of course, poverty was even worse abroad, he reminded his listeners. Going to Calcutta, Bombay, and London on his trip for *Everybody's* magazine, Russell encountered misery beyond what he saw in America. "While we feast," he wrote on Christmas Day, "the majority of the men, women and children upon this earth live in conditions unfit for human beings and have probably never once known what it is to have enough to eat." In the rest of the world, four out of five children were born into poverty. "The truth is that the world . . . is a pleasant or even a tolerable place for only the minority of the persons that live in it. Poverty and insufficiency," Russell concluded, "may be said to be the rule." That finding left Russell admittedly bitter. "A man that could spend somedays in the East End of London and write of it without bitterness has powers of self control I can never hope to emulate," he said. In fact, it was such passion that was making socialism popular. The socialists' anger at poverty and their fervent hope for a better world was finding a receptive audience.[12]

As Russell honed his message for public consumption and readied himself to run for governor in 1910, he used a constant refrain: capitalism and competition were the cause of American poverty and its problems. A bad system, not bad men, drove people to bad things. Again, he used a reporting anecdote to drive home his point. This time it was the Rubensteins, who lived in a two-room flat in Manhattan. The grandfather was a poor tailor who worked in a sweatshop, when he could. The grandson, Julius, was a cripple who sold newspapers while a granddaughter, Bertha, a pretty girl, worked in a department store. Russell kept up with the family through Julius, whom he met each day on his way to cover the courts. When Julius told him how Bertha had gotten a job in an all-night restaurant, Russell was suspicious. One night, coming from the theater, he spotted a group of women skulking on a side street. They were prostitutes, and Bertha was among them. When the grandfather learned of Bertha's fate, he committed suicide. Bertha never returned home. "A man need not be a puritan nor of any nice scruples about the recognized facts of life to be struck here into dumb disgust of the whole business," Russell wrote. "There are other causes for prostitution than the one great economic cause," he admitted, "but the economic cause is greater than all other causes together."[13]

For poor women, the choice was to sell their bodies or starve. But even the wealthy were forced by the system into selling women, Russell asserted. Just look at the American mania among the wealthy class to sell off their daughters in marriage to blue-blooded European aristocrats. In three articles for *Redbook*, he named Anna Gould, Gladys Vanderbilt, and forty-three others, information that "no man has had the courage to expose," the magazine asserted. He exposed a European company that was finding aristocrats for American women, a service that led to police scrutiny and arrests. The magazine ran a photograph of Russell and called him "the greatest investigator of his day," even though his articles seemed as much tongue-in-cheek as serious. Fictional dialogue and scenes were as prominent as facts, but nonetheless, his point was clear: the rich, trying to mimic the class system of old Europe, would prostitute their daughters just to get a title. "Lost women's souls and ruined lives are the product of this system," he believed. "It is not wise to buy and sell women."[14]

III. A GLASS BOTH EMPTY AND FULL

The issue of altering the balance of economic power between rich and poor was at the heart of both progressive and socialist causes in the years after the turn of the twentieth century. Progressives wanted to bring change by making the corporations and the wealthy industrialists susceptible to the control of the large majority of the people with taxes, regulations, and more opportunity. The socialists wanted to get at the root cause—competition and profit—and allow the people to own key industries. Underlying the belief system of Russell and the Socialists were two assumptions. First, capitalism was illogical, brutal, and destined to die. Russell called it "purely arbitrary, irrational, and unjust . . . a false system of society that makes enemies of men that otherwise would be friends." Not only was poverty "absolutely wrong" but it was also "utterly unnecessary."[15] Naively, Russell and his comrades argued, just get rid of capitalism and poverty would disappear. How to accomplish this—and what tactics to use—was a cause of disagreement among the socialists, however. The evolutionists, including Russell, believed that socialism would come gradually, evolving from capitalism, just as capitalism had evolved from feudalism. Russell repeated this consistently in speeches and writing, rebuking at the same time those who believed in revolution or violence to bring about the cooperative commonwealth. "Socialism is opposed to all violence, force and coercion and seeks its aims only through appeals to the reason," Russell explained. Success at the ballot box, however remote, was the means to a Socialist state for Russell's faction of the party. "The kind of revolution that socialists think of would never disturb our grandmothers," he noted. The second assumption was about the nature of mankind. Socialists felt that people shared a common fund of humanity and interdependence; the world was not a Darwinian jungle where beasts competed. It was the competitive nature of capitalism that turned people into animals. Without capitalism, people would be good, rational, and willing to sacrifice for common goals. To argue that without the possibility of personal gain and the pursuit of wealth there would be no incentive to work or achieve was "to take the lowest possible view of man, and to deny all that is good in him," Russell believed. "The greatest joy that life affords is something done for somebody else. The man that lives for himself dies within himself."[16]

Undoubtedly Russell was an optimist—as were most progressives and socialists. But whether he really believed that socialism would cure the world's ills is difficult to determine. Indeed he was gloomy about the state of America in 1910, a pessimism that would deepen over the next five years. He was absolutely unequivocal that reform would not help matters (even though his journalism was helping the reformers) and he was adamant that electoral change was unlikely to succeed because the political system was in the grip of corrupt ruling forces. All of which begs the question as to why he would even bother to run for office. The answer is that he constantly saw the glass as half empty *and* half full—at the same time. He trusted the people explicitly. "All they need is the facts," he observed, exactly what many of the muckraking journalists said. They can be "fooled, betrayed, bamboozled . . . but the heart of the people is true." Moreover, he said, "the time is coming when the people will get up and kick the system into the street. . . ."[17] The problem, if Russell's muckraking political reporting in the years leading up the governor's race was to be believed, was that the electoral system was so manipulated the people were powerless to make changes.

Russell believed there was little difference between the Republican and Democratic parties, that in fact they were one party controlled by the corporate interests. In reality, he said, it was the capitalist parties versus the socialist party. But "before we can have Socialism we must introduce the machinery of a genuine democracy," Russell explained, not an easy task as he tried to show with his reporting. Russell saw politics influenced in two ways—with direct and outright fraud at the polls and with corporate bribery and payoffs to legislators. He dug into his reporter's bag of tricks to prove it, writing two multipart series of articles for Hearst's *Cosmopolitan*. The articles display Russell at a logical point in his development as a journalist and ideologue. He was, as the *Times* called him, "the magazine writer," but clearly he was and wanted to be more. He wanted out from behind the pen—but the pen nonetheless was the way he reached his audience and would likely still have his greatest effect. His journalism, even after his declaration for socialism, showed him to be a careful muckraker on one hand and an ideologue-socialist on the other. Russell used the results of the 1905 mayoral campaign in New York City to show how the entrenched political parties kept power. Hearst lost this election by a scant number of votes in a contest that historians agree was stolen by ballot-box fraud. Russell, who had covered or coordinated election coverage in New York City for thirteen years, had spent Election Day at the polls witnessing "a vast, organized, articulate and profitable industry" of fraud. He used an anonymous source—a reformer from the West Side of Manhattan—to tell an insider's tale of how elections were manipulated. His tale began at 5:00 A.M. at a flophouse for vagrants in Manhattan where two-hundred men were rousted out of bed, given breakfast, and then brought to various polling places to vote under someone else's name for the machine's candidate, after which they were paid. At one location Russell saw 100 fraudulent votes cast out of a total of 380. "The respectable, intelligent, patriotic, right-minded citizen . . . has no knowledge of the stupendous size of this evil," he commented. The reformers, of course, did know—for example, how $25 was paid for someone to vote more than once—but when they complained or intervened, they ended up in the hospital, bloodied by the machine's goons. "And no one has ever been punished for any of these crimes, " he reported. "One can order any reasonable number of fraudulent votes with as much certainty as one would order oysters."[18]

When importing and paying voters to commit fraud was not enough, then a second method came into play. Tally sheets used to tote up the final vote were smeared, defaced, mutilated, blotted, or written over with acid and ink to distort results. Russell's detailed and meticulous reporting, impressive even by modern standards of investigative reporting, paints a convincing picture of fraud, which he said could be found in cities from Philadelphia to Denver to Portland. Russell could have called his four-part series of articles the "shame of the ballot box." It revealed a corrupt system that matched the one Lincoln Steffens had found five years earlier. But while Steffens often said he was not sure of what he had found in his look at American cities, Russell was quite clear. "Here is revealed one of the means by which the corporations elect their puppets, secure their franchises, obtain the laws they want, control legislative bodies [and] forestall investigation." How can Americans preach for fifty-one weeks about "the beauty of public purity, the duties of citizenship, and the grandeur of civic honesty," while on the fifty-second week the "very breath of republican government" is choked by a "gangs of thugs"? Russell's look at election fraud struck a responsive chord in the New York State Legislature, which began an investigation. A year after his articles, the legislature toughened its election fraud laws, giving it one of the better systems in the nation.[19] Russell took the same tact as Steffens who, when he finished his "shame of the cities" in 1902, went on to investigate the states. But Russell's six-part "What Are You Going to do About it?" articles, also in Hearst's *Cosmopolitan*, are less impressive. Written in 1910, the articles, although carefully documented, deal mostly with graft and corruption in five state legislatures a decade earlier. Moreover, they are much longer on rhetoric than on fact. His point, repeated often, is that bad men are not the problem. "The real culprit," he writes, "is the System that makes grafting inevitable . . . no matter how many men we put into jail nor how many families we break up, so long as we have the System, we shall have its results."[20]

IV. RUNNING FOR GOVERNOR

The "system" took center stage in the race for governor of New York, at least as far as Russell was concerned. The Socialists got a jump on the other parties by nominating Russell in June 1910, well before either Republican Stimson or Democrat Dix. Russell laughingly called the nomination "an act of derangement" by the party. But he was deadly serious about the issues: poverty, slum housing, the increased cost of living, the failure of regulation, corruption in government—and the concentration of power and wealth that "is as much a menace to free government as imperial authority might be in another country."[21] The cure for it all, he declared, was Socialism, "the next advance for democracy." Be assured, he said, "it is no dreamy Utopia." Winning the election might be a dream, but at least at the outset of the campaign it appeared the socialists were gaining strength.

Russell opened his campaign at a picnic in Astoria, Queens, in late August. More than two thousand people cheered as he made his entrance and a procession headed by a brass band accompanied him to a lectern. Russell said he appreciated the cheering, but he understood that the cheers were for socialism and not for him. The cheers died down quickly, however, as Russell spent the next eleven weeks campaigning throughout New York State often at places where virtually no one showed up, and when they did seemed not to care at all about what he said. "Few things in nature can be more comical than the spectacle of an elderly person scrambling madly from town to town and city to city, trying to tell people something they do not wish to hear," Russell recalled in his autobiography. In White Plains, New York, one night he addressed eleven people; in Rome, someone opened a switch on a railroad steam pipe so nothing he said could be heard. It could have been worse. One Socialist candidate was thrown into the Erie Canal after a speech. In Wellsville he spoke at a firehouse, but the townspeople all stood in the back, with no interest and no applause. The town gave him seventy-eight votes. In Bolivar his train arrived so late that he missed his engagement, found all the hotels closed, and a policeman had to sneak him into a room. One hotel in Rattlersville was so bad that Russell slept in his clothes with his head near the window to ease the smell. Was this the road to the Cooperative Commonwealth? If so, it was to be a bumpy road.[22] Meanwhile, the other candidates said little about concentrations of wealth or threats to democracy, but they also said little about issues relating directly to New York State. Because of his background as a lumber mill and bank executive, the Democrat Dix stressed that if elected he would bring efficiency to state government. He favored popular election of U.S. Senators, direct primaries, and a federal income tax. He saved his choicest words for Theodore Roosevelt, the former president angling to run again in 1912, who had hand-picked Henry Stimson as the Republican candidate. Dix denounced Roosevelt as a "public enemy" and "an agent of destruction." Russell was no kinder, calling TR that "wild-eyed person" and "skillful demagogue." The fastidious Stimson, a graduate of Yale and Harvard and a former U.S. attorney, was caught in a crossfire between President William Howard Taft and Roosevelt, Taft's predecessor who was mounting his comeback. Moreover, Stimson was unsuited for the mudslinging often associated with a New York campaign. The press tagged him with the nickname "the human icicle."[24]

The campaign heated up in early October when Russell addressed a crowd of ten thousand in Union Square in Manhattan. They had come to hear the Socialist gubernatorial candidates from New Jersey, Connecticut, and New York. Russell assailed both parties. The Republicans have "Boss

Roosevelt," he said to laughter. "He opposes all bosses except himself." As for the Democrats, they answer every question with: "Ask Murphy." Charles F. Murphy was the Democratic chief of Tammany Hall. "If you asked them what the weather was they replied, 'Ask Murphy.'" He then turned to the issue of poverty, noting, "Life grows harder and harder for the average man." Three days later he received a long ovation from one thousand people in Lower Manhattan where he was well known and where the Socialists had their greatest strength. "In both parties, the workingman has no friend, no representative," he declared. Only Socialism could help. "It proposes to abolish the system under which a few men can control everything."[23] In Brooklyn another friendly crowd cheered Russell as he made fun of Woodrow Wilson, "the new Messiah from New Jersey," and "Dr. Roosevelt," whose remedy was "down with the boss." Never mind, Russell said, "whether you can pay your grocery bills." Neither party could stop the trusts from overwhelming the people's interests. "The real remedy," he said, "is to let the nation own the trusts." Russell seemed to strike responsive chords with his audiences. After one speech, *The Call*, the Socialist daily newspaper, commented: "Russell was at his best. He spoke with a conviction and enthusiasm which sent a thrill through his audience." When he was finished one speech the crowd rushed to the platform to thank Russell for his "eloquent indictment" of the present system.[24] On October 15, the campaign's highlight came when Russell addressed a packed audience at New York 's Carnegie Hall. He gave an hour-long speech filled with sarcasm and repetition. After asking why he was a Socialist, he cited the troubling statistics on poverty, wages, and the trusts, ending each segment by telling the audience, "There is your answer." After attacking the Rockefeller-Morgan group, he thundered, "Let the nation own the trusts," adding, "our aim is not for today but for all the future." A moment of tension interrupted his speech when a woman stood up and demanded that Russell address the question of woman's suffrage. "Silence!" someone yelled. "Put her out," said another. But Russell waved the crowd to let her speak, and then replied, "I am for it. I believe in it without reservation." And he described what he had seen in New Zealand where women voted. The audience applauded. He concluded with the same refrain he had used when he had been criticized about his Trinity Church articles: How could anyone stand idly by in a "world filled with unnecessary horrors and never make a protest"?[25]

By November 1 Russell was feeling confident, writing, "We have a better opportunity than I had supposed." But he reminded his audience that electoral victory was not the real goal of the Socialists. "We are not seeking political power," he wrote in *The Call.* "We measure our advance by the spread of ideas."[28] Much like many of the other positions advanced by Russell, his stance on winning elections was embraced in almost lockstep fashion by members of the party. In fact, historian Daniel Bell points out that one of the flaws in the Socialist movement was its rather rigid adherence to a set of set party principles. While Russell did emphasize some positions and issues over others, he sounded remarkably like other Socialists in expressing the party line.

Perhaps the best measure of what Russell believed as the 1910 campaign drew to a close was his interview with the *Times* in which he was asked what he would do if elected. Of course, he said immediately, he would need a Socialist legislature to get his way, but if he had one, he laid out a vision that by today's standard does not seem very radical. First, he said he would institute recall and referendum, which would allow the people not to have to wait until Election Day to get rid of elected officials and policies they did not like. "In the long run, the people are always right," he said. Russell wanted "home rule," so that, for example, no legislator from upstate New York would tell New York City how to govern itself. "What human being is fit to decide an environment he does not know"? he asked.[26] Dix also advocated home rule.

Russell sought an eight-hour work day, overtime pay for any work beyond the normal work week, equal pay for men and women, limited overtime for women, a ban on children under sixteen years old in the work force, workers' compensation for injury, government-funded pensions for old persons, breakfast and lunch programs for school children, and a more rigorous civil service system. Except for limits on women's overtime, all those proposals are in place today. More controversial, however, was his desire to give free land upstate to people living in crowded urban areas; for municipalities to assume control of electric, water, telephone, and gas utilities; and for the state to take over certain natural resources, including oil, timber, and water power. Russell conceded to the *Times* that his proposals were not likely to lead to victory in November, but "we can march up and drop the ballots that register our protests, and sooner than people think there will be a Socialist government at Albany."[27]

In the last week before Election Day, Russell visited Auburn, Syracuse, Rochester, Buffalo and Schenectady, a Socialist stronghold where an overflow crowd heard Russell lash out at his opponents. Stimson and Dix were both selected "for the one purpose of permitting the capitalist class to go on fleecing and exploiting," he said, as applause erupted. On the eve of the election, back in New York City, he gave an impassioned speech, repeating his story of the coal workers in Pennsylvania, finishing with a tearjerker ending about a miner whose teenage son died in an accident in the mines. "Russell, it's better this way," the father said, holding the limp body of his son in his arms. "And it was better that way," Russell told the audience. "But what shall we say of a civilization in which it is better for a child to die than to live?"[28]

Election Day came. The socialists made great gains, sending the first Socialist ever to the U.S. Congress and winning the municipal elections in Milwaukee. German immigrants on the Lower East Side of Manhattan shouted, "Endlich! Endlich!" ("At last! At last!") But, alas, Russell garnered only 4.4 percent of the votes in New York. Dix won with 689,700 votes to Stimson's 622,229. Russell later recalled that on the eve of the election "the sidewalks were jammed with shouting people, the windows were full of smiling faces, old men and women wept and cried" in support of Socialism. "But when Election Day came around we did nothing of the kind. We had the cheering and the old parties had the votes."[29] Russell was not in the least disturbed by his defeat, however. He received a letter from his friend and Socialist colleague, Algernon Lee, who congratulated Russell on his showing. It brought tears to Russell's eyes. He replied, telling Lee about "the wonderful way that life has changed for me since I came into the Socialist Party." He added: "I don't quite understand it myself . . . nothing seems to annoy me very much now and I feel a kind of pleasure in living that I never felt before. It seems strange to me that what purports to be an economic philosophy should be a great moral force but I am sure I am a better man since I came into the Socialist Party. If I live long enough, I may be of use someday, but not yet."[30] Eagerly, Russell returned to his muckraking and, eventually, three more runs for political office.

CHAPTER TWELVE

GRAPPLING WITH THE OCTOPUS

I. MUCKRAKING IS DERAILED

WHILE HIS FIRST CAMPAIGN FOR GOVERNOR OF NEW YORK was underway in 1910, Charles Edward Russell began another multipart series of articles that would cause a reaction unlike one that he—or any other muckraker—had ever gotten. This time he turned to the topic of railroads, which first caught his attention during his 1904 investigation of the "beef trust." Russell had an obsession with the railroads, as did the rest of America. He wrote two books and dozens of magazine articles about them. More than likely the obsession stemmed from Russell's belief that his father's newspaper had been killed by the railroads many years before, much the same way the Rockefeller cabal had put Ida Tarbell's father out of the oil business.[1]

Such an explanation is too simplistic, however. Russell understood the actual and symbolic importance of the rails, just as he knew that Trinity Church was both a bad neighbor and a capitalist icon. As a reporter he had closely watched various groups grapple with "the octopus." Populists and farmers throughout the Gilded Age, angered by being at the mercy of the railroad companies, had sought a combination of tougher regulations and government ownership. The Interstate Commerce Commission was largely created to meet their demands. Yet the railroads controlled everything from the legislature to the press and represented a central element in the political, economic, and social development of the United States. But they represented much more than simply an engine of growth. As the railroads pushed westward and facilitated population expansion, they changed America. In the process, the men who built America's 250,000 miles of track from 1870 to 1900 became legendary heroes and epic villains, representing both the American Dream and nightmare. The robber barons and the "octopus" they controlled were made-to-order topics for the muckrakers who had been pounding away at various sources of concentrated power since the turn of the century.[2]

Benjamin Flower's *Arena* magazine began the scrutiny in 1904 by tracing "Twenty Five Years of Bribery and Corrupt Practices" by the railroads. A detailed look at high accident rates followed in *Leslie's*. And then Ray Stannard Baker put the railroads on trial in his famous muckraking articles in *McClure's* in 1905. The result, at least in part, was a public outcry and federal regulations in 1906 that revitalized the thirty-five-year-old Interstate Commerce Commission, but also put the brakes on demands for more drastic remedies. After his tour of the world in 1907, Russell returned to America convinced more than ever that government oversight of the rails was not enough. Blaming the poor condition of the American railroad system on "the dizzy financial juggleries of the Kings of Finance," and the "gentlemanly thieves of Wall Street,"[3] Russell sought to set the record straight in a 1910 series of articles in *Hampton's*. He wanted a history that would show, first, how consumers paid the price for a legacy of fraud by America's railroad tycoons and, second, what should be done about it.[4]

A handful of men built the rails in America. The best known were Jay Gould, William H. Vanderbilt, E. H. Harriman, Collis P. Huntington, and James J. Hill, all of whom were revered as examples of the great industriousness that typified America's best men, "the gifted generals of the commercial battlefield," Russell called them. "According to the entertained theory," Russell said, these men "have developed the railroads, built the factories, established the commerce, created the industries of the land." And the entire world looked up to them, which galled Russell who believed they were what today would be called white-collar criminals. If "thoughtful men" looked at how railroad fortunes were made in America, they would have to conclude that "the whole American railroad business was rotten with fraud and lying," Russell argued. So, Russell dipped back more than twenty years to trace how the railroad moguls built their lines—and made their fortunes. Anticipating criticism, Russell asked: "Why recite these things now? The Past is past: let it be." His answer: "I recite them because they have direct and absolute bearing upon the greatest public question that this generation will have to deal with." The railroads are "a power superior to the government, they levy and collect from every community whatever toll they please and every attempt to restrain them or control them ends in the same ridiculous failure."[5]

Take for example, the Canadian-born James J. Hill, the first railroad ty-
coon profiled by Russell. Not a surprising choice, since the financial shenanigans of Hill, Harriman, and J. P. Morgan had precipitated a stock market panic
in 1901 and led to a U.S. Supreme Court decision that shot down a merger of
their rail lines into the Northern Securities Company. While the merger made
Hill infamous and led to Theodore Roosevelt's ballyhooed decision to bust this
"trust," it was Hill's rail construction exploits that had made him legendary.[6]

In what was probably the greatest feat in railroad building in the United
States, Hill pushed his St. Paul and Pacific Railroad from Minnesota through
the Rockies, despite the appalling difficulties of the terrain. By 1893 the line
reached Seattle. Hill was "the most admired of our railroad kings," Russell
pointed out, often held up as "the perfect model for our aspiring youth." He
had industry, zeal, ability and integrity . . . or so it seemed. But such conclusions were reached, Russell noted, before "those vile creatures, the muck-rakers, had begun to cast their baleful shadows upon our fair land." To get the true
story, Russell ventured to Minneapolis, where his sister had since moved from
Davenport, Iowa, and he dug into documents in the federal courthouse.[7] What
he found was a lawsuit brought by one of Hill's early partners, who told of a secret arrangement in the 1870s to water the stock of Hill's fledgling company. In
court testimony the partner said had he told Hill, "We will have to keep this
thing to ourselves." Hill replied, "Certainly it won't do to let anybody know
anything about it." What the partners did, according to the testimony, was to
overcapitalize the stock of the company, thus allowing the partners to invest little and then reap large profits—if the company succeeded, which it did, as Hill
pushed its expansion and oversaw its great growth. The partner sued because
he was cut out of the eventual profits, an allegation the court did not believe
since, it concluded, the alleged oral agreement was too disputed to be trustwor-
thy. For Russell the real point was that fraudulent methods began the Hill empire and led to "colossal profits" from little or no investment. In thirty years, he
asserted, Hill and partners made $407 million profit! "Never before have there
been such marvelous results from a beginning so inconsiderable," he wrote.[8]

Russell's readers had to wait until the next month's installment to find out
more about Hill's dark deeds, about how when he pushed his rail line through
the Rockies he promised the people of Spokane, Washington, in his "large
warm patriarchal manner," that rail rates would be kept low if they helped him.
"The heart of Spokane leaped with joy," and Hill was given a right of way for a
mere $70,000. At last he reached the Pacific, but then, according to Russell's
account, Hill "had lapsus memoriae in its worst form." As to everything connected with his promises to Spokane his mind went blank, "a malady that "did

not effect his ability to keep things; only his power to remember things." His shipping rates amounted to extortion. To prove this Russell used complicated and virtually unreadable charts showing comparative rates. He reached three conclusions from the story of James J. Hill: first, the consumer invariably foots the bill for steep shipping costs in higher coal, food, and clothing prices. Second, the railroads "have the power" and can "levy and collect from every community whatever toll they please." And, third, no government is strong enough to stop them. These were sweeping conclusions from one look at the "money mill" of James J. Hill, but were they an accurate portrait or was Russell the Socialist bound and determined to use Hill's story for propaganda?[9]

Russell found nothing redeeming about Hill. Unlike Tarbell, who understood Rockefeller's genius and Standard Oil's corporate efficiency, Russell could see nothing but an evil system that had corrupted all men. Even Lincoln Steffens had found many of the corrupt bosses of American cities to be likable characters, but Russell would not be charmed by Hill. Was the lure of great profit the beneficent influence that drove Hill to push his rail lines to the Pacific? Russell could not even consider the possibility; it would debunk his belief that men were driven by the common good, not by private accumulation of wealth.[10]

And so it went in the rest of his articles as Russell insisted to *Hampton's* 425,000 readers that the railroads existed for no other reason but "to issue, to manipulate, and to possess railroad securities." In other words, the rails in private hands were solely a moneymaking tool and not an instrument of public service. Collis P. Huntington, Russell's other major focus, was much like Hill. The California storekeeper joined with Leland Stanford and two others to create a railroad company that had practical control of the West. Although his construction of a Pacific rail line was a magnificent physical victory, Russell depicted it as "a monstrous triumph of greed, fraud, and corruption." Moreover, the Southern Pacific displayed the evil influence of the rails over government. The company was a "truly imperial power that had seized the State of California," Russell charged. Huntington's "great political machine was much more efficient than Tammany's or any other machine that ever existed," and the people had no chance against its "colossal" might. Russell warned in his March article that this "steadily growing evil" was "more menacing than any problem any nation has ever dealt with." This was surely an exaggeration, but his words stung Huntington. Before his next article on Huntington appeared Russell received a telephone call from someone with "intimate" knowledge of its contents. The caller tried to refute some of the facts, urging Russell not to print his article, but he refused. In June, Russell reported that a federal judgeship was promised to a

Huntington friend because of the rail magnate's campaign contributions. The allegation was based on a source that allegedly overheard a conversation between Huntington, who had died in 1900, and the president, who, oddly, was not named. Russell's article, heavily documented and filled with charts and long quotations from various correspondence, made it almost unreadable, but nonetheless it was a damning portrait of money influencing politics at all levels of government.[11] Of course, such revelations and charges were nothing new for the muckrakers to make—or for the American public to hear.

Russell drew the ire of the rail companies once again in November 1910. Two weeks before publication of an article on William H. Vanderbilt's rail lines, a man who said he represented the New York Central Railroad called Russell, saying he knew the contents of the upcoming story. If the article was not suppressed, the rail line would withdraw advertising from the magazine, a common threat during the muckraking era. Undaunted, Hampton published the article in which Russell painted a dramatic a portrait of "Death Avenue," a rail crossing in crowded Manhattan where four hundred had been killed and hundreds maimed over the years because there were no crossing gates. Rail owner Vanderbilt was supposed to elevate the tracks but had not done so, which had long been a scandal in New York City. Russell was certainly not exposing a new problem, but his words were harsh and pointed as he told the story of Seth Low Hampton, the one hundred and sixtieth child to be killed at the crossing. His five hundred schoolmates wept as they marched behind his coffin. Men cursed, teachers cried. They knew, Russell wrote, that little Seth was a "needless sacrifice to the system that makes of public highways a private gift." If the Lows had been rich they could have met "bribery with bribery, lobby with lobby, influence with influence, wrong with wrong." But since they were poor, "they must submit to this monstrous perversion of justice and lawmaking." The Seth Low anecdote, which Hearst would have so loved, was placed deep in the article, however, and the "Death Avenue" story was not told as effectively as either Russell's Trinity or prison exposes. Nonetheless, when the articles appeared, the railroad followed through with its threat: it withdrew advertising from *Hampton's* next edition—not the first time a muckraker's taunts had irked a businessman.[12]

Even though, as Russell told the story, threats continued to the magazine, Russell and Hampton kept publishing the "stories of the great railroads." The series neared completion in October when a man who said he represented Charles S. Mellen, the president of the New York, New Haven, and Hartford Rail Company, came to *Hampton's* office to say the article, still in page proofs, was "full of lies." He identified four facts he said were false, but Hampton felt they were accurate. If the article was printed, the visitor threatened that the financial powers backing the New Haven railroad would ruin the magazine and Hampton. The threat notwithstanding, "The Surrender of New England" was published in November, a fitting ending to Russell's series as he used examples—again, many years old—to repeat his themes: that the Mellen rail companies cared only about watering stock and making profits; that they gobbled up all competition by quietly buying the stock of small owners; and that Mellen used his political influence to block anyone who stood in his way. When one Massachusetts businessman successfully led a fight to block Mellen's consolidation efforts, his credit at the banks was discontinued. Russell warned: "This shows what this Power really is— how tremendous, how many sided, how long armed." He asked: "Who are the real rulers of America? How long can we continue this process of piling up capitalization and increasing the cost of living?"[13]

With the articles completed, Russell and Hampton awaited reaction. It came swiftly. In late December Hampton wrote to Russell, apologizing for not paying him but explaining that he was having trouble getting loans from New York banks. A bank vice president had told Hampton that a loan was a "certain" proposition. But after ten days the vice president reported he would have to take the loan deal to the bank's president. "He seemed to think it was all right until he learned the name of the magazine. Then he declined to discuss it any further," wrote Hampton, who said he had visited twenty one banks; all of which refused to loan money. Hampton added that a friend who worked in banking "advises me that, in his judgment, it will be practically impossible for us to borrow any money at New York banks. Our proposition is all right, he says; bankers have to acknowledge that it is, but they do not like the magazine. All of which I am sure will interest you." Later Russell learned that the company's financial ledgers had been stolen by a newly hired accountant. Soon after, many of the company's stockholders in New York City were visited and told that Hampton was misusing company money and that he had bought an estate in the Adirondack Mountains and a Fifth Avenue mansion. The charges were ridiculous, Hampton insisted. "Mrs. Hampton and I were having a time to buy clothing for the children," he later recalled. "We were near the line of desperation."[14] But the *Hampton's* stockholders were stunned by the allegations; Hampton was unable to raise needed cash to pay expenses. For Russell it was déjà vu. Just as the rails had knifed his father, now he wrote, "Mr. Hampton was ruined according to prediction and his magazine was swept out of his hands." Despite a large circulation and a brisk advertising business, "not a bank in New York would advance it one dollar," noted Russell. By the summer of

1911, the octopus had strangled its enemy.[15] "The run that had been foretold to Mr. Hampton was come upon him," Russell concluded. Facing receivership, Hampton relinquished his magazine to a group of promoters who he later alleged looted the magazine, destroyed its financial records, and wrecked one of the few remaining muckraking magazines in the country. Concluded Russell: "Nothing is clearer than that the masters mean to absorb the monthlies and weeklies of liberal tendencies."[16]

Russell fully accepted the theory that a conspiracy existed to put the muckraking magazines out of business.[17] "Several chuckling gentlemen" had met in New York City and decided to halt the exposing of the facts, he wrote four years after *Hampton's* went under. "The Interests set out resolutely . . . to bring in the fiery untamed muckraking magazine and tether it in the corporation corral." The special interests, according to this view, then canceled advertising, bought certain magazines outright or forced banks to call in mortgages and loans, as with *Hampton's*. "There must be less muckraking, greater amiability toward business," one banker declared.[18] The overall results were spectacular: between 1905 and 1911, *Era, Ridgway,* and *Human Life* went out of business. Between 1911 and 1916 *Hampton's, Success, Twentieth Century,* and *Harper's Weekly* failed. By 1912 conservative business interests had taken control of *McClure's,* the *American,* and *Collier's.*

But the question remains: Did the "Morgan interests" really conspire to silence Russell and the muckrakers? The answer is yes and no. The powerful banker J. P Morgan did not convene a meeting to plot strategy. Little by little, however, the combined efforts of businessmen began to stifle muckraking and reform. But other factors also influenced the direction of the magazines' editorial content. Many of the changes the writers sought—food and drug controls, banking reform, an enlarged central government to tackle the excesses of industrialism—had come about. Eventually the public tired of exposé journalism and as circulation of the magazines began to drop, editors sought new approaches. Russell was the only writer of expose who kept pounding away consistently, but at times his style, replete with long quotations from documents and complex charts, may have turned off audiences. Moreover, his socialist ideology might have tainted his reliability. In the end many social factors combined to slow down and eventually stop the muckraking movement.[19] But in the case of *Hampton's,* the last of the attacking magazines, the rail interests clearly struck a direct blow at an opponent who was not only making damning allegations but who was proposing a remedy that threatened the rails' very existence as private companies. Russell declared at the end of one article: "The highways are the people's. Let us return them to the people from whom they have been taken chiefly by chicanery, bribery, and fraud."[20] Russell did not want to regulate the rails; he wanted to take them away from their owners. He *was* the enemy at a time when the enemy was making gains. For Russell, the attack on and demise of *Hampton's* was proof that the "people" were in a war with the "interests." And while most of the muckrakers turned to other pursuits, Russell kept fighting the war, becoming, in fact, more obsessed—almost paranoid—about the dangerous might of the capitalists.

II. QUARRELING COMRADES

If the muckraking magazines were being swallowed up by Wall Street, as Russell and others were convinced, only one choice remained for him and the socialists if they were to continue to educate the public: start independent publications free of advertising dollars and corporate ownership. If anyone had expertise on publishing to offer the Socialist Party it was Russell, who had edited some America's greatest newspapers. The Socialists' most widely read publication was the highly political *Appeal to Reason*, run out of Girard, Kansas. But some Socialists wanted a publication that would broaden their appeal, especially to families. Thus in 1910 they began to publish the *Coming Nation* as a supplement to the *Appeal*. Edited by Russell and Algie M. Simons, it featured complex articles on economics and politics, along with a children's page, a women's column, fiction, and drawings. Each week page one prominently featured an editorial written by Russell. Although financial problems continually plagued the publication in its run from 1910 to 1912, the *Coming Nation* was unique among radical publications. It attempted to move past politics and economic theory and fuse the concerns that people faced in everyday life with overarching issues about how to reach the "Co-Operative Commonwealth." Unfortunately Simons and Russell never had enough money to produce the quality publication they wanted. Furthermore, while the Socialists were preaching on their pages that under Socialism "democracy would be realized, the family would be strengthened and public morality would be improved," behind the scenes they were increasingly undermining this vision of harmony, acting like bourgeois capitalists fighting over a loose nickel.[21]

In his 1933 autobiography, recalling the days when Socialism was growing in leaps and bounds and hopes were high, Russell noted the conflicting strains in the Socialist Party. Upon entering the party, one automatically became "comrade." This custom, imported from Germany, "represented a beautiful ideal," Russell said, even though he felt it "was unsuited for America." It was even more unsuited for the fractious debate that often dominated party meetings. In New

York a central committee made all decisions on policy for the party's local branches. Russell was a delegate to the committee, which met every Saturday at East Eighty-fourth Street in Manhattan. "We sat always until 2 a.m. and sometimes later, ardently discussing the points of pins and the like vital matters," noted Russell sarcastically. There was no limit to debate and the factions often engaged in what Russell described as "acrimonious squabbling." The Socialists, in fact, had been squabbling ever since the party's creation in 1901. The party was born out of a wonderful ideal—that the people should own and share resources—but deciding how to get there, what tactics to employ, and who should lead the crusade split the comrades endlessly. "The great compensating fact about the whole business," Russell noted, "was the unmistakable spirit of devotion to a cause in which all believed implicitly." As Russell told friend Algernon Lee, "I could kick myself" for not joining the party earlier.[22]

But Russell had barely declared for Socialism in 1908 when he watched an angry dispute break out between Simons, his future co-editor, and William English Walling, with whom he would soon start the NAACP. Walling, not even a party member, wrote a letter seeking to oust five members of the party's national executive committee, including Simons. Walling wanted the party to ally itself with the union movement, a decision that many opposed because the unions were pro-capitalist. When Walling's letter outlining his reasons and calling for the ousters was read aloud at a party meeting, it caused uproar. Party mainstay Victor Berger said Walling was at the head of a "cabal" to disrupt the party. But there was no cabal; the party members just differed wildly on numerous key issues.[23]

The issue of labor unions was particularly tricky. The Socialists considered themselves the party of the workers; after all, they wanted the workers to own the factories . . . eventually. The labor movement, however, was more concerned with immediate improvements in salaries and working conditions. The American Federation of Labor, led by Samuel Gompers, staunchly opposed Socialism. Russell wrote and said little about labor. Even in speeches he gave scant attention to the question, except to note that wages were not keeping pace with costs. When he did write about labor, however, he was typically of two minds—Progressive and radical. Gompers, America's most important labor leader, was "sensitive, imaginative, kindly," Russell wrote in a 1909 profile, and he came away from an interview with Gompers with "increased respect" for how he had helped the unionists. But he noted that Gompers's concern for the workers would do little to halt poverty, slums, and breadlines. Powerful unions were not enough to ameliorate the gut issues that moved Russell.[24]

The other more vexing question raised by an alliance with labor concerned violence. Was "direct action" by unions and workers—strikes, slowdowns, and sabotage—ever justified? Should socialists obey injunctions and laws passed, interpreted and enforced by defenders of capitalism when those laws operated against the interests of the working class? Was violence to bring about the Co-operative Commonwealth ever justified? A 1910 dynamite bomb that killed twenty people in a labor dispute at the *Los Angeles Times*; the great 1912 strike in the textile mills of Lawrence, Massachusetts; and ongoing threats of "direct action" by "Big Bill" Haywood and the International Workers of the World all precipitated a heated quarrel over the efficacy of labor violence as the socialists prepared to go to Indianapolis. Even though Russell was signing his letters to other socialists "Fraternally yours," the party was clearly divided into two less-than-brotherly camps: the moderates and conservatives, also called the constructivists, were on one side. The radicals, sometimes known as "impossibilists," who believed in more aggressive action, were on the other. While Russell was impatient with social injustice and capitalism's flaws, he was nonetheless a conservative socialist, adamantly insisting that evolution, not revolution, was needed to bring about socialism. "Socialism is inevitable," Russell wrote, "because evolution, the process of conditions, the immutable laws of human development make it as certain as the sun."[25] The constructivists were generally content to educate and propagandize, and then turn to elections as the preferred route to socialism. This might mean a slow process of change, and some constructivists were willing to accept immediate changes in the form or government regulation. Certainly Russell's reporting, on prisons and on Trinity Church, for example, implied the need for immediate change and reform. But even on the matter of reform, the socialists were split. Some felt that to give in to reform was to accept and help capitalism. Others felt that Progressive changes were acceptable, for to reject them was to turn the Socialist Party into only a party of dreams. The impossibilists were not content to wait for the capitalists to reform their system; they wanted to use "direct action," in the form of strikes, for example. Some felt that violence was acceptable. In particular, the International Workers of the World—the Wobblies—were reputed to have anarchists in their ranks whose penchant for violence would ruin socialism's chances of attracting more Americans to the fold.

Not all the socialists' disputes were over policy and substance; at times the arguments were petty and personal. The writer Gustavus Myers, whose histories of corporate chieftains were much like his friend Russell's, was told to appear before the party's Central Committee to answer charges that he had criticized another party member in uncivil terms. Myers refused to appear, declaring, "If suspension is to be the price for freedom of speech in the Socialist Party, particularly in self defense, I shall very gladly pay the price." Myers quit the party. Even Eugene V. Debs, the party's presidential candidate in the three previous elections and the most well known and revered socialist in America, was involved in angry personal disputes with both New York's Morris Hillquit and Milwaukee's Victor Berger. "I have been silent under his insults a good many times for the sake of the party," Debs declared of Berger, "but [I will] tell a few truths about Berger the Boss and the bully that will put him right before the comrades."[26] Russell understood that some of the infighting had to with "personal ambitions . . . men that mixed much desire for limelight with a purpose to emancipate the working class." And the feuding troubled Russell. "We have not one moment to waste in internal quarrels," he declared.[27]

While Russell was as impatient for change to occur as some of the more left-wing party members, he was restrained and even cordial in his approach to those both in and out of the party. In fact, despite his bitterness toward capitalism, he always maintained warm friendships with those who had more conventional political beliefs. His closest friend was David Graham Phillips, the former newsman who turned out two novels a year after he left Pulitzer's fold in 1902. While Phillips flirted with socialism, he stuck to believing capitalism could be reformed; Russell stayed close to him nonetheless. Tragedy struck Phillips on January 21, 1911, when a deranged man who thought that a Phillips novel had maligned his Southern family shot him in Gramercy Park in Manhattan. Russell rushed to his friend's bedside, but Phillips died three days later. Russell's most frequent correspondent during this time was Julia Marlowe Sothern, who had been America's most famous actress before her retirement and permanent move to Europe. Russell spent two months each summer in Europe, often visiting Marlowe in Switzerland and Paris with his second wife, Theresa Hirschl, whom he had met in Chicago and married in 1909. Hirschl was a native of Davenport, Iowa, like Russell, but it is unclear if they had known each other growing up. Like Marlowe and Russell, Theresa shared a love of the arts, and she fit easily into his other orbit, the one centered on poetry, music, and theater into which politics and economics rarely intruded.

Russell also kept in close touch during this period with Arthur Brisbane, his former colleague who had become Hearst's second-in-command. Brisbane moved to the political right over the years and owned considerable New York real estate, yet that did not hinder his friendship with Russell, to whom he jokingly signed letters "Downtrodden proletariat."[28] For Russell, Brisbane the landlord was simply the logical product of a competitive system, a theme he repeated over and over in his 1911 book *Business: The Heart of the Nation*. He used harsh words about capitalism, but his actions were conciliatory. For example, he never commented publicly on the issues that split the party and seemed to think compromise was always possible. When a union disturbance threatened the editorial independence of the party's daily newspaper, *The Call*, Russell commented: "I think the men in the union must be reasonable persons and cannot want to insist upon conditions that would make publication impossible. I should think some kind of compromise would be feasible and much preferable to any row." Negotiate, talk, and settle differences the way a "reasonable man" would, he suggested.[29] He asked, "Is it impossible that the men in [the union] might be reasoned with?" As the party prepared for its presidential nominating convention in May 1912 in Indianapolis, Indiana, Russell tried to play the role of reasonable man, a task that would prove to be increasingly daunting.

III. Candidate for President

The year 1912 was a watershed in American politics. Teddy Roosevelt, who Russell called the "wild man from Oyster Bay," decided to come out of retirement, create a new political party, and challenge his hand-picked successor, William Howard Taft. Russell called Taft "the putterer" because he did little but putter around the golf course while America's problems mounted. The Democrats were pinning their hopes for a return to power on the man from Princeton University, Woodrow Wilson. Meanwhile, the optimistic Socialists were hoping to build on their strong showing in 1908 when Debs received 402,000 votes and drew large inspired crowds to Socialist rallies. Russell was downright ebullient in his *Coming Nation* column, declaring, "Socialism has advanced to the point where it is a serious menace to the exiting order." He added, "reaction cannot much longer be dominant in America."[30] Debs echoed Russell, commenting in early spring of 1912, "The outlook is positively inspiring . . . things are shaping rapidly for the undoing of the powers that are grinding the faces of the people." Indeed, Socialism had made gains, electing by 1911 one congressman, 18 state legislators, 33 mayors, 2 township chairs, and 313 other officials. Reflecting on the progress he saw the Socialists making, and with just a touch of hyperbole, Russell declared: "There has never been another time in the history of the world when it was so good to be alive."[31]

By mid-May the Socialists began gathering in Indianapolis, the city in which the party was born eleven years earlier. Representatives from every state except South Carolina were on hand, including the new kid on the block, Charles Edward Russell, who was attending his first national convention of Socialists. As a reporter he had covered the conventions of the Democrats and Republicans, but at this one he was a participant—and, as it turned out, a leading contender for the party's presidential nomination. Although a party member for only four years, he came to the convention riding a streak of victories as a writer-reformer, one of the only delegates who was known nationwide, and one with a reputation as an orator who could move and inspire audiences. New York's twenty-three-man delegation was enamored of Russell. Russell had to know, however, that the Socialist Party belonged to Eugene Victor Debs, the God of American socialism who had run for president in the three previous elections. Debs, like Russell, was an inspiring speaker known throughout the nation. As a paternal figure who tried to avoid becoming embroiled in party squabbles, Debs was also able to bridge the radical and conservative factions of the party.

There is no indication that Debs and Russell worked on any issues together before or after the convention. There are no letters between them and no reason to believe they had a personal friendship. This is not to say that they were enemies. In fact, in the one reference Russell makes to Debs in his writings, he calls him "the apostle and solider of the working class." On the other hand, there was some rivalry between the two, at least in Russell's mind. When Debs went to speaking engagements for the party, he was paid $100. When the party offered Russell only $50, he balked, even though he found it "painful and awkward" to voice his complaint. "It would be very difficult for me to think that you intended to offer me less than you paid to Comrade Debs," he wrote a party official. Russell saw himself as Debs's equal.[32] They clearly came from different worlds. Debs had been involved in labor and union activity since the great Pullman strike of 1894, and Socialism had been his milieu since before the turn of the century. Russell, meanwhile, has been immersed in journalism, writing about the activities of leaders such as Debs, but he was more comfortable in Progressive and reform circles than in radical activity. That the two had in common a passion for the common people is clear. Debs, however, was known to like a good time, while Russell the teetotaler was a less rough-and-tumble personality. There was no worry about social gatherings between the two at the 1912 convention: Debs chose not to attend, even though the convention was taking place in his home state, and his absence fed rumors that his often-problematic health had worsened. Moreover, his calming and lordly figure might have mellowed what was soon to be a stormy convention.

New York delegate Morris Hillquit opened the proceedings on May 18 by applauding the Socialist Party's growth from 10,000 members in 1901 to 100,845 dues-paying members in 1912, making it "a political party of the first

magnitude . . . a factor in the social, political and public life of this country."
But he added a warning: "Let us not waste time [on] petty, unimportant, in-
significant matters." On Day Two a Tennessee delegate tried to lighten the
mood by reminding the attendees that Socialism was "a movement for joy, for
happiness, for health, for laughter, for flowers, and for the good things of earth
in general." They applauded as he added, "This is the best world I ever got
into, in spite of the fact that it is run by the capitalist class." The "doggoned socialists," shouldn't "make such sour faces. You are not going to catch flies with
vinegar, and if you want to catch a bear use honey or molasses. Now, friends, be
cheerful about the thing and don't quarrel much, and when you do quarrel put
on a smiling face."[33] Laughter echoed through the hall. But then somber-faced
and sour John Spargo of Vermont got up to ask that foreign delegates be recognized, ignoring completely the previous speaker. It was time to do business,
and honey was not in the recipe. On Days Three bickering broke out about
whether a commission form of government gave Socialism a better chance to
take root. On Day Four fighting became nastier when a committee headed by
the *Coming Nation's* Simons urged that private farms be socialized. One delegate immediately challenged the report, but another questioned his right even
to speak on the convention floor. A third delegate followed by saying that only
farmers should enter into this discussion, not delegates from urban areas. Another then asked whether the report meant that all private property should be
communally owned or just farms. Didn't the people own all the earth's land?
Finally, someone reminded the convention that the party already had a position
on this issue and had rejected communal property. The debate ended, having
gone nowhere.[34]

The next day was more productive. Russell, making his first appearance on
the dais, praised the "spirit of socialist unity that has been such a beautiful and
attractive feature of this convention." He presented the delegates with recom-
mendations of the platform committee he chaired. They approved abolishing
convict labor for anyone under sixteen years of age, equal voting rights for men
and women, shorter work days, a day and a half off each week for workers,
more factory inspections, public works programs for the unemployed, old age
insurance, compulsory accident insurance, and a graduated income tax. A proposal to eliminate all federal courts was controversial. Russell defended it by
saying, " We take the federal courts of this country to be a source of infinite evil
in the community. Being a source of evil we think we should cut it out." Finally,
Russell agreed to change the wording of that proposal and a handful of others
also. He was gracious and moderate in making concessions. But then, as Russell's work was finished, the fireworks broke out.[35]

Jeb Harriman of California had alluded to a simmering issue when on May 22 he argued for more aggressive tactics by the party. "You don't scatter literature when a man is starving: you throw a beefsteak in his mouth," he observed. "The socialist party as I conceive it has but one purpose, and that is to apply its philosophy, not to theorize about it, but to apply it. " Harriman was not content to wait for the ballot box to reap dividends; his comments were a veiled attack on the party's moderates. But many party members feared where Harriman's brand of activism would lead. Syndicalists, anarchists, and the Wobblies—all wanted aggressive actions that many felt threatened Socialism's viability. Delegate Cassidy of New York rebutted Harriman, pointing to the "great danger, the tremendous danger that faces the movement today . . . from the end . . . that smells of violence and anarchy."[36] A secret caucus led by Victor Berger and Morris Hillquit drafted an amendment to the party's constitution that read: "Any member of the party who opposes political action or advocates crime, sabotage or other methods of violence as a weapon of the working class to aid in its emancipation, shall be expelled from membership in the party." The amendment was aimed directly at "Big Bill" Haywood and the IWW faction, and it touched off even angrier exchanges. "Sabotage means jack-ass methods of fighting capitalism. In the end it spells but the philosophy of the individualist," one delegate yelled. When a delegate from New York began telling a long story about how the anarchists had marred some New York rallies, he exceeded his allotted time and shouting ensued about whether he should continue. Another delegate tried to drown him out, declaring that the Socialists should not air their internal disputes in public. Responded another: "I don't believe this is a washing of dirty linen. This had better be thrashed now than to be held in abeyance."[37]

The party's organizers had planned that on Day Six, at three o'clock, all work would stop and the presidential nomination would take place. No one had expected that a debate on violence would be in progress. But the delegates voted to take a short break and then resume the debate. The nomination would have to wait. When they returned, Berger, perhaps the second most powerful Socialist in the party next to Debs, took to the floor. "Let us be perfectly sincere about this matter," said the man from Milwaukee. "The time has come when the two opposite trends of thought that we have had must clash again." He meant Socialism and Anarchism. "There never can be any bridge," he said, decrying those would use the party for "IWWism, sabotage, and syndicalism." Dramatically, Berger insisted, "I do not believe in murder as a means of propaganda; I do not believe in theft as a means of expropriation; nor in continuous riot as a free speech agitation." Berger then threatened to quit the party and take his considerable Midwest organization with him. When he finished, another delegate mockingly replied that Berger always threatened to quit, but never did. Berger's words, however, had aptly summed up the opposition to violence.[38]

Although Russell was silent at the convention about violence, the issue was one with which he had grappled. He made up his mind about it in the winter of 1907, while he was researching stories on New York City's rail lines. One night in a howling snowstorm he talked with young women who had just been dismissed from a factory job that paid meager wages. They were trying to decide if they had a nickel to take the trolley home. Just then a heated limousine carrying one of the factory owners who was wearing a fur-lined coat drove by. Russell was infuriated. "I began to understand what oppression meant," Russell recalled. Moreover, he added, "I began to feel coming up in my head the old jungle impulse for vengeance. I wanted something in my hand to throw." But Russell decided that violence would be foolish. "No act of violence could possibly help those victims of the system. Any act of violence would only degrade me to the level of the thief." Russell decided that the workers needed to unite, not fight. With the issue long decided in his mind, he thought the debate at the convention was a waste of time. "Nobody knows how [Socialism] is going to be established," he wrote shortly after the convention. "We might as well quarrel about how the wind is going to blow seven years from today." Furthermore, he said, "I don't give a hoot how it is established. All I care about is to get it and to get it in the shortest possible space of time, because every day that it is delayed costs hundreds of lives needlessly sacrificed to the blood-dripping profit system."[39] While one could interpret the "I don't give a hoot" comment to mean that Russell might support violence, the evidence points in an opposite direction. For Russell's wing of the party, especially the Socialists from New York, incremental change and gradual progress was acceptable. Ballots and not bullets would bring them to the Promised Land. And the majority of the party agreed, voting 191 to 90 in favor of the anti-violence amendment to the party's constitution.[40]

Having succeeded at getting its way on the sabotage question, the party's right wing now zeroed in on the presidency, which was somehow anticlimactic after the slugfest over violence. Debs had been the party's standard-bearer for every election since 1900, and his vote totals had improved each year. But the powerful Berger, with his Milwaukee and Chicago followings, wanted someone less independent than Debs, someone he could "boss," as Debs noted privately. The New York coalition sought a candidate who might better speak for the urban East. Russell was a logical choice. In fact, the *International Socialist Review* seemed to imply that the convention would look to either Debs or Russell when it asked the duo to write, side by side, articles on the party's strategy for 1912 in an issue published just before the convention. Oddly, Russell, the passionate writer, did not come across as well as Debs, the passionate orator, in detailing his position. Both agreed that the Socialists needed to stick to their principles and not to sell out to reform or the unions. "The moment [socialism] takes a seat at the grimy board is the moment it dies within," Russell wrote. Debs warned of giving in to "bourgeois reform." Getting elected was not worth giving up on the principles of socialism, he said. Russell used the examples of Australia and New Zealand, where socialism had flourished, to argue his point of view, but the story he told was obtuse and complicated. It hardly seemed that it would capture the imagination of Midwest farmers, Western miners, and Southern Populists. Only the immigrants of New York, if they could bear to read it, might relate to Russell's story. While he concluded on an inspirational note—"If this cause of socialism is worth believing in it is worth following to the end without compromise"—his message was likely lost on the delegates. Debs, meanwhile, was inspirational throughout, arguing clearly what socialism must stand for, what it must resist, and whom it must help.[41] As a biographer recounts, Debs could be a formidable force. Once at a rally in Illinois, two Irish women came to hear him speak. After Algie M. Simons addressed the crowd, one woman said to the other, "An' is that Debs?" The other replied, "Oh no, that ain't Debs—when Debs comes out you'll think it's Jesus Christ."[42]

The only question that remained was about Debs's health. Ever since the 1908 campaign, when he had periodically suffered from exhaustion, Debs had had recurring ailments, including throat surgery in 1910. But his allies made clear that the candidate was now healthy, rested, and eager for a new fight; he would accept the nomination. With that assured, the right wing of the party was no match for Debs. The Milwaukee-Chicago coalition nominated Emil Seidel, who was Milwaukee's socialist mayor. The New Yorkers nominated Russell. Since the Socialists eschewed the politics of personality, no nominating speeches were made. The candidates were named and the vote was taken. Debs received 165 votes, Seidel 56, and Russell 54. Even if the right wing had coalesced around one candidate, it would still have fallen short of defeating Debs. The nomination was his. Seidel immediately asked that the nomination be made unanimous. Russell responded: "I never had greater joy in my life than I have when I second that motion."[43] Russell then declined to be considered for the vice presidency; Seidel was thus chosen with 159 votes. In effect, the convention was over. The Socialists went home, and when Russell returned to New York he was quickly chosen by his party to be the nominee again for governor. With Indianapolis behind him, Russell began his second campaign as a Socialist political candidate.

CHAPTER THIRTEEN

THE DOVE BECOMES A HAWK

I. A RADICAL IN THE STOCK MARKET?

EVER SINCE HIS BREAKDOWN AND RECURRENT health problems began in 1902, Russell had taken a vacation each summer for at least a month. Without fail, he would sail to Europe, usually visiting France, Switzerland, or Germany. The baths at Carlsbad were one of his favorites. His good friends, Julia Marlowe and her husband, Edward Sothern, would anxiously await the arrival of "Charles and Theresa." The Russells and the Sotherns were an odd combination. Theresa, an ardent feminist, was active in the women's movement. Charles Russell was a sober, serious, and passionate social crusader, a workaholic. The Sotherns, meanwhile, were America's most famous theatrical couple. Edward, fifty three, scion of a distinguished British theatrical family, was a successful touring actor in the 1880s and 1890s. Marlowe, also English-born, first appeared on the New York stage in 1887, where she was an immediate success and soon after a national celebrity. Like the Russells, the Sotherns always spent summer in fashionable European locations. Eventually, Julia moved permanently to Europe and wrote often to Russell.[1] When the couples got together, it was a time of gaiety and fun. Russell could discuss the theater, poetry, and Shakespeare. Socialism took a backseat. This is not to say that Russell did not keenly observe economic conditions in Europe, especially in Germany, which he so admired. But public policy and social issues were mostly pushed aside when he was on holiday.[2]

Even though a governor's race beckoned in New York, the year 1912 was no different from others. Soon after the Socialists' convention in the spring, the fifty-one-year-old Russell set sail for Europe. He had long been planning this trip, writing regularly to Marlowe. Their correspondence reveals a different side of Russell, one that raises serious questions about his true commitment to the principles of socialism that had become so much a part of his public persona. Beginning in 1901, well before his conversion to socialism, Russell began investing money in the stock market for Marlowe. The investments were in his name, probably because Marlowe, who was famous, wanted her investments anonymous. Russell invested $19,000 in New York City municipal bonds; $10,000 in the International Paper Company, and $9,000 in the Metropolitan Street Railway Company.[3] In 1901 alone, Marlowe's investments earned $7,252.57, part of which Russell received as a commission. It was not until 1903 that Marlowe's name appeared on her investments, but nonetheless it was Russell who was choosing them, including a number of mortgages on various properties. Mostly, Russell recommended that Marlowe invest in government bonds. When she asked him about investing in railroad securities in 1912, he demurred. "I could not recommend them to anybody for I do not believe in them," he wrote, although he did not privately attack the rail moguls with the venom that he used in his magazine articles. Moreover, Russell did not seem to enjoy his investment advice, even though he profited. "The longer I live," he told her, "the clearer it seems to me that there is no satisfaction in anything connected with business."[4] He added, "I had much rather be a Socialist agitator on a pittance than a multi-millionaire."

Despite his disdain for the world of business, however, it is clear that Russell, the anti-capitalist, was playing the capitalist game.[5] It seems contradictory that Russell, so publicly angry about the inadequacies of capitalism, was privately engaging in the sport that was Wall Street. But his correspondence does indicate that almost all of the investments were municipal bonds, especially in the later years of his ongoing advice to Marlowe, which continued well into the 1930s. Some socialists believed that investment in cities and governments was not a contradiction and was an appropriate method of helping the nation's infrastructure. Even mortgages can be defended. The Socialist Party was quite emphatic that it was not opposed to private property. Only large and vital industries were to be socialized and taken over by the workers, although the list of which industries would be included was never clear. What is also not clear are the types of buildings that Russell owned with Marlowe and his old friend and former colleague Arthur Brisbane. Was Russell a landlord? And if so, was he a better landlord than Trinity Church? Did he own property that housed large businesses? There is no apparent answer to those questions, although when he died in 1941 he owned no real estate.

The evidence about his complicity in Wall Street activity indicates that Russell was not a revolutionary bent on remaking the world in radical ways. He admitted he knew little of Marxist theory. What he did understand was that the lust for profit drove people in directions that contradicted what he saw as man's true nature as a cooperative animal. He felt that the industrial world was inevitably headed down a path of monopolistic industries, but the profits would go not to Rockefeller or Morgan but to the workers. And he wanted to help make that transition come about with education and elections. Russell likely also saw the return on his investments as a means to allow him to do more work for the cause than to have to worry about making an income. During his freelance years from 1902 to 1915, he took various jobs as an editor—at *Hampton's*, at the *Coming Nation*, and at *Pearson's* magazine. Undoubtedly the steady income from his editing chores was useful to Russell, who traveled extensively to various American cities and to Europe. But he lived modestly, owning a house on I Street in Washington, D.C. Smoking good cigars was his only vice. At a time when he was bickering over what fee he should be paid for speeches, he wrote to one party official: "I prefer to make my service free, and I am going to strive to shape my affairs so that I can do these things without money and without price."[6] Julia Marlowe's investments gave him that chance. In the meantime, he needed the money he earned from his magazine articles and the $75 to $100 fees that he received for his speaking engagements. When he finished his vacation in Europe, speaking engagements beckoned. Russell went back on tour for the Chautauqua, a popular commercial enterprise that hired famous authors, scientists, musicians, and political leaders and sent them on tours of American cities to provide provincial entertainment and "culture under a tent." More urgent, however, was the 1912 race for governor of New York for which Russell had agreed again to be the Socialist Party candidate.

II. Reformed Reformer Campaigns

John Dix, who defeated Russell in the 1910 campaign, was a disappointment as New York governor. Independent Democrats hoped for a reform administration, but Dix had proved to be utterly subservient to the Tammany Hall party machine. Woodrow Wilson, running for president, also opposed his renomination; he wanted an unbossed candidate. The Democrats thus turned to William Sulzer, also known as "Plain Bill"" or the "boy spellbinder" because of his oratorical charm. Sulzer was a mixed character, giving lip service to reform causes but also maintaining close relationships with the bosses.[7] The Republicans nominated Jeb. E. Hedges, a prominent attorney, while the Progressive Party chose Oscar S. Straus, a well-known philanthropist and former member of Teddy Roosevelt's cabinet. For Russell, the three opposing parties were one and the same: only Socialism offered a different and real remedy. "The other three propose to maintain the existing system but to trim it a little and tinker it a little, if there is anything wrong," he said.[8] Russell attacked all three parties during the governor's race, but he reserved particular disdain for Roosevelt, the man who had coined the word "muckraker" just six years before.

Russell had been observing Roosevelt for many years, first when TR was New York's police commissioner, then its governor, and then as vice president and president. He especially resented Roosevelt's saying that he was a friend of the worker. As Russell reminded voters, when he was New York's governor, Roosevelt sent out the state militia in April 1900 to break up a protest by immigrant workers who were building a reservoir for New York City in the Hudson Valley. The workers were simply asking that their wages be raised to the going rate for construction. One state National Guardsman was killed in a confrontation with the workers. "A friend of labor?" Russell asked. "Spot him instantly as a fakir and fraud." Russell somewhat exaggerated Roosevelt's view of labor, however, since he was actually progressive in his tenure as New York's governor. His administration supported the workers' request for higher wages in the construction of the New York dam, and Roosevelt ordered an inquiry to see if the workers had been forced to work longer than allowed hours.[9]

Russell went after TR's Bull Moose Party because he believed that its ulterior motive was to thwart the rising socialist fervor. As the capitalists began to realize that Socialism was gaining, that "revolt was in the air," Russell said, "terror awoke in their hearts." They decided to develop a third party, not to defeat the Democrats or Republicans, but to siphon votes from Socialism.[10] Of course, while this may have in effect happened, Russell could not have truly believed that Roosevelt came out of retirement just to stop the revolution. While he was president, Roosevelt had written private letters saying that he feared the great unrest that was being caused especially by the muckraking exposes, but Roosevelt returned because he was unhappy with William Howard Taft and because he wanted to win. Nonetheless, the allegation always made it into Russell's standard stump speech—and the audiences loved it as he mocked the "big Bull Moose with shining white teeth."[11]

Russell made a more serious allegation during the campaign, one that created national headlines and led him to testify before a U.S. Senate Committee investigating campaign contributions. In early September, as the campaign heated up, Russell told a cheering audience that Roosevelt, while he was President, had demanded that financier J. P. Morgan contribute $100,000 to the Republicans if he wanted favorable legislation passed. Russell said one of his sources, whom he did not name, was with the New York banker as he had a telephone conversation with the White House; Morgan was reportedly furious at Roosevelt's demand. To Russell, the story was evidence of how the political parties were giving away the government to the highest capitalist bidder. When he first told the story, an audience applauded for eight minutes. A Senate Committee called Russell to Washington in October, insisting that he provide details. He used the platform to argue that both political parties regularly prostituted themselves for campaign contributions, and that only socialism would take the "for sale" sign off the government lawn. The committee demanded to know Russell's sources, and Russell obliged, saying a colleague at *Hampton's*, Judson Welliver, was his source. Welliver denied the story when he testified, but Russell said that when he reminded Welliver of the incident Welliver did not deny it. While Russell did not backtrack on his version, he told the committee that he could not verify that Roosevelt had pressured Morgan. He could simply say that a reliable source told him that Morgan said Roosevelt did. The investigation went no further, but Russell again was in the eye of the storm and able, as he liked to say, to agitate. The *New York Times* placed the story and his picture on page one.[12]

Aside from the flap caused by the Roosevelt allegation, the campaign of 1912 was much like the one two years earlier. Russell scooted all over the state to crowds of varying sizes, mostly very small upstate and often quite large in New York City, the Socialists' stronghold. Two days after the Roosevelt incident, for example, fifteen thousand people gathered in Madison Square Garden to hail Debs and Russell. Debs arrived late, but when he stepped to the podium thousands waved red kerchiefs, aprons, and flags, accompanied by clapping, stomping, cheering and whistling. "The effect was startling," wrote the *Times*.[13] Caught up in the moment, Russell and Debs, ostensible rivals, spontaneously hugged each other on the platform while the screaming throng cheered for twenty-nine minutes. Whatever tension had existed between the two was now gone. Russell spoke before Debs and jabbed the Progressive candidate for governor, Straus, who was the owner of Macy's department store. "You don't hear about the exploited women and children in his store," Russell charged. He suggested a torchlight parade of Straus employees, with coins jingling in their pockets to reflect their paltry salaries. Debs mocked the candidates for national office, Taft, Wilson, and Roosevelt. "Not one of them has ever had to look for a real job [or] been slugged by a capitalistic policemen," he said.[14]

The campaign was officially off and running, interrupted only slightly when the Socialist leaders all gathered in Schenectady in late October in support of the Socialist Mayor George R. Lunn, who was arrested for speaking at a rally in support of striking mill workers. Russell and others lambasted the police action and declared victory because Lunn had been quickly released. Russell went from Schenectady to Syracuse and then back to New York, emphasizing three points as the final days of the campaign approached. With the cost of living constantly going up, Americans were becoming "worse fed, worse housed, worse clothed," Russell pointed out. Stop building battle ships, he exhorted the government, "to defend ourselves against mythical foreign enemies. . . ." With World War I looming, however, he would soon change his tune on defense.[15] Next, he turned to the Morgan and Rockefeller group that he said controlled one-third of the nation's wealth. "These capitalists have practically abolished the republic. They own the government." Citizens had no chance against their colossal might. "The corporations dance on your laws and kick them full of holes," he argued. Monopolies did make sense, Russell told New Yorkers; the trust was an efficient mechanism. "The only trouble is that so far it has been privately owned and operated . . . for private greed. Now let it be owned and operated by the community and operated for the common good and the trust becomes the greatest blessing of the age." Finally, he stressed that reform and regulation would not undo the harm caused by the trusts. Capitalism must go, he declared, adding, "We have entered upon a war against this system that will never cease until we have swept it from the face of the earth."[16]

If the final days were any indication, the Socialists seemed poised—as they had in the 1910 campaign—to make a dent in the vote totals of the other parties. At an open-air rally in Manhattan's Union Square, ten thousand cheered twenty minutes for Russell before he could speak. When the crowd grew silent, he laid into Roosevelt 's "little 2–cent program of reform." "Let the working class rise" and take over the government, he told the roaring crowd.[17] The next night, with 3,000 people on hand, Russell became emotional, saying, "I would rather have one exploited worker take my hand in his hard hand and have him call me comrade than have any office on earth." Service to the world was "the only thing of any real value." The following night he told a group in Brooklyn that reform was futile. "This is something about which I ought to know. For, let me confess, I am myself a reformed reformer."[18]

On the final night of campaigning, a crowd estimated at fifteen thousand thronged the streets of the Lower East Side in Manhattan's Rutgers Square. People screamed, "Russell is coming, Russell is coming." He could hardly get through the streets. The people kept chanting. "Debs, Debs, Debs . . . Russell,

Russell, Russell." When he spoke, he told them, "We socialists are not fighting for votes or office. We are fighting to save human lives right now." Russell got in his car trying to cross the Williamsburg Bridge, but the car moved at a snail's pace as the crowds surged around it. Finally, Russell got out again near the bridge and spoke once more. "We are going to make such a dent in capitalism tomorrow," he said. Satisfied, the crowd let his car finally cross into Brooklyn. It must have been a heady evening for Russell. He insisted that Socialists did not run for office for personal gain, but the adoring crowds made him emotional and hopeful.[19] On Election Day, however, his hopes were dashed again. Republican Sulzer won with 664,488, Democrat Hedges got 448,918, Straus 380,899, and Russell 56,917. "It was a splendid fight and we have a made a splendid record," Russell observed. "Now let us go to it for the next great fight beginning today." Like a minister tending to his congregation, Russell wrote in *The Call*, "Praise socialism from which all blessings flow. " His friends, however, did not see any blessings. When Russell visited with them in Consodine's Restaurant in Manhattan after Election Day, they jeered him in a friendly way. Nobody votes for you . . . you pay your own expenses . . . you must be a lunatic, they laughingly told him, or, as he wrote in his autobiography, "the nation's incomparable dumb-bell." Nonetheless, he would do it again in less than a year.[20]

III. ONE MORE ROUND WITH THE OCTOPUS

The muckraking journalists not only made headlines with their startling and passionate exposes in the first decade of the century, they became headliners themselves in the process. When the Chautauqua tent circuit got in full gear by 1910, Lincoln Steffens, Will Irwin, and Charles Russell were among the attractions who agreed to travel around the country giving talks to audiences in cities large and small. The headliner, however, was William Jennings Bryan, the "great commoner" and erstwhile presidential candidate who consistently drew crowds of thirty thousand people a night. It was all part of the uniquely American phenomenon that started in Chautauqua, New York, in 1904 and sought to combine, as Russell pointed out, "culture and profits." The Chautauqua was a traveling tent enterprise that sent out a strange blend of inspiring and educational speakers along with entertainers, ranging from barbershop quartets to violin concertos. At its height, 30 million Americans a year attended Chautauqua evenings in twelve thousand different Main Street locations. "It is not to be denied that often the Chautauqua was a great educational factor," Russell observed in his autobiography, but nonetheless he hated the experience of being on the road, doing a talk each evening at a different provincial location. When radio invaded American homes in the 1920s, Russell said, it brought with it "much evil," but "glory be to it," he added, "for it killed the Chautauqua."[21]

Russell's problem with "being an attraction," as he called it, was that speakers often had to work a month straight, with nary a night off. They booked their own transportation, stayed in flea-bitten hotels, and tried to uplift their audience even when, as in Russell's case, their message was gloomy and foreboding. In one letter to Julia Marlowe, he complained that the Chautauqua was taking so much time and that he was longing for the baths of Carlsbad. Who could blame him? While it might have represented "the parliament of the people" and brought culture and enlightenment to the provinces, the tour was also backbreaking. On summer nights the tents were like a Turkish bath and a furnace combined. The audiences, often coming in from farms, could be at times hostile to the speakers, especially ones who preached Socialism, which Russell said they saw in the same category as smallpox or hog cholera.[22]

Nonetheless, Russell went on the road each spring, summer, and fall to tell audiences about the danger of what the Socialists call "the unconsumed surplus," a topic that must have been almost unintelligible to his audience. It had to do, in short, with the fact that scarcity and poverty were common in America on one hand, and yet great wealth and a surplus of goods existed on the other. The people needed access to that unconsumed surplus. When Russell concluded his warning, he was often followed by John Wesley Hill, a powerful orator who would always ask that Russell produce the surplus on the spot and allow the audience to consume it. "This invariably brought down the house and erased my feeble efforts," Russell said.[23] But, oddly, that did not seem to bother Russell as much as the bad food and long hours.

What is strange about this episode in Russell's career is that someone so passionate about the issues would allow himself to be part of what was often a traveling sideshow, the Progressive Era equivalent of a television crossfire of competing ideologies. The Chautauqua, was, in fact, a sizable industry and popular entertainment in an era before radio and television. It was a bit like a Pulitzer or Hearst newspaper, a combination of facts, entertainment, and vaudeville, both exciting and educational. And Russell was still willing to go along with this combination and laugh at himself a bit as he did it. He probably needed the money and liked the earnest folks who he met. For those folks, meeting and greeting the "talent," as they were called—the likes of Warren G. Harding, Walter Lippmann, Herbert Hoover, and Edna Ferber—was a thrill. Most importantly, however, Chautauqua was critical in stimulating thought and discussion on important political, social, and cultural issues of the day.[24]

Despite the diversion of Chautauqua, however, Russell's heart was still more focused on enlightening the public to the great threat to American values—an invisible cartel of monopolists who were grabbing control of the economy and democracy. This was his passion in the years from 1912 to 1915; it can be seen consistently in his writings, lectures, and especially in his run for the mayor of New York City in 1913. The obsession began in earnest when he wrote his 1904 beef -trust articles labeling the meat packers as "the power." Two years later, probing the insurance industry, he glimpsed "a very strange and subtle power that pulled unseen strings, exerted mysterious influences, compelled men to do its bidding."[25] When he joined the Socialist Party in 1908 he pointed to "a power seldom seen but always at work, much stronger and more subtle than any government, a power that we usually recognize by the name of the Financial Interests." As Russell elaborated more and more on this "mysterious octopus," he began to point to what he saw as its center—either J. P. Morgan, the Wall Street banker said to control the "banking trust," or John D. Rockefeller, whose Standard Oil tentacles seemed to wrap around every industry. His weekly column in the *Coming Nation* repeatedly cited the "the secret, malignant" power of a money trust controlled by "the Morgan gang."[26] "In the history of the world," Russell warned, "there was never a power to be compared with [them] . . . absolute, irresponsible, autocratic"[27]

How Russell believed these "Central Interests" worked secretly to get their way could be seen in his three-part series of articles in *Hearst's Magazine* in 1911. Turning away from the railroad owners, Russell focused his reporting on Frederick Weyerhaeuser, the timber king of America who owned 10 percent of the nation's forests. What was so different about the lumber industry, Russell found, was that no central force directing the timber owners could be detected. Nonetheless, Russell found "back of all the schemes were the vast Weyerhaeuser and allied Interests" in a loose but clear alliance that controlled four-fifths of America's lumbering, "pursuing a policy as definite as Standard Oil." Russell said this "remarkable" new development in the trust evolution made it impossible for the anti-trust prosecutors to bring Weyerhaeuser to court.[28] This, of course, also confirmed his persistent belief that oversight of industry was futile, "like a dog chasing its tail." Reform "may afford some harmless amusement to the spectators, but it never gets anywhere," Russell tartly commented. As for the Sherman Anti-Trust Act, he asserted that it was used by the corporations to "fatten and bulwark themselves" and to "confirm and strengthen their hold upon the country."[29] As he had done in his study of the railroads, Russell reached his conclusions by carefully tracing the history of the lumber industry and finding that its founders had a "burning frenzy to get rich, animal-like and irrational." He observed: "Any conception of pioneer heroics fades instantly upon a close examination of [this] sordid and filthy story."

Russell's reporting is impressive, a detailed behind-the-scenes look at an industry that had gotten little attention, coming also at a time when most of the muckrakers had turned to other pursuits. While Hearst's *Cosmopolitan* magazine had pointed a finger at Weyerhaeuser's influence in 1907, the attack of the muckrakers on the lumber moguls had, as one historian points out, "a popgun quality in sharp contrast with the howitzer bombardments that roared against the Harrimans, Rockefellers, Carnegies, and Morgans. Indeed, the entire lumber industry escaped lightly."[30] Russell tried to correct that as he put aside his socialist rhetoric to return to reporting, even though his themes were reminiscent of his railroad series and repeated what he was saying in public speeches. Using documents and a variety of sources, Russell pointed repeatedly to a "sinister power" that made great profits by passing along costs to the public. Speaking for the ignored consumer, he asked, "Where do we come in?"[31] The problem with Russell's articles, however, was that he missed the real story—and failed in his effort to transform the timber industry. Throughout the Gilded Age, the lumber companies had neutered forests from Minnesota to New York's Adirondacks. From 1880 to 1900 America's population increased 52 percent while its lumber cutting rose 94 percent; Americans used 400 feet of lumber per person while Europeans used only 60 feet apiece. Consumption was out of control, but Russell, who knew Europe so well, missed this fact. Moreover, he also overlooked how scientists, government officials, and lumber industry leaders—all aware of the problem of deforestation—were studying conservation and forest management techniques. In 1911 the Weeks Act was passed by Congress to facilitate the purchases of woodland tracts by the federal government, a good start in the creation of National Forests. In fact, a working alliance that would soon solve the problem of overcutting of forests was developing, with Weyerhaeuser an active and willing participant. But Russell was so stuck on the corporations as big, bad, and evil—"sinister" was the word he used repeatedly—that he could not see the forest for the trees: a progressive coalition was possible and emerging, and it needed a progressive publicist to encourage its development. America did not need socialism to regulate this industry. In his prison series only two years earlier, Russell was willing to hitch his articles to progressive reformers, but now he was less flexible.[32]

When Russell's articles on the lumber trust were completed, he made plans to travel again to Europe. His popularity with the Socialists was stronger than ever. The newspaper *The Masses* held a giant rally on May 27 in Carnegie Hall in honor of "Mother Jones," the Irish-born radical labor leader, eighty-three years old, who had just been arrested for organizing mine workers in Colorado. Max Eastman, the *Masses'* editor, was trying to spur the Socialists to more activism, and Mother Jones was the perfect model of consistent and insistent activism. Russell joined her onstage to give the keynote speech. He was met enthusiastically by the crowd, and he "held the vast audience in the grip of his eloquence," reported *The Call*.

The Socialists turned to Russell to be their mayoral candidate, which he accepted, although he informed the party that he would not return from Europe until late September. When he returned, he debarked from the *Princess Irene* on September 25 to find reporters waiting. "From all that I have been able to learn," Russell said, "the Socialists are in a better position than they have ever been in a New York City campaign."[33] Russell, too, was in his best position to make a run for elected office. He knew New York City intimately from his years as reporter and editor; the Socialists' strongest base of support was in the city's immigrant quarters, especially Manhattan; and municipal elections were the only ones Socialists had won, for example, in Schenectady and Milwaukee. Russell wasted no time in laying out his themes and going on the attack against thirty-four-year-old John Purroy Mitchell, who represented reformers in the Fusion Party, and Edward E. McCall, forty nine, the Democrat who was Tammany Hall's choice. Russell probably would not have run for mayor if the incumbent, William Gaynor, shot in the throat in 1910 by a disgruntled city employee, had been able to run. In his days crusading for reform in Brooklyn, Russell had portrayed Gaynor as a force for righteousness. It would have been difficult to oppose him, although Russell had come a long way in twenty years. Clean government and good people to run government were hardly the issue. The real concern, he decided, was the "invisible government" that controlled New York City and was trying to put its handpicked candidate—Mitchell—into office. It is the "Ryan-Belmont-Wall Street combine" that is the "real power" in the city, he said.[34] Thomas F. Ryan, the owner of a slew of franchises for city rail lines, and August Belmont, a financier and city power broker, took the place of Rockefeller and Morgan in what Russell called the "secret and intangible influences" that directed the government, perverted court decisions, and silenced the press. Standing before a crowd of 12,500 at the Hippodrome Theatre in Manhattan, Russell cited the "Central Financial Powers" who manipulated their politicians like puppets and operated a "Government of Strings." Only the Socialists, he roared, could make true changes. "The reform movement," he said, "known variously as Fusion, Con-fusion, Fusion-con" was a joke. If they won, Russell noted, it would be only because "they are financed by the millionaires."[35]

Russell could not, of course, really have believed the Socialists had a chance to win the mayor's race of 1913. Despite the gains the movement had made, it was still an under-financed blip-on-the-screen political party, largely misunderstood and often considerably distrusted by the public. In the winter of 1913 Russell suggested that the battle to beat capitalism had entered a "new and probably last stage of the conflict," but nonetheless he could offer no clues as to how the change to socialism would take place—or how the Socialists could make it occur. That same vagueness permeated his mayoral campaign. Despite his knowledge of New York issues and despite the fact that he kept assuring his audience, "We offer you the adequate and exact remedy for every evil that besets the city," he never offered specific plans. He ignored the detailed platform that the socialists had adopted in May when Russell was nominated. In fact, more often than not, Russell sounded like any other politician, offering platitudes.[36] He complained about police corruption, while at the same time he lionized police officers he had known who were heroic and brave. He lamented the decline of the public school system, said it was headed for "extinction," and then offered the obvious: "The public school system is one of the foundations of any republic." He argued that more money was needed for school construction, but he did not say where the money would come from, except to charge that if Belmont and Ryan were not stealing so much, the taxpayers would have more to spend. Russell's solutions to the problems the city faced—population congestion, failing transportation facilities, neglected streets, increasing crime, inadequate health care—called for more money and an enlarged government, solutions that befitted a Progressive as much as a Socialist.[37]

Russell would have balked at any suggestion that his reform goals had anything in common with the other candidates. In fact, a key point of his campaign was mocking the reformers.

"No matter which man wins, the man behind the curtain will still hold the puppets and manipulates them as he pleases," he said.[38] Only the Socialists could cure what ailed New York, he insisted, and he pointed to the bitter fight in the state capitol of Albany that played itself out during the campaign. William Sulzer, the Tammany Hall Democrat who defeated Russell a year earlier, was impeached. His crime—taking bribes before he was ever elected to office—had been exposed by Tammany Hall partisans who were upset that Sulzer, when elected, refused to go along with Tammany chief Murphy's constant demands. In an unprecedented public spectacle, Sulzer was removed from office, which so split the Tammany Hall vote that the Fusion candidate Mitchell swept into office. Even Sulzer, once ousted, stumped for Mitchell as a way of retaliating against Tammany Hall.[39] Russell saw it all as confirmation of his grand theory of a conspiracy. Sulzer's sin was his refusal to go along with the demands of Wall Street. "If he had never antagonized the Financial Powers," Russell wrote, "he would be sitting this day in the office of Governor." But come Election Day, Sulzer was on the sidelines, as was Russell, who garnered 32,000 votes. Mitchell became the city's "boy mayor," sweeping into office with the greatest plurality in the city's history.[40] Russell told the voters what he saw as the hard lesson of the election. "You have turned out of office a set of men marked Tammany and turned into office a set of men marked Fusion." But in the end, "not one of your present hardships will be lessened." Reform, he wrote, was a "Hollow Mockery and Sham."[41] Despite his continuing pessimism about capitalism and the chances for progressive change, Russell should have been encouraged. He increased the Socialist mayoral vote by 200 percent. Maybe Socialism was gaining. Unfortunately, with dark war clouds on the horizon, the advances of both Socialism and Progressivism were soon to be halted.

CHAPTER FOURTEEN

THE AMATEUR DIPLOMAT

I. RECLAIMING HEROES AND FACTS

WITH THE MAYORAL ELECTION BEHIND HIM, the fifty-three-year-old Charles Edward Russell plunged into various new projects, most notably the writing of a biography of Wendell Phillips, the abolitionist reformer from Boston who was his lifelong hero. This was the second of eight biographies that Russell wrote. Coming from a family that had been actively engaged in fighting slavery, Russell would know about and admire Phillips. In fact, many of the positions Russell took in his life resembled those of Phillips, who died in 1880 after a long and distinguished life as a powerful orator. Phillips came to prominence after a speech in Boston's Faneuil Hall in 1835 following the assassination of abolitionist editor Elijah P. Lovejoy. He was unrestrained in his criticism of slaveholding and of Abraham Lincoln's moderate views on the emancipation of slaves. Moreover, it was not enough for Phillips that slaves be freed; he insisted that the government owed blacks land, education, and full civil rights, the radical position Russell espoused in his work for the NAACP. Even after slavery was abolished, Phillips found new unpopular social reform causes to support, just as Russell did throughout his life.[1] Phillips fought for women's suffrage, the abolition of capital punishment, and the rights of labor well before there were unions to protect workers. Perhaps most telling was Russell's admiration for the fact that Phillips adopted positions that were indistinguishable from socialism. It was that allegiance to a non-competitive system that, in Russell's view, made historians forget Phillips. "He championed the cause of labor, he made war upon the wage system . . . and for this reason alone his name is slighted and his services forgotten," Russell charged. To Russell, Phillips was a neglected and ignored American hero who needed to be reclaimed. Unfortunately, no mainstream publisher agreed, and *The Story of Wendell Phillips: soldier of the common good,* was put out in 1914 by the socialist publisher C. H. Kerr in Chicago. Nary a book review of Russell's works appeared, and it took 44 years before another biography of Phillips came out.[2]

But the second project that was engaging Russell's attention had greater potential to attract an audience. He was nearing completion of his first autobiography, entitled *These Shifting Scenes,* which was a whimsical mix of growing-up-in-Iowa tales and adventures in the news business.[3] He recalled the offbeat characters that he encountered in his father's newsroom, told the tale of the Johnstown flood, and described the gruesome sight of the first hanging he witnessed as a reporter. One reviewer called the book "a collection of 'stories' such as will not be found in any newspaper [coming from] the most alert and imaginative reporter's pen." Another reviewer complained, rightly, that Russell was long-winded and that he made "two words do the duty of one."[4] Nonetheless, the reviewer concluded, Russell's "romantic fascination" with journalism made the book worthwhile. The book ends at the turn of the century with Russell romanticizing his days in Joseph Pulitzer's newsroom but inexplicably ignores any mention of his years working for William Randolph Hearst. It stops well before his nervous breakdown, his muckraking crusades, and his turn to political activism.[5] Politics and social issues take a backseat to his narrative of the first part of his life and career, the journalism years that he knew were now over forever. This book was meant to be fun for a reading public that had seen his name in headlines for nearly a decade.

If readers wanted Russell's political voice, they would have to turn to a third book that he brought out in 1914, again for Kerr, *Doing Us Good and Plenty.*[6] The two years he spent writing weekly sarcastic and scorching columns of criticism of capitalism and the establishment in the *Coming Nation,* seen only by those in the Socialist reading community, were collected in this edition, but much of it already seemed dated—as well as overly polemical—when the book appeared.

Alongside his book projects, Russell continued reporting in his new outlet, *Pearson's* magazine, which gave him great freedom to make his argument that reform was folly and that the tentacles of the Morgan cabal extended everywhere. Originally an English monthly, *Pearson's* started publishing in America in 1901. By 1904, as it began muckraking, its circulation went as high as 250,000, but it could not compete with the larger and more effective monthlies such as *McClure's*, *Everybody's* and *Cosmopolitan*. Nonetheless, editor Arthur W. Little, the son of the publisher, kept trying. At a time when Russell was warning the nation of the attempts by banker J. P. Morgan to swallow up the magazines, Little scoffed at this idea, saying: "Mr. Morgan's partner has not been to see me with a proposition for the purchase of *Pearson's*, and I am not expecting this."[7]

Assured that *Pearson's* would not be swallowed up by the corporations, Russell went to work for the magazine as part-time editor and freelance writer. He used *Pearson's* to continue his assault on America's railroad companies with three articles just before the mayoral campaign of 1913. Then in the fall of 1913 he turned to what he saw as the next great threat to American democracy: the takeover of the nation's news media, which, except for Will Irwin's 1911 exposé of the press in *Collier's*, had escaped scrutiny. Like most Progressives, Russell had profound faith in public opinion. "Nothing helps a bad situation so much as some good competent X-raying," he observed. "To right any wrong in the United States is, after all, a simple process. You only have to exhibit it where all the people can see it plainly."[8]

The problem in America, as Russell saw it, was that the "Controlling Interests" were making it impossible for the true facts to surface. Russell had long given up on the newspaper as the "tribune of the populace." Once, around the turn of the century, "it lay bare what was wrong, pilloried malelfalctors, [and] indicated improvements" but now "the real editors are the advertisers. And back of them are the Central Financial Interests."[9] Such a view was greatly exaggerated, of course. Advertisers had certainly changed the face of the newspaper and did influence news decisions at various times.[10]

To assert that the advertiser ruled the newspaper reflected a paranoia that could not be backed up by facts, but it was consistent with Russell's obsession with a dark and mysterious force that was turning democracy into plutocracy. "How can we have an enlightened public opinion," he wondered, "when the public is not allowed to know what is going on in this country?"[11] Equally worrisome to Russell was the power of the Associated Press, the newsgathering agency that took its name at the turn of the century and had grown quickly to provide information and facts to hundreds of newspapers. Often, in smaller newspapers, the only view of the outside world came from the AP. Describing the AP as "an engine that causes 30,000,000 minds to have the same thought at the same moment," Russell argued it could not be trusted to give the truth.[12] To document how the AP was misrepresenting news events, Russell went to the scene of a labor disturbance in the Calumet region of upper Michigan, where seventy-two copper miners, their wives, and children had died in a community center in late December. The deaths occurred during the fifth month of a strike when, with sheriff's deputies blocking exits from the town center, someone yelled fire and in the ensuing panic a stampede killed the workers who had gathered for a Christmas celebration.

Why, Russell wondered, did the country know so little of this? He pointed the finger of blame at the Associated Press, which he found simply did not report accurately what happened. Russell, the meticulous investigator, did his own research, which he printed side by side with the AP account. He called his version "fact."[13] His point was made with a question: "Are there any limits . . . to the actual power of the Controlling Interests?" The AP was a tool for corporate interests, not the people. And the only vehicle left to get out the truth, the magazine, was being gobbled up by the big corporations. In three subsequent articles on "the kept press," Russell tried to show how advertisers and interlocking corporate ownerships made it unlikely that facts that damaged the establishment would ever surface. Russell's articles were smooth, well argued, and well ahead of the time, but they contained few of the "facts" that had made the Calumet article so much more effective. Rhetoric and Russell's obsession with the might of a centralized corporate force took precedence over his normal fidelity to evidence.[14]

II. WAR IS INSANITY

When winter of 1914 ended, Russell went back on the Chautauqua speaker's circuit, pointing still to the need for the public to take over the big corporations. "There is but one way to peace and justice and that is through the cooperative commonwealth," he continued to tell audiences. Russell also showed a new intolerance of modern industrialism as he mocked the fashion industry and pointed to how it attempts "by one childish device after another, to compel the small percentage of the population that has purchasing power to buy things that they do not need." The people owning the trusts, Russell insisted, was the only way to end "the present insane system."[15] President Woodrow Wilson came in for special criticism for telling the public that the "trust" problem had been solved in America. Candidate Wilson was a "roaring champion of the people against the robbers," but once elected, Russell argued, he "turned his back so he could not see the robbers at work," acting as if "the trusts had become good, the octopus had turned angel, the monster had become as a little child."[16] Wilson's foreign policy was also misguided, Russell declared in an angry speech in April, a speech with special significance as war loomed in Europe. When Wilson became President he inherited a troubling situation in

Mexico. In 1911 General Victoriano Huerta had deposed and murdered Francisco I. Madero, who in turn had overthrown the democratically elected Porfirio Diaz. The Wilson Administration had not recognized Huerta's government, although the United States had a policy of extending de facto recognition to revolutionary governments. Wilson saw Huerta as a military usurper and was revolted by the bloody means he had used. Relations, already tense, were worsened when on April 10 the crew of an American naval vessel was arrested after it docked without permission at Tampico. The crew was quickly released with an apology, but Wilson saw it as an opportunity to move against Huerta and hasten his downfall. He received congressional approval to send troops to Veracruz, where a shipment of ammunition from the Germans was to be received. In a bloody battle on April 22, twenty-six Mexicans and nineteen Americans were killed. The American public was dazed, and Russell was indignant. "I want to love the land wherein I was born," he told an audience on April 27. "And I want to honor the flag that floats over it. But I want that flag to stand for liberty, justice, democracy and the rights of the people." The Mexican intervention, Russell alleged, was made to satisfy the American oil companies and "when a nation should turn international bandit and make the streets of an undefended city run with blood, then the flag of that nation is nothing but a filthy rag." After calling Wilson a "jingo," Russell added, "If I should be drafted I would refuse to serve."[17] Of course, this was an almost comical threat since as a fifty-four-year-old with a number of health problems, Russell was hardly a prime candidate to fight a war. Moreover, his claim that the oil interests were behind the intervention was off base. The oil companies actually wanted Wilson to recognize Huerta because he represented a stable market. More important, however, was Russell's intimation that he would not adhere to what was long the socialists' adamant position against all wars. A just war—that Russell could support.

On July 28, 1914, after a busy year working on three books, various magazine articles, and touring on the Chautauqua and Socialist lecture circuits, Charles and Theresa set sail from Hoboken, New Jersey, for Rotterdam in the Netherlands, marking his twelfth visit to Holland.[18] Russell was to be a delegate at the International Socialist Congress to be held in Brussels on August 22, the first such conference since 1907; when it was over he would get some needed rest and relaxation. But on June 28 Archduke Francis Ferdinand, heir to the Austria-Hungary throne, was killed in Sarajevo, and war clouds began rumbling over Europe. Despite the widespread belief that enlightened countries and modern governments would not go to war, Russell believed otherwise. In fact, the previous fall, when he returned from Europe, he had tried to convince editors to allow him to write magazine articles about a coming war in Europe. "They laughed me to scorn," he later recalled. "It was my only chance to appear as a prophet and I muffed it."[19]

As he sat in his cabin on the trip to Europe, Russell began to harken back to all the years he had visited Germany and to how much he had grown to admire the Germans. "I know them well, esteem their good traits, like to visit their country," he later wrote. But for as long as he could recollect, Germany had "thought war, dreamed war, sung war, dined upon war, lived with and clove to the image of war." He remembered sitting near the Rhine River in 1898, watching the German army march by. "What a sight," he recalled. Miles of marching men, like machines, in step, identical motion, no deviation, no weakness, perfect coordination. "Nothing missing," he said, "except a black cloud of smoke ahead for a conquered town." A year later in Heidelberg, on a perfect Sunday, he watched civilians cower as army officers passed. The following year he watched the cowering of the soldiers themselves as they deferred meekly to their own officers. Once in 1902, while at the baths in Carlsbad, he observed an officer knock over three old women and never even stop to help them recover.[20]

As early as 1906, when he returned from his worldwide trip, Russell had warned publicly about the "Germanizing of the world." He wrote in *Cosmopolitan* about a "new gothic invasion" by a "persistent, tireless, indefatigable" German nation seeking to spread its commercial tentacles. He hinted that it was eyeing both of its small neighbors, Netherlands and Belgium, spurred by a government that was "urging, encouraging, advising, pushing." The only question was when Germany would make its move, Russell warned. "To study, to wait and at the right moment to move with intelligence and gathered resources," that is Germany's plan. Only socialism, which preached that "dominion and aggrandizement are not the chief end of man," could stop the Germans. Or so he believed in 1906.[21]

As his steamship approached Europe, Russell recalled other ominous signs; how in 1908, he entered a restaurant only to be confronted with a sign: "Jews not allowed." It was not clear if his wife, Theresa Hirschl, who was Jewish, was with him. He then went over in his mind what he had seen on a small South Seas island on visits in 1905 and 1911 when the Germans had taken over the island. The natives, once happy and smiling, no longer danced and were presided over by military officers with guns. What was once one of the happiest spots on earth, he thought, is now "one of the most wretched and sorrowful. "[22]

As Russell's ship approached Europe, it was boarded by a French naval vessel, which he knew was very unusual. The French intimated that war was at hand, which was no surprise to Russell. The previous year, while he was on holiday in Carlsbad, he noted how "the air was tense, nervous, and charged with electric expectation. I had never seen the like there. All the talk was about the war." Pan-Germanic literature was everywhere, urging the creation of a German empire. "The thing that had been surmised about and dreaded for thirty years was about to burst upon us," he knew. On August 3, days before he landed, news came over the wireless radio that war between France and Germany had been declared. Germany had invaded tiny Belgium, just south of the Netherlands. Russell asked in his diary, which he began to keep on regular basis: "Will there be any France when all this is done? Never thought before of a world without France." He worried most about the "terrible, unequaled, unapproached German war machine." As passengers listened to the news on August 5 that England had declared war on Germany, a Wall Street financier on board commented that the United States would never allow England and France to be crushed. "I wonder," Russell wrote.[23] On August 7, France invaded Alsace Lorraine. A day later Wilson declared American neutrality in the conflict, prompting Russell to ponder how anyone would remain neutral in this war. "Only neutrals are in the cemetery. For the living it's one side or the other," he observed in his diary. But what side to take? That was the momentous question that Russell was about to face. The Socialist Party had consistently opposed war for many years as the product of competition, capitalism, and imperialism. All wars were fought for markets, and nothing else. Workers had no stake in fighting wars, and they should always oppose them at all costs. Every war was a rich man's war, but a poor man's fight, wrote Socialist Oscar Ameringer, who along with Meyer London, Emil Seidel, Victor Berger, and Morris Hillquit, were to attend the international congress with Russell.[24] You could not belong to the Socialist Party and support the capitalists' wars. In 1914, at least, Russell embraced the Socialist position that the search for "commercial supremacy" was always the cause of war which is "only competition carried to its logical limits."[25]

Such a simplistic position, however, left out the possibility that nationalism, old rivalries over borders, and oppressed ethnic minorities were as important in Europe as economics. But for now Russell adhered to the party line.[26] Russell got off his steamer and he was hit square in the face with the first chaos of what he called "the insane war dance . . . the lunatic business of war." Because of the fighting, the socialist congress was postponed. More devastating were the first reports of those fleeing Belgium. Russell must have thought back to arriving at the Johnstown flood when he was told he would not believe what he would soon see. Except this would be much worse. By the end of the first year of the war two million were dead. In the face of such devastation, could he and should he remain neutral?[27]

When the Russells' hotel room proved too expensive, they looked for another and saw signs of chaos everywhere. "I have not known a tenser atmosphere," Russell said. Thinking they were British, some restaurants would not
take his money and waiters would not serve the Russells. The Dutch still resented the Brits for their part in the Boer War, and many seemed to support
Germany, a stance that would fade, of course, when Germany overran the
Netherlands. One man, whom Russell did not know, approached him and declared that the result of the war would be socialism throughout Europe. Russell
suspected he was a spy, a suspicion that proved true. Once, while looking in the
window of a store, a man sidled up to Russell, saying he was an American who
had German parents. He wanted to get back home, he said in an accent that
Russell felt could only have been learned in a German gymnasium. Russell listened and then asked, "Where did you live in the United States?" The man
replied, "In Wisconsin." And where, Russell asked, is Wisconsin? "It's in Milwaukee," the man replied. Russell wished him good morning and went on,
knowing he had just had a conversation with a German spy probably trying to
find what he could from the famous American socialist.[28]

Russell found the Dutch resolute in the face of the war reports. There was
no sensationalism in the press, no panic in the streets, no harsh words, but people
were tense, grave, and hushed as they went about their business. Sympathy began
to turn against Germany as Belgians began arriving after having walked miles
lugging suitcases. Many told horror stories. One woman, a famous opera singer,
whom Russell did not name, told of being detained with her husband, strip
searched four times, and paraded in front of German officers. "All Europe is
crazy . . . mad as a hatter," Russell concluded. When he learned that hundreds of
refugees were besieging the American embassy in the Hague and seeking help,
Russell went there and offered aid to the ambassador, Henry Van Dyke. But Van
Dyke saw Russell as a "detested socialist," as Russell put it, and declined his offer.
A few days later, Theresa visited the embassy and convinced the Ambassador that
she and Charles were respectable citizens whose volunteer work could help the
overwhelmed embassy. He accepted her offer and Russell, with Corona cigar in
hand, reported for work the next day at what he called "the switchboard of Europe." It was the beginning of his career as an "amateur diplomat."[29]

Since Russell could read Dutch, he took over the task of translating dozens
of telegrams and letters at the embassy from those seeking to find relatives and
friends in France, Germany, and England. Two Wall Street lawyers and Van
Dyke's son also had volunteered; all were kept busy with a steady stream of ex-
asperated Dutch, French, English, and American citizens. Many fleeing Belgium had no clothing, others were without money while some simply had lost

relatives and spouses. After about two weeks, reports of the Germans abusing noncombatants began to wane. Russell believed that the Germans, acutely aware of public opinion, had made clear to their troops that they needed to behave better. The Germans even began to inquire if they could compensate victims. "Somebody in the mad dance of nations had experienced a lucid interval," he observed. "They may be mad in Berlin but they are not stupid," he wrote in his diary.[30] But Van Dyke, privy to more information than Russell, was privately warning President Wilson that Germany was "waging this war with a purpose of making Terror her ally." The war, as he was learning from eyewitnesses, "has been marked by great atrocities." Meanwhile, in the embassy, the Germans were trying to cull information with their spies. Late in August a man came to Russell's desk to inquire about his daughter who he believed was near the border. As he sobbed on Russell's shoulder, he inquired about the border situation. Van Dyke signaled Russell that the man was a known spy. "I got rid of him as soon as I could," Russell said. "It was a clumsy performance."[31]

Russell tried to go about his life normally, but when he visited the coastal resort town of Schnevigan, which usually bustled, he found it deserted. He noted, "Never have I seen anything more melancholy." Once he was inexplicably detained while on a train, but was released shortly after. "There is no sense to a hundred things we see about us," he remarked. A few days later the conservative New York newspaper and magazine publisher Frank Munsey visited Russell, one of a steady stream of journalism luminaries who would stop by to see him in Europe during the war years. Meanwhile, Russell's publisher, Kerr, was pressing him to submit his final manuscript on Wendell Phillips. His diplomatic work had put him behind schedule. Russell knew that he would have to travel to England to do library work to finish research and writing. He began reluctantly to plan his exit. His diary entry on September 3 noted: "Not very happy to go because work has been interesting and was glad to feel myself of some slight use." A few days later: "It has been a really inspiring time. And odd thing is that while we worked for nothing, we worked hard." In his autobiography years later he elaborated, writing: "Every emergency proves that men will do for service that they will never do for hire. . . . The greatest of all incentives is . . . merely the joy of being of use."[32]

III. "Is there nothing to stop them?"

In England, Russell worked mornings at the British Museum but spent the rest of the day observing how the Brits were responding to war. What he saw led only to "drooping spirits." The Brits' "extraordinary lack of interest in the war" and downright hostility led him to quip, "goodnight to the Empire." Even as the body counts mounted, he found the English bored. Worse were the British troops—"dwarfs and scarecrows," he called them, a conclusion he reached on September 10 as he watched the Prince of Wales lead a group of soldiers on a public march. "The Prince!" someone yelled as the crowd cast reverential looks at a white-haired, smallish man who walked with a limp from blistered feet and looked about fifteen years old. With his cap falling awkwardly over his ears and his rifle causing his shoulders to slump, he appeared to Russell "highly grotesque and unprincely." The Prince was a "most uninspiring figure," Russell concluded, but, unfortunately, he was a man who typified the British troops.[33]

Russell was not only glum but increasingly bewildered by the war. Walking in an English garden on September 14, he observed: "Crazy is this race to fight when it might grow flowers." On September 25 he celebrated his fifty-fourth birthday quietly by drinking a bottle of Australian burgundy. A few days later, as the Germans pushed further into Belgium, Russell's concern mounted. "Is there nothing to stop them?" he asked. "I was never able to believe that the world was destined to slip back into the autocratic theory of government and civilization after all these centuries of sacrifices and martyrs, but I am beginning to think so now."[34]

By late September Russell was ready to head back to the United States with Theresa, but not before he stirred a bit more of controversy. While publicly he adhered to the Socialists' antiwar stance, privately he showed very mixed feelings. On the one hand, he said, "if we don't like war why don't we abolish the thing that makes war"—that is, capitalism. On the other hand, he would not endorse America's neutrality. "When war is forced upon us by an enemy whose principles are absolutely false to liberty and the hope of democracy . . . then we must fight," he wrote in his diary, a harbinger of things to come. Russell shared these private thoughts about the need to support war against Germany with British Socialist Henry M. Hyndman, who also favored the war. He wrote Hyndman a long letter, which, to Russell's surprise, Hyndman sent to the *London Telegraph* for publication. When the letter made its way back to the States, the comments caused great consternation among the American Socialists. "What a nine weeks," Russell commented as he prepared to set sail, return home and to run, once again, as a Socialist candidate for elected office, this time for the U.S. Senate from New York.[35]

Russell's run for the Senate in 1914 was hardly a run at all. No one—including candidate Russell—paid it much attention. The mass rallies and throngs of adoring crowds that marked his previous efforts never materialized. The *New York Times*, which had been so respectful in past elections, hardly mentioned him. Even the *New York Call*, the Socialists' daily newspaper, made no reference to Russell's campaign. And when he did campaign, Russell was more likely to talk about the war in Europe than New York issues or his opponents, Republican James W. Wadsworth, Jr. and Democrat James W. Gerard, the U.S. ambassador to Germany. There are a number of explanations for this. First was the obvious fact that war in Europe had begun to dominate Russell's thinking and that of America, although it was ostensibly neutral. Russell left Europe reluctantly, unhappy that he had to return for another losing effort in a political campaign; his heart was still in the American embassy in Holland. Second, by most accounts, Socialism's heyday had passed. Russell would not admit this, nor would the party's hierarchy, but nearly a decade of exposés and the resulting Progressive reforms had taken some of the wind out of the Socialist sails. Perhaps he had also tired of losing and seeing few gains among the socialists. Russell was also beginning to chafe at the rigidity and inflexibility of the socialists on many issues but especially on the war. His letter in the *London Telegraph* eroded some of his support in New York. His public pronouncements that Germany's brutal "savagery" in prosecuting the early parts of the war and his criticism of the kaiser likely lost him German American votes, a key part of the Socialist constituency in New York City. Russell also split with the party on tactics; he wanted to blame the war on capitalism's lust for profit and markets, but he also wanted to especially criticize German behavior as beyond excuse. The party told Russell not to do this, and he went along—for a while. In mid-October, at the biggest rally of the campaign at New York City's Carnegie Hall, Russell blamed the war in Europe on "the system" that was "more powerful than kings or Kaisers." The search for foreign markets, he declared, had driven both Germany and England to war. The only solution to war was Socialism— "the taking over [of] producing machinery for the benefit of the people."[36]

Russell did take a few effective jabs at his opponents, especially Gerard who he claimed was callous and inept in his handling of the problems of Americans trapped in Europe at the start of war. He said Gerard's work compared unfavorably with his own in Holland. More biting was Russell's allegation that Gerard's appointment at ambassador was his reward for a $115,000 campaign contribution to the Democratic Party. Publicly at least the Socialists were hopeful of making gains, predicting that they would win 20,000 more votes than Russell had garnered in the governor's race two years earlier.[37] The 1914 Senate race was also the first time that the people could actually directly vote for the Senate seat, thanks to the Seventeenth Amendment to the Constitution. Ironically, it was Russell's best friend, David Graham Phillips, whose 1906 articles had so powerfully made the argument for direct elections that was finally adopted in 1913. But the people did not choose Russell or Socialism. In fact, he received slightly fewer votes—a total of 55,266—than he had in running for governor. Wadsworth squeaked out victory over Gerard while the Progressive Party candidate received about 1,000 more votes than Russell did. It was Russell's last try at political office, although he probably did not know that in 1914. His name was still mentioned frequently as the likely nominee of the Socialists for the presidency in 1916, mostly because Eugene V. Debs had said he would not run again. War in Europe and Russell's emerging position on the war would intervene, however, and lead to a fractious and bitter fight between Russell and the political party that had not too long ago made him feel as if he had finally found a home. Now, as he had done throughout his life—leaving friendly Davenport for bigger Midwestern cities, leaving the Midwest to confront New York, leaving both Pulitzer and Hearst for the challenges of muckraking; and leaving muckraking to embrace the religion of Socialism—Russell prepared to break again with the comforts of his Socialist Party home.[38]

CHAPTER FIFTEEN

AT WAR WITH
HIS PARTY—AND GERMANY

I. WAR, LUNATICS, AND DEGENERATES

WHILE PLAYING AMATEUR DIPLOMAT in Holland in 1914, Charles Edward Russell, the inveterate tourist, traveler, and reporter, one day slipped across the border into the small Belgium town of Herve, a quaint, picturesque village of crooked streets and queer old houses. Nearby fields were green with beets and yellow with wheat, as in a Millet painting. Three weeks later Russell returned to the village after the Germans had invaded. Nearly all of the town's 500 houses had been destroyed; most of the inhabitants were dead. He found one elderly couple, insane, "mumbling and muttering" as they overturned dead bodies. The wheat fields were strewn with severed heads, arms, and legs. He saw three heads split open by sabers, the brains splattered about. A stream ran red with blood. Russell described the stench as "intolerable," far worse than he had encountered in the tenements of Trinity Church. "Atrocity is as much a part of war as bullets," Russell knew, but the German atrocities seemed by far worse than anything the Allies had done.[1] If only Woodrow Wilson, who was adamant about maintaining strict American neutrality in the European conflict, would listen and allow America to enter the war.

Americans were dumbfounded by and unprepared for the war in Europe. For more than a decade, reform of the economy and politics and the drive for social justice had taken center stage. Progressives, including Wilson, were bent on perfecting the world, and many of the most important reforms of the era were close to fruition. War could not be allowed to undermine the forward movement.[2] Consequently, European politics barely registered for Americans, who knew little of the issues that had so roiled the continent. Wilson agreed with Progressives and Socialists on the war's causes and on the need to remain neutral, at least at war's outset. The nationalism of the Austro-Hungarian Empire, Russia's need for access to the Mediterranean, France's desire to recover Alsace Lorraine, Germany's challenge to Britain's naval and commercial supremacy, and the imperialistic rivalries of early twentieth century all contributed to the outbreak of war. But Wilson, who abhorred using violence to achieve national objectives, felt that going to war would favor only the financiers and industrialists. America must follow a strict policy of neutrality, he insisted. Since all sides shared in the blame, Wilson told his advisers that he would listen to no stories of atrocity, German or otherwise.[3]

The German misdeeds that Russell had learned about in Holland, however, were not the only or even the most important factors that influenced his views on the war. In a series of articles in *Pearson's* magazine in the winter and spring of 1915, Russell laid out the themes that dominated his war thinking for the next four years, led to a public feud with the Socialist party, and killed his chances of becoming the Socialist Party's presidential nominee for 1916. Two overarching issues were inextricably linked for Russell—capitalism and democracy. The "ultimate origin of the war," Russell declared in January, is "commercialism and the competitive system." In February he repeated: "That system was the final cause and origin of this war. It has been the cause of all other modern wars." Privately he insisted that "this war results from the competitive system and will be followed by other wars still worse unless that system is abolished." Many years later in his autobiography, he reiterated, "The last and worst of the war culprits was and is and always will be Capitalism."[4] Russell conceded that nationalism—"almost the strongest impulse among men"— helped bring about war. But even this "strange, subtle, irrational, bone-bred and atavistic loyalty" was stirred by commercialism which, Russell argued, "keeps alive the instincts of the jungle" and "creates a situation in which good men, sincere men, men that hate war, are nevertheless convinced that . . . war is justifiable." Russell's public views echoed the sentiments of Socialists. Fellow New Yorker Morris Hillquit, the party's dominant theorist and tactician, summed up the party's doctrine: "The basic cause [of war] is capitalism . . . [a] modern Frankenstein which is destroying its own creators."[5]

Explaining the cause of war actually came quite easily to Russell: he had been warning about commercialism's effect for years on the Chautauqua circuit in his speech about the "unconsumed surplus," a concept that bewildered his audiences. Britain and Germany have gone to war because they are trying to sell their excess goods in the same markets. As Victor Berger, soon to become Russell's archenemy, put it, "Modern wars are between rival nations for commercial supremacy." The "ruthless struggle for markets," added Russell, "that is the reason why we had this war."[6] In short, imperialism was the cause. Again, Russell and the Socialists were quite in agreement, although this position was hardly radical. Even Progressives condemned imperialism. But privately Russell disagreed with the Socialists, telling Carl Thompson, the secretary of the party's executive committee, that its pacifist suggestions—disarmament, courts of arbitration, international police—were "foolish" and "wasted effort." Treaties and agreements were useless, given the competition for markets. "The first work before civilization is to restore a basis of faith upon which civilization may proceed," he wrote. And increasingly for Russell that meant stopping the Germans' march.[7]

Where Russell began to split publicly with his comrades, however, was over what he saw as a secondary—and perhaps equally important—issue. The rulers of England and Germany, King Edward and Kaiser Wilhelm, who were chosen by no one, had made true democracy impossible. "So long as we have the ridiculous and pestilent survival of the Middle Ages that we call monarchies we shall have great wars," Russell observed. If the people could choose, they would not choose war. But the ruling monarchs represent "a denial of democracy, a peril to popular government, a drag upon the footsteps of civilization, and a well-spring of war." Moreover, he said, because royalty needs to keep the line of descent intact, it tends to resort to intermarriage. The result: "some of the crowned heads of Europe are now in mad houses, others ought to be." God help the nations of Europe who have committed their destinies to this race of "lunatics and degenerates."[8] Russell's nasty allegations won him no fans in England, as he would soon find out, or among the many German-born American Socialists, like the Austrian-born Berger, who once told a Russell friend that he hated the kaiser but "when I see the world taking arms against him I feel that I must seize a rifle and take my place in the ranks and fight for him." Russell's words stung Berger and his ilk. But they put him more in line with the view of most Progressives who, as Lincoln Steffens commented, believed that the war in Europe was "the product of an inegalitarian and undemocratic social order."[9] Russell was equally critical, however, about his own country, which he said was no more a democracy than England or Germany. In America "rich men practically rule"; the kings are the capitalists. "In subtle, secret, unrevealed ways . . . wealth gets what it wants," he explained, a theme he had been repeating for a decade. The King, the Kaiser, Carnegie—all were "archaic, monarchial and disastrous."[10] Only France won Russell's admiration as a true republican democracy and a threat to the European aristocracy. "She is fighting democracy's battle," he wrote.[11]

Eventually, Russell's passion for democracy led him to worry less about commercialism and more about German authoritarianism. Even in the spring of 1915, when hardly anyone, let alone a socialist, was arguing for American entry into the war, Russell edged toward a stance of preparedness, the first step to war. "It is time we should come out of our trance," he wrote in *Pearson's* in January. "If you are determined to keep the cause of war, then prepare for the war that impends." In February, he urged that the government take over all munitions making, writing: "Preparedness never prevents war; it causes war. But *if we are going to be forced to prepare for war,* let's do it ourselves, without profit to any private owners."[12] Was this a criticism of capitalism or a call for America to take up arms? Russell was not clear; Woodrow Wilson was. The president still called for absolute American neutrality even though the Germans had begun attacks on unarmed merchant ships. Despite this clear German threat, Russell decided in April to return to the war front. With Theresa, who was to attend a women's conference on socialism in the Hague, and her mother, Charlotte Hirschl, he boarded the steamship *S. S. Lusitania* headed for Liverpool, England. Speaking to reporters at the dock in New York, Russell denied reports that he was going to investigate how prisoners of war were being treated. His mission: to research and write articles on how European countries would pay off the tremendous debt they were piling up.[13]

II. "A TERRIBLE PALL ON EVERYTHING"

The Russells never had an Atlantic voyage quite like the one of April 1915. The luxurious *Lusitania*, especially popular with the rich, was the largest passenger liner afloat. However, ever since February, when the Germans had declared the waters around England as war territory, passengers had stayed away from such cross-Atlantic ocean liners. Even advertisements for the Cunard-owned British ship told potential passengers of the threat from submarines. No wonder the Russells were able to get a cabin he called a "peach." Despite the superb accommodations, the trip was harrowing. "If a sub wants to hit this ship it will," the captain told Russell, adding grimly, "It was a chance but all war was a chance." Joining Russell on board was seventy-four-year-old Richard Croker, who throughout the 1890s was the "boss" of Tammany Hall, the Democratic political machine in Manhattan.[14] As a reporter Russell had dealt regularly with Croker, whom people on board clamored to see. "I expect to see a mob batten down with a fire axe the door to the Croker rooms," Russell wrote in his diary.

Once, while strolling the deck, passengers excitedly pointed at Russell and Theresa, mistaking them for Croker and his new bride. Mostly, however, those aboard were more interested in keeping watch for German submarines. "We kept scanning the surface for a periscope," Russell recalled. To avoid being detected, the liner's lights were covered with blankets. "It was gruesome business, there is no doubt about that." During one dinner a cabin door loudly blew open and seven hundred people began screaming, all their faces turning pale. "I hadn't before had the sensation of sitting moment after moment expecting to be blown up," Russell confided. One evening during a concert the tension overcame Russell as the music moved him to tears. "I was crying and had clearly forgotten where I was," he said. On April 10, the crew and passengers spotted Liverpool. Russell observed, "I don't know that I ever felt such a grand and glorious feeling. It was as if every nerve had been stretched and painful for many hours. I breathed again and felt that life was good."[15]

Before debarking the next day, Russell exchanged pleasantries with Croker, but as soon as he touched British soil a Scotland Yard detective pointed to him and said, "They're Socialists." Moments later a man with a bleeding finger asked Russell to help him with a bandage but then used the opportunity to ask questions about where he was going and why. Russell suspected he was a British spy. "Watched all the time," he noted in his diary. "When war comes at the door wisdom flies out the window." Russell set out to investigate the debt question, but he was more interested in how unprepared the Brits seemed. The terrible conditions of the tenement dwellers had caught up with them, he concluded. The French, reared on farms and outdoor life, were better able to field a vigorous fighting force. The Germans, nurturing their men for years just for the purpose of war, were fearsome. But the typical English soldier had pipe-stem arms, a hollow chest, pasty face, blotchy skin, and a feeble mind. Often he was drunk, but if you lived in England's slums, Russell commented, "you would go out and get soused . . . and so should I." Visiting a London friend, Russell learned that 250,000 British women were pregnant with illegitimate children, the fathers off to war. "War is insanity," he concluded."[16]

Early in May Russell met for three days with British socialist Henry M. Hyndman, a staunch supporter of the war despite his socialist credentials. The sixty-four-year-old strongly influenced Russell, who left the meetings bleak about the prospects for an Allied victory. "I don't see where the Allies have a chance," he wrote in his diary. A German victory would mean "the end of everything." But "that is what we shall have and no human being or people can make Americans see this."[17] Three days later Russell left to see if conditions were better in France. Paris shocked him. As he walked down the Rue de Rivoli on a Sunday, the streets were silent. Five women out of seven—grieving widows and mothers—wore black. The cafes were largely empty. A "terrible pall on everything," Russell noted, "all so sharply contrasted with the Paris I used to know." But "it was the look on the faces that got me most," he found. He sat on a curb and cried like a baby, making "a ridiculous exhibition of myself. The gayest city in Europe has become the Place of Tears. . . . grim and hideous." The news got worse the next day when he read that the *Lusitania* had been torpedoed by the Germans, killing 1,198 people, including 124 Americans. Russell's life had been spared by days. "The Germans must be insane," he thought, using the submarine "like a monstrous mad devil fish, sinking indiscriminately friend and foe."[18] He thought of his steward, Wilson. "How can it help Germany that this quiet little man is killed?" When reporters asked him for a statement, he said, simply, it would now be difficult for the United States to maintain both neutrality and self-respect.

Russell's views on the war crystallized as he visited Italy before returning to Britain to sail home in April 1915. A friend told him that the Brits were unenthusiastic about war because the Socialists—"Writers like you," Russell was told—had poisoned the debate. Russell scoffed at that idea. He blamed the British press and the government's inability to enunciate clearly what was at stake: "The war is not a struggle between nations but between ideas." It was democracy—"the hope and the weapon of the working class"—on one side and "the autocratic idea" on the other. Someone needed to tell the people, Russell reasoned, and he prepared to head back to America with a new mission in mind. If France and England go down to defeat, "democracy around the world suffers its deadliest blow."[19]

Russell arrived home to learn that his 1910 book, *Why I am A Socialist*, had gone into a second printing, perhaps in anticipation of his receiving the Socialist Party presidential nomination, which was expected in 1916. The book stuck nicely to the Socialist line that war was nothing more than "competition in its final form," but his chapter opposing the making of armaments clashed with his evolving war views. He now believed that America needed those weapons to prepare for war.[20] He learned also when he returned that the president now agreed with him; the sinking of the *Lusitania* had forced Wilson to reevaluate the American position. The nation would trade more extensively with the Allies, prepare to defend itself, and also seek to end the conflict with mediation. For his part Russell went back on the Chautauqua lecture circuit again, this time ending up in the Northwest—and unexpectedly finding a new cause.

As a young farmer drove Russell by automobile from one North Dakota town to the next, he saw a farming landscape in disarray: fields turned to weeds, barns in disrepair, houses abandoned. One in every five farms was idle as banks foreclosed with regularity. "If they keep on, they'll own them all," Russell was told. "Hardly on the East Side of New York had I seem anything so depressing," Russell observed. Paris might be the place of tears, but North Dakota was "the Land of Broken Lives." After lecturing one night, a man who Russell did not know, A. C. Townley, offered to drive him to his next engagement. Townley was a thirty-five-year-old refugee from the Socialist Party who feared for the future of the state's farmers and had ideas on how they could be saved. "Long automobile rides have no charms for this old traveler," said the fifty-five-year-old Russell, but "I was so curious to know why he thought another movement was better than Socialism that I agreed." Russell heard from Townley a tale he had been hearing for more than thirty years: the banks, railroads, storage houses, legislators all had the farmers at their mercy. Townley's solution was a novel one: no third party, like Populism or Socialism, just a nonpartisan alliance of farmers and voters using an aggressive campaign of publicity. The agenda: elect the most qualified candidates who supported a combination of reformist measures—strict regulation of fraud and freight rates and state insurance for weather-related crop damage—along with more radical solutions such as state ownership of flour and grain mills. In essence, Townley wanted to combine a socialist and a progressive agenda, one similar to what Russell had been pursing for a decade. Townley asked Russell to help with the publicity for what Townley called the Nonpartisan League. Surprisingly, he agreed. "As soon as I was done with the horrors of Chautauqua for that season," Russell said, "I railed back to North Dakota" to start a newspaper.[21]

Why would Russell—so focused on the war in Europe, steadily writing articles for *Pearson's* magazine, with a presidential nomination beckoning and a reputation as one of America's foremost journalists—agree to start a newspaper for a group with little resources and no public recognition? Answer: Russell loved a fight, loved a challenge, was excited by the prospects of a new radical-progressive agenda, and his heart broke when he saw the farm families of North Dakota. He was still angry with the businessmen who took advantage of the farmers. He wrote: "They lived in beautiful houses in the choicest regions. They went to church and prayed on Sunday and the next day donned the black mask and went upon the road, pistol in hand. Praying on Sunday and preying the rest of the week." Russell grew up with farmers like these in Davenport, Iowa; the farmers' revolt that became Populism—which was a mix of socialism and reform—fascinated him in the 1880s. Just before he met Townley, in fact, Russell had written four articles on farm conditions.[22]

By late summer a group consisting mostly of socialists joined Townley and Russell in an abandoned church in Fargo. They had to enter the building by a plank through a window, but it did not deter their progress in mobilizing and putting out the first edition of the *Nonpartisan Leader* on September 23, 1915. It was a classic party newspaper: direct news and information about the group while guiding members to action and seeking to combat bitter opposition from banks and large businesses. It had a breezy conversational style, editorials written by Russell, large cartoons, state political news, items from Washington, and foreign news. The first editorial was classic Russell, gruff and folksy. "Well, we're here! Your friends, the enemy, said we wouldn't get here but we did. What's more, we're here to stay." Warned Russell: "Do not believe anything you read about [the Nonpartisan League] unless you read it in your own journal or in journals that you know are absolutely with you."[23] War abroad might be bleak and insane, but Russell was holding on to his optimism and his zeal.[24] Moreover, the league was a truly novel experiment on the American political scene—an organization proclaiming public ownership and regulation as a solution for economic ills. And it soon became an effective vehicle for change and a potent force in North Dakota, Minnesota, Montana, Idaho, Wisconsin, and Colorado. Russell was neither the brains of nor the brawn behind the league, but his publicity work in the first three months of the league's existence set a tone and enabled it quickly to become an influential player in farm politics. It's not clear if he quite understood that he was tacitly embracing reform again as a partial solution to industrialism's ills. In April he had written that "every governmental remedy has been tried and re-tried . . . and not a condition has changed." Yet only six months later he was promoting the league's amalgam of public ownership and strict regulation. Many years later, he understood the value of the league, writing, "To all persons really believing in the forward march of man, every struggle for his emancipation is an instruction and an inspiration. The name and the shape of the enemy he confronts will change from century to century. . . . The men of the American Revolution fought it in one shape; the Nonpartisan League confronted it in another." Russell concluded, "Progress is slow, but surely there is something gained."[25]

III. WARNING THE NATION

Russell's next enemy, ironically, became the Socialist Party. In late fall of 1915 the "cooperative commonwealth" comrades splintered over the issue of American preparedness. The break was inevitable. It became public when a columnist for the *San Francisco Bulletin*, Pauline Jacobsen, an old friend of Russell, interviewed him for a nationally syndicated article. Jacobsen reported that Russell was in San Francisco to recuperate from his war-related travels, but he actually had been back in America for four months. She found that his hair had whitened, his rosy complexion had become sallow, and he was gloomy. Look at this war, he said, "poisoned wells, asphyxiating gas bombs that kill 10,000 at once, shrapnel that sends shells like rain; 'Big Berthas' that with one shell can raze a stone building and bury two hundred men underneath. . . . barbed wire fences fitted with heavy dynamos so that men charging through . . . are instantly killed." And for what? In the end, Germany would win this war, he declared: "I can't see anything that will defeat her now." Meanwhile, Americans resembled "an exalted order of mutts who still prate of peace, peace, peace, when there can be no peace now." He added: "We are fatuous lunatics. We won't abolish the cause of war, and we can't do anything to defend ourselves." All that Progressives and Socialists have stood for—democracy, suffrage, social justice, industrial freedom—would be swept away. The interview ended when Russell sighed, went silent, and then muttered: "I think I'd like to go somewhere in the country where I could raise roses—and forget."[26]

Russell did not become a gardener, of course. Instead, he went on the stump to warn the nation about the threat from the German autocracy. In late November he told a Socialist gathering in Philadelphia that democracy was in danger and that America needed to prepare by developing the world's largest militia. "The world has refused to prevent war by abolishing the competition system," he declared, "and now we must fight." Did not this position disqualify him as a member of the party?, he was asked. "If my convictions as to preparedness interfere with my being a Socialist, which I believe they do not, then I will get out of the Socialist Party," he announced. "If Germany wins, good night to Socialism and every progressive cause."[27] Since the speech received widespread publicity, Russell's comrades saw it. Morris Hillquit said immediately that Russell's stance did disqualify him from the presidential nomination. "Mr. Russell's views are not consistent with the ideals of the Socialist movement," he explained. Eugene Debs demurred, saying, "There's no instance in American politics where a man in order to be true to his own conscience deliberately forfeited the nomination for the president of the United States. Such men, however mistaken, are all too rare in the world." The lone Socialist in Congress, Meyer London from New York City, argued that Russell's call for preparedness was "psychological," showing only his fear of Germany's might. The party faithful sided with Hillquit, however, publicly rebuking Russell in late December, saying that the nation, in no danger of being attacked, did not need to prepare for war. Those who wanted war—bankers, ammunition makers,

speculators—did so to fatten their own coffers.[28] But Russell scoffed at that notion, calling it a "flight of fancy" without the "slightest evidence." Privately
Russell told Upton Sinclair that the party's "blunders" may "wreck its existence." Didn't they understand, he asked, that the world was faced with "an
overshadowing autocracy, menacing the surviving democracies of the world"?
He added: "I don't know any reason why we should stand about mum and mo-
tionless when there is an emergency like this at hand."[29] But Russell was hardly
mum. The war of words was on . . . and the exchanges became only harsher.
The party met in May to nominate its candidates for the fall election. With
Russell in disrepute because of his pro-preparedness stance, the party turned to
Allan Benson, a little-known journalist who had worked in the Midwest. Russell was officially persona non grata. For the first time in six years he was not
running for office.

    In June Russell headed once more to Europe, this time as a correspondent
for the Newspaper Enterprise Association, a subsidiary of Scripps-Howard
Newspapers. He hoped to get to the French front where the war was stale-
mated, but he ran into surprises in both Britain and France. "Feeling here
against Americans is most bitter I have ever seen," he wrote on July 1 when he
landed in Liverpool. Three days later he was asked to leave his hotel by the
proprietors because he was overheard in his room loudly complaining that the
$5 million spent each year on the royal family should go for the troops. "Found
another good hotel," he wrote. As he left England for Holland, after waiting in
line for hours, he was grilled at midnight by Scotland Yard: "You say you want
to learn the economic and industrial conditions in Holland. What do you want
to learn that for? Who are you going to see?" At 2:00 A.M. his passport was
stamped, but he was roused early in the morning to stay on deck in case a submarine should torpedo his ship. "It gives you an uncanny sensation to feel an
unseen eye is watching you," he noted. When he reached Holland, more questions were posed. His cigar box was dumped out and searched. He gave a cigar
to a searcher. "I was here playing the part of Christian," he quipped.[30] But the
French portion of his trip was delayed because Russell was denied permission
by the American Embassy to visit the war front, allegedly because he had criticized the president's peace overtures early in 1916. A New York congressman
took up Russell's heated complaint that his free speech rights were violated.
This was ironic because eventually, when America did enter the war, the government clamped down hard on Socialist publications, but Russell said very little.[31] Nonetheless, Russell went back to England before returning to America
and he was interrogated thoroughly again. All these questions, Russell sighed,
"because I once wrote an article arguing that that if Great Britain had abol-

ished her slums 20 years ago she would today be in a better position to fight this war." What Russell fails to note, however, and what the British did not know, was that Russell had been an Anglophobe for a decade.[32]

In the second week of August Russell received permission to visit the battlefield at Marne, where the Allies had repulsed a German offensive in July. He saw nothing but crosses where soldiers had died, "a wonderful, sad and moving sight, that vast silent graveyard." A week later he traveled with a correspondent from *Collier's* magazine to the city of Rheims, which was under fire as he arrived. "It is a terrible sight," he noted. "I have never seen anything more ghastly and horrible." An elderly couple told him that their church was bombed at noon on a Sunday as people left services. They gave him shards of precious stained glass from a cathedral to bring back to America to show its citizens. Next they visited the trenches where soldiers wore gas masks "like fearsome prehistoric animals." The Germans were only three hundred meters away and a soldier—"in the midst of hell"—was playing his flute. Russell climbed out of the trench to a clump of nearby bushes when machine-gun fire broke out. It was "amazing," he commented, "how quickly some humble journalists disappeared." Back in Rheims he watched an old woman harvesting in the fields while bombs dropped about. "The whole business is unreal," he said. Three days later a group of journalists gave a dinner in his honor but the speeches so moved him that he could hardly speak. Seeing the stalemate at the front was horribly depressing, but even more so was the thought that if Germany won "life for a democrat would be intolerable."[33] It was clear to Russell that he must continue trying to alert the nation. Preparing to return home again, he wrote in his diary, his most explicit thoughts on the war: "Nothing on earth can save this situation and rescue democracy but the United States. We shall have to go in and end this war if it is to be ended. . . . Everything depends upon America, the fate of the world in her hands and there is nobody or influence to arouse her. I think it [America] will wake up too late."[34]

Woodrow Wilson was still not that influence. He ran for his second term in November, a climactic year for progressivism. Louis Brandeis, who believed strongly in the regulation of capital, was appointed to the Supreme Court, federal banks to help struggling farmers were created, and workmen's compensation and child labor laws were also enacted. Almost all the legislation Progressives wanted had been pushed through by Wilson. But he insisted that America would not go to war, that it would continue to attempt mediation and be prepared if war should come. He was a virtual peace candidate. Russell predicted that Wilson would win the election because people gave him credit for keeping the nation out of war. "That means a lot to the inland Americans," he said.[35] Wilson was re-elected but, as his biographer points out, the war led America into "one of the bitterest and most portentous debates in its history."[36]

Russell's fight with the Socialists mirrored the larger national debate. He applauded the pacifists for not wanting war. "Nobody wants war," he said, but "a quarrel has been forced upon us" by the Germans. Socialist Algernon Lee fired back that entry into the war would only hurt the nation's "material and moral interests," and that Socialists were duty-bound to oppose it. Russell answered Lee, saying, "I am not yet convinced that it is impossible for one to be a Socialist and at the same time to be an American. But if it is, I am American."[37] He was even clearer in a letter to a friend from New Jersey. About the Socialists, he said, "they must go their way and I mine. That we should still have the United States of America and that it should still mean an ideal and a faith are infinitely more important than any friendships of mine." Patriotism and democracy demanded that America go to war. "We should be shameful descendants of Valley Forge . . . if we were indifferent to such a catastrophe," he wrote.[38]

Germany unexpectedly resumed unrestricted submarine warfare on February 1, and soon after, several American ships headed for Britain were sunk. The United States then broke diplomatic relations with Germany. In early March the press revealed a note from German Foreign Minister Arthur Zimmermann to the government of Mexico, proposing a German-Mexican alliance should America enter the war. The public was outraged. War could no longer be resisted. On April 2 Wilson asked Congress for a declaration of war and received one. Russell would get his way. Meanwhile, the socialists were planning a special convention in St. Louis to protest American entry in the war.[39] Behind the scenes, Russell was intensely lobbying like-minded Socialists, including William English Walling, his NAACP co-founder; millionaire James Graham Phelps-Stokes; and Vermont's John Spargo to join him in resisting the party's antiwar stance. A flurry of letters passed between those who would become known as the "pro-war socialists." They were especially indignant that some party leaders were openly supportive of Germany, a sentiment they felt bordered on treason. Stokes, the handsome Yale graduate, urged Russell to make clear that the party "has betrayed the interests of democracy, and that democracy is the *sine qua non*."[40] Russell agreed fully and composed a formal statement that amounted to the group's final break with the Socialist Party. He hoped to deliver it in dramatic fashion at the St. Louis convention with the dissenting comrades walking out en masse as they resigned.[41]

Russell's basic principle was simple: without democracy, there could not be socialism. "The world is rent with the greatest of all struggles between the opposing principles of democracy and autocracy. The future of the democratic cause everywhere depends upon the issue," he declared. By not opposing Germany, the party was betraying "the interests of the working class." In closing he said, "Between men of these convictions and men that feel their first loyalty is to monarchy and Germany there can be no association."[42] Stokes, however, convinced Russell not to deliver the resignation statement, but to allow Spargo to elicit support for their position: the war needed to be won by the Allies, with civil liberties kept intact, a referendum offered before any draft, full government cooperation with the unions, and state ownership of war industries. But the convention overwhelmingly rejected their views. Russell did not attend because he was busily preparing to undertake a new diplomatic mission at the behest of the Wilson administration. Without Russell's keen sense of publicity to help them, the pro-war socialists—eventually including novelist Upton Sinclair; historian Gustavus Myers; 1916 Presidential candidate Allan L. Benson; author William J. Ghent; and Chester M. Wright, the editor of the *New York Call*—chose not to resign en masse at the convention. The dissenters thus missed a chance to grab headlines and emphasize their differences with the party. Nonetheless, a considerable flap arose as the resignations of the group became known. Their numbers were few, but since they were well-known intellectuals and writers, the press gave the resignations widespread publicity. Their departure "robbed the Socialists of some of their most eloquent spokesmen, imaginative leaders, and best-known members," observes one historian. Moreover, the party lost some of its respectability since the pro-war sentiments of the defectors underscored the party's seemingly unpatriotic attitude.[43]

On the surface, the split was about a bitter feud between the war's supporters and its detractors. Indeed, the dissenters were angry. When Ghent resigned he wrote Hillquit a letter that ended with: "You are my enemy and I am, Yours." In a speech in Madison, Wisconsin, Russell is reported to have said: "The Socialists who are opposed to the war are dirty traitors [who] should be driven out of the country." And he hurled nasty epithets at Progressive Wisconsin Senator Robert La Follette for his opposition to the war. "I admit that I have been a friend of Robert La Follette in the past, but in this supreme hour I have no brother. I have nothing but the Republic." But the resignations went deeper than the war issue. For Russell, the Socialist Party—not socialism—had outlived its usefulness. The "damned party," he told Sinclair, "is going to hell and let it go . . . the sooner it got there the better."[44] He wanted a movement with a broadened appeal, one that allowed reform to co-exist with radicalism. This is evident in the report that Spargo presented at the St. Louis conference, urging the party to work more closely with both labor groups and Progressives and to pursue reform goals while still seeking Socialism. In reality, this had been what Russell's journalism had argued for all along—incremental changes that, while they did not get at root causes, made life better. The dogmatic Socialists were, in the end, just too inflexible for Russell. Stokes, Spargo, and Russell began to discuss a new political party, perhaps fashioned along the lines of the Nonpartisan League, but first the war with Germany would have to be won. With his break with the party complete and the war officially declared, Russell made clear to Woodrow Wilson's advisers that he would be willing to help the war effort. The president called shortly thereafter.[45]

CHAPTER SIXTEEN

PROPAGANDIST IN RUSSIA

I. IMPLORING THE RUSSIAN PEOPLE

THE TRIPLE ENTENTE WAS AN ODD ALLIANCE. France, a democratic republic, had much in common with America, including a revolutionary beginning. But Great Britain, although a parliamentary democracy, was headed by a monarch who oversaw a striated society that Russell and the Socialists hated. Russia was ruled by the despotic Czar Nicholas, oppressing a people who were poor and fed up, yet fighting nobly on the Eastern Front against their German neighbor and foe. And to be allied with the czar was particularly difficult to reconcile with the Wilsonian slogans about saving the world for democracy. One can only imagine the rejoicing then when, three weeks before the president declared war, the Russian people finally revolted, toppling the czar. No one was more gleeful than Charles Edward Russell, who, always prone to hyperbole, called the first Russian revolution "the greatest event in human history," adding that "the Man with the Hoe had come literally into his own at last."[1] On the very day America entered the war, Wilson sent a message to Russia, welcoming the world's newest democracy and making clear that a fresh political and economic relationship would be welcomed. Moreover, Wilson indicated that it would be vital for Russia to stay with the alliance and keep fighting the Germans. If the new government made peace with Germany—as many pro-German Socialists in America wanted—it would free up two million German soldiers to do battle with the Allies on the Western Front in Europe. The Allies might never recover.[2] Desperately wanting to avoid this, the Wilson administration, at the urging of Secretary of State Robert Lansing and New York businessman Oscar Straus (who had opposed Russell in a mayoral election) began to prepare to send a diplomatic delegation to Russia.

The composition of the mission was politically controversial. Despite being a war president, Wilson was deeply involved in its makeup, saying he wanted "men of large view" and "tested discretion" who are "genuinely enthusiastic for the success of the revolution."[3] His most important decision was naming the head of the commission. He settled on Republican Elihu Root, a former U.S. Senator and Secretary of State under Theodore Roosevelt, who had chosen William Howard Taft over Root as his successor. The seventy-two-year-old Root had made his name as a lawyer for American corporations, representing the likes of Thomas Fortune Ryan and William Whitney, the men Russell so lambasted for their accumulation of "lawless wealth." Six years earlier Russell had called Root "one of the most dangerous men in public life today, a bitter reactionary . . . a sly foe of democracy."[4] Of course, Russell was not alone in distrusting the choice of Root. A confidante of Roosevelt told the ex-president that "Root in revolutionary Russia was as welcome as the small pox. . . ."[5]

Not even Root wanted the job, however. Russia was a dangerous maelstrom of conflicting political currents, from the moderates then in power to the Leninists lurking in the wings. A Russia expert warned the State Department that Russia "is full idealists, pacifists, socialists & half-baked reformers, who all think that the nation can be saved & made prosperous & happy only through the adoption of their visionary & impracticable schemes." Root knew little about this but was nonetheless wary. He told Taft, "You have no idea how I hate it, but is just like our boys going into the war: there can be no question about doing it."[6]

The rest of the mission's makeup was equally problematic. John R. Mott, a champion of the YMCA, was an innocuous choice because of his philanthropic work. Cyrus H. McCormick, whose International Harvester Company had interests in Russia, New York banker Samuel R. Bertron, and Charles P. Crane, an industrialist with experience in Russia, were chosen to represent business. But who would represent the workers? And would it make sense to appoint a Socialist who might share common ground with the radical elements of the provisional but moderate Russian government? Wilson wanted Samuel Gompers, the powerful leader of the American Federation of Labor, to join the mission, but his fierce anti-socialist views made such an appointment unwise. His vice president, seventy-four-year-old James F. Duncan, equally anti-socialist, was chosen instead.[7]

Initially Wilson opposed the idea of picking a Socialist. But he soon changed his tune, prompting the *New York Times* to ask, "Socialist Going to Russia?" Probably at the suggestion of Gompers, the president first considered William English Walling, an antiwar Socialist who was also a Russia expert.[8] But Walling was committed to staying in the United States, in part to lead the fight against Morris Hillquit, Victor Berger, and the Socialists whom he considered a threat to the war effort. Lansing focused next on Russell whose ideas, he told Wilson, "are more in accord with what I conceive to be the best suited to influence the Russian socialists." Through an intermediary, Wilson now made the offer to Russell. He immediately accepted and told the president he could travel within forty-eight hours. At fifty-seven years old, Russell was no longer an amateur diplomat, but as "envoy extraordinary" he had become a member of a U.S. delegation that one historian described as "elderly, distinguished, thoroughly Anglo-Saxon Christian and conservative."[9] No wonder the Socialists balked.

Russell had long stopped signing "fraternally yours" in letters to his comrades. In fact, as Wilson pondered his appointment, Russell and Walling were launching broadsides against the Socialists. In public pronouncements, they attacked an international peace conference being planned in Stockholm as "the most dangerous of the Kaiser's plots," insisting that the Germans wanted to use it to pressure Russia to either make a separate peace or force a civil war. All the delegates attending, including the Americans, they insisted, "will be under the influence of Berlin." A cable sent to European Socialist leaders declared: "There is only way to bring the war to an early end. The Kaiser must go." Privately Russell told Secretary of State Lansing that the conference was "sinister," and Lansing agreed that Hillquit was "a natural intriguer" and "utterly unreliable."[10] The Socialists struck back as soon as Russell's appointment was announced. First they asked Russell not to join the mission. Then they insisted that he was one of a "very slight minority" of Socialists who opposed the war. Hillquit accused Russell and Walling of lying. In her magazine Emma Goldman mocked the "ravings" of both Russell and Walling, but said that it should come as no surprise that Russell had become a "conferee of Root." After all, she said, "nothing else could ever be expected from a journalist."[11] A prominent Socialist journal praised Russell "as honest and as square as any man who ever called himself a socialist," but added about the man who was almost the party's presidential candidate, "he never understood socialism." He worked for too many years with publishers and owners to understand the workers truly. Neither Root nor Russell "will be able to find any common ground with the revolutionists." From Russia the novelist Maxim Gorky wondered why Wilson would choose a Socialist who did not truly represent the Socialist Party.[12]

II. "HURRAH AMERICANSKY"

In late spring of 1917 Russia was a confused and boiling cauldron, overrun with political agents and military troops from Britain, France, Japan, Poland, Austria, and, of course, Germany. Common ground did not come easily for anyone, let alone for a group of mostly aging capitalists that totaled seventeen including military and diplomatic attachés. They arrived in Russia on June 3, after encountering stormy seas that left them tired. On the trip over Root and Russell sparred, as was inevitable, when Russell showed Root a telegram he had sent Wilson, expressing his view about the need for a full-scale publicity effort in Russia. "Root did not like it," Russell wrote in his diary, "but he said I was free to follow my own judgment." They discussed the issue of private property and seemed to agree. When not terribly ill from the ocean voyage, they all read books on Russia, had long discussions, and got along well, to Russell's surprise. "American democracy," he called it. "I humbly give thanks that it is still possible." But Russell warned the group to expect a hostile greeting. The Socialists have been sending "false reports" about the mission and they will do us "great harm unless promptly met and denied." Many "Russian Jews from New York" were on their way to make trouble, he said. Anticipating this problem before leaving America, Russell had brought with him letters of reference and praise from the likes of *Jewish Daily Forward* editor Abraham Cahan, Rose Pastor Stokes (Walling's wife), and Algie M. Simons.[13] The mission faced the problems of agitators almost immediately on landing when a pro-German Socialist Russian just back from America began to harangue them. When a group he was with tried to stop the mission's train, soldiers threatened to shoot them. The mission was hustled out of Vladivistok to a secret location.[14]

Russia became a blur of fascinating and frightful images for Russell and the delegation. At Vladivistok he saw 800,000 tons of freight—munitions, steel, shoes, food—piled high. With the Russian train system in chaos, the freight just sat on the ground, "one of the strangest sights in the world," Russell commented. The mission was then put aboard what had been the czar's private nine-car blue train, a terrible symbolic choice since, at times, the Russians thought that the czar was trying to return to the capitol at Petrograd, causing them to scream at the train. When the train would stop, they did not know if it would be met with violence or people cheering "Hurrah Americansky." Mostly, however, there were cheers. Wearing workman's clothing and holding up both his union and Socialist Party cards, Russell addressed one group at a depot, saying that he represented "the plain people of America . . . the workers, the radicals, the American socialists" who have "united fervently" because democracy is in "deadly peril of extinction." "We make war that we may have peace," he said. "And our word to you is, Lead on. You know the road. Where the great Russian democracy goes we are proud and glad to go with you."[15] Russell quickly showed himself to be a keen practitioner of public relations—the old clothes, the union cards, the inspiring rhetoric and symbols. At one speech he took off a bright red tie he had purposely chosen and waved it as a symbol of Russia's red flag. *San Francisco Bulletin* reporter Bessie Beatty accompanied Russell when he made the speech, saying the Russians "listened to his message, but it had no meaning for them." Revolution, not unions, was on their minds.[16] Of course, little did Russell know that holding up the card of the Socialist Party was about to become a fraud. While traveling in Russia his ex-comrades formally expelled him. Before he left America he had been asked to appear before the New York Socialists. The party had a rule that no member could take a government position without its approval. When he refused to appear, they revoked his membership—in absentia. When word came to Russia about the party's action, Russell issued a formal response: "I have not been repudiated by the Socialists of America. It is quite likely that some such action may have been taken by the Germans, pro-Germans, and wild-eyed Kaiserites that constitute a wing of the Socialist party . . . but these persons are not Americans." In his diary he wrote, angrily, "I was no more obligated to consult them about my course than to consult the Kaiser. So far as I am concerned they could repudiate until they were blue in the face."[17] But the Socialists' actions complicated matters for the mission. Their lone Socialist was no longer considered a Socialist. At a train stop shortly thereafter two socialist city commissioners requested a meeting with Russell, asking how a socialist could support this war. He had a ready response: "I said they didn't disbelieve in war any more than I did nor hate it any more." But "whether the democratic principle should survive or perish" was at stake; all would be lost if the Russians made a separate peace. They left agreeing with him, but not many others would.[18]

Arriving in Petrograd, the mission found silent throngs of people outside the huge bullet-scarred Winter Palace, the main residence of the czars since the 1700s, where the delegation was to be housed. Located on the bank of the Neva River, this Baroque-style palace had 1,786 doors, 1,945 windows, and 1,057 halls and rooms. Russell was escorted to a room with a bathtub that "you could swim in," he quipped. After formal meetings with American Ambassador David R. Francis, Russell huddled at midnight with a reporter he knew from New York, then retired to his room to collect his thoughts. The people thronging the streets bewildered him. "Everywhere we saw public meetings, in the streets, in the squares, in the parks . . . Orators haranguing them and the great crowds silently listening." He called it "unchained Russia . . . delighting in its new-found freedom." But he worried: "A voice tells me it is something more . . . the vast, inexpressive throngs, listening and thinking and gathering power, nobody knows what they may mean."[19] The second Russian revolution was coming. Russell saw it in that first night in Russia, but he was nonetheless optimistic that the mission could succeed in keeping the Russians in the democratic family—and in the war. Just as he had convinced the two socialists, the mission had to convince the Russian people.

The mission's first formal telegram to the United States was pessimistic about its ability to do much good, however. This angered Russell. "Wasted time all morning which is the usual thing," he complained on June 21, adding that "looking pleasant and eating copiously" were the mission's specialties. Russell disliked the formal receptions. "The country is being ruled by its peasants and working man," he noted, "and the ministers to whom we pay so much attention are only bureau chiefs." Just as he had wandered the streets of Lowell, Massachusetts, while covering the Lizzie Borden murders, he wanted to mingle more with the people.[20] When the mission balked at his suggestion for a massive publicity blitz in Russia, he said: "Objections are what to we do best. It seems like the sum total of what we do will be negatives. At a time like this!" Although Russell praised some of Root's speeches, he was worried when at a reception Root urged a group of Americans then in Russia "to teach these people democracy," comparing the Russians to kindergarten children. "Pray God that remark does not get out or our usefulness is done for here," Russell commented.[21]

The mission's usefulness, as Russell began to realize and argue, was in spreading the gospel, "propaganda work," he called, to "arouse the people on the peril to democracy." Just as he had done for a decade as a muckraking journalist, he now felt that progressive publicity could work in soon-to-be Communist Russia. Even Root agreed, telling Lansing in a cable: "We think the people of Russia—particularly the soldiers—are going to decide whether Russia stays in the war, and we have got to get at them in some way." Russell wanted $5 million immediately and $100 million overall for public relations work—films, newspapers, speakers, mailings, leaflets, rallies. The mission asked for $100,000.[22] Russell was so adamant that publicity was needed that he cabled Lansing, asking for permission to stay behind after the mission departed. But no answer came back from the States about either his request or the money.

Meanwhile, of more immediate danger were the agitators assailing the U.S. delegation. Russell witnessed a parade of thousands of people in a Petrograd square. They waved banners proclaiming: "Down With the Ten Capitalist

Ministers," "Down With the War for All Countries," and "Bread, Peace and Liberty." One speaker, a hoarse red-faced little man who said he was an American, yelled to one gathering that the Root mission was sent by the capitalists to deceive the Russian people. Later Russell confronted the man. "I asked him how much of an American he was," Russell said. He did not know Milwaukee from Minneapolis, conceding to Russell that he had visited America only briefly many years earlier.[23]

Journalist Rheta Childe Dorr, then in Russia, told Russell that many of the negative stereotypes Russians had of Americans were the work of Lincoln Steffens, who had just traveled the country. He seems to have done "a prodigious amount of mischief," Russell said, but the real villains he believed were the East Side of New York radicals sent by Hillquit to spew their lies. Given the task they faced, Russell was aghast when many of the mission's members agreed to go to Moscow for what amounted to a sightseeing trip at a time when, he noted, "hell is poppin and the world is teetering."[24]

Further complicating matters were the constant rumors that swirled around the mission about violence. So dangerous were conditions that on June 30 the mission was asked to relocate to Finland to avoid possible attacks. "I was not going out of Petrograd," Russell told a resentful Root, even though Russell observed, "tomorrow the city may be drenched in blood." It is difficult to determine if Russell was being brave, careless, or exaggerating the threat. Nonetheless, he and Duncan, along with military attachés, not only stayed but traveled out of Petrograd to a huge old casino to address a large gathering that included Vladimir Lenin, who with the help of Germany had just recently returned from exile. Russell's speech was delayed, however, when he was told that if he made references to the war a riot would ensue. He was asked to avoid such references, but he refused. A second official then said that since he did not represent the U.S. Socialist party, he should not speak at all. Furious, Russell replied: "It would be a cold day when I stood hat in hand at the door of anybody on earth asking permission to speak." If the Council of Workmen, Soldiers, Peasants, and Deputies did not want him to speak, "It could go to hell for me."[25]

Finally, a cabinet minister relented and Russell spoke—mostly about the war. Russell said he was received with enthusiasm, except for "the strange figure of Lenine," who sat still and did not applaud. He later recalled Lenin as a magnetic personality but an "obstinate fanatic" with a "lust for power." A few days later Russell also encountered, by chance, Leon Trotsky, soon to be Lenin's Bolshevik deputy in the communist revolution. He liked Trotsky who he saw as a "dreamy, hotheaded Utopian Jew, bushy haired, sanguine, highly smug, excitable and a gifted talker." Little did he know that Trotsky was writing that Russell was a tool of the Morgan banking interests.[26]

Russell, ever the optimist, believed that the mission was making progress even as he grumbled more about having to meet with "ministers and mummies" when "everything depends upon the plain, hard-fisted, unwashed multitudes." At a speech twenty-five miles outside of Petrograd to six thousand peasants and soldiers, he and Duncan were interrupted with constant applause when they spoke at one in the morning after watching hours of traditional Russian dances and songs. But still no answer from Washington about the publicity money. Russell went to Ambassador Francis, who sent a cable on the spot reiterating the request. Root had also pleaded for the publicity money, insisting that German propaganda "can be prevented only by active and immediate counter attacks by same weapons." On July 5 he had a good meeting to discuss a plan to help Russia's decrepit rail system, his specialty.[27] At another meeting a cabinet minister leaned over and whispered, What do you really think about the chance for democracy to survive in Russia? Russell pointed out the window to a line of people waiting for bread. "They will tolerate it in the summer but come winter they will not," he advised. The next day he asked Root if he could be allowed to stay behind when the mission left. Root bitterly told Russell that the publicity business was now finished; he could not stay; the group would depart in four days. "It was an unsatisfactory session," Russell wrote. The night before the mission's departure, he was melancholy, writing, "I am overwhelmed . . . that we are going away just as the prospect opens before us of opportunity and power to do good." On July 10 the mission members boarded their train, "a silent crew," Russell observed, "utterly worn out." Obviously forgetting his breakdown just after his first wife died in 1901, Russell added: "I have never been so tired or so depressed."[28]

III. STAINS OF BLOOD EVERYWHERE

Most of the mission members slept as they headed back to Vladivistok, awakening only when a bridge they were to cross was burned down by anti-American agitators. After a thirty-six-hour delay, they had another close call when a building near their train was torched. The mood lightened at one stop as the mission was greeted by cheering crowds. After Russell spoke to a large gathering of soldiers, praising their revolution, one officer threw his arms around him and kissed Russell. By July 22 they were sailing for Seattle. Root wrote to his wife, "We all feel that we have accomplished far more than we dared to hope. . . ." But the reception in Seattle was lukewarm. Root declared that Russia would stay in the war against Germany and remain a democracy, He was wrong on both counts, of course. Russell sounded like a reactionary patriot, declaring: "If a man now says, 'My wages before my country,' or 'My balance sheet before my country,' or 'My class or creed or association before my country,' he is not an American." No one can or should criticize or disagree with the war effort, he insisted. "Talk of peace at this time and arguments against sending our boys to France," he added at a speech in Chicago, "is utter rot."[29] The mission then traveled cross-country to Washington, D.C., to meet the president and deliver its report, the highlight of which was a request for a huge publicity program. The request was sent to George Creel, head of the government's giant war propaganda machine. Feeling the mission was poorly treated, Root concluded many years later that Wilson only wanted a "grandstand play," adding, "When we delivered his message and made our speeches, he was satisfied; that's all he wanted." His criticism may have been unfair. Wilson was immersed in countless details of running a massive war effort. No one in his administration quite understood the dynamics that had been unleashed in Russia, as he was bombarded from all sides with advice. He wrote to Russell some weeks later that, "all sorts of work in Russia now is rendered extremely difficult because no one channel connects with any other."[30] Root, for his part, had a limited view of the mission's goals—and while there he liked to get up late, read books, and see the sights as much as deliver speeches. Moreover, as a corporate patrician he was an unlikely figure to understand the plight of a poor country on the verge of explosion. Root liked only very slow change. The "filth" of the country appalled him, as did the political dynamic at work. Only Russell seemed to make a real effort to mix it up with the "people" of Russia. But he was so obsessed with the propaganda question that his vision too was narrow. His diary contains some acute analysis, but it reads best when he re-creates scenes and people, as befitting the good journalist he always was. The Root mission was off the mark in its prediction that Russia could maintain its new democracy, but nonetheless Lansing concluded that the group was "as capable of judging the situation and giving advice as any this Government could have sent out."[31]

From Washington, Russell headed to New York, where his Socialist comrades had expelled him a few weeks before, to appear before the patriotic Union League. His target was Robert La Follette, the liberal Senator from Wisconsin whom Russell once lauded as "a different species from the rest." Now he attacked La Follette for his opposition to the war, calling him a "disloyal American, a traitor in disguise" who does "the dirty work of the Kaiser."[32]

La Follette's Midwestern isolationism made him vote against American entry, and Russell had heard his words repeated all throughout Russia like "a poisoned dagger plunged toward the heart of your country." Russell was always prone to rhetoric and exaggeration in his writing and speeches, but now he was downright demagogic. In speeches across America he went on the attack, as if obsessed with proving his patriotism over his radicalism. Russell, the man who one Russian observer called "a most interesting and queer soul," had become overwhelmed by the lunacy of war . . . just like the rest of the world. The muckraker had turned superpatriot.[33]

Aware that his rhetoric was soaring to new heights, Russell defended himself at a giant pro-war rally at New York's Madison Square Garden, explaining his fiery support of the war: "It is not because we have grown any weaker in our advocacy of social reform, social justice and industrial democracy, but because, more than ever, we are committed to those reforms. It is because we see that the very foundation of the cause we represent is in deadly peril." And then he attacked La Follette again, comparing him to traitor Benedict Arnold and declaring: "I admit that I have been a friend of LaFollette in the past, but in this supreme hour I have no friend, I have no brother, I have nothing but the Republic."[34] In fact, Russell's view was a mirror of Progressives and muckraking journalists like Will Irwin, Ray Stannard Baker, Ida Tarbell, and Jane Addams, all of whom moved from assailing the city boss and the large corporation to attacking the Kaiser and German militarism. Russell summed up the issue bluntly in a letter to Upton Sinclair, saying "We are confronted with the destruction of democracy and the domination of the world. . . . Until that imminent peril is averted there is nothing else worth talking about or thinking about." Over the next three months Russell devoted himself to two things: writing a book about Russia and going on the lecture tour for Creel's Committee for Public Information (CPI). He wanted very much to return to Russia to head up a government publicity program there, lamenting to Creel that the publicity program the Root mission wanted was not implemented. "We knew perfectly well what was needed," he said. "I should have kept on the job until we got what was needed."[35] Creel wanted to send Russell back to Russia but some in government felt he could not be trusted. As a socialist, even a patriotic one, he might propagandize more for socialism than capitalist democracy. Russell the free spirit, the man who poked fun at so many public figures and institutions, was, not surprisingly, just not safe enough to represent the government abroad. But this did not stop Creel from asking him to embark on a lecture tour for the CPI. Creel knew that in Russell he had a well-known national figure who was passionate about the war and who loved the stump. Baker called the touring ex-journalists "the vigilantes."

Russell gave fifty-eight fire-and-brimstone addresses between October and February 1918, one of the 15,000 speakers that the CPI eventually sent out across America working for $10 a day and travel expenses. In Chicago alone during the war years 451 speakers gave 50,000 talks to 25 million people. Russell mostly spoke to labor audiences, addressing particularly large crowds in Cleveland, Des Moines, and New Orleans, where he gave twelve talks. In the South he accompanied visiting French speakers, the Marquis and Marquise de Courtivron and the Marquis and Marquise de Polignac. One observer compared his "forceful presence and dramatic instinct" to the Reverend Billy Sunday.[36] But Russell warned Creel not to book him into churches because "a church is a deadly place for the kind of meetings I want to hold," and in Nashville, Tennessee, some residents complained about his vitriolic attacks on members of Congress. For his part Russell felt that German saboteurs were shadowing him and disrupting his speaking tour. "There is spy work going on," he told Creel.[37] The CPI speakers were extremely successful in rousing Americans to a fever pitch, but it is likely they were also equally responsible for the unprecedented attack on civil liberties that occurred throughout the war years. In reporting on the suppression of more than one hundred radical newspapers, the *Times* gleefully observed that the antiwar newspapers had caused "such influential men as John Spargo and Charles Edward Russell to withdraw from the Socialist Party." Russell, in fact, was still lambasting the Socialist Party, mocking its "iron-clad regulations" promulgated by "gentlemen with unpronounceable names and a tangled dialect."[38]

Creel was pleased with Russell's speaking tour, telling him, "I hear remarkable comments from everywhere." Russell's reward came in the spring of 1918, as the war entered its final stage, when Creel asked Russell to head up the CPI's publicity office in Great Britain, of all places, the country that Russell had been privately and publicly grumbling about for nearly twenty years. "You are the man of all men for the work in England," he told Russell.[39] With a Russia assignment out of the question, Russell accepted and joined the growing list of former journalists who plunged into the propaganda business. By April 26, with son John accompanying him, Russell was aboard an ocean liner that was zigzagging the Atlantic to avoid German submarines. "In this climate," Russell quipped, "the normal operation of the mind can only be attained with the aid of a reasonable amount of alcoholic stimulation."[40]

Russell's three months in England were notable for three things: his inability to get along with the British and to accomplish much for the propaganda effort; his increasingly irascible attitude toward everything and everyone; and the starkly contrasting images he drew between life's delights and war's horrors.

Russell began immediately to scrap with the Brits when they hassled him over his passport papers. "Madness on one side and official arrogance on the other," he commented. When he tried to get favorable news from the CPI placed, he received little cooperation from British newspaper editors, who distrusted him. "Do they think I am a German spy?" he asked. His counterpart in the British war publicity office told Russell that indeed there was "manifest suspicion" of him, but Russell wrote it off to typical "British chilliness and bad manners." His disdain for the English must have been evident.[41]

Before Russell left for England he told Creel that he and Will Irwin, the muckraking journalist who was then overseeing CPI publicity efforts in foreign countries, had found a way to make the Allies share information. The plan did not work in England, however, as he met constant resistance from the press, causing him to be miserable. He complained about everything: English Jews were annoying because they so hated America; Scotland Yard was surely shadowing him and John; German spies undoubtedly had sabotaged one of his luncheon meetings; English youngsters were "lifeless, hopeless."[42] Concluding that he was in an "almost impossible position" to influence the English positively, Russell begged Creel to relieve him from his CPI duties. While he waited for an answer he carefully observed wartime Britain where food was scarce, prompting him to note, "I should think myself fortunate in being a vegetarian if there were any vegetables." Most astounding to Russell were the regular air raids on London. On May 21 Russell and his son were reading in their room when the air raid sirens went off. While the sky lit up in yellow and red with shrapnel from bombs dropping around the house, they gathered downstairs with other boarding house guests to watch the "astounding drama," as Russell called it. When the "all-clear" siren sounded, he concluded, "The human race has gone mad."[43]

Russell's only solace came when he and John took leisurely Sunday boat rides up the Thames. He gazed at the majestic homes lining the river, the flowering spring bushes blooming—"idyllic, beautiful restful delightful . . . like heaven." How can this exist with "a world gone mad"? he asked. He wired Creel again, asking for relief. Meanwhile, he sought the counsel of H. G. Wells, the fifty-two-year-old science fiction writer who also was an adamant socialist. Despite Wells's high-pitched voice and incessant talking, Russell concluded that he had "never met a shrewder, quicker or more certain mind." When the two discussed why Americans in England so disparaged the United States, Wells noted that whenever he discussed abolishing the monarchy someone quoted to him remarks from Americans about how dismal a failure their republic was. "I don't suppose your countrymen ever think of the harm their loose remarks do to the republican cause in Europe," Wells observed. One can only wonder if he was talking about Russell.[44]

Russell's old friend, the reformer and former mayor of Toledo, Ohio, Brand Whitlock, visited Russell in London. Whitlock, who was America's ambassador to Belgium during the war, was thin and haggard. "He seemed to be contemplating horrors," Russell felt. Two days later Creel finally told Russell he could leave his CPI post and John, then thirty-three years old, could take over. Russell was joyous, packing immediately for Paris where he planned to join a small delegation of Socialists—including old comrades John Spargo and Simons—who were going to tour France and Italy at the behest of the CPI to bolster the morale of labor groups and Socialists.[45] Paris shocked Russell again; almost all the women were in black; most of the men were one-legged or maimed. One day, as bombs rained down on the city, he hustled across a bridge to reach a shelter; moments later, the bridge was destroyed. On August 2, British reporter Herbert Bailey, whom he knew from Russia, took Russell through the countryside for four hours. He was shocked to see villages he had known in 1916 wrecked, replaced by battlefields covered with airplanes, gas canisters, and bodies. At one stop Russell and his comrades cut off buttons from dead German soldiers; Spargo took a bayonet as a souvenir. They all shuddered as they stood over an American soldier who died holding the book *Oliver Twist*, which he had apparently been reading when he was hit. Returning to Paris, they passed endless lines of soldiers—"one long avenue of war, war, war," Russell wrote in his diary. Back in Paris, Russell met with Alexander Kerensky, the now-deposed Russian leader, and discussed ways of preventing Russia from signing a peace treaty with Germany. Clemenceau, the French prime minister, met with the traveling delegation and then arranged to meet privately the next day with Russell, who told him, "Every man has now two countries—his own and France." But France told the story of the war: "the dark stains of blood were everywhere," Russell said. "I have had enough. The human race has gone insane."[46] Russell prepared to sail home again one more time from war-torn Europe.

NEW CAUSES IN THE FINAL YEARS

I. A RETURN TO WRITING

WHEN WORLD WAR I WAS FINALLY OVER, it was difficult for any of the Progressives and pro-war Socialists to be gleeful. More than 100,000 Americans had died; 10 million soldiers lay dead in battlefields stretching from Europe to Asia; another 20 million had been wounded. The economy of Europe was in ruins, and 3.5 million American soldiers now prepared to return to America. Who could predict what was in store for the American economy? Pacifists, Progressives, Socialists, pragmatists, Romantics—all were thoroughly disillusioned by the outcome of war, confirming what many feared: brute impulse, not reason and compassion, still ruled. The triumph of progressivism was not inevitable after all.[1] In March 1918, Russia signed a separate peace treaty with Germany. It was official: the Root mission had failed to persuade the Russians to keep fighting. The agreement was the fruit of long and bitter negotiations with Germany conducted by Leon Trotsky, soon after he and Lenin took power in the Bolshevik Revolution, which occurred only four months after the Root Mission. As Russell commented, Russia "walked six months in freedom and allowed itself to be snared by another autocracy."[2] The treaty forced Russia to make numerous concessions to Germany, but when World War I finally ended in November 1918, many of the concessions were voided. Russell, the superpatriot, got at least part of what he wanted: the Kaiser and autocracy were defeated. Nonetheless, Russell was glum.

The fifty-nine-year-old Russell now had to reconcile the war's results with his eternal optimism about mankind. "A period of general depression" followed the war's end, he conceded, and Russell was shook as he wondered about the cost of victory. "That eleven little children playing at hop-scotch should be blown to pieces, in what way did that help to win the war?" he asked. "That a mother should claw frantically in a heap of ruins to find and clasp the headless corpse of her infant, wherein did that make for triumph?" Even Russell had to concede that "all the decent, kindly instincts in man [were] seemingly gone," revealing him as a "strange, ingenious, crafty, murderous creature, worse than any wild beast." And yet "amidst all the killing and mayhem and bloodshed he rushes into burning buildings to save little children, pulls a life boat through a storm, gives life to save others, endures pain, privation for an altruistic faith." Hope is not lost, he concluded, because "new things were about to come upon the world worth even this price." The glass was still half full for Russell. He still yearned and hoped for what he had been seeking since his conversion to Socialism in 1908: a "democracy of opportunity." Even more, however, the preacher's grandson was hoping still to convince mankind that "the only real happiness on this earth is spiritual and intellectual, that in the pursuit of the material there is literally nothing but ashes and bitterness, vacuity and sorrow." For Russell, "making our fortunes the god of our idolatry, and our business its religion, all this is but sorry employment for the aspiring human soul."[3] The question now for the gray-haired journalist-turned-socialist-turned patriot was what pulpit would he choose to preach from? He was, after all, a man without a political party.

The Social Democratic Federation offered some possibilities as a left-of-center political party that embraced reform and Socialism. In the winter of 1919 Russell and William English Walling, both officers in the party, sailed to Europe to visit Britain and France and to meet with other Socialists in an attempt to sell Woodrow Wilson's "Fourteen Points," including a League of Nations that might prevent more world wars. But the SDF never gained any ground. Russell turned again to what he knew best—writing. In the immediate aftermath of the war he wrote three books in three years on Russia—on his trip there, on the Bolshevik revolution, and on the dangers posed to the world by an authoritarian society, no matter how noble its goal.[4] From the end of World War I to his death in 1941, Russell wrote seventeen books, including one that won the Pulitzer Prize for biography. Russell's books displayed his dual passions—politics and art—as he carefully blended history and biography to both the delight and harsh criticism of reviewers—and the occasional anger of those who he continued to attack.

For the first few years after the end of the World War, Russia obsessed him, especially the brutality he saw in Bolshevism, which would soon become authoritarian communism. Lenin—and the American intellectuals who supported Bolshevism made Russell furious. He said about Bolshevism what he had been saying for years: there is never a justification for using violence to bring about political goals. How could the "intellectual Bolsheviks," who opposed American entry into war on the ground that "peace is a holy thing," now support "cruel and bloodthirsty" Bolshevism? Men and women Russell had met in Russia were facing firing squads soon after Lenin took power. He worried and warned about the spread of Bolshevism in America, writing, "We want no violence in this country, no street fighting, no barricades and no class warfare." And the way to prevent Bolshevik revolution in America, he said, was to keep workers' wages at the high level of wartime and to continue to make progressive social changes. Compulsory high-school education, state-funded university education, stricter child labor laws—these would surely keep the people from turning to Bolshevism. "Men that believe they are fairly and honestly treated do not listen to Bolshevism," he wrote. "Where there is no wrong there is nothing to revenge. The true bulwark against Bolshevism [is] good-will, kindness, equity, the modernizing of industry."[5]

In 1920, Russell published his book on the Nonpartisan League, a further affirmation that he admired a combination of progressive reforms and state-funded cooperative measures to protect workers and farmers. He wrote and said little overtly about bourgeois politics and popular elections, although he raised eyebrows when he came out against using animals for experimentation, arguing that the real cure for disease is the rejection of materialism and the embrace of spiritualism.[6] For the preacher's son, the search for the spirit became a hallmark of his last twenty years of life. "The world has no need of any affirmation of materialism," he said in an anti-vivisection speech. "It has only need of the affirmation of spirituality." After one vivisection debate, a listener told Russell he had "annihilated" his opponent.[7]

II. THE PULITZER PRIZE

The early 1920s were relatively quiet—at least by Russell's standards. "I am glad you are well and IDLE," Hearst editor Arthur Brisbane wrote him. But Russell did publish articles on woman's suffrage and prohibition of alcohol, as well as a highly technical book on railroad regulation, and two others on the prospects of Filipino independence. His interests continued to be widespread. In a flash of insight in 1925, he warned after a summer trip to Carlsbad that Germany should be watched. "Trying it again," he said, was the idea that "most dominates" the imagination of the average German. No one paid much attention, perhaps at least in part because Russell had developed a reputation as a bit of an eccentric. "I'm a crank, you bet, right down to my corns," he told a friend.[8] He told one interviewer that splitting wood and feeding the fire took of most of his time. "I don't do anything interesting; just knock out a few pieces on my old type-writer, and yawp a little," he said. This was mere modesty, however, because Russell was actually beginning not only to research new books but to champion new causes. Irish independence especially interested him because it was "a great cause" and "great spirits enlisted in it," something he first learned as a nineteen-year-old reporter in 1880 when an Irish nationalist spoke in Iowa about seven centuries of struggle with Britain.[9] He regularly visited Ireland during the war. In April 1916 the British crushed an Easter rebellion, executing many rebels. Eamon De Valera, one of the rebels, was spared because he was an American, born in New York City. Exiled from Ireland, De Valera became a friend of Russell, who accompanied him on a U.S. speaking tour. When De Valera returned in 1920 to Ireland, civil war was under way and his political organization, Sinn Fein, was engaged in a widespread guerrilla campaign against British forces. In 1924, Russell visited De Valera, then the head of the Irish Republican troops. He was in hiding. Russell had to be smuggled to meet him, driving from sundown till midnight on a wild journey to a remote location – all this for a man of sixty-four years who was, for all intents and purposes, "retired." The two men talked until daybreak; Russell found De Valera "calm, steady, reasoning, unemotional, iron-nerved," even though he faced death.[10]

When Russell returned to America he went on a speaking tour and lashed out at Britain's intransigence. "They tell me I am a proponent of the gospel of hatred because I step forward and say that Ireland deserves to be free and independent. I am. I hate Great Britain," he told one audience. "I hate it and everything connected with it and the life of it." After years of discreet diary entrances about his distaste for Britain, Russell finally pulled no punches. This was characteristic of his final years when he became blunt, forthright, opinionated, and, for better or worse, downright cranky. He reserved some of his harshest words for Britain, which he labeled "the champion of oppression." England, he declared, "perpetrates swindle in the name of religion and commits murder in the name of Christianity."[11] The British must have heard Russell's voice. In late May 1926, he was enough of a power, enough of a threat to refuse him entry into the country. Officials told him that the Irish Free State, still part of the British Empire, had labeled him an undesirable because of his support of Irish independence. The incident made national headlines. When Russell got to Paris, he told waiting reporters he hoped the ban would be permanent. "The world was full of places I had rather be in," he quipped. But he immediately fired off a letter to Britain's Secretary of State for Home Affairs, refusing to agree not to travel to Ireland. To do so would be "degrading, disgusting and an affront to the nation of which I am a citizen," he wrote. "I am a friend of the Republican movement in Ireland. I am a friend of every Republican movement everywhere in this world. To my mind any other form of government in the Twentieth century is a grotesque absurdity." Hicks replied promptly, saying tartly: "If you are as bellicose in your acts as you appear to be in your correspondence," it is no wonder you were barred from entry. But Hicks insisted the refusal came from the Irish Free State. "What a mess, Charlie," a friend told him.[12] Eventually the matter was taken up in Parliament and son John watched as the House of Commons voted to allow his father to enter the country. "Undesirable" Russell, sixty six, with an aching back and persistent stomach problems, could still enter the eye of the storm.

III. "SLOWLY BUT SURELY WE GO UP"

Beyond politics, however, there were other projects. He was writing two biographies that crowned his lifelong interest in music and art, an interest he had put aside in 1904 when he joined the muckraking movement. In fact, Russell's two most consistent correspondents in the last twenty years of his life were Ernest McGaffey, a poet from California, and Julia Marlowe, the famous actress-expatriate. Russell handled Marlowe's finances up until his death in 1941. She dedicated her 1954 memoirs to him, writing that his "watchful care and regard for my fortunes have perhaps been a more potent influence than that of any one person I have known."[13] In 1926 Russell published what can only be called an authorized biography of Marlowe in which he never reveals their relationship. He wrote not only a glowing story of her life but also a history of the development of theater in America. Like everything else he had ever written, Russell was not objective in this case. He clearly had a conflict of interest, and one publisher rejected the book as too admiring. The book, deservedly perhaps, received mixed reaction. One critic cited "too much adulation, a lack of critical discrimination in discussing her art . . .some inexcusable errors of fact." Another said it was "too long, and it is not equally interesting in all its parts." But other critics called it careful, well informed and "an excellent survey of one aspect of the progress of the American stage."[14]

The ink was hardly dry on the Marlowe book when Russell brought out his fourth biography, of a lifelong hero, Theodore Thomas (1835–1905), an orchestra conductor who was largely unknown to the American public. When Russell was a youngster, Thomas stayed at the Russell household in Davenport as he toured the country promoting symphonies, then unheard of in rural America. As he popularized the music of the great European masters and planted the seed for local symphony orchestras in cities across America, his route became known as the "Thomas Highway." "If I say that no other man of his period exerted upon mankind an influence so great and lasting, I shall be looked upon as lunatic, although that is what I honestly believe," Russell wrote. Certainly there was little doubt that Thomas deserved acclaim, but Russell's admiration of him related to the beliefs that drove much of his work: if America could more fully embrace the highbrow arts, such as symphony orchestras, "it might change the whole American character; it might scourge us of material-ism."[15] The critics were kind to this book, with the *New York Times* calling it "comprehensive, widely ranging, illuminating, valuable, interesting."[16]

In the end, Russell's comprehensive review of the development of the American orchestra, not offered through the lens of a music critic, made the reading compelling. The following year Russell was awarded the Pulitzer Prize for writing America's best biography. Russell was typically understated about receiving the award. He never mentioned it in the autobiography that he wrote six years later. Others were more impressed. Benjamin Hampton, the editor who published so much of Russell's biting journalism, sent a note. "Trying to get in touch but no luck. But now after the Pulitzer, I assume there is no hope in the world of my ever seeing you," he wrote. "Gosh, there is no way in the world to keep a guy like you down."[17]

Hampton had a point. Russell was a difficult man to slow down. The year after winning the Pulitzer he wrote a memoir about life on the Mississippi River at a time—his childhood—when rafts still rode the water. "Not a dull page in the book," one reviewer said.[18] The next year, two more books ap-peared—on boating and poetry. He followed a year later with an odd biogra-phy—of Charlemagne, the king of the Holy Roman Empire, a larger-than-life figure who was responsible for the fusion of the Christian, Germanic, and Roman cultures that yielded European civilization. Although his armies domi-nated the battlefield, he was also known as a "light in the Dark Ages," a tireless reformer who improved his people's lives. Russell, at the age of seventy, was still trying to tell interesting and meaningful stories. The critics were mixed again, however, calling Russell "an industrious writer " and "careful scholar" whose writing was "as humdrum as his subject is unusual."[19]

Criticism did not stop him, however. He quickly followed up with a biog-raphy of Haym Salomon. It would be Russell's last great cause and interest. Sa-lomon was a young Polish Jew living in America who was instrumental in raising funds for the American Revolution and who barely escaped execution to help the revolutionary cause. In his development from penniless fugitive to respected businessman, philanthropist, and defender of his people Salomon was a hidden hero. But Russell chose him because injustice and oppression of the underclass was always his passion. He feared, especially in the early 1930s, for the fate of Jews worldwide. He wrote in 1939, "Millions of our fellow beings in Central and Eastern Europe are undergoing extermination by the most cruel means of death. What answer is civilization to make?"[20] Again Russell was taking up a cause that few were aware of—and he wrote about it with passion and anger. In the early 1930s Russell helped form and became president of the Pro-Palestine League of America, a Christian organization that was arguing for the creation of a protected homeland for Jews in the Middle East, an area then controlled by the British. He was publicly rebuking England for making it difficult for Jews to enter Palestine to escape German persecution. He urged Americans to "stand and protest" against the "Middle Age ferocity" of the Nazis. After all, he noted in one speech, "The Jews are the only world family."[21] At his death, one Jewish leader hailed Russell as "the foremost Christian champion of the Zionist cause." As usual, however, his words often caused controversy. After one bitter magazine attack on Adolph Hitler, an editor asked him to tone down his words. "We are flooded with letters of protest" about your opinions, he wrote.[22]

In 1936 Julia Marlowe wrote Russell, "Charles, go slowly for the rest of your life." It was not possible for him. "I have been so rushed with the business of saving Ireland, Palestine, Manila and Madrid that I haven't yet had a chance to get to the library," he told one friend. "Your energy continues to astound me," another friend told him."[23] But the truth was that Russell was growing increasingly nostalgic, referring to himself as a "fossil." He and Theresa now spent the summers in Vermont to escape Washington's heat, as one ailment or another often kept him idle "I look out upon the White Mountain Range, miles and miles away, across foothills and valleys. That is enough to exalt even one so dull as I am," he wrote. "Nothing really counts but the spirit, which is the intelligence that is bestowed upon each of us. The material existence is after all a kind of dream, the spiritual is reality."[24]

Russell alternated between despair and hope. The reality of worsening conditions in Europe depressed Russell. "The world has been poisoned by this man Hitler," Julie Marlowe wrote him. A 1939 poem captured Russell's emotions. "The sadness of the world oppresses me like somber-sounded moanings of the sea," he wrote. "The sunset's grief, the dawn's pathetic plea, the dead leaf dropping from deserted tree. What is there left to light with rosy gleam the sadness of the world?"[25] Novelist Fannie Hurst often wrote to Russell to cheer him up. "There are certain people I like to think about because just knowing they are on the planet gives me the courage to carry on," she said "You are one of the few who keep alive confidence that we are ultimately going to right the universe."[26]

In fact, of course, Russell had slowly come to the conclusion that the work he had done and the movements in which he participated had played a key role in improving America. "The world does not grow worse, does not stand still, but slowly grows better," he concluded. Reform is a "vast, complicated and often mysterious evolution. It is not to be had with the naiveté of a single push." It calls for the persistence of each generation. "Slowly but surely we go up," he felt. He still saw the need to get rid of the "outworn, poisonous system" of capitalism, but incremental changes were needed while the world moved inevitably away from competition toward cooperation.[27]

Russell 's life story mirrors the conflict so many reformer-utopians faced in the years between 1880 and 1920—his most important professional years. Industrialism had produced wondrous new riches for America, improved living conditions, and brought affluence never before seen. But it had also spawned dreariness and poverty, horrid living condition in urban ghettos, a threatening and dangerous industrial workplace, and a terrible despoliation of politics. The world for many was truly a dangerous and dismal place. For Russell, the excesses of the competitive marketplace and industrialism outweighed its glories, introducing conditions that he could not tolerate and that he had to fight to change up until the day he died. While the rest of the muckrakers got on with their lives, Russell kept trying to slay the beast. He grew to despise the fact that for so many Americans the goal of life was to accumulate as much wealth as possible. He wanted people to glory in the pleasure that came from cooperation, not competition. The question, of course, was how to get there. He rejected the religious solution of his parents and grandparents, which was to save souls. Instead, he grew to believe that the goodness of man could be realized only by changing the conditions that produced the misery. At first he became a reformer, a believer that by changing laws and instituting regulations many of the evils could be eliminated. But when he ousted the Boss of Brooklyn in 1888 and then watched the Boss quickly return to his throne, he realized that the people's wrath and reform solutions were short-lived indeed. Thus Russell turned to a more radical solution—socialism, the ownership by government of key industries, although he never outright rejected more temporary palliative measures.

Russell might be best remembered as the muckraker who sought both long- and short-range solutions to society's ills. He was associated with every major reform movement from the 1880s to the end of World War I. First he brushed up against the agrarian revolt known as Populism. Then, as a newspaperman and magazine writer, he was in the thick of the crusading zeal of the 1890s and the first part of the twentieth century, which led to some of the most important reforms in American life. But reform was not enough for him, and he joined the political party that sought to transform capitalism. He was the only muckraker who became so passionate about the social issues of the era that he came out from behind his pen to make four runs for political office. But he continued to straddle the worlds of journalism and politics, because even during his runs for office he kept up a steady stream of both commentary and exposé journalism in magazines and books. While journalism has always had activist and neutral strains, Russell was unique in that he successfully presented fact and opinion at the same time and thus succeeded in some of his major efforts, most notably in his triumph over Trinity Church. But his overlooked "beef trust" articles in 1904–1905 also had a major effect. Coupled with the work of Upton Sinclair and Samuel Hopkins Adams, Russell helped force the creation of the Food and Drug Administration, the federal agency which still today is the major overseer of everything from fish to drugs to meat. Its creation was a significant twentieth-century development. Russell's work in helping start the NAACP is more difficult to characterize. It is his lone significant accomplishment that did not involve his journalism or writing. He was purely a social activist, not a journalist, in pushing for the formation of this group, which became the premier advocate for civil rights up until the 1960s when so many other more militant organizations supplanted it. But for the most part Russell was a journalist who used his writing and research to make a difference.

In his final years, Russell seemed satisfied that he had made a contribution. "Nothing in this world softens the melancholy fact of increasing years and approaching death except the reflection that one has been of use, one has served one's times, helped one's fellows, brightened some lives, contributed some service that Society required," he observed. Tributes that poured in to Russell in his last few years certainly echoed those sentiments. The Literature Lovers of America gave him a testimonial dinner, as did a Jewish group in New York City and the YWCA in Washington. A little of his old spirit still remained. At the Washington dinner the eighty-year-old walked slowly to the podium. The event's sponsor went to fix the microphone. "Take it away," Russell thundered. "If I can't make myself heard in this little place, I'll crawl back in my cradle." The audience roared, and then they listened raptly as he castigated the nation for its continued discrimination of black Americans.[28]

Russell still tried his hand at some writing, including a short story (never published) about Jewish victims of Hitler in Germany. Julia Marlowe perhaps spoke for them both when she wrote, "I am sorry but life seems to be too much." His good friend Ernest McGaffey wondered how Russell could keep "aiding in so many uplift enterprises and not get tangled up in some sort of physical reaction."[29] Just a few months later, however, Russell succumbed. He was at his typewriter on April 23, 1941 when he became ill. He went to a couch to lie down. Soon after, Theresa came in and found her husband dead. "C. E. Russell Dies From Overwork," one newspaper reported.[30] Unknowingly, Russell wrote his own epitaph. When his close friend William English Walling died, Russell spoke at a memorial service. He could have been talking about himself when he said: "He lived with unswerving loyalty; he fought the good fight; he loved his fellow man and served him. Greater achievement is not allowed to any upon this earth."[31]

NOTES

PROLOGUE

1. "Charles Edward Russell, 80, Dies After Brief Illness," *Washington Tribune*, April 26, 1901. Russell Papers, Library of Congress, Washington, D.C.
2. Telephone interview with Janet Sims Woods, April 18, 1994.
3. "Charles Edward Russell, 80, Dies After Brief Illness," *Washington Tribune*, April 26, 1901, "Charles Russell, Noted Writer, Socialist, Dies," Associated Press Story, April 24, 1941. "Charles Russell, Journalist, Dies," *New York Times*, April 24, 1941, 44.
4. Russell, *Theodore Thomas and the American Orchestra* (Garden City, N.Y.: Doubleday, Page & Co., 1927).
5. There is no biography, only a Ph.D. dissertation: Donald H. Bragaw, "Soldier for the Common Good: The Life and Career of Charles Edward Russell," Syracuse University, 1970. See also David Mark Chalmers, *The Social and Political Ideas of the Muckrakers* (New York: Citadel Press, 1964).
6. Justin Kaplan, *Lincoln Steffens: A Biography* (New York: Simon and Schuster, 1974); Russell Horton, *Lincoln Steffens* (New York: Twayne Publishers, 1974); Kathleen Brady, *Ida Tarbell: Portrait of a Muckraker* (New York: Seaview/Putnam, 1984); *More than a Muckraker: Ida Tarbell's Lifetime in Journalism*, edited, with an introduction, by Robert C. Kochersberger (Knoxville: University of Tennessee Press, 1994); Louis Filler, *Voice of the Democracy: A Critical Biography of David Graham Phillips, Journalist, Novelist, Progressive* (University Park: Pennsylvania State University Press, 1978); Isaac F. Marcossen, *David Graham Phillips and His Times* (New York: Dodd, Mead & Company, 1932); William A. Bloodworth, *Upton Sinclair* (Boston: Twayne Publishers, 1977); Leon A. Harris, *Upton Sinclair, American Rebel* (New York: Crowell, 1975); Robert C. Bannister, *Ray Stannard Baker: The Mind and Thought of a Progressive* (New Haven: Yale University Press, 1966); John E. Semonche, *Ray Stannard Baker: A Quest for Democracy in Modern America, 1870–1918* (Chapel Hill: University of North Carolina Press, 1969).
7. Tarbell, *The History of the Standard Oil Company* (New York: McClure, Phillips, 1904); Sinclair, *The Jungle* (New York: Doubleday, Page & Co., 1906); Steffens, *The Shame of the Cities* (New York: Hill and Wang, 1904, reprinted 1986).

CHAPTER ONE

1. Russell, *These Shifting Scenes* (New York: Doran Co., 1914), 146, noted the challenge of such routine stories, saying, "To make an annual event a story fresh and

new was a test of workmanship." "Police in New Suits Out on Parade," *New York Herald*, April 1, 1889, 9.

2. A good summary of the Penny Press is Michael Schudsen, "The Revolution in American Journalism in the Age of Egalitarianism: The Penny Press," *Discovering the News* (New York: Basic Books, 1978), 12–60. For overviews, see Frank Luther Mott, *American Journalism* (New York: Macmillan Co., 1941), 228–252 and Michael and Edwin Emery, *The Press and America* (Englewood Cliffs, N.J.: Prentice-Hall, 1988), 6th ed., 115–143.

3. *Shifting Scenes*, 147.

4. Wardman had the most successful career of "The Big Four." He stayed with the *Tribune* until 1895 and became editor of the *New York Press* until 1916. Kenney became an assistant to New York City's mayor, while Farrelly became a top editor at three of William Randolph Hearst's newspapers.

5. *Shifting Scenes*, 148. Russell briefly recounted how he got to the scene of the disaster in "Herald Enterprise," June 10, 1889, 3. The *Herald's* first two pages were always filled with advertisements. Thus page 3 is the equivalent of its page 1.

6. *Shifting Scenes*, 149–1450. "Herald Enterprise." Kenny's account of the journey is in "The Road to Johnstown," *New York Times*, June 2, 1889, 2.

7. "Herald Enterprise."

8. Reporters knew this rule well. In New York the *Sun*, *World*, and *Herald* had long been at war. See W. A. Swanberg, *Pulitzer*, "The Feud with Dana" (New York: Scribner's, 1967), 136–144.

9. *Shifting Scenes*, 153–154.

10. Ibid., 157. The telegram was reported by Kenney, "Road to Johnstown."

11. "Herald Enterprise." George T. Ferris, *The Complete History of Johnstown and Conemaugh Valley Flood* (New York: H. S. Goodspeed, 1889). Ferris also confirms the outline of Russell's account of how they came to Johnstown. On the flood, see also Frank Connelly, *Official History of the Johnstown Flood* (Pittsburgh: Journalist Pub. Co., 1889).

12. *Shifting Scenes*, 162.

13. Ibid. Russell, "After the Deluge," *Herald*, June 4, 1889, 3.

14. "Woe Wrought by the Wrath of the Waters," *Herald*, June 3, 1889, 3.

15. "Hundreds of Lives Lost in a Flood," *Herald*, June 1, 1889, 3. "Victims Numbered by Thousands," *Herald*, June 2, 1889, 3. In total, the *Herald* printed fourteen stories on the first day of its coverage.

16. "Victims Numbered by Thousands," 3–4. On the Hungarians, see, for example, "Lynching the Ghouls" and "Hungarians on the Loose," both page 3. David G. McCullough, *The Johnstown Flood* (New York: Simon & Schuster, 1968), refutes the tales of the Hungarians, 211.

17. McCullough's chapter on the press coverage of Johnstown is entitled "No pen can describe . . . ," 205–229. "Chaos and Death," *Herald*, 3. "Waters Subside on Scenes of Desolation," *Herald*, 5. "Shadows of Despair," *Herald*, 6.

18. "Digging for the Dead," *Herald*, June 6, 1889, 3.

19. "Death, Ruin, Plague," *Herald*, 3.

20. Ferris, 299. Richard O'Connor, *Johnstown: The Day the Dam Broke* (New York: J. P. Lippincott, 1957), 179–180. Russell, *Shifting Scenes*, 167.

21. McCullough, 208.

22. *Shifting Scenes*, 168–169. Russell eventually said his success at Johnstown was "blind and irresistible chance." *Why I Am a Socialist* (New York: Doran Co., 1910), 152.

23. Kenney describes the Cafe Hungaria, "Road to Johnstown." Ferris, 298. *Shifting Scenes*, 165. O'Connor, 182; and McCullough, 215–216; both retell the Davis anecdote. See also Arthur Lubow, *The Reporter Who Would Be King* (New York: Scribner's, 1992), 37–39. "Thugs at Their Work," June 2, 1889, 4 and "In Unwholesome Company," June 6, 1889, 3.

24. *Shifting Scenes*, 165.

25. "Death, Ruin, Plague," June 5, 1889, 3. "Shadows of Despair," June 4, 3. "Waters Subside on Scenes of Desolation," June 4, 1889, 3.

26. "Digging for the Dead," June 6, 1889, 3. "Mud, Ashes, Dead" and "Decaying Bodies Breed Pestilence," both June 7, 1889, 3.

27. "Flood of Money for the Flood Stricken," June 4, 1889, 4. "Gloomy, Muddy Johnstown," June 12, 3. "Mud, Ashes, Dead," June 7, 1889, 3.

28. Kenney notes the nickname in "How the Correspondents Live," *New York Times*, June 2, 1889, 2. Ferris, 287. O'Connor, 164. Despite what O'Connor wrote, Russell reported that thirty priests, mostly from Pittsburgh, were on the scene by June 4. See "Waters Subside."

29. "Swept from the Face of the Earth," June 9, 1899, 11. *Shifting Scenes*, 170.

30. Russell, "The Noblest Ambition," *The Academy Student*, 4. Claire Johnson of St. Johnsbury, Vermont, supplied a copy of this article to the author.

31. *Shifting Scenes*, 132.

32. Ibid., 169.

33. That Russell believed this is noted in a letter from William English Walling to Willoughby Walling, May 26, 1919: "Remember Mr. Russell's motto: 'The public doesn't know a fact until it has been printed sixteen times.'" Strunsky Walling Papers, Box 1, Folder: Correspondence 1917–1928, Yale University.

34. "Rational Political Action," March 1912. It is unclear where this article appeared. It is in the Russell Papers, Library of Congress, Washington, D.C. He makes a similar comment in "Old Reporter Looks at the Mad-house World," *Scribner's*, October 1933, 225.

35. *Shifting Scenes*, 260. McCullough, 224.

36. The cause of the dam burst is described by McCullough, 51–58, 76–77, and 247–250. See also O'Connor, 29–33. McCullough notes that "very few newspapers ever went so far as to mention any specific names" of the members of the South Fork Fishing and Hunting Club, 250.

37. *Shifting Scenes*, 168.

38. Ibid., 167. Lincoln Steffens, "A Muckraker," *Lincoln Steffens Speaking* (New York: Harcourt, Brace & Co., 1936), 157. His comments appeared originally in a book review of Russell's *Bare Hands and Stone Walls* in the *Nation*, December 20, 1933, 713.

CHAPTER TWO

1. *A-rafting on the Mississipp'* (New York, London: The Century Co., 1928), 4.

2. Ibid., 6. A profile of William Rutledge is found in *History of Scott County, Iowa* (Chicago: Inter-State Publishing Co., 1882), 633–635. Russell describes his grandfather in *A Pioneer Editor in Early Iowa; A Sketch of the Life of Edward Russell* (Washington, D.C.: Ransdell Inc., 1941), 43–47.

3. *A-rafting*, 8.

4. The column appeared in *The Coming Nation*, a socialist weekly newspaper, in 1911–1912. His work there will be discussed in chapters 11 and 12.

272 THE PEN IS MIGHTIER

5. On Davenport's history, see *History of Scott County*, ibid.; on Iowa, see Louis Atherton, *Main Street on the Middle Border* (Chicago: Quadrangle, 1966).
6. An article describing this adventure, "A Mad Engineer," *New York Dispatch*, April 10, 1887, is in the Russell Papers, Library of Congress.
7. Russell made this comment in a United Press International obituary, "Charles Edward Russell, 80, Davenporter who won fame as author, newsman, dies," supplied to the author by the Davenport Public Library. The comment about Edward Russell, *History of Scott County*, 578.
8. *Pioneer Editor*, 4, 7.
9. Ibid., 1–11. The connection between temperance advocates such as Rutledge and the Russells and reform causes such as abolitionism can be found in Alice Felt Tyler, *Freedom's Ferment: Phases of American Social History to 1860* (Minneapolis: University of Minnesota Press, 1944).
10. *History of Scott County*, 579; *Pioneer Editor*, 16.
11. On the press and partisanship, see Michael Schudson, *Discovering the News: A Social History of American Newspapers* (New York: Basic Books, 1978). On political patronage and newspapers, see *Iowa: A Guide to the Hawkeye State* (New York: Hastings, 1949), 125.
12. Russell wrote about Johnson: "He began almost at once to exercise the dictatorial instincts of his brutish mind by removing from office all persons that had displeased him or opposed his policies." *Pioneer Editor*, 41. See also *History of Scott County*, 580; "Iowa Imprints Before 1861," *Iowa Journal of History and Politics* 36, 1938. v. 9. The Andrew Johnson Papers, V. 9, 315, also state that he was the first official removed by Johnson. The papers cite the above two sources. Letter to the author from Hans L. Trefousse, a Johnson biographer, September 24, 1996.
13. Trefousse, *Andrew Johnson: A Biography* (New York: Norton Co., 1989). *Pioneer Editor*, 4.
14. On the politics of Reconstruction, see Howard K. Beale, *The Critical Year: A Study of Andrew Johnson and Reconstruction* (New York: Ungar, 1958); Martin E. Mantell Johnson, *Grant and the Politics of Reconstruction* (New York: Columbia University Press, 1973); Eric L. McKitrick, *Andrew Johnson and Reconstruction* (Chicago: University of Chicago Press, 1960).
15. The *Gazette's* history is described in *History of Scott County*, 575–578 and "There goes the Gazette Block," *Quad City Times*, August 28, 1981, supplied to the author by the Davenport Public Library. *Bare Hands and Stone Walls* (New York: Scribner's Sons, 1933), 4.
16. Russell describes this incident in *Bare Hands*, 5–8. On the *Gazette's* award, "There goes the Gazette Block," ibid.
17. *Shifting Scenes* (New York: Doran Co., 1914), 5.
18. Ibid., 14–15.
19. *Catalogue, St. Johnsbury Academy* (St. Johnsbury, Vt.: C. M. Stone Co., 1881), 20.
20. Edward Russell's abstinence is noted in *History of Scott County*, p. 581. *St. Johnsbury Catalogue*, 21.
21. *Bare Hands*, 10. To understand the academy, I used Arthur F. Stone, *The First Hundred Years* (St. Johnsbury, Vt., Alumni Fund, St. Johnsbury Academy, 1942) and St. Johnsbury Academy admission catalogue, 1990.
22. *Bare Hands*, 25. *The Story of Wendell Phillips: Soldier of the Common Good* (Chicago: C. H. Kerr & Co., 1914).

23. Russell's views on free trade can be seen in "The Reason Why A Republican Free Trader Gives His Reasons for Opposing What is Falsely Called a Protective Tariff," *Iowa State Leader,* 1881. *Bare Hands,* 23.

24. *St. Johnsbury Catalogue,* p. 19. *Bare Hands,* 11.

25. *Bare Hands,* 12, 14.

26. David D. Anderson, *Robert Ingersoll* (New York: Twayne, 1972).

27. *Bare Hands,* 9, 15.

28. Discussed in E. T. Fairbanks, *Town of St. Johnsbury, Vt.; A Review of One Hundred Twenty-five Years to the Anniversary Pageant* (St. Johnsbury, 1912), 249.

29. On Fairbanks, see *Dictionary of American Biography* (New York: Scribner's Sons, 1959), 248–251. Sons of the founders were active in the town when Russell attended the academy, but there is no indication that he had relations—good or bad—with any of them.

30. *Bare Hands,* 16, 21.

31. The chapter in *Bare Hands* discussing Dow is entitled, "Old Jim Dow, Notcher of Beams," 8–25.

32. Russell made these comments in an introduction to Caro Lloyd, *Henry Demarest Lloyd, 1847–1903, A Biography, V. 1* (New York: G. P. Putnam's, 1912), vi, viii. A better biography of Lloyd is Chester McArthur Destler, *Henry Demarest Lloyd and the Empire of Reform* (Philadelphia: University of Pennsylvania Press, 1963).

33. *Bare Hands,* 16.

34. Telephone interview with Newell, September 6, 1996. Letter to the author from Mrs. Johnson, February 7, 1990.

35. *The Uprising of the Many* (New York: Doubleday, Page & Co., 1907), 12. Introduction to Caro Lloyd, *Lloyd,* see note 32, vii.

36 *Bare Hands,* 27. He discusses his cousin in a letter, CER to J. B. Oakley, May 1, 1929, Haldeman Manuscripts, Lilly Library, Indiana University.

37. *Bare Hands,* 27. The Populist revolt is best described by John Hicks, *The Populist Revolt: A History of the Farmers' Alliance and the People's Party* (Minneapolis: University of Minnesota Press, 1931); Norman Pollack, *The Populist Response to Industrial America: Midwestern Populist Thought* (Cambridge, Mass.: Harvard University Press, 1962); and Lawrence Goodwyn, *Democratic Promise: The Populist Moment in America* (New York: Oxford University Press, 1976).

38. *Bare Hands,* 31. "The Reason Why." See note 23.

39. Perry, *Principles of Political Economy* (New York: Scribner's, 1891), 503. Carroll Perry, *Professor of Life: A Sketch of A. L. Perry* (Boston: Houghton Mifflin Company, 1923.)

40. Russell letter to Gurney C. Gue, August 31, 1888, quoted in "The Bravery of Iowans in Storming of Chapultepec," *The Annals of Iowa* VXXVIII, October 1946, 148.

41. Russell briefly sketches his activities during this time in Arthur F. Stone, *History of the Class of Eighty-One, St. Johnsbury Academy* (St. Johnsbury: C. M. Stone & Co, 1883), 17. *Bare Hands,* 32.

42. "The Bravery of Iowans," see note 40, 147. *Pioneer Editor,* 51.

43. Ibid., 51–52. He repeats this anecdote in *Bare Hands,* 58–59.

44. Background on the Hennepin Canal is in John J. Steinbach, "History of the Illinois and Mississippi Canal," M.S. thesis, Illinois State University, 1964, 1–32 and Gerald A. Newton and Donald Griffin, *History of the Hennepin Canal* (Macomb, Ill.: Institute for Regional Studies, 1984). Edward Russell's early advocacy is

noted in *History of Scott County*, 581. See also Roald Tweet, *A History of the Rock Island District, 1866–1983* (Rock Island, Ill.: U.S. Army Corps of Engineers, 1984) and Gerald A. Newton, *History of the Hennepin Canal* (Macomb, Ill.: Western Illinois University, 1984).

45. *Pioneer Editor*, 66, Steinbach, ibid., 15. See also Illinois and Mississippi River and Canal Improvement Commission, *Cheap Transportation and the Hennepin Canal: Proceedings of the Convention* (Davenport, Iowa: Gazette Co., 1981).

46. *Pioneer Editor*, 68.

47. The U.S. Army Corps of Engineers found that prices could be cut in half when the railroads had waterway competition. See Steinbach, 25. Government agency was U.S. Army Corps of Engineers, *Annual Report*, 1891, quoted in Steinbach, 31. A similar discussion of reduced rates is in Major W. H. H. Benyaurd, *From Lake Michigan to the Mississippi River: Reasons for the Construction of the New Canal* (Davenport, Iowa: Michigan and Mississippi Canal Commission, 1884).

48. *Pioneer Editor*, 70–71.

49. "Edward Russell," *Davenport Sunday Democrat*, December 20, 1891, 2. Russell's active and organizing role can also be seen from the minutes of the 1881 conference he organized on the canal. *Proceedings of the River and Canal Improvement Convention* (Davenport, Iowa: Gazette Printers, 1881).

50. Henry C. Adams, in an introduction to F. H. Dixon, *State Railroad Control: A History of its Development in Iowa* (New York: Crowell, 1896), 8. *Pioneer Editor*, 70.

51. *Pioneer Editor*, 71.

52. *Star Tribune: 125 Years of History in the Making* (Minneapolis: Star Tribune, 1992). D. L. Sullivan to Russell, February 6, 1885, Russell Papers, Library of Congress.

53. Ted Curtis Smythe, "A History of the *Minneapolis Journal*, 1878–1939," Ph.D. dissertation, University of Minnesota, 1967. The comment about his editing is from an undated article that has a small drawing of Russell. Gelatt's comments are in two letters, one addressed "To whom it may concern," the other Gelatt to CER, both dated June 10, 1886. Both are in Russell Papers, Library of Congress.

CHAPTER THREE

1. *These Shifting Scenes* (New York: Doran Co., 1914), 31.

2. The letter from his father is in Russell Papers, Library of Congress. *Shifting Scenes*, 39.

3. *Shifting Scenes*, 32.

4. *Shifting Scenes*, 34, 40.

5. Many of Russell's early newspaper articles were carefully pasted and saved in a scrapbook that I have used to understand his early reportage. In his papers, Library of Congress. "Broadway Oddities," *Commercial Advertiser*, July 20, 1887.

6. "An Aged Voodoo's Life," *Mail & Express*, October 1886. "An Old Grave Digger," *Brooklyn Eagle*, December 19, 1886.

7. "Women Bird Fanciers," November 14, 1886, and "The Thieves of the Hill," February 6, 1887, both *Brooklyn Eagle*.

8. "Wonderful Crimes," *New York Dispatch*, December 5, 1886. In another story, he gave over two full columns for one of the city's oldest detectives to talk about his years of crime solving. "Detective Life," *Commercial Advertiser*, January 22, 1887.

9. "Barrel House," *Brooklyn Eagle*, November 7, 1886.

10.   "Victims of the Tremens," *Commercial Advertiser,* May 22, 1887.

11.   The journal is in the Russell Papers.

12.   On reporters and space rates, see Ted Curtis Smythe, "The Reporter, 1880–1900: Working Conditions and their Influence on the News," *Journalism History* (Spring 1980), 1–10. "A Widower's Wonderful Cat," *Mail & Express,* September 1886; "A Family of Gum Chewers," *Mail & Express,* October 24, 1886; "Anaconda's Bath," *Brooklyn Eagle,* December 10, 1886. "Women at the Market," *Commercial Advertiser,* June 8, 1887; "Dyspepsia," *Commercial Advertiser,* February 26, 1887.

13.   "An Arkansas Mystery," *New York Dispatch,* September 12, 1886; "A Tale of Three Lives," *Mail & Express,* September 1886; and "The Demon of Gottingen," *Dispatch,* February 27, 1887.

14.   "Hunting a Ghost," *Dispatch,* February 6, 1887. Quoted in Hazel Dickens-Garcia, *Journalistic Standards in Nineteenth-Century America* (Madison: University of Wisconsin Press, 1989), 199.

15.   "A Woman Dies for his Love," *Mail & Express,* January 8, 1887; "In a Very Bad Fix," *Mercury,* March 6, 1887; "Two Trades," March 29, 1887, *Brooklyn Eagle,* and "Whims of Abused Women," *Mail & Express,* November 20, 1886.

16.   *Shifting Scenes,* 38. *The Autobiography of Lincoln Steffens* (New York: Harcourt, Brace & Co., 1931), 311.

17.   *Shifting Scenes,* 47. *Recollections of a Varied Life* (New York: Holt & Co., 1910), 294. He cites Russell as one of the outstanding reporters who worked for him, 260. On Eggleston's life, see also *A Rebel's Recollections.*

18.   *Shifting Scenes,* 55. He wrote this originally in "The Police Justices Oe (sic) Gotham," *Mail & Express,* February 5, 1887.

19.   *Shifting Scenes,* 56. "And They Were Married," *Commercial Advertiser,* September 22, 1886.

20.   *Shifting Scenes,* 52. *Bare Hands and Stone Walls* (New York: Scribner's Sons, 1933), 90.

21.   *Bare Hands,* 87.

22.   Ibid., 81.

23.   *Shifting Scenes,* 49. *Bare Hands,* 79.

24.   Eggleston, *Recollections of a Varied Life,* 293.

25.   *Shifting Scenes,* 21. He tells about the incident in "The Case of William Heilwagner," 18–30.

26.   Henry David, *The History of the Haymarket Affair* (New York: Collier Books, 1963), 58–79.

27.   Russell's version is "The Haymarket and Afterward," *Shifting Scenes,* 80–110.

28.   "The Growing Menace of Socialism," *Hampton's,* January 1909. Reprinted in *Studies in Socialism,* a pamphlet, September 1910, 1–21.

29.   *Bare Hands,* 193. *Shifting Scenes,* 212.

30.   "The Story of the Crime," *World,* November 12, 1886, 2. It is difficult to determine which stories, aside from the one noted here, were Russell's. Clearly, however, he was the second writer behind Henry Guy Carleton.

31.   "Autobiography of an Author," *Notes on Books and Authors* from Doubleday, Page. & Co., found in Russell Papers. His two articles on Haymarket are: "The Haymarket and Afterwards, Some Personal Recollections," *Appleton's,* October 1907, 399–412 and "Chaos and Bomb Throwing in Chicago," *Hampton's,* March 1910, 307–320. *Shifting Scenes,* 94. He carefully traced how pipe bombs, like the one used in Chicago, could be bought in "Infernal Machines," *Commercial Advertiser,* August 24, 1887.

32. *Shifting Scenes*, 96. The *World* is quoted in David, 273.
33. *Shifting Scenes*, 105, 104.
34. "No Parade, No Red Flags," *Boston Globe*, November 12, 1888. *Shifting Scenes*, 204.
35. On the prison, *Sing Sing Prison: Its History, Purpose, Makeup and Program* (Albany, N.Y.: Department of Correction, 1953). Russell, "In Sing Sing," March 1, 1887; "Sing Sing Inmates," March 2, 1887, both in *Commercial Advertiser.*
36. "The Capital Punishment Question," *New York Times*, August 12, 1890, 12.
37. Russell, "McElvaine in the Death Chair," *Herald*, February 9, 1892, 5. *Brisbane, A Candid Biography* (Westport, Conn.: Greenwood Press, 1937), 97.
38. "McElvaine in the Death Chair," ibid.
39. "Execution of Murderer Cotto," *Herald*, March 29, 1892, 3. See also, "Cowardly Cotto Will Die To-day," *Herald*, March 28, 3. Russell wrote to a Davenport, Iowa, friend, Ralph Cram, on the letterhead of the American League to Abolish Capital Punishment, located in New York City, Russell to Cram, August 3, 1939.
40. *Shifting Scenes*, 22. Detective journalism was almost a journalistic genre. See Russell A. Mann, "Investigative Reporting in the Gilded Age: A Study of the Detective Journalism of Melville E. Stone and the *Chicago Morning News*, 1881–1888," Ph.D. dissertation, Southern Illinois University, 1977.
41. The article is in the Russell Papers and appeared in the *World*, May 7, 1887.
42. *Shifting Scenes,*132.
43. "Where Was the Danmark?" *Shifting Scenes*, 132–145. He discusses his love of boating, 249.
44. The reference to Riis and Russell is in a fragment of a magazine article found in the Russell Papers. *Why I Am a Socialist* (New York: Doran Co., 1910), 97.
45. Russell also wrote many stories on the murder of Carl Ruttinger. See "Puzzling Mysteries of the Arthur Kill Murder," March 13, 1891, 4. "W.W. on the Handkerchief; William Wright Missing," March 14, 1891, 3; "Ruttinger's Life Insured for $21,000," March 16, 1891, 4; "Murder and Suicide Fit Wright's Character," March 20, 1891, 4. "Wright May Have Died With Ruttinger," March 15, 1891, 4; "More Mystery in the Strange Case of Carl Ruttinger," March 17, 1891, 4; "Startling Testimony that Evans Was Wright," March 18, 1891, 3; "Again All Theories Fail in the Ruttinger Case," March 21, 1891, 5; "Wright Seemed then on the Verge of Despair," March 22, 1891, p. 22; "Probably Ruttinger and Probably Not," April 1, 1891, 6, all in the *Herald. Shifting Scenes*, 190. "Ghastly Butchery By a New York Jack the Ripper," *Herald*, April 25, 1891, 3.
46. "No 'Ripper' Yet For All the Hard Work," *Herald*, April 29, 1891, 7. His other stories in the *Herald* include "New York's 'Ripper' Known to the Police," April 26, 1891, 17; "The 'Ripper' Left a Fairly Plain Trail," April 27, 1891, 3; "Four Days Gone and No 'Ripper' Found Yet," April 28, 1891, 5.
47. "No Motive Yet Found for the Borden Murder," *Herald*, August 7, 13, 1891.
48. "Mrs. Borden Was Dead A Full Hour Before Her Husband Came," *Herald*, August 8, 3, 1891.
49. Ibid.; "Borden Mystery May Soon Be Solved," *Herald*, August 9, 1891, 3. There are various accounts of the Borden murder. However, the most thorough is Edward D. Radin, *Lizzie Borden: The Untold Story* (New York: Simon and Schuster, 1961). Radin concluded that Lizzie Borden was innocent. He carefully and con-

vincingly repudiates the biased account of Edmund Pearson, *Trial of Lizzie Borden* (New York: Doubleday, Doran & Co., 1937).

50. Radin, 4. Russell, *Why I Am A Socialist*, 84.
51. *Why I Am a Socialist*, 88.
52. Ibid., 85–86.
53. *Bare Hands*, 80.

Chapter Four

1. "Harrison Men fear Blaine's name may create a cyclone," *Herald*, June 4, 1892, 3.
2. "The Bravery of Iowans in Storming of Chapultepec," *The Annals of Iowa* VXXIII, October 1946, 148.
3. Russell describes this incident in *A Pioneer Editor in Early Iowa: A Sketch of the Life of Edward Russell* (Washington, D.C.: Ransdell Inc., 1941), 58–59. It is discussed also in *History of Scott County, Iowa* (Chicago: Inter-State Publishing Co., 1882), 581.
4. *Business: The Heart of the Nation*, 13. Russell said both the Republican and Democratic parties started with noble ideals, but both became corrupt. See "The Breakup of the Parties," *Success*, January 1909, 5–10; February, 80–82, 111–122.
5. Business: *The Heart of the Nation*, 20–24. He devotes a chapter to Weaver, "Greenback the Weaver," in *Bare Hands and Stone Walls* (New York: Scribner's Sons, 1933), 57–78. Frederick E. Haynes, *James Baird Weaver* (New York: Arno Press, 1975).
6. "Life in A Big City," October 1886; "Detective and Clerk," January 2, 1887. Both articles are in the Russell Papers.
7. *These Shifting Scenes* (New York: George H. Doran, 1914), 112, 119.
8. Ibid., 120.
9. A Blaine biographer asserts that both Blaine sons were actively working for their father's nomination. David Saville Muzzey, *James G. Blaine: A Political Idol of Other Days* (New York: Dodd, Mead & Co., 1963) 375. Quote from Russell, *Shifting Scenes*, 130.
10. *Shifting Scenes*, 113.
11. Although the dates are not clear, Russell always especially liked Minneapolis, where he would often go for summer vacations, splitting logs and rowing on the state's lakes. He also regularly visited his brother's sisters in Minneapolis. Later, he often used Minnesota examples in his reporting.
12. Muzzey, 463. See also Homer E. Socolofsky and Allan B. Spetter, *The Presidency of Benjamin Harrison* (Lawrence: University of Kansas Press, 1987), 110.
13. On relations between Harrison and Blaine, see Muzzey, 462–466 and Socolofsky and Spetter, 197–198.
14. "Blaine comes on a personal errand" and "Blaine Gets Nearer to the nomination," *Herald*, May 24, 1892, 3.
15. *Shifting Scenes*, 214–215, 213.
16. "Blaine will accept if nominated," *Herald*, June 3, 1892, 3; *Shifting Scenes*, 216; "Blaine will accept, that seems sure," *Herald*, May 27, 1892, 3.
17. "Mr. Platt Dissects President Harrison," *Herald*, June 1, 1892, 3. On Platt's dissatisfaction with Harrison, *The Autobiography of Thomas C. Platt* (New York: B. W. Dodge, 1910), 206 207 and Socolofsky and Spetter, 195–197.
18. "Harrison men mean to make a hard fight," *Herald*, June 2, 1892, 3.

19. Ibid.; Muzzey, 472–474; "Blaine's resignation sets Minneapolis wild," *Herald*, June 5, 1892, 3.

20. *Shifting Scenes*, 217, 213.

21. "Neck and neck are the leaders at Minneapolis," *Herald*, June 7, 1892, 3.

22. "Harrison ahead, but bartered votes will decide it," *Herald*, June 8, 1892, 3.

23. *Shifting Scenes*, 219. James P. Boyd, *Life and Service of Honorable James G. Blaine* (New York: Publishers Union, 1893), 174.

24. "Harrison ahead, but bartered votes will decide it," *Herald*, June 8, 1892, 3.

25. *Shifting Scenes*, 227.

26. Ibid., 237. "Still hard at work to save democracy from defeat," *Herald*, June 22, 1892, 3.

27. Russell wrote an admiring description of Whitney in a letter to Whitney's biographer. See Mark D. Hirsch, *William C. Whitney: Modern Warwick* (New York: Archon Books, 1969), 393.

28. Russell wrote an admiring portrait of Whitney for the *Herald* as well. "Whitney's able battle," June 20, 1892, 4,5.

29. Russell's allegations came in *Shifting Scenes*, 243–244. Whitney's biographer denies that Whitney had to make promises in return for Cleveland's election (411), although he concedes that Whitney's modus operandi was to meld business and politics. Hirsch, 469. Cleveland biographer Allan Nevins also makes no mention of possible vote buying, saying only that Whitney was "suave, cool and indomitable." *Grover Cleveland: A Study in Courage* (New York: Dodd, Mead & Co.), 490.

30. *Shifting Scenes*, 243, 113.

31. Russell described the encounter with Kelly in *Bare Hands*, 117–119.

32. Profiles of McLaughlin include Harold Zink, " 'Old Man' Hugh McLaughlin," *City Bosses in the United State* (Durham, N.C.: Duke University Press, 1930), 178–193, and Henry Claflin Wells, *Urban Political Development and the Power of Local Groups: A Case Study of Politics in South Brooklyn, 1865–1935* (New York: Columbia University Press, 1986), 119–136. Wells says McLaughlin was one of the first bosses in America. For contrasting views on the political boss, see Samuel P. Orth, *The Boss and the Machine* (New Haven: Yale University Press, 1920); Bruce Stave and Sondra Astor Stave, eds., *Urban Bosses, Machines, and Progressive Reformers* (Lexington, Mass.: Heath, 1972) and John D. Haeger, ed., *The Bosses* (St. Charles, Mo.: Forum Press, 1974).

33. *Bare Hands*, 119. Russell details the grievances against the McLaughlin machine in "Here, There, and About the City," Brooklyn supplement, October 15, 1. See also Russell's "Why Brooklyn is bankrupt," a less impressive story, October 21, 4.

34. "Ring Ridden Brooklyn in Revolt," October 8, 1893, 5–6.

35. Ibid.

36. *Bare Hands*, 121; *Shifting Scenes*, 210.

37. *Bare Hands*, 120.

38. *City Bosses*, 192, 182–183.

39. "Further Mayoralty Comments," August 13, 1893, Brooklyn supplement, 1. Russell's criticism of Boody can be seen also in "Mr. McLaughlin as Talker," September 3, Brooklyn supplement.

40. " 'Boss' McLaughlin returns," September 15, 1893, 8, *New York Times*. The *Tribune* article, November 2, 1877, 4, is cited in *City Bosses*, 183.

41. Ibid., September 15, 1893. Russell discussed the opposition in "Mr. Boody in Danger," September 17, 1893, Brooklyn supplement.

42. "Specific Charges for Boody," October 19, 1893, 1; "Specific Charges, He Demands, and Here They Are," October 20, 1893, 5, both in the *New York Times*. Russell analyzes the political situation in "Mr. Boody in danger," September 17, 1893, Brooklyn supplement.

43. Russell's story on the Committee of 100 is "For Brooklyn's emancipation," September 29, 1893, Brooklyn supplement. "Brooklyn Demands a Fighter for Good Government," *New York Times*, October 1, 1893, 13.

44. "Ring Ridden Brooklyn in Revolt," October 8, 1893, 5–6.

45. Ibid. On McLaughlin's wealth, see *City Bosses*, 191–192.

46. "Honeycombed with corruption," October 9, 2; "Brooklyn citizens declare for their champion," *New York Times*, October 13, 1893, 1.

47. "Throttled by the Brooklyn ring," October 22, 1893, 6. He elaborates in "Find the ring hard to beat," October 25, 1893, 6.

48. "Brooklyn demands a fighter for good government"; "Closing the lines around the ring," *Herald*, October 29, 1893, Brooklyn supplement, 3, a knowledgeable commentary on Brooklyn politics and the issues posed by the election.

49. "Specific charges for Boody," *New York Times*, October 29, 1893, 1.

50. "McKane and his Sunday school," October 1, 1893, 6.

51. Ibid. on McLaughlin, see *Bare Hands*, 122.

52. "War on floaters in Kings County," *Herald*, November 1, 1893, 1; "The issue in Brooklyn," October 27, 1893, 6.

53. "War on floaters," ibid.; "'Boss' M'Kane to the Bar," *New York Times*, November 1, 1893, 1.

54. "Fighting for a citizen's spoils," November 2, 7. Blaine A. Brownell and Warren E. Stickle, eds., *Urban Political Development and the Power of Local Groups: Bosses and Reformers in Urban Politics in America, 1880–1920* (Boston: Houghton-Mifflin, 1973), 1. The authors portray rigid dichotomies such as Russell's as simplistic and offer a revisionist view that the bosses were important to stability and in providing municipal services.

55. "M'Kane's Crowning Outrage," *New York Times*, November 6, 1893, 1; " 'Boss' McKane still defiant," November 6, 1893, 1. Russell described the police effort to influence voters in "Police muster for Boody," October 27, 1893, 5.

56. "Why Brooklyn's ring must fail," November 3, 1896, 6. Russell discusses campaign money in "'Boodle' for the campaign," October 18, 1893, 6.

57. "Brooklyn ring annihilated," *New York Times*, November 8, 1893, 1; "All praise the Herald," November 9, 1893, 1.

58. *Bare Hands*, 122, 123.

59. Zink, *City Bosses*, discusses McLaughlin's various comebacks and his final days, 186–189.

60. *Bare Hands*, 126.

CHAPTER FIVE

1. "Controls All the Ice," April 23, 1896, 3. Discussions of the trust problem can be found in all the major literature on the Gilded Age and the Progressive Era. See Eliot Jones, *The Trust Problem in the United States* (New York: Macmillan, 1928) and George Mowry, *The Era of Theodore Roosevelt* (New York: Harper and Row, 1958).

2. *World*, April 1, 1896, 1, 3, 4, 5, 13.

3. *World*, April 23, 1896, 1, 2, 3, 5.

4. "Began a Fight, Got Shot," *World*, May 6, 1896, 1.

5. James W. Barrett, *Joseph Pulitzer and His World* (New York: Vanguard, 1941), 97.

6. Charles Edward Russell, *These Shifting Scenes* (New York: Doran Co., 1914), 286.

7. There are three biographies about Phillips: I. F. Marcossen, *David Graham Phillips and His Times* (New York: Dodd, Mead, 1932), Abe C. Ravitz, *David Graham Phillips* (New York: Twayne Publishers, 1966) and Louis Filler, *The Voice of Democracy: A Critical Biography of David Graham Phillips, Journalist, Novelist, Progressive* (University Park: Pennsylvania State University Press, 1978).

8. Marcossen, 11. Russell and Phillips authored a book together called "Dictionary of things as they are." It contained such musings as: "Success—Gouging your way to the front with lies, fakes, and the strangling of your fellows." And "Friendship—The interest that Mr. A. pretends in Mr. B for the sake of some advantage he expects to win from Mr. B." No publisher was interested in this book. Marcossen, 184.

9. *Shifting Scenes*, 289.

10. "Was Alive in His Coffin," *World*, April 29, 1896, 1.

11. "A World Picture Did It," *World*, May 5, 1896, 1.

12. "Now Comes a Hypnotist," May 4, 1996, 3, "Dead in the River Mud," April 13, 1896, 2, both in the *World*.

13. "Knife Stuck in Skull," December 1, 1997, 3 and "Zavoli's Wife No. 4 to Be Exhumed To-morrow," December 12, 1897, 4, both in the *World*.

14. George Juergens, *Joseph Pulitzer and the New York World* (Princeton: Princeton University Press, 1966), 84. Juergens provides the best analysis and discussion of the themes that clearly emerge in the news pages of Pulitzer.

15. Quoted by Juergens from a *World* editorial, May 6, 1884.

16. Juergens, quoting Pulitzer, *World*, May 27, 1884, 70–71.

17. Almost none of the editors and reporters wrote memoirs about their years in Pulitzer's newsroom. Given the fact that the *World* was considered an admirable—if not august—newspaper, this is odd. It is understandable that they were too busy to write letters during their days as reporters; however, it is inexplicable that their memoirs reflect so little of their news days. Perhaps, since many went into careers as writers of fiction, they considered their news days as merely training grounds, with little lasting value.

18. Russell, *Shifting Scenes*, 285.

19. Russell, *Business: The Heart of the Nation* (New York: John Lane Co., 1911), 123.

20. Ivy Lee to CER, January 4, 1909, Russell Papers, Library of Congress.

21. *World*, April 13, 1884, 4, quoted in Juergens, 70.

22. Phillips's journalism is detailed in Robert Miraldi, "The Journalism of David Graham Phillips," *Journalism Quarterly* 63 (Spring 1988): 83–88. This article is a summary of a Ph.D. dissertation of the same name, New York University, 1985.

23. *Shifting Scenes*, 286.

24. "Death Hid in the Stove," December 3, 1897, 3 and "Her Husband a Felon," July 3, 1896, 3, both in the *World*.

25. "Burglars Rob Old—and Perhaps Young," *World*, September 9, 1897. Juergens, 52. A good discussion of the "story" techniques found in Pulitzer's *World* is Michael Schudsen, "Stories and Information: Two Journalisms in the 1890s," *Discovering the News* (New York: Basic Books, 1978), 88–120.

26. *World* editorial, December 7, 1883, quoted in Juergens, 50.

27. John Tipple, "Big Businessman and a New Economy," *The Gilded Age*, ed. H. Wayne Morgan (Syracuse: Syracuse University Press, 1975).

28. The articles appeared April 3–8, 10–15, 1893, with headlines such as "Smash This Trust!" and "Kill these Trusts." They are discussed in my dissertation (note 22), 71–75.

29. Undated, unsigned memo, about 1900, in the Pulitzer Papers, Columbia University, New York City.

30. "Boodle to Buy Votes," March 11, 1895, 1. "Can't Stand the Light," March 15, 1895, 1, both in the *World*.

31. Ibid.

32. "Controls All the Ice," *World*, April 23, 1896, 1–2.

33. Other stories on the ice monopoly included "Fight the Ice Trust," April 24, 1896, 2, "May Kill the Ice Trust," April 26, 1896, 4, and "Morse's Ice Trust," May 4, 1895, 4. Less crusading but equally adamant was a story about a court hearing on an injunction to halt a wallpaper manufacturer from controlling that industry in New York. "Wages Cut and Rivals Crushed," read a headline over the story, another example of the public outrage over lack of competition. "Fighting a Big Trust," *World*, April 26, 1895,1.

34. April 28, 1895, *World*, 1. The meat packers, later to become Russell's archenemies, were particular targets that month. See stories attacking the beef trust on April 11, 13, and 16, 1895. Further indication of the Pulitzer obsession with the trusts' control is "At the Mercy of the Trusts," May 6, 1895, 2, which was a summary of how the trusts were overcharging consumers.

35. "Shoes Will Come High," *World*, May 3, 1895, 1.

36. "Secret of the Kinsgbridge Road Big Franchise Grab," *World*, September 27, 1897, 1.

37. "Mind-Reading A Trick," *World*, February 18, 1895, 6. Two months after this article appeared, Cochrane married and ended her illustrious and controversial reporting stint at the *World*.

38. Pay for Bail Bonds," *World*, April 24, 1896, 1.

39. Alleyne Ireland, *An Adventure with a Genius: Recollections of Joseph Pulitzer* (New York: Johnson Reprint, [1969] 1920), 115.

40. See note 36.

41. Stories on the franchise grab appeared on September 19–20, 27–30, and October 6, 1897.

42. "The World's 'Halt' Holds the Franchise Grab," *World*, September 30, 1897, 1.

43. September 20, 1897, 1; "A Philadelphia Engineer Examines N.Y. Streets for World," October 4, 1897, 5; "Chaos Collins Causes Water to Flood," October 11, 1897, 1, both in the *World*.

44. Quoted in Juergens, 92.

45. Russell, *Shifting Scenes*, 285.

CHAPTER SIX

1. W. A. Swanberg, *Pulitzer* (New York: Charles Scribner's Sons, 1967), 136–147.

2. In the "new journalism" of the 1880s, see Edwin and Michael Emery, *The Press and America*, 6th ed. (Englewood Cliffs, N.J.: Prentice-Hall, 1988), 203–212. The *World* was reaching 450,000 people, an unheard of number.

3. David Nasaw, *The Chief: The Life of William Randolph Hearst* (New York: Houghton-Mifflin, 2000), 98.
4. Swanberg, 207. A glimpse at the New York newspaper world can be seen in Allen Churchill, *Park Row* (New York: Rinehart, 1958).
5. Ben Procter, *William Randolph Hearst, The Early Years* (New York: Oxford, 1998), 81.The Goddard story is retold in Ferdinand Lundberg, *Imperial Hearst: A Social Biography* (New York: Equinox Cooperative Press, 1936), 54–55; John K. Winkler, *W. R. Hearst: An American Phenomenon* (New York: Simon and Schuster, 1928), 106–107); Swanberg, 206; and Nasaw, 103–104.
6. Nasaw, 120, 104.
7. Swanberg, 207; Nasaw, 105; Proctor, 87; Lundberg, 56.
8. Russell, *These Shifting Scenes* (New York: Doran Co., 1914), 272–273.
9. Don Seitz, Joseph *Pulitzer: His Life and Letters* (New York: Simon and Schuster, 1924), 211–212. Russell, *Shifting Scenes*, 277.
10. Abbot, *Watching the World Go By* (Boston: Little, Brown and Co., 1933), 207–208. Russell, *Shifting Scenes*, 310.
11. The secret Pulitzer code names are listed on the inside cover of Swanberg's biography, *Pulitzer*. Russell's name is omitted. However, his code name is listed in the Joseph Pulitzer Collection, Columbia University, Container No. 1, Box 1896–1898.
12. Oliver Carlson, *Brisbane: A Candid Biography* (Westport, Conn.: Greenwood Press, 1937), 107–8.
13. I. F. Marcossen, *David Graham Phillips and His Times* (New York: Dodd, Mead & Co., 1932), 190.
16. Procter, 87; Nasaw, 113; Abbott, 134–135.
17. *New York Journal*, January 3, 7, 1897, 1. "Crime and passion . . .were the most pervasive themes in every *Journal* paper," concludes Procter, 98.
18. There are various accounts of the war coverage. See Charles H. Brown, *The Correspondents' War* (New York: Scribner's, 1967); Walter Millis, *The Martial Spirit: A Study of Our War with Spain* (Boston: Houghton Mifflin, 1931); Marcus M. Wilkerson, *Public Opinion and the Spanish-American War* (Baton Rouge: Louisiana State University Press, 1932); and Joseph E. Wisan, *The Cuban Crisis as Reflected in the New York Press* (New York: Columbia University Press, 1934).
19. Russell, *Shifting Scenes*, 276, Procter 137–138.
20. Lundberg, 59; Procter, 99.
21. *New York Journal*, January 2, 1898, 45; Procter, 97–97; Nasaw, 102.
22. Russell, "William Randolph Hearst, 791.
23. Russell, ibid., 790. "Trolley defies law's edict," January 1, 1897; "Shea and His Duty," January 6, 1897; and "Officers Board the Bridge Loop," January 3, 1897, all in *New York Journal*.
24. Procter, 97. Nasaw (121) agrees on this point, writing, "Hearst and his paper kept a careful eye on the process, ever alert to new swindles, new payoffs, new 'grabs' by the trusts."
25. Russell, "William Randolph Hearst," 791.
26. Procter, 96; Abbot, 142; Russell, "Hearst," 790.
27. Russell, "Hearst," 790.
28. "Journalism for Revenue Only," unpublished manuscript, Russell Papers, Library of Congress.
29. Ibid.
30. Ibid.

31. Ibid.

32. Procter, 152. The rise of journalistic objectivity is traced in Michael Schudsen, *Discovering the News* (New York: Basic Books, 1978) and Robert Miraldi, *Muck-raking and Objectivity: Journalism's Colliding Traditions* (Westport, Conn.: Green-wood Press, 1991).

33. Phoebe Apperson Hearst to Orrin Peck, May 3, 1899, in Orrin M. Peck Collection, Department of Manuscripts, Huntington Library, San Marino, California. See note 17, Nasaw, 621. May 3, 1899, quoted in Judith Robinson, *The Hearsts* (New York: Avon, 1992), 326.

34. Telegram Hearst to Bryan, May 19, 1900. Box 24, Bryan Papers; James K. Jones to Bryan, April 21, 1900. Box 24, Bryan Papers, Library of Congress, Washington, D.C.

35. John Tebbell, *The Life and Good Times of William Randolph Hearst* (New York: E. P. Dutton & Co., 1952), 153, 133. Bryan to Hearst, July 4, 1900. Box 24, Bryan Papers.

36. Emmett Dedmon, *Fabulous Chicago* (New York: Atheneum, 1981), 192–193. See also Harold M. Mayer and Richard C. Wade, *Chicago: Growth of a Metropolis* (Chicago: University of Chicago Press, 1969); Edward Wagenknecht, *Chicago* (Norman: University of Oklahoma Press, 1964).

37. "A Word to the *American*'s Friends," *American*, September 27, 1901

38. Salisbury, *The Career of a Journalist* (New York: B. W. Dodge & Co., 1908).

39. Salisbury, 170.

40. Russell identified the reporter in *Bare Hands and Stone Walls* (New York: Charles Scribner's Sons, 1933), 137. The major stories on the water diversion are "Water Thieves Caught," September 7; "Grand Jury at Work on Water Steal," September 10; "Grand Jury Follows the Lead of the American and Indicts a Packer for Theft of Water," September 28; "Water Thieves Are Watched"; and "Cut Off Water from the Thieves," October 1900.

41. Lundberg, *Imperial Hearst*, asserts that Hearst's newspapers ceased their attacks on companies once they began to advertise in his newspapers, 62–63. In his groundbreaking criticism of the press, Will Irwin alleges that Hearst newspapers regularly gave favorable play reviews for Broadway shows that advertised in his newspapers. Irwin, "The American Newspaper," *Collier's*, February 18, 1911, and June 3, 1911. Hearst filed a $500,000 lawsuit against Irwin and *Collier's*. "Armour's Plant Fed by Stolen Water," November 9, 1900; "One of the Stealers of the City Water Confesses," January 14, 1901; "First of the Water Thieves Is Guilty," January 18, 1901.

42. The major gas trust stories are "People Fight the Gas Infamy," September 5, "Has $6,000,000 to Fight Gas Trust," September 6, "Chicago Proceeds to Own a Gas Plant," September 8, "The Gas Group," September 9. In total seventeen stories were published on the gas trust.

43. "Municipal Ownership," September 10, 4; "The Socialism of the Trusts," August 26, 1900; "Notes About Municipal Ownership," February 4; "A Great Metal Trust," February 6; "Do It Now," February 25, all 1901. Mark H. Rose, *Cities of Light and Heat* (University Park: Pennsylvania State University Press, 1995). Frederic Lundberg asserts that Hearst's real motivation was to take the leadership out of the hands of true reformers and to assume it himself. Then he could use it to get advertising and to gain more influence in municipal politics. Lundberg's proof is weak, however. *Imperial Hearst*, 62–64.

44. About Chicago journalism, see John J. McPahul, *Deadlines and Monkeyshines* (Englewood Cliffs, N.J.: Prentice-Hall, 1962); Tebbell, 97.

45. Salisbury, 177–179.

46. Salisbury, 523–524. Russell never discusses the incident, even though his two autobiographies were published after Salisbury's book. In fact, except for one three-page article in *Harper's Weekly*, Russell oddly never discusses his years with Hearst.

47. Clippings of obituaries were found in Russell's Papers, Library of Congress.

CHAPTER SEVEN

1. "Charles E. Russell Goes Abroad to Remain a Year," *New York Telegraph*, March 2, 1902. The article indicated he suffered from rheumatism as a result of his Johnstown flood reporting, and that he was accompanied by a stepson. I have found no evidence that he had a stepson. The article is in the Russell Papers, Library of Congress, Washington, D.C.

2. Russell to Julia Marlowe, June 10, 1900; Marlowe to Russell, June 3, 1905, Russell Papers.

3. Russell to Rice, September 2, 1906. Rice Papers, Newberry Library, Chicago. Although this letter is written later than the period being discussed, it is accurate about Russell's state of mind in 1902. John Edward Russell was at Northwestern University for two years. He did not graduate, however, but went into newspaper work before writing fiction and movie screenplays in Hollywood. His application form was supplied to the author by Northwestern.

4. See "Dead Music," 124, and "Memories of the Riffelberg," 126, in *Such Stuff as Dreams* (Indianapolis: Bowen Merrill Co., 1901) which was dedicated to the memory of Abby Osborne Russell. There are also seven poems written about Julia Marlowe. Russell wrote three other volumes of poetry: *The Twin Immortalities and Other Poems* (Chicago: Hammersmark Publishing Co., 904), *Songs of Democracy* (New York: Moffat, Yard & Co., 1909), and *An Hour of American Poetry* (Philadelphia: Lippincott & Co., 1927).

5. Russell Papers, no date. CER to Rice, December 17, 1901, Newberry Library.

6. Russell, *Bare Hands and Stone Walls* (New York: Scribner's Sons, 1933), 136.

7. John A. Cassidy, *Algernon C. Swinburne* (New York: Twayne, 1964); Edmund Gosse, *The Life of Algernon Charles Swinburne* (London: Macmillan & Co, 1917); Edwin Williams, "Algernon C. Swinburne as Poet-Prophet," Ph.D. dissertation, University of North Carolina, 1972. Russell, *The American Orchestra and Theodore Thomas* (Garden City, N.Y.: Doubleday, Page & Co., 1927).

8. *Bare Hands*, 136.

9. Russell, "Confessions of a Muck-Raker," an epilogue to *Lawless Wealth* (New York: B. W. Dodge & Co., 1908), 282.

10. "Confessions," 283.

11. Ibid., 282.

12. Gabriel Kolko, *Railroads and Regulation, 1877–1916* (Princeton: Princeton University Press, 1965), 55, and I. F. Sharfman, *The Interstate Commerce Commission: A Study in Administrative Law and Procedure* (New York: Harper & Row, 1931), 46. For background on railroad regulation, see Balthasar H. Meyer, *Railway Legislation in the United States* (New York: Arno, Press, 1973).

13. "Confessions," 283.

14. Various historians view the Progressive Era in this way. See John Chamberlain, *Farewell to Reform* (New York: John Day Co., 1932); Eric Goldman, *Rendezvous with Destiny* (New York: Vintage Press, 1955); and Louis Filler, *The Muckrakers* (University Park: Pennsylvania State Press, 1976), published originally in 1939 as *Crusaders for America Liberalism.*

15. "Confessions," 283, and *Bare Hands,* 137.

16. *Bare Hands,* 137.

17. A. M. Simons, *Packingtown* (Chicago: Charles H. Kerr & Co. 1899).

18. Quoted from a review of Tarbell's 1902 book, *A History of Standard Oil,* "Miss Tarbell," *Chicago Examiner,* December 17, 1904, 6. Found in a Russell scrapbook, Russell Papers. Hofstadter, *The Age of Reform/From Bryan to F.D.R.* (New York: Vintage, 1955), 186. "It is hardly an exaggeration," he wrote, "to say that the Progressive mind was characteristically a journalistic mind. . . ."

19. "Miss Tarbell," ibid.; *Bare Hands,* 141.

20. Russell, *The Greatest Trust in the World* (New York: The Ridgway-Thayer Co., 1905). Reprinted by Arno Press in 1975 as part of its series on American farmers and the rise of agribusiness. The book version of Russell's work was published after it first appeared in *Everybody's.* The page numbers cited here are from the magazine articles that appeared from February to September 1905. February, 151–156; March, 291–300; April, 502–516; May, 643–654; June, 779–792; July, 61–74; August, 218–227; September, 380–384. The two quotations included in this note are from 650, 783.

21. "Confessions," 284. On the meat-packing industry, see Louise Wade, *Chicago's Pride: The Stockyards, Packingtown, and Environs in the Nineteenth Century* (Urbana: University of Illinois Press, 1987).

22. *Bare Hands,* 132, 133; "Confessions," 284. Lawson's articles are collected in *Frenzied Finance, The Crime of Amalgamated* (New York: Ridgway-Thayer Co., 1905).

23. On Tarbell being threatened, see Kathleen Brady, *Ida Tarbell/Portrait of a Muckraker* (Pittsburgh: University of Pittsburgh Press, 1984), 122–123. Sullivan discuses being shadowed in *The Education of an American* (New York: Doubleday, Doran & Co., 1938), 186–187. "Confessions," 284.

24. "Confessions," 284.

25. "The Greatest Trust," 63, 155, 148, 149, 151.

26. Ibid., 151.

27. Ibid., 134, 90. On Armour, see B. C. Forbes, *Men who are making America* (New York: B. C. Forbes Co., 1917).

28. Ibid., 90, 131.

29. Ibid., 107, 115, 14.

30. Sinclair, *The Jungle* (New York: Doubleday, Page & Co., 1906). Sinclair to Russell, January 25, 1905, Russell Papers.

31. On Tarbell, see Brady, 144–145. Russell outlines these sources in "Confessions," 285–286.

32. Kolko, 94.

33. Kolko, 95. "The Greatest Trust," 215.

34. "Greatest Trust," 645. Armour was particularly indignant at this allegation. Armour said Iowa state officials reported that the bank failures were because of "unwise speculations and reckless banking methods," not the manipulations of the meat packers. Armour, *The Packers, the Private Car Lines and the People* (Philadelphia: Altemus Co., 1906), 127–128. A reliable history of the meat packers is David

Gordon, "The Beef Trust, Anti-Trust Policy and the Meat Packing Industry, 1902–922," Ph.D. dissertation, Claremont College, 1983.

35. "Beef Trust Resolution of Inquiry," *Congressional Record*, House Resolution 347, 5406.

36. The Sherman Act is discussed in Hans Thorelli, *The Federal Anti-Trust Policy/Organization of an American Tradition* (Baltimore: John Hopkins University Press, 1985), 587. Roosevelt's moderate approach is best summarized in George Mowry, *Theodore Roosevelt and the Progressive Movement* (New York: Hill and Wang, 1960) and John Morton Blum, *The Republican Roosevelt* (Cambridge, Mass.: Harvard University Press, 1954).

37. *Report of the Commissioner of Corporations on the Beef Industry*, March 3, 1905 (Washington, D.C.: Government Printing Office, 1905), 83. Armour, ibid., 70

38. Kolko, *Railroads and Regulation or Triumph of Conservatism*, 81.

39. "They had shaped the terms of the investigation," wrote Jack M. Thompson, "James R. Garfield: The Career of a Rooseveltian Progressive, 1895–1916," Ph.D. dissertation, University of South Carolina, 1958, 106.

40. "The Greatest Trust," 784, 785, 789. See Gordon, note 34, 157–169, in which he analyzes Russell's articles. Although Gordon applauds Russell's overall impact on the meatpackers, he wrote in regard to the Garfield report: "He continued to misread or misrepresent" it (164).

41. Gordon, ibid., discusses the trial in "The Garfield Commission and an 'Immunity Bath,'" 90–125. Garfield's diaries contradict his testimony at the trial. See Thompson, 106.

42. "The Greatest Trust," 781, 217. Roosevelt's comments are in Elting S. Morison, ed., *Letters of Theodore Roosevelt*, 5 (Cambridge, Mass; Harvard University Press, 1952) March 22, 1906, 189–90.

43. Ibid., 650, 647, 89, 224, 227, 208.

44. *Bare Hands*, 139. Many of the muckrakers opted for fiction. See Jay Martin, "The Literature of Arguments and the Arguments of Literature," *Muckraking: Past, Present and Future*, eds. John M. Harrison and Harry Stein (University Park: Pennsylvania State University Press, 1973), 100–117. See also James R. Bailey, "David Graham Phillips: Novelist of the Progressive Era," Ph.D. dissertation, Indiana University, 1971; and Louis Filler, *The Voice of Democracy: A Critical Biography of David Graham Phillips* (University Park: Pennsylvania State University Press, 1978). On Phillips's muckraking fiction, see Robert Miraldi, "The Journalism of David Graham Phillips," Ph.D. dissertation, New York University, 1985, 153–206.

45. The best account of Sinclair is in William Bloodworth, "The Early Years of Upton Sinclair: A Study of the Development of a Progressive Christian Socialist," Ph.D. dissertation, University of Texas, 1972. Bloodworth, *Upton Sinclair* (New York: Twayne, 1977), 44–45, 48. See also Jon A. Yoder, *Upton Sinclair* (New York: Ungar, 1975) and Walter Miller, *Upton Sinclair's The Jungle: A Critical Commentary* (New York: Monarch Press, 1983).

46. Good summaries of the Adams influence on the FDA are in John Crunden, "It Is Sin to Be Sick: The Muckrakers and the Pure Food and Drug Act," *Ministers of Reform: The Progressives' Achievement in American Civilization, 1889–1920* (New York: Basic Books, 1982), 163–199, and James H. Cassedy, "Muckraking and Medicine: Samuel Hopkins Adams," *American Quarterly* 16 (Spring 1964),

85–99. See also Samuel V. Kennedy, "The Last Muckraker," Ph.D. dissertation, Syracuse University Press, 1993 and *Samuel Hopkins Adams and the Business of Writing* (Syracuse: Syracuse University Press, 1999).

47. Roosevelt said that the David Graham Phillips articles and *The Jungle*, which he labeled as "lurid sensationalism," prompted his denunciation of the muckraking writers. His comment on revolution: Roosevelt to William Howard Taft, March 13, 1906, *Letters of Roosevelt*, 5, 183–184. A discussion of how to build "media and policy agendas" in order to achieve social change can be found in David L. Protess et al., *The Journalism of Outrage: Investigative Reporting and Agenda Building in America* (New York: Guilford Press, 1991), 231–257.

48. Gordon, "The Beef Trust," 168.

CHAPTER EIGHT

1. Charles Edward Russell to Wallace Rice, June 16, 1905. Rice Papers, Newberry Library. Russell, "Empty Ways," *The Twin Immortalities and Other Poems* (Chicago: Hammersmark Publishing Co., 1904.)

2. Russell, *Bare Hands and Stone Walls* (New York: Scribner's Sons, 1933), 237–239. Much of America was equally concerned about the route of capitalism. See, for example, Samuel P. Hays, *The Response to Industrialism, 1885–1914* (Chicago: University of Chicago Press, 1973) and Robert H. Wiebe, *The Search for Order, 1877–1920* (New York: Hill and Wang, 1967).

3. Sinclair, *The Jungle* (New York: Doubleday, Page & Co., 1906). Of course, Sinclair's purpose was to recreate a harsh competitive environment that completely condemned capitalism. The ending of his novel, although simplistic and naïve and severely attacked by critics, suggested that socialism would create new incentives and cure the ills of industrialism, a position much like the one Russell would soon adopt. Richard Hofstadter, *Social Darwinism in American Thought, 1860–1915* (Philadelphia: University of Pennsylvania Press, 1944). See also David Noble, *The Paradox of Progressive Thought* (Minneapolis: University of Minnesota Press, 1958.)

4. Hearst's campaign is described in *The Chief: The Life of William Randolph Hearst* (New York: Houghton-Mifflin Co., 2000), 168–185. Ralph W. Cram, "A Big Circus Tent for Roosevelt Rally," *Davenport Democrat and Leader*, 1935. Article supplied to the author by the Davenport Library. Russell and Wallace Rice exchanged numerous letters during this period, mostly discussing poetry. Russell makes various references to meeting Rice at the *American* offices in Chicago.

5. For years critics had assailed the Senate as a bastion of the wealthy. Reformers had long sought direct election of senators, instead of the method then used whereby state legislatures, often notoriously corrupt, chose senators. David Rothman, *Politics and Power: The United States Senate, 1869–1901* (London: Oxford University Press, 1966). Russell, *Bare Hands*, 142–143.

6. Phillips's articles appeared originally in *Cosmopolitan*, March to November 1906. They are reprinted in George Mowry and Judson A. Grenier, eds., *The Treason of the Senate* (Chicago: Quadrangle Books, 1964), and discussed in Robert Miraldi, "The Journalism of David Graham Phillips," Ph.D. dissertation, New York University, 1985, 244–275.

7. Quoted from *The Uprising of the Many* (New York: Doubleday, Page & Co., 1907). The articles appeared originally in *Everybody's* magazine as "Soldiers of the Common Good," April 1906, 380–383; May, 597–601; June, 753–765; July, 42–55; August, 178–179; September, 340–352; October, 465–482; November, 774–792; December, 3–13. Citations from the articles are taken from *Uprising*.

8. Russell diary, Russell Papers, Library of Congress. February 21, October 20, 1905. The diary is extremely difficult to read and he does not make entries on a regular basis or even throughout his many months abroad.

9. Russell diary. February 21, 1905. Russell, "Coronation Ode," *Twin Immortalities*, 71. His clear contempt for British caste can be seen in "England's system of snobbery," *Cosmopolitan*, January 1907, 276–285.

10. *Uprising*, 42, x-xi, 39.

11. Russell, *Uprising*, 66, 68. Russell, "England's system of snobbery," *Cosmopolitan*, January 1907, 276–285. Russell discussed class distinctions in Europe in "Caste in Various Countries," *Cosmopolitan*, February 1907, 448–456.

12. *Uprising*, 153. Diary, November 9, 15, Russell Papers. Russell became ill after his trip to India. See article in *New York Herald*, Paris edition, 1907, in Russell Papers. A feature story about Russell has an accompanying photograph of Russell on an elephant, Frank Marshall White "Charles Edward Russell," *Human Life*, December 1908. His anger with the British is evident also in Russell, "Caste— Curse of India," *Cosmopolitan*, December 1906, 276–285. Russell devoted a chapter to New Zealand in his autobiography, *Bare Hands and Stone Walls*, 171–182

13. Russell Diary, Russell Papers, October 23, November 2, 1905. Russell, *Uprising*, 155. Bernard S. Cohn, *Colonialism and its Forms of Knowledge: The British in India* (Princeton: Princeton University Press, 1996).

14. Russell, *Uprising*, 23, 24, 17. He wrote a separate article about the council, "Socialistic Government of London," *Cosmopolitan*, February 1906, 368–376. In the book version detailing his trip abroad, Russell added a chapter on cooperative movements in America, 26–39, but little in it seems freshly reported or novel as he recounts various communal efforts in America. Throughout this book I have capitalized socialism only when referring to the American Socialist Party.

15. Ibid., *Uprising*, 91.

16. Ibid., 101, 100.

17. Ibid., 123

18. Ibid., 129, 127, 138.

19. Ibid. 278, 309, 303, 278, 14. See also Russell, "More Light on the Common Good: How New Zealand Bans Trusts," *The Coming Nation*, July 22, 1911, 3–4; John Bell Condliffe, *The Welfare State in New Zealand* (London, Allen & Unwin, 1959). Russell devoted a chapter to New Zealand in *Bare Hands and Stone Walls*, 171–182.

20. Russell, *Uprising*, 235, 164–165. Neil Harris, *The Land of Contrasts: 1880–1901* (New York, G. Braziller, 1970)

21. In a subsequent meeting at the White House with Lincoln Steffens, Roosevelt indicated that Sinclair and Phillips were his true targets. Lincoln Steffens, *The Autobiography of Lincoln Steffens* (New York: Harcourt, Brace & Co., 1931), 581. Russell agreed, *Bare Hands*, 143. But David Nasaw's recent Hearst biography asserts that Hearst was his real target. Most likely, Roosevelt had all three in mind. He wanted to stop the muckrakers and those who subsidized their exposes: Nasaw, *The Chief: The Life of William Randolph Hearst* (New York: Houghton-

Mifflin, 2000), 190–191. See also Judson A. Grenier, "Muckrakers and Muckrak-ing: An Historical Definition," *Journalism Quarterly* 37 (Autumn 1960): 552–558; and John Semonche, "Theodore Roosevelt's 'Muckrake Speech': A Reassess-ment," *Mid-America* 46 (April 1964): 114–125.

22. Theodore Roosevelt, "Theodore Roosevelt's Views on Socialism," *Outlook*, March 20, 1909, 85–86.
23. "The Growing Menace of Socialism," *Hampton's*, January 1909, 4–5.
24. A good chronology of muckraking and Progressivism is Louis Filler, *Crusaders for American Liberalism* (New York: Harcourt, Brace and Co., 1939), 395–402. On Phillips, see Miraldi, ibid. John Semonche, "The American Magazine of 1906–1915: Principle vs. Profit," *Journalism Quarterly* 40 (Winter 1963): 39–40. Peter Lyon, *Success Story: The Life and Times of S. S. McClure* (New York: Charles Scribner's Sons, 1963).
25. "The Red Game Cock," Bare *Hands*, 46–56, 52. In the mayoral election, George received more votes than Theodore Roosevelt. Howard H. Quint, *The Forging of American Socialism: Origins of the Modern Movement* (Columbia: University of South Carolina Press, 1953). Chester McArthur Destler, *Henry Demarest Lloyd and the Empire of Reform* (Philadelphia, University of Pennsylvania Press, 1963). John L. Thomas, Alternative *America: Henry George, Edward Bellamy, Henry De-marest Lloyd, and the Adversary Tradition* (Cambridge, Mass.: Belknap/Harvard University Press, 1983). Henry Demarest Lloyd, *Wealth Against Commonwealth* (New York, Harper, 1894).
26. Ghent, *Our Benevolent Feudalism* (New York: Macmillan Co., 1903) and *Mass and Class, a Survey of Social Divisions* ((New York: Macmillan Co., 1904).
27. Russell, *Bare Hands*, 205. Morris Hillquit, *Loose Leaves from a Busy Life* (New York: Dacamp Press, 1924).
28. Although Phillips never declared for Socialism, often the leading characters in his popular novels were Socialists. Victor Dorn in *The Conflict* (New York: D. Appleton & Co., 1911) is a figure much like Socialist leader Eugene V. Debs. Robert Hunter, *Poverty: Social Conscience in the Progressive Era* (New York: Harper and Row, 1965). Hillquit, 58.
29. *Outlook* 87: 543, November 9, 1907; *Literary Digest* 35: 678, October 19, 1907; *Review of Reviews* 36: 758, December 1907; *Dial* 43: 256, October 16, 1907.
30. The muckrakers had styles that varied from factual to literary to advocacy. See Miraldi, *Muckraking and Objectivity: Journalism's Colliding Traditions* (Westport, Conn.: Greenwood Press, 1992), 30–46.
31. In Russell's Papers, Library of Congress, is a scrapbook with thirty pages of clip-pings from newspapers across the country. There are various accounts of the rise of socialism. David A. Shannon, *The Socialist Party of America: A History* (New York: Macmillan, 1955); Daniel Bell, *Marxian Socialism in the United States* (Princeton: Princeton University Press, 1967); James Weinstein, *The Decline of Socialism in America, 1912–1925* (New York: Monthly Review Press, 1967); Morris Hillquit, *History of Socialism in the United States* (New York: Russell & Russell, 1965).
32. "Chas. E. Russell Joins Socialists," *New York Call*, October 23; "Chas. Edward Russell Joins Socialists," *Davenport Democrat and Leader*, October 28; "Russell Now a Socialist," *New York World*, October 29; "C. E. Russell now an enrolled socialist," *New York Times*, October 29; "Russell enrolls as a socialist," *New York Tribune*, October 29; "Charles E. Russell to Join Socialists," *New York American*, October 29; "Newspaper man Turns Socialist," *Davenport Times*, October 31;

"Russell a Socialist," *St. Louis Globe Democrat*, November 8, all 1908, clippings in Russell Papers, Library of Congress. *Bare Hands*, 197.

33. Russell, *Why I Am a Socialist* (New York: George H. Doran Co, 1910), 286; *Bare Hands*, 191.
34. "C. E. Russell on 'Socialism,'" *Yonkers Statesman*, December 18, 1908, clipping in Russell Papers, Library of Congress.
35. Steffens, 632.
36. Russell, "The Growing Menace of Socialism," *Hampton's*, January 1909, 92; *Bare Hands*, 196; Weinstein, 20; Russell, "The Church and Socialism," pamphlet published by Socialist Party, ca. 1915, Tamiment Library, New York University; Russell, "Socialism: Just Where it Stands To-Day," *Hampton Columbian*, January 1912, 759.

CHAPTER NINE

1. Russell, *Why I Am a Socialist* (New York: Hodder & Stoughton, George H. Doran Co., 1910), 3, 140. Accounts of life in lower Manhattan can be found in Moses Rischlin, *The Promised City: New York's Jews, 1870–1914* (Cambridge, Mass.: Harvard University Press, 1962) and Irving Howe, *World of Our Fathers* (New York: Harcourt, Brace, Jovanovich, 1976).
2. Russell's three articles are "Trinity: Church of Mystery," *The New Broadway Magazine*, April 1908, 1–12, subsequently referred to as "Mystery"; "Trinity Corporation: A Riddle of Riches," *The Broadway Magazine*, May 1908, 187–195, referred to as "Trinity"; and "Tenements of Trinity Church," *Everybody's*, July 1908, 47–57, referred to as "Tenements." For a history of the church, see Clifford P. Morehouse, *Trinity: Mother of Churches: An Informal History of Trinity Parish in the City of New York* (New York: Seabury Press, 1973).
3. Russell, "Tenements," 47. *Bare Hands*, 94. Discussions of Progressive attitudes toward housing and poverty are in Roy Lubove, *The Progressives and the Slums: Tenement House Reform in New York City, 1890–1917* (Westport, Conn.: Greenwood Press, 1962), and Robert Bremner, *From the Depths: The Discovery of Poverty in the United States* (New York: New York University Press, 1956).
4. Russell, "Trinity," 195.
5. Russell, "The Cry of the Slums," *Everybody's*, December 1907, photographs of the slums by Bessie March and a short essay by Russell and "The Slum as a National Asset," *Everybody's*, February 1909.
6. Lincoln Steffens, The *Shame of the Cities* (New York: Hill and Wang, 1957). Steffens's life is chronicled in Justin Kaplan, *Lincoln Steffens: A Biography* (New York: Simon and Schuster, 1974). Steffens tells his story in *The Autobiography of Lincoln Steffens* (New York: Harcourt, Brace, 1931). Tarbell's expose is reprinted in *The History of Standard Oil* (New York: McClure, Phillips & Co., 1904). Her life is recounted in Kathleen Brady, *Ida M. Tarbell* (New York: Macmillan, 1984) and in her autobiography, *All in a Day's Work* (New York: Macmillan, 1939).
7. The best account of the muckraking movement is still Louis Filler, *The Muckrakers* (University Park: Pennsylvania State University Press, 1976). A recent account of various episodes in the muckraking saga is Robert Miraldi, ed., *The Muckrakers: Evangelical Crusaders* (Westport, Conn.: Praeger, 2001).
8. Phillips's articles are reprinted in *The Treason of the Senate*, eds. George Mowry and Judson A. Grenier (Chicago: Quadrangle Books, 1964), which has a fine in-

troduction by Mowry and Grenier. The articles are analyzed also in Robert Miraldi, "The Journalism of David Graham Phillips," Ph.D. dissertation, New York University 1985: 242–275, and Miraldi, "The Journalism of David Graham Phillips," *Journalism Quarterly* 63, No. 1 (Spring 1986): 83–88. Russell was originally supposed to write the Treason articles. *Bare Hands and Stone Walls* (New York: Scribner's Sons, 1933), 143–144.

9. Roosevelt's speech is reprinted verbatim in *Bookman* 33 (March 1911), 12, and in David Graham Phillips, *The Treason of the Senate*, eds. George Mowry and Judson A. Grenier (Chicago: Quadrangle, 1964), 216–225. A good discussion of the speech's development is in Grenier, "Muckrakers and Muckraking: An Historical Definition," *Journalism Quarterly* 37 (Autumn 1960).

10. *Bare Hands*, 143.

11. On Phillips's assassination, see Louis Filler, "Murder in Gramercy Park," *Antioch Review* 11 (December 1946), 495–508.

12. *Bare Hands*, 144, 146. Filler, *Crusaders*, 260. On the reasons why muckraking fades, see Miraldi, "Muckrakers are Chased Away," *Muckraking and Objectivity: Journalism's Colliding Traditions* (Westport, Conn.: Greenwood Press, 1991), 57–80.

13. The magazine was originally called *Hampton's* but changed its name a number of times, owing mostly to financial problems that beset Benjamin Hampton. The problems of the muckraking magazines are traced in Peter Barry, "The Decline of Muckraking: A View From the Magazines," Ph.D. dissertation, Wayne State University, 1973.

14. Russell, "Autobiography of an Author. Chas. E. Russell Tells About Himself," *Notes on Books and Authors* (Doubleday, Page & Co.'s, no date), Russell Papers, Library of Congress.

15. "Tenements," 48. Attempts to improve housing in New York in general and not just that of Trinity's, had been taking place since the 1880s when, under the leadership of Richard Watson Gilder, various groups and city commissions proposed legislation. Russell noted Gilder's work in a letter to the *New York Times*, "Tenement Reform," May 8, 1909, 6. And Gilder summarized Trinity's housing record in a letter to the *New York Evening Post*, "Trinity and the Tenements," December 28, 1908. On the evolution of tenement reform, see Richard Plunz, *A History of Housing in New York City* (New York: Columbia University Press, 1990) and James Ford, *Slums and Housing* (Westport, Conn.: Negro Universities Press, 1936). Lincoln Steffens's "Shame of the Cities" appeared originally in *McClure's*, beginning in October 1902.

16. "Tenements," 52. Ibid., 56–7.

18. Russell, "Trinity's Tenements—The Public's Business," *Everybody's*, February 1909, 279.

19. Russell, *Business: The Heart of the Nation* (New York: John Lane Co., 1911), 177, 197.

20. Letter to the *Times*, note 15. "Trinity's Tenements, 279.

21. "Tenements," 54.

22. Various histories discuss Trinity. See Morehouse, note 2; John C. Goodbody, *One Peppercorn: A Popular History of the Parish at Trinity Church* (New York: Parish of Trinity Church, 1982); *A History of the Parish of Trinity Church in the City of New York*, ed. Morgan Dix (New York: Putnam, 1898).

23. "Mystery," 5, 6.

24. Dix attacked the press in a long letter to the *Churchman*, December 22, 1894. 834–835, in which he defended the church leaders. Russell's responses are in "Trinity," 194.

25. Ibid., 190–191.

26. "Trinity," 1, 8.

27. "Tenements," 47. "Mystery," 5. "Tenements," 47, 52, 57.

29. Baker, "The Case Against Trinity," *American*, May 1909, 15. The article became part of Baker's book on religion, *The Spiritual Unrest* (New York: Frederick A. Stokes, 1910), 1–48. On Dix's death, *New York Times*, April 30, 1908, 1, and Russell, *Bare Hands*, 147. *Call*, June 26, 1908. Satirical cartoons about Trinity appeared also in the evening *New York World*, January 6, 1909, and the *New York Evening Mail*, January 20, 1909. Summaries and reactions to the article appeared in the *Houston Post*, *Columbus Journal*, *Seattle Times*, *Arkansas Gazette*, and *Springfield Republican*, among others. Clippings in Russell Papers.

30. Baker, ibid., 3.

31. Cammann made this statement to the *New York Evening Post*; reprinted in *The Churchman*, August 15, 1908, 10.

32. That the muckrakers were generally moderate can be seen from the work of David M. Chalmers, *The Social and Political Ideas of the Muckrakers* (New York: Citadel, 1964). A good summary of the views and interpretations of muckraking is Harry H. Stein, "American Muckrakers and Muckraking: The 50-Year Scholarship," *Journalism Quarterly* 56 (Spring 1979): 9–17, and Filler, "The Muckrakers in Flower and Failure," *Essays in American Historiography*, ed. Harvey Shapiro (Boston: Heath and Co., 1968).

33. On the various approaches to writing by the muckrakers, see Miraldi, *Muckraking and Objectivity*, 23–56. The quotation from Baker, "The Case Against Trinity," ibid., 15. On Baker's life and work, see John Semonche, *Ray Stannard Baker: A Quest for Democracy in Modern America, 1870–1918* (Chapel Hill: University of North Carolina Press, 1969) and Robert C. Bannister, Jr., *Ray Stannard Baker: The Mind and Thought of a Progressive* (New Haven: Yale University Press, 1966). On the "information" mode, see Michael Schudson, *Discovering the News* (New York: Basic Books, 1978). Russell, "The Slum as a National Asset," 180.

34. "Trinity's Tenements," a report compiled and published by Trinity, written by Dinwiddie, 2. A copy of the report was supplied to the author by the church. A slightly different version of the report was reprinted as "The Truth About Trinity's Tenements," *Survey V.* 23, February 26, 1910. Dinwiddie's comment is not in that version.

35. Ibid., 15.

36. "To Have Charge of Trinity Tenements," *The Common Welfare*, 1912, 145–146. "Manning Hits Back at Trinity Critics," *New York Times*, April 19, 1909, 9.

37. Charles T. Bridgeman, *A History of the Parish of Trinity Church in the City of New York* (New York: Trinity Church, 1962), 119. Bridgeman discusses the St. John's controversy, 77–101. Manning's comments are in the *New York Times*, ibid.

38. "Trinity Explains How It Uses Funds," *New York Times*, January 2, 1909, 1, 5. Bridgeman discusses the church's finances, 128–131. *The St. Louis Mirror* wrote an editorial on Trinity; quoted in "A Notable Victory for Publicity," *Printers' Ink*, January 27, 1909, 36. Based on correspondence with the former librarian of Trinity's archives, the author believes that the church has copies of not only the original reports made on the 1908 controversy but a number of internal memos

that discuss the church's actions. In 1992 the church temporarily closed its
archives, however, and church officials refused to respond to numerous written
and telephone requests for access to the documents.

39. "Trinity Will Sell All Its Real Estate," *New York Times*, February 7, 1909, 1.
40. "Manning Hits Back at Trinity Critics," *New York Times*, April 19, 1909, 9. Russell, *Bare Hands*, 146.
41. Bridgeman describes the improvements made by the church in its properties and the favorable response of the New York media, 125–126.
42. Russell, *A Pioneer Editor in Early Iowa* (Washington, D.C.: Runsdell, 1941), 8.

CHAPTER TEN

1. The story or the Progressive Era is told by various historians, although, as Irwin Unger and Debi Unger point out, "The concept of Progressivism turns out to be curiously elusive." *The Vulnerable Years: The United States, 1896–1917* (New York: New York University Press, 1978). See also William O'Neill, *The Progressive Years: America Comes of Age* (New York: Harper and Row, 1975); Eric Goldman, *Rendezvous with Destiny* (New York: Vintage, 1959); Gabriel Kolko, *The Triumph of Conservatism* (Glencoe, Ill.: The Free Press, 1963); James Weinstein, *The Corporate Ideal in the Liberal State, 1900–1918* (Boston: Beacon Books, 1968); David Noble, *The Paradox of Progressive Thought* (Minneapolis: University of Minnesota Press, 1958).
2. Letter from Steffens to Upton Sinclair, September 25, 1932, in Ella Winter and Granville Hicks, eds., *The Letters of Lincoln Steffens*, V. 2 (Westport, Conn.: Greenwood Press, 1938), 928.
3. Russell, *Lawless Wealth* (New York: B. W. Dodge & Co., 1908), 287.
4. Letter from Steffens to Ray Stannard Baker, March 3, 1904, quoted in Robert C. Bannister, Jr., *Ray Stannard Baker: The Mind and Thought of a Progressive* (New Haven: Yale University Press, 1966), 106. Herbert Shapiro, "The Muckrakers and Negroes," *Phylon* 31 (1970), 78.
5. Steffens, "What the Matter is in America and What to Do About it," *Everybody's*, June 1908, 723.
6. Russell, "Rockefeller—An Estimate of the Man," *Human Life*, January 1908, 9, 11.
7) Russell, "Morgan—Master of the Money Mart," *Human Life*, May 1908, 7.
8. Russell, "Forward Citizens to the Firing Line," *Everybody's*, November 1908, 707.
9. The article appeared originally as Russell, "A Burglar in the Making," *Everybody's*, June 1908, 753–760, hereafter referred to as "Burglar." It is reprinted in Arthur and Lila Weinberg, eds., *The Muckrakers* (New York: Capricorn, 1964), 322–337. Russell encountered prison conditions as a reporter twenty-five years earlier as he recounts in "One Woman Who Has Done Great Work," *Human Life*, December 1908, 7–8, 29.
10. Russell, "Burglar," 754, 759. W. E. B. Du Bois, "The Spawn of Slavery: The Convict Lease System in the South," *Missionary Review*, October 1901, 737–738.
11. Russell, "Burglar," 759. "Forward Citizens to the Firing Line," *Everybody's*, November 1908, 709. Russell reached similar conclusions when he wrote about New York City's courts and prisons. See Russell, "The Night Court of New York," *Human Life*, September 1909, 7–8, 30.
12. Russell, "Beating Men to Make Them Good," *Hampton's*, October 1908, 486; "Burglar," 755.

13. "Burglar," 756.
14. Ibid., 759, 760.
15. McKelway, "The convict lease system of Georgia," *Outlook*, September 12, 1908, 72. "Attacks 'Neer Beer' and Convict System," *Atlanta Constitution*, July 20, 1908, 3.
16. "Men Are Named to Apply Probe," *Atlanta Constitution*, July 18, 1908, 7; Weinberg, 323.
17. "Report Made on Convicts," July 11, 1908, 4. "Men Are Named to Apply Probe," July 18, 1908, 7. "Convict Probe Under Way by Committee," July 22, 1908, 1; "Stories of Cruelty to State Convicts Told to Committee," July 23, 1908, 1, 5, all in the *Atlanta Constitution*.
18. Blake McKelvey, *American Prisons: A Study in American Social History Prior to 1915* (Montclair, N.J., Patterson Smith, 1968 [1936]), 71. The *Atlanta Constitution* made the plea twice in editorials: "Get Away from the Lease System," July 15, 1908, 6, and "The Convicts and the Good Roads situation," July 18, 1908, 8.
19. Quoted in Weinberg, 323. No one account details the Georgia reform of its prison system. However, see "Georgia's Convict Lease System Remedied," no author, *The Common Welfare*, September 26, 1908, v. 20, 721. *Thirteenth Annual Report, Prison Commission of Georgia* (Atlanta: The Commission), June 1909–May 1910 was circumspect, simply noting that prisoners were now on road gangs and that "there is careful watch on the part of competent Inspectors to see that there are no abuses," 97. Bill Herring, "Rise, Fall and Rebirth of the Georgia State Penitentiary, 1816–1946: A Social and Legislative History of Georgia State Penitentiary," Ph.D. dissertation, Valdosta State College, 1993.
20. "Russell, "Beating Men to Make Them Good: Signs of a Better Era for Those that Go Wrong," October 1909, 486, 491. Russell's other two articles were "Beating Men to Make Them Good: An Illuminating Glance Behind the Walls of American Prisons," September 1908, 312–323, and "Beating Men to Make Them Good: the Decline of the Punishing Idea," November 1908, 609–620.
21. Russell, *The Passing Show of Capitalism* (Girard, Kansas: The Appeal to Reason, 1912),
19; Russell, "Beating Men," October, 494; November, 617.
22. On prison history, see John Bartlow Martin, *Break Down the Walls; American Prisons: Present, Past, and Future, 1915–1987* (New York, Ballantine Books, 1954), Mark Colvin, *Penitentiaries, and Chain Gangs: Social Theory and the History of Punishment in Nineteenth-Century America* (New York: St. Martin's Press, 1997); and McKelvey.
23. "Beating Men," October, 495, 485, 491 494.
24. Ibid., 496.
25. David M. Chalmers discusses the importance of concentrated wealth for the muckrakers in "Law, Justice and the Muckrakers," *Muckraking: Past, Present and Future*, eds., John M. Harrison and Harry H. Stein (University Park: Pennsylvania State University Press, 1973), 77. Russell, "Forward Citizens to the Firing Line," *Everybody's*, November 1908, 709.
26. The most comprehensive account of the Springfield riot is Roberta Senechal, *The Sociogenesis of a Race Riot: Springfield, Illinois in 1908* (Urbana: University of Illinois Press, 1990). See also James Crouthemal, "The Springfield Race Riot of 1908," *Journal of Negro History* 45 (July 1960): 164–181.
27. Senechal, 1.

28. David Levering Lewis, *W. E. B. Du Bois: Biography of a Race, 1868–1919* (New York: Henry Holt & Co., 1993), 387.

29. James Boylan, *Revolutionary Lives: Anna Strunsky and William English Walling* (Amherst: University of Massachusetts Press, 1998).

30. Russell, "Rockefeller—An Estimate of the Man," and "Morgan—Master of the Money Mart," notes 6 and 7, and "Samuel Gompers, Labor Leader," April 1909, 6–7. See also "Philander Chase Knox—the New Secretary of State," May 1909, 7–8; "Senator Platt—The Yaller Hawk of Politics," July 1908, 7–9; "One Woman Who Has Done a Great Work," December 1908, 7–8; "The Mystery of Edward the Seventh," November 1908, 5–6; "Dr. Parkhurst, Preacher & Man," February 1909, 5–7; and "The Next King of Erford," November 1909, 5–6, all in *Human Life.*

31. Robert C. Bannister, Jr., "Race Relations and the Muckrakers," in *The Muckrakers: Past, Present and Future.* As John Hope Franklin wrote, "The Negroes could look neither to the White House nor to the muckrakers for substantial assistance." *From Slavery to Freedom,* 2nd ed. (New York: Knopf, 1956).

32. E. C. Stickel to Russell, May 14, 1904, Russell Papers, Library of Congress, Washington, D.C. Noted also in Bannister, note 29, 431.

33. Baker, *Following the Color Line: American Negro Citizenship in the Progressive Era* (New York: Doubleday, Page and Co., 1908), 117–118. Bannister, ibid., 54.

34. Russell's comments came in a speech, reprinted in Anna Strunsky et al., *William English Walling: A Symposium* (New York: Stackpole Sons, 1938), 75–76.

35. "The Race War in the North," *Independent* 65 (September 3, 1908), 530–531.

36. Ibid., 529. Boylan, 154.

37. Walling, ibid., 534.

38. Walling quote, speech by Russell, Chicago, November 1912, Russell Papers. Boylan, ibid., 156. Russell, *Bare Hands and Stone Walls* (New York: Charles Scribner's Sons, 1933), 225.

39. Russell retells this story in *A Pioneer Editor in Early Iowa: A Sketch of the Life of Edward Russell* (Washington, D.C.: Ransdell Inc., 1941), 29, passim.

40 Russell made these comments in a speech, "National Unity, National Defense and the Color Line," January 26, 1941, to the Inter-racial Committee of the District of Columbia. In Russell Papers.

41. Russell, *Pioneer Editor;* ibid., 13; "About Race Prejudice," *Coming Nation,* August 12, 1911, 1.

42. Russell, *Bare Hands,* ibid., 227, 224. Speech, "Address of Charles Edward Russell," no date, Russell Papers.

43. Russell, ibid., 224. For a discussion of the Niagara movement, see Lewis, ibid., 297–342.

44. Lewis, 389. The call is reprinted as an appendix to Warren St. James, *The National Association for the Advancement of Colored People: A Case Study in Pressure Groups* (New York, Exposition Press, 1958), 166–167. Russell speech, "Leaving It to the South." Oswald Garrison Villard, *Fighting Years: Memoirs of Liberal Editor* (New York: Harcourt, Brace and Co., 1939).

45. Russell notes his trip through the South in *Why I Am A Socialist* (New York: George H. Doran Co., 1910) 83, 93. White, *The Walls Came Tumbling Down* (New York: Harcourt, Brace and Co., 1947), 107. Walling, "The Founding of the N.A.A.C.P.," *The Crisis,* July 1929, 226. Other accounts of the early history of the NAACP include Charles F. Kellogg, *NAACP: A History of the National Association for the Advancement of Colored People,* Vol. 1, 1909–1920 (Baltimore: John

Hopkins University Press, 1967); Langston Hughes, *Fight for Freedom: The Story of the NAACP* (New York: W.W. Norton & Co., 1962); and Robert L. Jack, *History of the NAACP* (Boston: Meador Publishing Co., 1943).

46. *Walling Symposium*, 98; *Bare Hands*, 225–226.

47. Ovington, ibid., 105.

48. *Proceedings of the National Negro Conference, 1909* (New York: Arno Press, 1969), 98. *Bare Hands*, 226–227.

49. Du Bois, *The Autobiography of W. E. B. Du Bois* (New York: International Publishers, 1968), 391. Ovington, ibid., 105.

50. *Bare Hands*, 219.

51. Louis R. Harlan, *Booker T. Washington: The Wizard of Tuskegee, 1901–1915* (New York: Oxford, 1983); Lewis 394.

52. Stephen R. Fox, *The Guardian of Boston: William Monroe Trotter* (New York: Atheneum, 1972); Ovington, 106; *Proceedings*, 104; Russell speech, "Leaving It to the South," National Association of Colored People reprint, no date.

53. Russell, T*he Passing Show of Capitalism*, 156.

54. Lewis, 395; "To Raise $500,000 for a Negro Uplift," *New York Times*, June 2, 1910, 9.

55. Ovington, 107; Barnett, *Crusade for Justice: The Autobiography of Ida B. Wells* (Chicago: University of Chicago Press, 1970), 325; Lewis 398.

56. Du Bois, *Dusk of Dawn: An Essay Toward an Autobiography of a Race Concept* (New York: Harcourt, Brace and Co., 1940), 271. The effectiveness of the NAACP can be seen, for example, in August Meier and John H. Bracey, Jr., "The NAACP as a Reform Movement, 1900–1965: 'To Reach the Conscience of America,'" *Journal of Southern History* 49 (February 1993): 3–30; and Robert L Zangrando, *The NAACP Crusade Against Lynching, 1909–1950* (Philadelphia: Temple University Press, 1980).

57. Russell, *Bare Hands*, 225, *Walling Symposium*, 78; "About Race Prejudice," 1.

CHAPTER ELEVEN

1. "Charles Edward Russell, Socialist Candidate for Governor," *New York Times*, August 30, 1910, Part 5, 5.

2. Daniel Bell, *Marxian Socialism in the United States* (Princeton: Princeton University Press, 1967), 55.

3. "Where Did You Get It, Gentlemen?" *Everybody's*, August, 201–211; September, 348–360; October, 503–511; November, 636–645; December, 118–127, 1907.

4. "Mr. C. E. Russell and Muckraking," *Cleveland Plain Dealer*, July 12, 1908; *New York Times*, June 27, 1908. Found in Russell Papers, Library of Congress.

5. Steffens, *The Autobiography of Lincoln Steffens* (New York: Harcourt, Brace & Co., 1931), 575. From Russell's weekly column in *The Coming Nation*, October 1, 1910 in Russell Papers. Many of his columns, which appeared for two years, are reprinted in *The Passing Show of Capitalism* (Girard, Kansas: The Appeal to Reason, 1912).

6. *The Coming Nation* and other Socialist publications are discussed in James Weinstein, *The Decline of Socialism in America* (New York: Monthly Review Press, 1967), 84–92. Hillquit, *Loose Leaves from a Busy Life* (New York: Da Capo Press, 1971), 91.

7. Russell, "Rational Political Action," *International Socialist Review*, March 1912, 2. *The Story of Wendell Phillips* (Chicago: Charles H. Kerr, 1914), 184. *Coming Nation*, January 28, 1911, 2.

8. Frank Marshall White, "Charles Edward Russell," *Human Life*, December 1908, 88; *Why I Am a Socialist* (New York: George H. Doran Co, 1910), 17. Bell, 56–57.

9. Russell, *Why I Am a Socialist*, 99, *The Passing Show of Capitalism*, 70.

10. Russell, "What About Stuyvesant Fish?" *Human Life*, April 1908, 6. "The Passing of the Poorhouse," *The Broadway Magazine*, December 1908, 744. *Lawless Wealth* (New York, B. W. Dodge & Co., 1908), 168–169.

11. Russell, *Why I Am a Socialist*, 4; *The Coming Nation*, June 19, 1910, 4; December 2, 1911, 4.

12. "Claims drink is boon to real poor," *Philadelphia Record*, March 11, 1908; "Rum the only relief of starving poor," *Philadelphia Telegraph*, March 11, 1908; "Would give the poor rum," *New York World*, March 24, 1908. All in Russell Papers.

13. Russell, *Why I Am a Socialist*, 146, 140, 162, 57; *Coming Nation*, December 24, 2.

14. Russell, *Why I Am a Socialist*, 77, 79.

15. "The Price the Woman Pays," *The Redbook*, November 1908, 33, 48; "Billions for Bad Blue Blood," September 1908, 610–624. The third article was "The Curse of the Coronet," October 1908, 785–800. These articles are very similar to David Graham Phillips's "Swollen Fortunes," December 22, 1907, 3–4, and January 12, 1907, 10–11, 29–30, and "Curing Rich Americans," May 13, 14–15, 35, all in the *Saturday Evening Post*.

16. Russell, *Why I Am a Socialist*, 89, 283. *Coming Nation*, December 2, 1911, 2.

17. Russell, "Socialism: Just Where It Stands To-day," *Hampton-Columbian*, January, 1912, 761; *Why I Am a Socialist*, 283, 286. "The Growing Menace of Socialism," *Hampton's*, January 1909, 14.

18 Compare Russell's comment with that of Ray Stannard Baker, who said, "The people need "economic facts." Quoted in David Mark Chalmers, *The Social and Political Ideas of the Muckrakers* (New York: Citadel, 1964) from the notebooks of Baker, note 13, 122. *Coming Nation*, April 29, 1910, May 10, 1911.

19. Ibid., 157; Russell "At the Election," January, 1908, 259–271; "At the Throat of the Republic: After the Election," 361–368, all in *Cosmopolitan*.

20. Russell, "Postscript—The Election of 1907," 480. *Bare Hands and Stone Walls* (New York: C. Scribner's Sons, 1933), 140–141.

21. Russell, "What Are You Going to Do About it? Graft as an Expert Trade in Pittsburg [sic]," August 1910, 292. The other articles are "Legislative Graft and the Albany Scandal," July, 146–160; "The Jack-Pot in Illinois Legislation," September, 466–478; "The Man the Interests Wanted," October 1910, 592–601; "Colorado—New Tricks in an Old Game," December, 45–58. "Senator Gore's Strange Bribe Story," January 151–162, all in *Cosmopolitan*.

22. "Russell for Governor," *New York Times*, August 20, 1910, 2. "What the Socialist Candidate for Governor of New York has to Say in Accepting Nomination." Copy of speech in Russell Papers.

23. "Russell Opens Campaign," *New York Times*, August 22, 1910, 4; *Bare Hands and Stone Walls*, 215, 216.

24. "Henry L. Stimson, Republican Nominee for Governor," *New York Times*, October 2, 1911, Part 6, 5. Godfrey Hodgson, *The Colonel: The Life and Wars of Henry Stimson, 1867–1950* (New York: Knopf, 1990), 71.

25. "Socialists meet in Union Square," *New York Times, October* 2, 1910, 2; "Battery crowd cheers Russell," *New York Call,* October 5 1910, 1.

26. "Russell Rouses Brooklyn Crowd," *New York Call,* October 8, 1910, 1; " Socialist Speakers Fill Opera House," *Call,* October 24, 1910, 2; "Russell Pillories both Old Parties," *Call,* October 25, 1910, 2; "Russell Addresses Two Big Meetings," *Call,* 1.

27. "Socialism and the National Crisis," Speech at Carnegie Hall, October 15, 1910, copy in the Russell Papers. Russell had actually come out strongly in favor of women's voting rights in 1908. See "Obstructions in the Way of Justice," speech to annual convention of the National American Woman Suffrage Association, October 20, 1908. Russell Papers. On women and socialism, see Weinstein, 53–62.

28. "Socialist Growth Enthuses Russell," *New York Call,* Nov. 1, 1910, 1.

29. "Charles Edward Russell, Socialist Candidate for Governor," *New York Times,* August 30, 1910, Part 5, 5.

30. Ibid. Russell's positions were common among Socialists, dating back to before the turn of the century. See Bell, 53–54.

31. "Russell Speaks on Real Issues," *Call,* November 7, 1910, 1.

32. Russell, *Bare Hands,* 200.

33. Russell to Algernon Lee, November 9, 1910, Lee Papers, Tamiment Institute, New York University.

CHAPTER TWELVE

1. Russell, *Stories of the Great Railroads* (Chicago: C. H. Kerr & Co., 1912), *Railroad Melons, Rates and Wages: A Handbook of Railroad Information* (Chicago: C. H. Kerr & Co., 1922). Kathleen Brady, Ida *Tarbell: Portrait of a Muckraker* (Pittsburgh: University of Pittsburgh Press, 1989), 22.

2. Gabriel Kolko, *Railroads and Regulation, 1877–1916* (Princeton: Princeton University Press, 1965); Leo Marx, *The Machine in the Garden; Technology and the Pastoral Ideal in America* (New York: Oxford University Press, 1964); Samuel Hays, *The Response to Industrialism, 1885–1914* (Chicago: University of Chicago Press, 1957); Frank Norris, *The Octopus: A Story of California* (New York, Doubleday, Page & Co., 1901).

3. Russell, "Wall Street Greed and Railroad Ruin," *Ridgway's,* December 29, 1906, 13, 14. See also Russell, "Seven Kings in Mexico," *Cosmopolitan,* July 1907, 271–279. Louis Filler, *Crusaders for American Liberalism* (New York: Harcourt, Brace and Co., 1939), 203–216.

4. His articles were collected in *The Stories of the Great Railroads* but appeared originally in *Hampton's:* "Great Millionaire's Mill," April, 478–491; "Winning and Empire and the Cost of Winning," *Hampton's,* May, 603–617; "Scientific Corruption of Politics," June, 843–858; "Speaking of Widows and Orphans, " *Hampton's,* July, 79–92; "Remedy of the Law," August, 217–230; "Railroad Machine as it Works Now," September, 364–376; "Surrender of New England," December, 759–770; "Paying of the Bill," October, 507–520; all 1910; and "Speed," October, 444–576, 1911.

5. Russell, *Lawless Wealth* (New York: B. W. Dodge & Co., 1908), 9, 62; *Stories of the Great Railroads,* 451, 56. Russell's articles on the rails appeared initially in *Hampton's.* Citations here are from the book version.

6. The Northern Securities merger is treated in many Progressive Era histories. See Jean Strouse, *Morgan: American Financier* (New York: Random House, 1999), 438–443, 460–463, 533–535.

7. Russell, *Stories of the Great Railroads*, 13, 23.
8. Ibid., 28, 32.
9. Ibid., 43, 46, 38, 56.
10. Stewart Hall Holbrook, *James J. Hill: A Great Life in Brief* (New York: Knopf, 1955) covered much the same ground as Russell and concluded that Hill was a mixed character. Other biographies of Hill include Martin Albro, *James J. Hill and the Opening of the Northwest* (New York: Oxford University Press, 1976); Joseph Gilpin Pyle, *The Life of James J. Hill*, (Gloucester, Mass., P. Smith, 1968 [1944]); and Glenn Chesney Quiett, *They Built the West: An Epic of Rails and Cities* (New York, London, D. Appleton-Century Company, 1934).
11. Russell, *Stories of the Great Railroads*, 23, 127, 160. On Huntington, see Oscar Lewis, *The Big Four: The Story of Huntington, Stanford, Hopkins, and Crocker, and of the Building of the Central Pacific* (New York: A. A. Knopf, 1938), and David Lavender, *The Great Persuader* (Garden City, N.Y.: Doubleday, 1970).
12. Ibid., 100, 101. For examples of business reaction, see Robert D. Reynolds, "The 1906 Campaign to Sway Muckraking Periodicals," *Journalism Quarterly* 56 (Autumn 1979): 513–520.
13. Russell describes the reaction in an epilogue to *Stories of the Great Railroads*. Other Russell quotations, 321, 332.
14. Upton Sinclair, *The Brass Check: A Study of American Journalism* (Pasadena, Calif.: The author, 1919), 231.
15. Russell, *Stories of the Great Railroads*, 7. Hampton to Russell, December 20, 1910, Russell Papers, Library of Congress, Washington, D.C.
16. Russell, "The Magazine Soft Pedal," *Pearson's*, February 1914, 180. Russell tells in detail the story of *Hampton's* demise in this article, 187–189. Filler, *Crusaders*, retells the story, 366–368. Russell, *The Coming Nation*, February 25, 1911, 1.
17. Newsman Walter Lippmann said he was told many times about such a conspiracy. *Drift and Mastery: An Attempt to Diagnose the Current Unrest* (Madison: University of Wisconsin Press, 1985), 3. Filler, *Crusaders*, 359, accepts the theory also.
18. Russell, "The Magazine Soft Pedal," 182. Mark Sullivan, *Education of an American* (New York: Doubleday, Doran & Co.1938), 286–287.
19. The rise and fall of muckraking is described in Peter Barry, "The Decline of Muckraking: A View from the Magazines," Ph.D. dissertation., Wayne State University, 1973. See also Miraldi, "The Muckrakers are Chased Away," *Muckraking and Objectivity: Journalism's Colliding Traditions* (Westport, Conn.: Greenwood Press, 1990), 23–80 and Michael D. Marcaccio, "Did a Business Conspiracy End Muckraking?" A Reexamination," *Historian* 47 (November 1984): 58–71.
20. *Stories of the Great Railroads*, 133.
21. Kreuter, 585.
22. Russell, *Bare Hands and Stone Walls* (New York: C. Scribner's Sons, 1933), 198. Russell to Algernon Lee, November 9, 1910, Lee Papers, Tamiment Institute, New York University.
23. David A. Shannon, *The Socialist Party of America: A History* (New York: Macmillan, 1955), 71. Victor Berger to A. M. Simons, December 6, 1909, New York Socialist Papers, Tamiment Institute, New York University. James Boylan, *Revolutionary Lives: Anna Strunsky and William English Walling* (Amherst: University of Massachusetts Hospital, 1998), 168–170.

24. "Samuel Gompers, labor leader," *Human Life*, April 1910, 7. See "John R. Commons, "Karl Marx and Samuel Gompers," *Political Science Quarterly* (June 1926): 282–286.
25. Russell, "Growing Menace of Socialism," *Hampton's*, January 1909, 14.
26. Typewritten note on bottom of a letter, Myers to Julius Gerber, July 22, 1912, New York Socialist Papers, Tamiment Institute. Debs is quoted in Nick Salvatore, *Eugene V. Debs, Citizen and Socialist* (Urbana: University of Illinois Press, 1982), 249.
27. Russell, *Bare Hands and Stone Walls*, 199. "What Next?" *International Socialist Review*, January 1913, 334. Milton Cantor, *The Divided Left: American Radicalism, 1900–1975* (New York: Hill and Wang, 1978).
28. Louis Filler, "Murder in Gramercy Park," *Antioch Review* 11, December 1946. Brisbane to Russell, May 1, 1935, Russell Papers, Library of Congress, Washington, D.C.
29. Russell, *Business: The Heart of the Nation* (New York: John Lane Co., 1911). Russell to Gerber, April 2, 1912 and March 22, 1912, New York Socialist Papers, Tamiment Institute.
30. Russell comments on Roosevelt, Taft, and socialism, November 25, 1911 and October 22, 1911, all in *Coming Nation*.
31. See also Ray Ginger, *The Bending Cross: A Biography of Eugene Victor Debs* (New Brunswick: Rutgers University Press, 1949; rpt. Thomas Jefferson University Press at Northeast Missouri State University: Kirkville, Missouri, 1992) H. Wayne Morgan, *Eugene V. Debs, Socialist for President* (Syracuse: Syracuse University Press, 1962). The tally of Socialist gains was compiled by William Ghent in an undated 1911 memo, New York Socialist Papers, Tamiment Institute. Russell, October 22, 1911, *Coming Nation*.
32. Russell, *Socialism the Only Remedy* (New York: The Socialist Party, 1912), 20. William H. Carwadine, *The Pullman Strike* (Chicago: Charles H. Kerr and Company, 1973). Russell to Fred Warren, April 13, 1913, Haldeman Papers, Indiana University.
33. Socialist Party of America Papers, *National Convention of the Socialist Party Held at Indianapolis, Indiana, May 12 to 18, 1912*. Chicago, 1912, 33.
34. Ibid. A lengthy and detailed description of the convention is "The National Socialist Convention of 1912," *International Socialist Review*, June 1912, 807–831.
35. Ibid., 102.
36. Ibid., 99, 135.
37. Ibid., 122, 129.
38. Ibid., 130–131. Peter Carlson, *Roughneck: The Life and Times of Big Bill Haywood* (New York: W.W. Norton, 1983), and Joseph Robert Conlin, *Big Bill Haywood and the Radical Union Movement* (Syracuse: Syracuse University Press, 1969). Sally M. Miller, *Victor Berger and the Promise of Constructive Socialism, 1910–1920* (Westport, Conn.: Greenwood Press, 1973).
39. Russell, "What Next?" *International Socialist Review*, January 1913, 526.
40. Various histories of the socialist movement interpret the divides in the party differently. Some see them along regional lines, while others cite the split over violence; some emphasize the question of reform versus revolution; still others stress the personality clashes. The truth is that all of these splits fractured the party. I have used the following to understand socialism: Ira Kipnis, *The Ameri-*

can *Socialist Movement, 1897–1912* (New York: Columbia University Press, 1952); Daniel Bell, *Marxian Socialism in the United States* (Princeton: Princeton University Press, 1967); James Weinstein, *The Decline of Socialism in America, 1912–1925* (New York: Monthly Review Press, 1967); Albert Fried, ed., *Socialism in America: From the Shakers to the Third International* (New York: Doubleday & Co., 1970); and Milton Cantor, *The Divided Left: American Radicalism, 1900–1975* (New York: Hill & Wang, 1978).

41. Russell, "What Comes of Playing the Game," 31, and Debs, "Danger Ahead for the Socialist Party in Playing the Game of Politics," *International Socialist Review*, January 1911.

42. Salvatore, 223.

43. "The National Socialist Convention of 1912," 828.

CHAPTER THIRTEEN

1. Russell wrote Marlowe's biography, *Julia Marlowe, Her Life and Art* (New York, London: D. Appleton and Co., 1927). Russell tried to convince Marlowe to become involved in social issues but failed. See Russell to Marlowe, April 15, 1912, Marlowe-Sothern Papers, New York Public Library. Redmond & Co. to Julia Marlowe, June 25, 1913, Marlowe-Sothern Papers.

4. Russell to Marlowe, April 15, 1912, Marlowe-Sothern Papers. Donald Bragaw believes that Russell was "betraying his cause, his beliefs and his fellow workers of the world." "Solider for the Common Good," Ph.D. dissertation, Syracuse University, 1971, 226.

5. Russell to Fred Warren, May 1, 1929, Haldeman Papers, Indiana University.

6. Jacob Alexis Friedman, *The Impeachment of Governor William Sulzer* (New York: Columbia University Press, 1939), 15–37.

8. Russell, *Socialism: The Only Remedy* (New York: the Socialist Party, 1912), 2.

9. Ibid., 12. G. Wallace Chessman, "The Needs of Labor," *Governor Theodore Roosevelt: The Albany Apprenticeship, 1898–1900* (Cambridge, Mass.: Harvard University Press, 1965), 221–225. Chessman writes a chapter that portrays Roosevelt as sympathetic to the needs of workers.

10. "Russell Slashes Bull Moose Party," *New York Times*, October 4, 1912, 6.

11. Roosevelt to William Howard Taft, March 13, 1906, *Letters of Roosevelt 5*, ed. Elting S. Morrison (Cambridge, Mass.: Harvard University Press, 1952), 183–184.

12. "Says Colonel Asked $100,000 of Morgan," *New York Times*, September 2, 1912, 1. "Asked Morgan for $100,000 for TR's Fund, says Russell," *The Call*, September 2, 1912, 1. "Russell Testifies at Senate Inquiry," *New York Times*, October 8, 1912. 1.

13. "Socialists Cheer Debs 29 Minutes," *New York Times*, September 30, 1912, 5.

14. Nick Salvatore, *Eugene V. Debs, Citizen and Socialist* (Urbana: University of Illinois Press, 1982), 264. "MSG Rings With Wildest Cheers to Greet Socialist Candidates," *The Call*, September 30, 1912, 1, 2.

15. "Socialist Victory Complete in Battle for Free Speech," *The Call*, October 22, 1912, 13. "Socialism: The Only Remedy," 3

16. Ibid., 8. 11., 12, 23.

17. "Open-Air Socialist Meeting," *New York Times*, November 3, 1912, 4.

18. "Socialists Pack New Star Casino," *The Call*, November 4, 1912; "Remarkable Brownsville Rally Winds Up Campaign," *The Call*, November 4, 1912, 3.

19. "Crowd Abandons Sulzer to Hear Russell," *The Call*, November 5, 1912, 1.

20. Russell, *Bare Hands and Stone Walls* (New York: C. Scribner's Sons, 1933), 217.

21. *Bare Hands*, 321.

22. Ibid., 312. G. Frank, "The 'parliament of the people,'" *Century*, 98, July 1919. There are various accounts of Chautauqua, including Victoria Case, *We Called It Culture: The Story of Chautauqua* (Garden City, N.Y., Doubleday, 1948); William L. Slout, *Theatre in a Tent: The Development of a Provincial Entertainment* (Bowling Green: Bowling Green University Popular Press, 1972); Charles Francis Horner, *Strike the Tents; The Story of the Chautauqua* (Philadelphia: Dorrance, 1954); and Harry P. Harrison, *Culture Under Canvas: The Story of Tent Chautauqua* (New York: Hastings House, 1958).

23. *Bare Hands*, 215–219. Chautauqua provided a variety of political opinions, including the Socialists. Carl Thompson, a prominent Socialist propagandist, also traveled extensively on the Chautauqua circuit.

24. Case, 36. In 1912 there were forty-four lecturers and thirty entertaining companies on the 1912 Chautauqua circuit. The headliners were Bryan and Bohumir Kryl's Bohemian band. See Harrison, 118.

25. Russell, *Lawless Wealth* (New York: B. W. Dodge & Co., 1908), 9.

26. *Why I Am a Socialist* (George H. Doran Co., 1910.), 126; *The Coming Nation*, August 5, 1911.

27. "Socialism and the National Crisis," Speech at Carnegie Hall, October 15, 1910. "A Struggle for a Billion," *Ridgway's*, November 3, 1906, 9–10; November 10, 11–12; November 17, 13–14; November 24, 15–16; December 1, 15–16; December 8, 15–16. 1906.

28. "The Mysterious Octopus," *World To-Day*, April 1911, 2080. The articles are February, 1735–1750, March, 1960–1972; *Hearst's Magazine*, April, 2074–2085. The magazine was renamed *Hearst's Magazine* in April. A government investigation eventually did not find evidence of monopoly behavior by the lumber moguls.

29. *Coming Nation*, October 8, 1911. This conclusion mirrors the one reached in 1963 by Gabriel Kolko in his study of the railroad industry, *The Triumph of Conservatism* (Glencoe, Ill.: The Free Press, 1963).

30. Russell, "The Mysterious Octopus," March 1960. Ralph W. Hidy, Frank E. Hill, and Allan Nevins, *Timber and Men: The Weyerhaeuser Story* (New York: Columbia University Press, 1963), 300–301.

31. "The Mysterious Octopus," April 1911, 2085.

32. Various industries and disciplines were modernizing and meeting the challenges of industrialism See Robert Wiebe, *The Search for Order* (New York: Hill and Wang, 1967). *Timber and Men*, note 29, 310. Nevins says the Russell articles give "the impression of a halfhearted effort written under Hearst orders."

33. *The Call*, February 27, 28, 1913, 1. Russell to City Campaign Committee, undated, Social Democratic Federation Papers, Tamiment Institute, New York University. "Russell Confident of Socialist Jump," *The Call*, September 26, 1913, 1, 4.

34. "Russell Declares Ryan Has Control of Both Candidates," *The Call*, September 27, 1913, 1, 4. For Belmont's role in New York City, see Irving Katz, *August Belmont: A Political Biography* (New York: Columbia University Press, 1968), and David Black, *The King of Fifth Avenue: The Fortunes of August Belmont* (New York: Dial Press, 1981).

35. Russell speech, "The Invisible Government," October 12, 1913, New York Public Library. "Red Army Invades Hippodrome," *The Call*, October 13, 1913, 1. "The Invisible Government Visible At last," *The Call*, October 10, 1913, 1. "Russell, "This is Your Cause, Citizens!" *The Call*, September 30, 1913, 1.

36. Russell, "What Next?" *International Socialist Review*, January 1913, 525. "Mud-Slinging Vital Problems? Which Do You Prefer?" *The Call*, October 31, 1913, 1. The complete Socialist platform for New York City is in the Socialist Party Papers, Duke University.

37. "Schools the Basis of the Republic, Declares Russell," October 17, 1913, 1. "Private Palaces or Public Schools," *The Call*, October 22, 1913, 1. "How About the Real Issues?" *The Call*, October 30, 1913, 6.

38. "The Two Manikins, " October 28, 1913, p. 6, *The Call*. Russell, "The Power Behind the Campaign," *The Call*, November 3, 1913, 1.

39. Jacob Alexis Friedman, *The Impeachment of Governor William Sulzer* (New York: Columbia University Press, 1939).

40. Russell, "Sulzer Gets His," *The Call*, October 17, 1913, 6. Edwin R. Lewinson, *John Purroy Mitchell: The Boy Mayor of New York* (New York: Astra Books, 1965).

41. "Russell, "Mr. Voter," *The Call*, November 6, 1913, 6. See also Russell, "Reform, Oh Blessed Reform," *Pearson's*, June 1914, 702–716.

CHAPTER FOURTEEN

1. Russell, *The Story of Wendell Phillips: Soldier of the Common Good* (Chicago: C. H. Kerr & Co., 1914), 10.

2. Ibid., 182. Oscar Sherwin, *Prophet of Liberty: The Life and Times of Wendell Phillips* (Westport, Conn.: Greenwood Press, 1975). Other biographies include Lorenzo Sears, *Wendell Phillips: Orator and Agitator* (New York: Doubleday, Page & Company, 1909); George Edward Woodberry, *Wendell Phillips: The Faith of an American* (Boston: Woodberry Society, 1912); Irving H. Bartlett, *Wendell Phillips, Brahmin Radical* (Boston: Beacon Press, 1961); and George L. Austin, *The Life and Times of Wendell Phillips* (Chicago: Afro-Am Press, 1969).

3. Russell, *These Shifting Scenes* (New York: George Doran Co., Hodder & Stoughton, 1914). Journalists writing autobiographies is common enough. See Howard Good, *The Journalist as Autobiographer* (Metuchen, N.J.: Scarecrow Press, 1993).

4. *Dial*, 56:423, May 16, 1914, 350. *Boston Transcript* May 2, 1914, 10.

5. *Book Digest Index* 10, June 1914, 406.

6. *Doing Us Good and Plenty* (Chicago: Charles H. Kerr & Co. Co-Operative, 1914).

7. "Reflections of the Editor," *Pearson's*, April 1911, 549–550. See also Peter N. Barry, "The Decline of Muckraking: A View from the Magazines," Ph.D. dissertation, Wayne State University, 1971, 341.

8. Russell, *The Story of the Nonpartisan League* (New York: Harper and Bros.), 64.

9. Russell, "The Keeping of the Kept Press," January 1914, 34, "How Business Controls the News," May 1914, 406, both in *Pearson's*.

10. Will Irwin's articles appeared originally in *Collier's* from January 21 to July 29, 1911. Irwin's work is described in Robert V. Hudson, *The Writing Game: A Biography of Will Irwin* (Ames, Iowa: Iowa State University Press, 1982).

11. Russell, *Doing Us Good and Plenty*, 46.

12. A good history of the Associated Press is Oliver Gramling, *AP: The Story of News* (Port Washington: N.Y., Kennikat Press, 1969). See also Victor Rosewater, *History of Cooperative Newsgathering in the United States* (New York: Appleton-Century-Crofts, 1930).

13. "Russell, "The Associated Press and Calumet," *Pearson's*, January 1914, 437–447. Russell's account is much the same as that of investigator Leslie H. Marcy, "Calumet," *International Socialist Review*, February 1914, 453–461. Russell later said that the Associated Press made a "loud squeal" after his article appeared and blacklisted him for many years. Russell to Upton Sinclair, July 6, 1919, Sinclair Papers, Lilly Library, Indiana University.

14. Russell, "The Keeping of the Kept Press," *Pearson's*, January 1914, 33–43; "The Magazine Soft Pedal," *Pearson's*, February 1914, 179–189; "How Business Controls News," *Pearson's*, May 1914, 546–557.

15. Russell, *Doing Us Good and Plenty*, 150, 171.

16. Ibid., 111–113.

17. *New York Times*, April 28, 1914; Arthur Link, "Mexico: Interference and Defeat, 1913–17," *Woodrow Wilson and Progressive Era, 1910–1917* (New York: Harper & Row, 1954), 107–144. See also Robert E. Quirk, *An Affair of Honor: Woodrow Wilson and the Occupation of Veracruz* (Lexington: University of Kentucky Press, 1962).

18. While Russell was a draw on the lecture circuit, he felt audiences saw him as "a wild-eyed Socialist [and] a rude unmannerly disturber of the peace of good men." With his careful dress, close clipped gray hair, and gentlemanly manner this was hardly likely. He made variations on this comment twice. *Bare Hands and Stone Walls* (New York: Charles Scribner's & Sons, 1933), 265 and in Russell Diary, August 13, 1914, Russell Papers, Library of Congress.

19. *Bare Hands*, 263. I have used three separate accounts by Russell to recreate the early days of the war in Europe. They are, *Bare Hands and Stone Walls*, 256–279; his diary while in the Netherlands, Russell Papers; and an unpublished account he wrote of his days there, "When Holland Looked at the Cloudburst," Russell Papers. All accounts provide new evidence but no discrepancies in his version of events.

20. Russell, "When Holland Looked at the Cloudburst," 8, Bare *Hands*, 258.

21. Russell, "Germanizing the World," *Cosmopolitan*, February 1906, 275–278, 282.

22. Russell, *Bare Hands*, 258. His full account of the island is "In the Outposts of Germany's Advance," *World To-day* October 1907, 999–1008. See also Russell, *After the Whirlwind A Book of Reconstruction and Profitable Thanksgiving* (New York: George H. Doran Co., 1919), 146–178.

23. Russell, *Bare Hands*, 263. Russell Diaries, August 3. Russell describes his knowledge of German plans in more detail in *After the Whirlwind*, 23–46.

24. Russell Diaries, August 7, 1914. Ameringer, *If You Don't Weaken* (New York: Henry Holt & Co., 1940), 300–301.

25. "Facts about war," ca. 1914, a pamphlet, Tamiment Library, New York University, Radical Pamphlets Collection.

26. Various books discuss socialism and the war. See James Weinstein, "The Socialists and the War," *The Decline of Socialism in America, 1912–1925* (New York: Monthly Review Press, 1967), 119–176; William E. Walling, ed., *The Socialists and the War* (New York: Garland, 1972 [1915]); Mary E. Merle Fainsod, *International Socialism and the World War* (New York: Octagon Books, 1966 [1935]). On

the war's cause see Luigi Albertini, *The Origins of the War of 1914* (London: Oxford University Press, 1952), Sidney Bradshaw Fay, *The Origins of the World War* (New York: Free Press, 1966); H. W. Koch, *The Origins of the First World War: Great Power Rivalry and German War Aims* (New York: Taplinger Pub. Co., 1972); and Denna F. Fleming, *The Origins and Legacies of World War I* (Garden City, N.Y.: Doubleday, 1968).

27. Russell, "When Holland Looked at the Cloudburst," 12, 18. "Source List and Detailed Death Tolls for the Twentieth Century Hemoclysm," http://users.erols.com/mwhite28/warstat1.htm/.

28. "When Holland Looked at the Cloudburst," 4. *Bare Hands*, 272.

29. Russell Diaries, August 12, 16, 1914. *Bare Hands*, 265.

30. Russell, *Bare Hands*, 273. Russell Diaries, August 23, 1914.

31. Quoted in Tertius Van Dyke, *Henry Van Dyke: A Biography* (New York: Harper & Bros., 1935), 329. *Bare Hands*, 272–273. Russell noted other spying incidents in unpublished manuscript, "Book Fragments," 15, Russell Papers. On German spying, Harold D. Lasswell, *Propaganda Technique in the World War* (New York: Peter Smith, 1938). Frederick C. Luebke, *Bonds of Loyalty: German-Americans and World War I* (DeKalb: Northern Illinois University Press, 1974).

32. Russell Diaries, August 18, September 5, 1914. *Bare Hands*, 274.

33. Russell, "This King and Kaiser Business," *Pearson's*, January 1915, 28.

34. Russell Diary, Aug 29, 1914.

35. Russell Diary, September 28, 1914, 30, Russell Papers. *Bare Hands*, 285–286. Hyndman was a prominent socialist who carried on a long correspondence with Russell over many years. Russell called him "one of the most remarkable minds I have ever known."

36. Russell, "Speech in Carnegie Hall," *New York Times*, October 11, 1914.

37. "Socialists Expect War to Help Them," *New York Call*, October 25, 1914, 2.

38. Miraldi, "The Treason of the Senate: Muckraking's High Point?" in "The Journalism of David Graham Phillips," Ph.D. dissertation, New York University, 1985, 264–275. C. H. Hoebeke, *The Road to Mass Democracy: Original Intent and the Seventeenth Amendment Author* (New Brunswick, N.J.: Transaction Publishers, 1995). Melvin Dubosky, "Success and Failure of Socialism in New York City, 1900–1918: A Case Study." *Labor History* IX (Fall 1968): 361–375.

CHAPTER FIFTEEN

1. Russell, "Will You Have Peace or War?" *Pearson's*, March 1915, 324.

2. John A. Thompson, *Reformers and War: American Progressive Publicists and the First World War* (Cambridge: Cambridge University Press, 1987) and David M. Kennedy, *Over Here: The First World War and American Society* (New York: Oxford University Press, 1980).

3. Arthur S. Link, *Wilson the Diplomat, A Look at His Major Foreign Policies* (Baltimore: The John Hopkins Press, 1957) and *Woodrow Wilson and the Progressive Era* (New York: Harper and Row, 1954) and Harvey A. DeWeerd, *President Wilson Fights His War: World War I and the American Intervention* (New York: Macmillan, 1968).

4. Russell, "This King and Kaiser Business," *Pearson's*, January 1915, 26. Russell to Carl Thompson, January 15, 1915, Socialist Party Papers, Duke University. *Bare Hands and Stone Walls* (New York: C. Scribner's Sons, 1933), 285.

5. Russell, "Some Obscured Lessons of the War," *Pearson's*, February 1915, 163. William English Walling, ed., *The Socialists and the War* (New York: Garland Publishing, 1972) notes that many socialists did not blame economics alone, 468. Progressives and Socialists agreed on many causes of war. See John A. Thompson, *Reformers and War: American Progressive Publicists and the First World War* (Cambridge: Cambridge University Press).

6. Berger in *The American Socialist*, January 9, 1915, quoted in Walling, 388. Russell, "Will You Have Peace or War?" *Pearson's*, March 1915, 327.

7. CER to Thompson, January 15, 24, 1915, Socialist Party Papers. Discussed also in Donald Bragaw, "Solider for the Common Good," Ph.D. dissertation, Syracuse University, 1971, 236–237 and David Shannon, *The Socialist Party of America: A History* (New York: Macmillan, 1955), note 12, 286.

8. *Who Made This War,* unpublished manuscript, Russell Papers. This long article repeats many of the themes of his *Pearson's* articles. It is in the form of a page proof, but it apparently was never published. "This King and Kaiser Business," 24–25.

9. *Bare Hands*, 288. Thompson, 101. See also C. Roland Marchand, *The American Peace Movement and Social Reform, 1898–1918* (Princeton: Princeton University Press, 1973).

10. "This King and Kaiser Business," 39. Russell especially mocked the peace efforts being put forth by steel magnate Andrew Carnegie, asking: "How will you have peace so long as capital controls the nations and capital finds that its profits are blocked in a way that can be relieved only through war?" *Who Made This War.*

11. Russell, "France and the Common Good," 492 3.

12. Russell, "This King and Kaiser Business," 34, "Some Obscured Lessons of the War," 167, 169.

13. "C. E. Russell Off for War," *New York Times*, April 12, 1915, 3. He discusses debt in "Why England Falls Down," *Pearson's*, August 1915, 201–219 and in *After the Whirlwind/ A Book of Reconstruction and Profitable Thanksgiving* (New York: Doran Co., 1919), 198–222. Russell concluded that the debt could not be paid off under capitalism. Under government ownership, however, the profits would go to the state, not individuals, and then the debt could be cleared.

14. Russell Diary, Russell Papers, Library of Congress, April 5, 1915. Lothrop Stoddard, *Master of Manhattan: The Life of Richard Croker* (New York: Longmans, Green and Co., 1931). 492 3.

15. Russell Diary, April 10, 1915. Adolph and Mary Hoehling, *The Last Voyage of the Lusitania* (H. H. Hold and Co., 1956) and Colin Simpson, *The Lusitania* (Boston: Little, Brown, 1973).

16. Russell Diary, April 11, 1915. "Why England Falls Down," 207. Russell fails to note, however, that Britain hardly needed an army because its navy was so superior. Russell Diary, April 21, 25, 1915.

17. Russell Diary, May 4, 1915. Frederick Gould, *Hyndman, Prophet of Socialism* (London, Pub., G. Allen & Unwin, 1928); *H. M. Hyndman and British socialism*, ed., Henry Pelling (London: Oxford University Press, 1961).

18. Russell describes Paris in "France and the Common Good," but he omits the crying scene, which is only in his diary, March 8, 1915. *After the Whirlwind*, 15.

19. Russell Diary, May 24, 1915. "France and Common Good," 493. H. C. Peterson, *Propaganda for War: The Campaign Against American Neutrality, 1914–1917.* (Port Washington, N.Y.: Kennikat Press, 1968).

NOTES 307

20. Russell, "The Men Behind the Dreadnaughts," *Why I Am A Socialist* (New York: Doran & Co., 1915), 114.

21. Russell, "In the Heartbreak Country," *Bare Hands*, 324, 325, 330.

22. *Bare Hands*, 328. The articles are "The Revolt of the Farmers," April 1915, "The Farmers' Battle," May, "Grain and the Invisible government," December, all *Pearson's*, 1915, and "The Farmer Versus the Great Interlocked," January, *Pearson's*, January 1916. On Populism, see John D. Hicks, *The Populist Revolt: A History of the Farmers' Alliance and the People's Party* (Minneapolis: University of Minnesota Press 1931) and Lawrence Goodwyn, *Democratic Promise: The Populist Moment in America* (New York: Oxford University Press, 1976).

23. Editorial, *The Nonpartisan Leader*, September 23, 1916, 7. See also Mary M. Cronin, Fighting for Farmers: The Pacific Northwest's Nonpartisan Leaguer Newspapers," *Journalism History*, Autumn 1997, 126–136.

24. Robert L. Morlan emphasizes the "crusading zeal" and optimism of the group's members in *Political Prairie Fire: The Nonpartisan League, 1915–1922* (Minneapolis: University of Minnesota Press, 1955), 38; Herbert E. Gaston, *The Nonpartisan League* (New York: Harcourt, Brace and Howe, 1920); Russell, *The Story of the Nonpartisan League* (New York: Harper and Bros., 1920).

25. Russell, "The Revolt of the Farmers: A Lesson In Constructive Radicalism," 426. *Bare Hands*, 340 345.

26. "Charles Edward Russell, an Optimist Turned Pessimist, Tells Pauline Jacobsen America will be forced to Fight a Victorious Germany," *San Francisco Bulletin*, October 30, 1915, clipping in Russell Papers

27. "Socialist Leader Warns U.S. to Arm," *New York Sun*, November 29, 1915, clipping Russell Papers. "Russell Angers Socialists," *New York Times*, November 30, 1915, 7. He was adamant that being a Socialist and going to war were compatible. "Nothing in the fundamental Socialist creed forbids a Socialist to take part in a just and righteous war," he wrote in *After the Whirlwind*, 97.

28. Debs is quoted in Shannon, 89. "Repudiated C. E. Russell," *New York Times*, December 25, 1916, 3.

29. "Russell, "A Socialist View," February 9, 1917, *New York Times*, 8. He reiterates this in *Bare Hands*, 292. Russell to Sinclair, February 22, 1916, Sinclair Papers, Indiana University.

30. Russell Diary, July 5, 16, 1916.

31. American Embassy official Robert W. Bliss denied Russell permission to go the war's front lines. A congressional investigation ensued but it was found Bliss did not err in his denial. Eventually Russell received the pass, however. "Takes Up Russell's Case," *New York Times*, September 8, 1916, 6; Bragaw, 353; Harry N. Schrieber, *The Wilson Administration and Civil Liberties, 1917–1921* (Ithaca: Cornell University Press, 1960).

32. Russell Diary, July 16, 1916. The article was "Why England Falls Down."

33. Russell Diary, August 14, 21, 1916.

34. Russell Diary, September 3, 6, 1916.

35. "Russell Goes to France," *New York Times*, June 17, 1916. Robert H. Ferrell, *Woodrow Wilson and World War I, 1917–1921* (New York: Harper and Row, 1985.

36. Link, *Wilson: Campaigns for Progressivism and Peace, 1916–1917* (Princeton University Press, 1965), 173.

37. Russell, "The Socialists' Stand," *New York Times*, February 15, 1917, 8. Algernon Lee, "Socialists Oppose a War," *New York Times*, February 12, 1917. Russell

insisted in his memoirs that financiers did not unduly influence the entry into the war. "If they had," he insisted, "I should have known the fact." *Bare Hands*, 292. H. C. Petersen and Gilbert C. Fite, *Opponents of War, 1917–1918* (Seattle: University of Washington Press, 1968). David S. Patterson, *Toward a Warless World: The Travail of the American Peace Movement, 1887–1914* (Bloomington: Indiana University Press, 1976).

38. Russell to Mrs. Charles Whiting Baker, February 25, 1917, Baker-Wheeling Family Papers, University of Virginia Library.
39. The Party's position is reprinted in full in "St. Louis Manifesto of the Socialist party," ed. Albert Fried, *Socialism in America* (New York: Doubleday & Co., 1970), and in "St. Louis Manifesto," *International Socialist Review*, May 1917. See also James Weinstein, "Antiwar Sentiment and the Socialist Party, 1917–1918," *Political Science Quarterly* 74, (1959): 215–239.
40. Stokes to Russell, April 8, 1917, Phelps-Stokes Papers, Columbia University. The letters started in March, Stokes to Russell, March 9, 10, 19, 20, 1917; Russell to Stokes, March 15, 1917.
41. Russell to Stokes, April 8, 1917, Stokes Papers.
42. Russell to Stokes, April 12, 14, 1917; Stokes to Russell, April 16, 1917, Stokes Papers. Russell's editor at *Pearson's*, Frank Harris, could not understand why Russell was so "bitten with the German bug." Harris to Upton Sinclair, May 19, 1917. Quoted in Upton Sinclair, *My Lifetime in Letters* (Columbia: University of Missouri Press, 1960), 178.
43. Kenneth Hendrickson Jr., "The Pro-War Socialists, the Social Democratic League and the Ill-Fated Drive for Industrial Democracy in America, 1917–1920," *Labor History* 11, 304–322. Shannon, 304.
44. Shannon, 101, 102. *New York Times*, September 7, 1917. Russell to Sinclair, May 4, 1917, Sinclair Papers.
45. William Bauchop Wilson, the President's Secretary of Labor, was the first to sound out Russell about the possibility of him doing diplomatic work for the Administration. Woodrow Wilson to Russell, May 10, 1917, and Russell to Wilson, May 11, 1917, Ray Stannard Baker. *Woodrow Wilson: Life and Letters* 6 (Garden City, N.Y., Doubleday, Page & Co., 1927–39), 262, 280.

Chapter Sixteen

1. Russell speech, June 12, 1917, *America's Message to the Russian People: Addresses by the Special Diplomatic Mission* (Boston: Marshall Jones Co., 1918), 143. Russell, *Unchained Russia* (New York: D. Appleton & Co., 1918).
2. I have used various secondary sources to describe the Russia trip, including George Kennan, *Russia Leaves the War* (Princeton: Princeton University Press, 1956); Norman E. Saul, *War and Revolution / The United States and Russia, 1914–1921* (Lawrence: University Press of Kansas, 2001); William Appleman Williams, *American Russian Relations, 1781–1947* (New York: Rinehart & Co., 1952); Robert Lansing, *War Memoirs* (New York: Bobbs-Merrill, 1935); and T. Bentley Mott, *Twenty Years as Military Attaché* (New York: Oxford University Press, 1937).
3. Lansing to Wilson, April 12, 1917, *The Lansing Papers, 1914–1920* (Washington, D.C.: U.S. Government Printing Office, 1939), 326.
4. Russell, March 4, 1911, *The Coming Nation*. I have used two Root biographies: Richard W. Leopold, *Elihu Root and the Conservative Tradition* (Boston: Little,

Brown & Co., 1954), and Phillip C. Jessup, *Elihu Root* (New York: Dodd, Mean & Co., 1938)

5. Samuel Gompers privately urged Wilson not to choose Root, as noted in Ronald Radosh, *American Labor and United States Foreign Policy* (New York: Random House, 1969), 76. See also his article, "American Labor and the Root Commission to Russia," *Studies on the Left* III (1962), 34–37. Raymond Robbins to Theodore Roosevelt, Aug 24, 1917, cited in Jessup, 366.

6. Kennan is quoted in Saul, 110. 356. Root to Taft, April 30, 1917, Jessup, 366.

7. "Root an Ambassador for Mission to Russia," *New York Times*, May 165, 1917, 9.

8. *New York Times*, April 29, 1917, 5. Wilson to Lansing, April 19, 1917, Wilson to Lansing, May 3, 1917, 196. Ray Stannard Baker, ed., *Woodrow Wilson, Life and Letters*, V. II, (Westport, Conn.: Greenwood Press, 1969 [New York: 1927–1939]), 29, 232 and Radosh, *American Labor,* 77–78.

9. Lansing to Wilson, May 3, 1917, and William Bauchop Wilson to WW, May 9, 1917, *Wilson: Life and Letters.*, ed. Ray Stannard Baker (New York, Greenwood Press, 1968 [1927], 212, Saul, 109.

10. "Socialists Here See German Trick," *New York Times*, May 9, 1917, 3. "Say the Kaiser 'Must Go,'" *New York Times*, May 13, 1917. Russell to Lansing, May 15, 1917, Lansing to Wilson, May 18, 1917, *Wilson Letters*, ibid. "Gen. Scott Joins the Root Mission," *New York Times*, May 12, 1917, 9. On the Stockholm conference, see Radosh, *American Labor,* 103–121.

11. "Ask Russell Not to Go," *New York Times*, May 16, 1917, 9. Hillquit to Lansing, May 10, 1917, 268, Wilson Letters. "The black scourge of war," *Mother Earth* 12, June 1917, 101–102.

12. Editorial, "The Passing Show—'Root'—ing in Russia," *International Socialist Review*, July 1917. "Gorky Hostile to Mission," *New York Times*, May 18, 1917, 6. Gorky's comments were published in *Jewish Daily Forward* in New York. See also Max Eastman, "Syndicalist-Socialist Russia," *International Socialist Review* (1917), 78.

13. Rose Pastor Stokes to Katerina Breshkovskaya, May 3, 1917, Cahan to Russell, May 17, 1917, Allen Benson to Russell, May 14, 1917, Russell Papers, Library of Congress, Washington, D.C. McCormick's diary confirms that International Harvester representatives had told him about American agitators stirring up the people before the mission arrived, May 22, 26, 1917, McCormick Papers, State Historical Society of Wisconsin, Madison, Wis.

14. Russell Diary, June 3, 1917, Russell Papers.

15. Russell Diary, June 5, 1917. While I have relied mostly on Russell's account, McCormick's diary also confirms many of the incidents on the trip. CER speech to Council of Workmen's, Soldiers' and Peasant Delegates, June 12, 1917 International Typographical Union, *America's Message to the Russian People*, 145–147. Some of the speeches are also in *The U.S. and the War: The Mission to Russia Political Addresses*, ed. Robert Scott and James Brown Scott (Cambridge: Harvard University Press, 1918). The complete itinerary of the mission is in "Special Diplomatic Mission of the United States of America to Russia," along with a summary of the Mission's activities sent to Secretary of State Lansing, copies in Russell Papers.

16. The incident is recounted by Beatty, *The Red Heart of Russia* (New York: Century, 1918), 39–40. While sailing to Russia, Russell told the Mission members that he was planning to do this. See McCormick diary, June 10, 1918. Russell's attempt

to appear as a proletarian was scorned by the American socialists. See Radosh, *American Labor*, 91.

17. "Vote Out C. E. Russell," *New York Times*, June 11, 1917, 18. Telegram to Socialist Party, Russell Papers, June 14, 1917. Russell Diary, June 14. 1917.

18. Russell Diary, June 6, 1917.

19. Russell Diary, June 13, 1917. Russell's analysis of Russia takes the name *Unchained Russia*.

20. Russell Diary, June 21, 26. Root wrote his wife that he liked the fact that everyone got up late in Russia. Jessup, 361.

21. Russell Diary, June 20, 21.

22. Root cable to Lansing, June 17 1917, Root Papers, Library of Congress. On publicity and Russia, see James R. Mock and Cedric Larson, *Words that Won the War: The Story of the Committee on Public Information, 1917–1919* (New York: Russell and Russell, 1939), 300–320, and Jessup, 365. See also John A. Thompson, *Reformers and War: American Progressive Publicists and the First World War* (Cambridge: Cambridge University Press).

23. Russell first warned about agitators on the trip to Russia. McCormick diary, May 21, 1917. Russell Diary, July 1, 1917.

24. Steffens discusses his time in Russia in *The Autobiography of Lincoln Steffens* (New York: Harcourt, Brace & Co., 1931), 741–777. Diary, July 1, June 21, 1917.

25. Russell Diary, June 25. 1917. Russell in *Assault on Democracy*, a fifteen-page unpublished manuscript in his Library of Congress papers, said he had documents to prove that Lenin was being paid by the Germans but that his trunk containing the proof had been stolen.

26. Russell, *Bare Hands and Stone Walls* (New York: Charles Scribner's Sons, 1933), 351. Russell Diary, June 27, 1917. Herbert Bailey, "Russell Foils Tricks of Socialists Here," *New York Times*, June 28, 1917, 2.

27. Diary, July 4, 1917. A U.S. delegation headed by John F. Stevens was in Russia at the same time as the Root mission. The Stevens mission was trying there to advise the Russians on their rail woes, but the mission interfered with the Root mission work. Saul, 142–144.

28. *Assault on Democracy*, 155. Russell Diary, July 7, July 10. Jessup, 365.

29. Root's letter home is noted in Jessup, 369. "Root Has Faith Russia Will Stand," *New York Times*, August 5, 1917, 1, 2. "Russell Would Stop Criticism of Russia," July 6, 1917, 3. "We can depend on Russia, Root Says," *New York Times*, August 12, 1917, 1, 3.

30. Root to Jessup, September 16, 1936. *Elihu Root*, 356. Wilson blamed Root for failing to win over the Russians. Leopold, 119. Wilson to Russell, November 10, 1917. *Wilson Letters*, 558. Wilson said he agreed with Russell's thinking on Russia. Wilson passed along Russell's letter to Creel, calling it "important." Note 1, *Wilson Letters*, 349.

31. "Memorandum on the Russian Situation," December 7, 1917, The Conduct of American Foreign Affairs, Lansing Papers, as noted on Radosh, note 213, 160. A Root biographer writes that the only fair criticism of Root was that "that he did not show himself [to be] wiser than all those around him." Jessup, 370.

32. "Robert Marion LaFollette," *Human Life*, July 30, 1909, 30. Russell speech, Union League Club of New York, August 15, 1917, *America's Message to the Russian People*, 150.

33. Fred Greenbaum, *Robert Marion La Follette* (Boston: Twayne Publishers, 1975). Joshua Butler Wright, a counselor to Ambassador Francis, described Russell, Diary, July 28, 1917. See Saul, note 116, 134.

34. Speech in Minneapolis before a labor loyalty rally, "Loyal Conference Defines War Aims," *New York Times*, September 7, 1917, 12.

35. Russell to Sinclair March 25, 1918, Sinclair Papers, Lilly Library, Indiana University, Bloomington. Russell to George Creel, October 29, 1917, CPI Papers, National Archives, Maryland. Stephen Vaughn, *Holding Fast The Inner Lines: Democracy, Nationalism and the Committee on Public Information* (Chapel Hill: University of North Carolina Press, 1980), 38.

36. The touring Progressives are discussed in Stuart I. Rochester, *American Liberal Disillusionment in the Wake of World War I* (University Park: Pennsylvania State University Press, 1977). Baker, *American Chronicle* (New York, C. Scribner's Sons, 1945), 303. Vaughn, 131.

37. Russell to Creel, January 4, and February 23,1918, CPI Papers. Vaughn, 307.

38. Vaughn, 140. "100 Radical Papers May Be Suppressed," *New York Times*, September 16, 1917. "Russell, "The New Socialist Alignment," *Harper's Magazine*, 569.

39. Creel to Russell, November 9, 1917, Creel to Russell, April 22, 1918, CPI Files.

40. Russell Diary, May 12, 1918. See, for example, Robert V. Hudson, "Propagandist," *The Writing Game, A Biography of Will Irwin* (Ames: Iowa State University Press, 1982), 109–128.

41. Russell's distaste for England was signaled in earlier articles, "Strange Lineage of a Royal Baby," *Cosmopolitan*, September 1907, "The Mystery of Edward the Seventh," *Human Life*, November 1908 and "The Next King of Erford," *Human Life*, November 1910, 5, 6, 23, 27. Russell Diary, May 8, 24. July 3, 1918.

42. Russell to Creel, April 21, 1918, CPI Files.

43. Russell Diary, May 25, 21, 1918.

44. Russell Diary, May 8, July 8, 1918. Vincent Brome, *H. G. Wells: A Biography* (Westport, Conn.: Greenwood Press, 1951); Lovat Dicksong, *H. G. Wells: His Turbulent Life and Times* (London: Macmillan, 1969).

45. Russell and other pro-war Socialists had formed the Social Democratic League as a second American Socialist Party soon after their split in 1917. The League never gained momentum and was more a paper organization than a real political party. There are various accounts of its existence. See Kenneth E. Hendrickson, Jr., "The Pro-War Socialists, the Social Democratic League and the Ill-Fated Drive for Industrial Democracy in America, 1917–1920," *Labor History* 11 (Summer 1970): 304–322 and Frank L Grubbs, *The Struggle for Labor Loyalty: Gompers, the AF of L and the Pacifists, 1917–1920* (Durham, N.C.: Duke University Press, 1968).

46. Russell Diary, July 26, 1918. The trip to Europe is also described in Marion Simons Leuck, "The American Socialist and Labor Mission to Europe, 1918, Background Activities and Significance: An Experiment in Democratic Diplomacy," Ph.D. dissertation, Northwestern University, 1941; Kent Kreuter and Gretchen Kreuter, *An American Dissenter: The Life of Algie Martin Simons, 1870–1950* (Lexington: University of Kentucky Press, 1969). Simons retells the story in *Vision for Which We Fought: A Study in Reconstruction* (New York: Macmillan, 1919).

EPILOGUE

1. Stuart I. Rochester, *American Liberal Disillusionment in the Wake of World War I* (University Park: Pennsylvania State University Press, 1977), 63. On the war and its effect on Progressivism, see also Arthur Link, "What Happened to the Progressive Movement in the 1920s?" *American Historical Review* 64 (July 1959): 833–81.
2. John Wheeler-Bennett, Brest-*Litovsk: The Forgotten Peace* (London: Macmillan and Co., 1918) Russell, *The Assault on Democracy*, unpublished manuscript in Russell Papers, Library of Congress.
3. Russell, *After the Whirlwind: A Book of Reconstruction and Profitable Thanksgiving* (New York: George H. Doran Co., 1919), 14–15, 21, 22, 300, 302–303.
4. *Unchained Russia* (New York, London: D. Appleton and Co., 1918), *After the Whirlwind, Bolshevism and the United States* (Indianapolis: Bobbs-Merrill Co., 1919).
5. Russell, *Bare Hands and Stone Walls* (New York: C. Scribner's Sons, 1933), 324, 335, 358. Russell wrote a series of articles on postwar America for the *McClure's* syndicate: "Labor as it Used to Be and as It is Now," March 23, "War Revelations About Labor," March 30, "A Reasonable Position of American Labor About the Present High Wage Scale," April 6, "Educational and Other Reforms That Are Most Needed," April 13, "The Great Need of Co-operation," April 20, "The Danger of Bolshevism in the United States," April 27, "Bolshevism and the United States," May 4, all 1919, clippings in Russell Papers.
6. *The Story of the Nonpartisan League: A Chapter in American Evolution* (New York, London: Harper & Bros., 1920). Russell's wife Theresa caused a flap in 1920 when she claimed to have been in contact with the spirit of feminist champion Susan B. Anthony who told her that Americans should vote for Eugene V. Debs, then in jail for his antiwar comments. Debs did get a million votes for the presidency in the 1920 election. "Miss Anthony, Dead, For Debs," October 3, 1920, *New York Sun*, clipping in Russell Papers, no date.
7. Russell, "The Ethics of Vivisection: Materialism vs. Humanity," speech before the Society for Humane Regulation of Vivisection, February 16, 1920. Copy of speech, Russell Papers. Sue M. Farrell to Russell, October 2, 1925, Russell Papers.
8. Brisbane to Russell, January 9, 1926, Russell papers. Russell, "Is Woman Suffrage a Failure?" March 1924, 724–730, "Is the World Going Dry?" January 1924, 323–333, and "At the European Switchboard, February 1925, 454, 452–463, all in *The Century Magazine*. Russell, *Railroad Melons, Rates and Wages: A Handbook of Railroad Information* (Chicago: C. H. Kerr & Co., 1922); *The Outlook for the Philippines* (New York: The Century Co., 1922); *The Hero of the Filipinos: The Story of Jose Rizal, Poet, Patriot and Martyr*, with E.B. Rodriguez (New York, London: The Century Co., 1923); Russell to John Spargo, December 19, 1926, Spargo Papers, University of Vermont Library.
9. Untitled profile in the papers of William Stanley Braithwaite, ca. 1925. Russell, *Bare Hands*, 375.
10. "Charles E. Russell, Now Famed Journalist, Early U.S. Writer to Sponsor Irish Freedom," *Washington Post*, July 24, 1938, clipping in Russell Papers, Library of Congress. Russell, *Bare Hands*, 385. "The True Dimensions of the Irish," February, 1,7, "British Propaganda in America," March, 1,7, and "The Growing Shadow of Imperialism," April, 3, 7–8, all *American Irish Review*, 1924. Mary Cogan Bromage, "Mission to America," *De Valera and the March of a Nation*

(New York: Noonday Press, 1956), 90–107, and Frank P. Longford, *Eamon de Valera* (Boston: Houghton Mifflin, 1971).

11. Russell recounts the incident in *Bare Hands*, 391–392. His speech is in "British Bar Russell for Cincinnati Talk," *Cincinnati-Times Star*, May 28, 1926, copy in Russell papers.

12. *Bare Hands*, 392. Russell to Hicks, June 7, 1926. Hicks to Russell, June 11, 1926. Russell papers. Unsigned letter to Russell, May 31, 1926, from a reporter with the *London Daily Express*. "British Bar Russell for Cincinnati Talk," *Cincinnati-Times Star*. Unsigned editorial, "Britain Chucklehead," *Cincinnati-Times Star*, May 28, 1926, clippings in Russell Papers.

13. E. H. Sothern, *Julia Marlowe's Story* (New York: Rinehart & Co., 1954) v, vi.

14. Russell, *Julia Marlowe: Her Life and Art* (New York, London: D. Appleton and Co., 1926). Book reviews: *New York Herald Tribune*, September 19; *New York Times*, August 15, 1926, 7; *International Book Review*, September 26, 1926, 611; *Boston Transcript*, August 28, 4, all 1926. A later biography was Adelaide A. Ovington, *The Star that Didn't Twinkle* (New York: Vantage Press, 1961).

15. Russell, *Theodore Thomas and the American Orchestra* (Garden City, N.Y.: Doubleday, Page & Co., 1927), vii. 312–313.

16. Theodore Caskey Russell, "Theodore Thomas: His Role in the Development of the Musical Culture in the United States, 1835–1905," Ph.D. Dissertation, University of Minnesota, notes "numerous inaccuracies" in Russell's book. See also Ezra Schabas, *Theodore Thomas: America's Conductor and Builder of Orchestras, 1835–1905* (Urbana: University of Illinois Press, 1989); *New York Times*, April 8, 1928, 18. See also *Boston Transcript*, January 14, 1928, 4; the *Nation*, January 4, 23; and *New York Evening Post*, November 12, all 1928.

17. Hampton to Russell, May 8, 1928, Russell Papers.

18. *A-rafting on the Mississipp'* (New York, London: The Century Co., 1928). *New York Herald Tribune*, November 11, 1928, 7. See also *New York Times*, October 7, 1928, 14.

19. Russell, *An Hour of American Poetry* (New York, London: J. B. Lippincott Co., 1929), *From Sandy Hook to 62 degrees; being some account of the adventures, exploits and services of the old New York pilot-boat* (New York, London: The Century Co., 1929). F. L. Robbins, *Outlook*, May 28, 1930, 145. Russell, *Charlemagne, First of the Moderns* (Boston, New York: Houghton, Mifflin Co., 1930). See also Richard Winston, *Charlemagne: From the Hammer to the Cross* (Indianapolis, Bobbs-Merrill, 1954) and Harold Lamb, *Charlemagne: The Legend and the Man* (Garden City, N.Y., Doubleday, 1954).

20. Russell, *Haym Salomon and the Revolution* (New York: Cosmopolitan Book Corp., 1930). Russell, Introduction to Zelig Tyler, *Let's Talk It Over: Present-Day Jewish Problems* (New York: Defense Publishing, 1939). See also Howard Fast, *Haym Salomon, Son of Liberty* (New York: J. Messner, 1941) and Laurens R. Schwartz, *Jews and the American Revolution: Haym Salomon and Others* (Jefferson, N.C.: McFarland, 1987).

21. The federation billed itself as "the voice of Christian America in behalf of the Jewish national home." See Russell, "The Truth about Palestine," article in Russell Papers, ca. 1936. "C. E. Russell Blames England for Arabs' Clash with Jews," newspaper clipping, December 15, 1936, "Russell Signs Petition Sent Britain by Jews," Newspaper clipping, October 26, 1940, both in Russell Papers. "Russell, Nazi Foe, Hailed By Mayor," *New York Times*, February 13, 1934. Russell speech,

"Hitlerism and the Jew," at the American Christian Conference, December 15, 1936, in Russell Papers.

22. Comments made by Edmund I. Kaufmann, "C. E. Russell's Funeral to Be Held Tomorrow," *Washington Post*, April 25, 1941, 25. Historian Henry Steele Commager said Russell's biography on Solomon did "a grave injustice" with its "indiscriminate enthusiasm" and "grotesque" interpretation of the American Revolution. Commager *Books*, November 30 1930, 10.

23. Marlowe to Russell, February 4, 1936, Russell Papers. Russell to Ralph Cram, November 21, 1936, Cram Papers, Newberry Library. John F. Finerty to Russell, July 29, 1938, Russell Papers.

24. Russell to Margaret Tolson, Letter book, July 18, 1937, New York State Library, Albany, New York. This letter book contains Russell letters from 1937 to 1940, a poignant collection of his final days and thoughts.

25. Marlowe to Russell, April 27, 1939. Unpublished poem in Russell Papers, "The sadness of the world."

26. Hurst to Russell, February 2, 1939, Russell Papers. Hurst (1889–1968) is known for her sentimental novels. It is unclear how she and Russell became friendly. See Brooke Kroeger, *Fannie: The Talent for Success of Writer Fannie Hurst* (New York: Times Books, 1999).

27. Russell, "Old Reporter Looks at the Mad-House World," *Scribner's*, October 1933, 225–220 and "Toward the American Commonwealth: Social Democracy: Constant Gradualism as the Technique for Social Advance," *Social Frontier*, October 1938, 22–24. *Bare Hands*, 421–425.

28. Russell, *Why I Am a Socialist* (New York: Hodder & Stoughton, George H. Doran Co., 1910), 286. "100 Honor Well Known Author and Publicist," *Washington Tribune*, April 19, 1934, clipping, Russell Papers.

29. Marlowe to Russell, March 5, 1940. McGaffey to Russell, March 7, 1940, both Russell Papers.

30. "Charles Edward Russell, 80, Dies After Brief Illness," *Washington Tribune*, April 26, 1901; "Charles Russell, Noted Writer, Socialist, Dies," Associated Press Story, April 24, 1941; "Charles Russell, Journalist, Dies," *New York Times*, April 24, 1941, 44; "Estate of C. E. Russell, Poet, Valued at $70,609," *Washington Star*, May 9, 1941; all in Russell Papers.

31. Russell speech in *William English Walling: A Symposium* (New York: Stackpole Sons, 1938), 79.

PRIMARY SOURCE BIBLIOGRAPHY

BOOKS

Such Stuff as Dreams (Indianapolis: The Bowen-Merrill Co., 1901).
The Twin Immoralities and Other Poems (Chicago: Hammersmark Publishing Co., 1904).
The Greatest Trust in the World (New York: The Ridgway-Thayer Co., 1905).
The Uprising of the Many (New York: Doubleday, Page & Co., 1907).
Lawless Wealth: The Origin of Some Great American Fortunes (New York: B. W. Dodge & Co., 1908).
Songs of Democracy and on Other Themes (New York: Moffat, Yard and Co., 1909).
Thomas Chatterton: The Marvelous Boy, The Story of a Strange Life, 1752–1770. (London: Richards, 1909).
Why I Am a Socialist (New York: Hodder & Stoughton, George H. Doran Co., 1910 [1915]).
Business: The Heart of the Nation (New York: John Lane Co., 1911).
The Passing Show of Capitalism (Girard, Kansas: The Appeal to Reason, 1912).
Stories of the Great Railroads (Chicago: C. H. Kerr & Co., 1912).
Doing Us Good and Plenty (Chicago: C. H. Kerr & Co., Co-Operative, 1914).
These Shifting Scenes (New York: Hodder & Stoughton, George H. Doran Co., 1914).
The Story of Wendell Phillips: Soldier of the Common Good (Chicago: C. H. Kerr & Co., 1914).
Unchained Russia (New York, London: D. Appleton and Co., 1918).
After the Whirlwind: A Book of Reconstruction and Profitable Thanksgiving (New York: George H. Doran Co., 1919).
Bolshevism and the United States (Indianapolis: Bobbs-Merrill Co., 1919).
The Story of the Nonpartisan League: A Chapter in American Evolution (New York: Harper & Bros., 1920).
Railroad Melons, Rates and Wages: A Handbook of Railroad Information (Chicago: C. H. Kerr & Co., 1922).
The Outlook for the Philippines (New York: The Century Co., 1922).
The Hero of the Filipinos: The Story of Jose Rizal, Poet, Patriot and Martyr. Written with E. B. Rodriguez (New York, London: The Century Co., 1923).
Julia Marlowe, Her Life and Art (New York, London: D. Appleton and Co., 1926).
The American Orchestra and Theodore Thomas (Garden City, N.Y.: Doubleday, Page & Co., 1927).
A-rafting on the Mississipp' (New York, London: The Century Co., 1928).
An Hour of American Poetry (New York, London: J. B. Lippincott Co., 1929).
From Sandy Hook to 62 Degrees; being some account of the adventures, exploits and services of the old New York pilot-boat (New York, London: The Century Co., 1929).
Haym Salomon and the Revolution (New York: Cosmopolitan Book Co., 1930).

Charlemagne: First of the Moderns (New York: Houghton Mifflin Co., 1930).
Blaine of Maine: His Life and Times (New York: Cosmopolitan Book Corp., 1931).
Bare Hands and Stone Wall: Some Recollections of a Sideline Reformer (New York: C. Scribner's Sons, 1933).
A Pioneer Editor in Early Iowa: A Sketch of the Life of Edward Russell (Washington, D.C.: Ransdell Inc.), 1941.

MAGAZINE ARTICLES

1887
"The Clergyman's daughter," *Waverly*, March, 48.

1900
"Greatest World's Fairs," *Munsey*, November, 161–184.

1901
"Story of the Nineteenth Century," *Munsey*, January, 551–559.
"Are There Two Rudyard Kiplings?" *Cosmopolitan*, October, 653–660.
"Old St. Saviour's Southwark," *Harper's Magazine*, November, 878–884.

1904
"William Randolph Hearst," *Harper's Weekly*, May 21, 790–792.
"Notable Dramatic Achievements," *Critic*, December, 525–531.

1905
"The Greatest Trust in the World," *Everybody's*, February, 151–56; March, 291–300; April, 502–516; May, 643–654; June, 779–792; July, 61–74; August, 218–227; September, 380–383.
"Popularizing Classical Music," *Reader*, July, 40–47.

1906
"Germanizing the World," *Cosmopolitan*, January, 274–282.
"Socialistic Government of London," *Cosmopolitan*, February, 367–376.
"Marshall Field, A Great Mercantile Genius," *Everybody's*, March 1, 1906, 291–302.
"Soldiers of the Common Good," *Everybody's*, April 1906, 380–383; May, 597–601; June, 753–765; July, 42–55; August, 178–189; September, 340–352; October, 469–482; November, 774–792; December, 3–13.
"Mr. Hearst as I knew Him," *Ridgway's*, October, 279–291.
"That Blessed Word Regulation," *Wilshire's*, November, 9–11.
"A Struggle for a Billion," *Ridgway's*, November 3, 1906, 9–10; November 10, 11–12; November 17, 13–14; November 24, 15–16; December 1, 15–16; December 8, 15–16.
"Caste—the Curse of India," *Cosmopolitan*, December, 124–135.
"The Retirement of Mr. Hitchcock," *Ridgway's*, December 15.
"Could These Be Elected By the People?" *Ridgway's*, December, 7–8.
"Wall Street Greed and Railroad Ruin," *Ridgway's*, December 29, 12–13.

1907
"Soldiers of the Common Good," *Everybody's*, January, 187–196; February, 318–328; March, 490–501; April, 581–593; May, 784–795; June, 15–23.
"England's System of Snobbery," *Cosmopolitan*, January, 448–456.

"Caste in Various Countries," *Cosmopolitan*, March, 448–456.

"The Growth of Caste in America," *Cosmopolitan*, March, 524–534.

"Forgotten Capital of the Orient," *Harper's*, March, 622–632.

"The Message of David Graham Phillips," *Bookman's Monthly*, April, 511–513.

"The American Language," *Saturday Evening Post*, June 15, 6–7.

"Seven Kings in Mexico," *Cosmopolitan*, July, 271–279.

"The Suez Canal," *Everybody's*, July, 94–103.

"Where Did You Get It, Gentlemen?" *Everybody's*, August, 201–11; September, 348–360; October, 503–511; November, 636–645; December, 118–127.

"Strange Lineage of a Royal Baby," *Cosmopolitan*, September, 465–476.

"Abdul—the Snake Charmer," *Human Life*, October, 7–8.

"River of the Pagoda Land," *Harper's*, October, 674–683.

"In the Outposts of Germany's Advance," *World To-day*, October, 999–1008.

"Humanitarian Rule in Paris," *World's Work*, October, 9426–9430.

"The Haymarket and Afterwards," *Appleton's*, October, 399–412.

"Swinburne and Music," *North American*, November, 427–441.

"The Cry of the Slums," with Bessie Marsh, *Everybody's*, December, 34–40.

"At the Throat of the Republic: Before the Election," *Cosmopolitan*, December, 1907, 146–157; "At the Election," January, 1908, 259–271; "After the Election," February, 361–368; "Postscript—The Election of 1907," March, 475–480.

1908

"Where Did You Get It, Gentlemen?" *Everybody's*, *January*, 342–353.

"Rockefeller—An Estimate of the Man," *Human Life*, January, 9–10.

"Gravity, Yard and other Shambles," *Independent*, January 30, 233–238.

"Governor Johnson—New Style Politician," *Everybody's*, April, 494–503.

"What About Stuyvesant Fish?" *Human Life*, April, 5–6, 134.

"Trinity: Church of Mystery," *The Broadway Magazine*, April, 1–12.

"Trinity Corporation: A Riddle of Riches," *The Broadway Magazine*, May, 187–195.

"Morgan—Master of the Money Mart," *Human Life*, May, 753–760.

"A Burglar in the Making," *Everybody's*, June, 753–760.

"Governor Johnson—New Style Politician," *Everybody's*, June, 494–503.

" A Rational Plan for American Peerage," *Broadway Magazine*, July, 21–28.

"Senator Platt—The Yaller Hawk of Politics," *Human Life*, July, 7–9.

"Tenements of Trinity Church," *Everybody's*, July, 47–57.

"Billions for Bad Blue Blood: Training for the Title," September, 610–624; "The Curse of the Coronet," October, 785–800; "The Price The Woman Pays," *The Redbook*, November, 33–48.

"Forward Citizens to the Firing Line," *Everybody's*, November, 701–709.

"The Mystery of Edward the Seventh," *Human Life*, November, 5–6.

"One Woman Who Has Done Great Work," *Human Life*, December, 7–8, 29.

"The Passing of the Poorhouse," *The Broadway Magazine*, December, 742–750.

1909

"The Break-Up of the Parties," *Success*, January, 5–10; February, 80–82, 111–122.

"The Growing Menace of Socialism," *Hampton's*, January, 119–126.

"Reducing the Tariff—Yes?" *Hampton's*, February, 156–166.

"Slum as a National Asset," *Everybody's*, February, 170–180.

"Dr. Parkhurst, Preacher & Man," *Human Life*, February, 158–166.

"Trinity's Tenements—The Public's Business," *Everybody's*, February, 278–279.

"The Grand Orchestra in America," *Cosmopolitan*, March, 376–388.

"Samuel Gompers, Labor Leader," *Human Life*, April, 6–7, 31.

"The Heart of the Railroad Problem," *Hampton's*, April, 452–473.

"Philander Chase Knox—the New Secretary of State," *Human Life*, May, 7–8.

"Assumptions Versus Facts: A Satire," *Arena*, July, 451.

"Rescuer of Ruined Lives," *Missionary Review of the World*, July, 451–456.

"Robert Marion LaFollette," *Human Life*, July 7–8, 24.

"Unto the Least of These," with Lewis W. Hine, *Everybody's*, July, 75–87.

"The Night Court of New York," *Human Life*, September, 7–8, 30.

"Beating Men to Make them Good: Signs of a Better Era for Those that Go Wrong," *Hampton's*, 312–23.

"Beating Men to Make Them Good: An Illuminating Glance behind the Walls of American Prisons," *Hampton's*, September, 312–323.

"Beating Men to Make Them Good: the Decline of the Punishing Idea," *Hampton's*, November, 609–620.

"The American Diplomat Abroad," *Cosmopolitan*, November, 739–749.

"The Next King of Erford," *Human Life*, November, 5–6, 23, 27.

1910

"The Story of Charlemagne," *Cosmopolitan*, January, 127–140; February, 369–379; March, 501–510; April, 643–653; May, 781–790; June, 60–68.

"Chaos and Bomb Throwing in Chicago," *Hampton's*, March, 435–447.

"Sanity and Democracy for American Cities," *Everybody's*, April, 435–447.

"Great Millionaire's Mill," *Hampton's*, April, 478–491.

"The Mystery of Dreyfus," *Human Life*, April, 9–10, 29.

"Winning and Empire and the Cost of Winning," *Hampton's*, May, 603–617.

"Monometallism and Water," *Cosmopolitan*, June, 21–24.

"Scientific Corruption of Politics," *Hampton's*, June, 843–858.

"What Are You Going to Do About it? Legislative Graft and the Albany Scandal," July *Cosmopolitan*, 146–160.

"What Are You Going to Do About it? Graft as an Expert Trade in Pittsburg [sic]," *Cosmopolitan*, August 1910, 283–293.

"What Are You Going to Do About it? The Jack-Pot in Illinois Legislation," *Cosmopolitan*, September, 466–478.

What Are You Going to Do About it? The Man the Interests Wanted," *Cosmopolitan*, October 1910, 592–601.

"What Are You Going to Do About it? Colorado—New Tricks in an Old Game," *Cosmopolitan*, December, 45–58.

"What Are You Going to Do About it? Senator Gore's Strange Bribe Story," *Cosmopolitan*, January 151–162.

"Speaking of Widows and Orphans, " *Hampton's*, July, 79–92.

"Remedy of the Law," *Hampton's*, August, 217–230.

"Railroad Machine as It Works Now," *Hampton's*, September, 364–376.

"Surrender of New England," *Hampton's*, December, 759–770.

Paying of the Bill," *Hampton's*, October, 507–520.

"Heir of the War Lord," *Cosmopolitan*, March, 464–468.

1911

"The Mysterious Octopus," *World To-Day*, March, 1960–1972; *Hearst's Magazine*, April 2074–2085.

"What Comes of Playing the Game," *International Socialist Review*, January.
"Speed," *Hampton's*, October, 444–457.
"A Muckraker Off Duty," *Twentieth-Century*, November, 23–29, 34–48.

1912

Socialism the Only Remedy, a pamphlet, the Socialist Party, 1912.
"Socialism: Just Where It Stands To-day," *Hampton-Columbian*, January, 752–762.
"Rational Political Action," *International Socialist Review*, March, 545–548.
"The Mysterious Octopus," *World To-Day*, February, 1735–1750, March, 1960–1972; *Hearst's Magazine*, April, 2074–2085.
"The Heir of the War Lord," *Cosmopolitan*, March, 464–468.
"Progress and Politics," *Cosmopolitan*, July, 286–288.

1913

"What Next?" *International Socialist Review*, January, 524–527.
"Railroad Revolution," February, 129–39; March, 321–331; April, 382–399; May, 497–508; all *Pearson's*.
"Things as They Are," *Pearson's*, 511–512.
"Pure Food Law: A License to Poison," *Technical World Magazine*, July, 642–648.
"Is America on the Map?" *Harper's Weekly*, October 25, 26–27.

1914

"Reform, Oh Blessed Reform," *Pearson's*, June, 702–716.
"The Keeping of the Kept Press," *Pearson's*, January, 33–43.
"The Magazine Soft Pedal," *Pearson's*, February, 179–189.
"The Associated Press and Calumet," *Pearson's*, April, 437–447.
"How Business Controls News," *Pearson's*, May, 546–557.
"These Days in Journalism," *International Socialist Review*, October, 210–216.

1915

"As to Making Peace," *Review*, January, 20–22.
"This King and Kaiser Business" *Pearson's*, January, 24–33.
"Some Obscured Lessons of the War," *Pearson's*, February, 161–171.
"Will You Have Peace or War?" *Pearson's*, March, 323–333.
"France and the Common Good," *Pearson's*, April, 483–493.
"The Revolt of the Farmers: A Lesson in Constructive Radicalism," *Pearson's*, April, 417–427.
"The Farmer's Battle," Pearson's, May, 516–527.
"No More Foes Without and None Within," *Pearson's*, June, 691–699.
"Why England Falls Down," *Pearson's*, August, 201–219.
"Skinning Our Indians," *Pearson's*, October, 389–397.
"Grain and the Invisible Government," *Pearson's*, December, 515–527.

1916

"The Farmer Versus the Great Interlocked," *Pearson's*, January, 32–43.

1917

"The Nonpartisan League," *Publications of the American Sociological Society*, XI, 31–36.
"Origin and Aim of the Farmer's Nonpartisan League," *Community Center*, March 17, 20–21.

"Democracy in Russia," *Collier's*, September 22, 8–9, 34, 37, 39.
"Ruyssia's Women Warriors," *Good Housekeeping*, October, 22–23.

1918
"Russell, "The New Socialist Alignment," *Harper's Magazine*, March, 563–570.
"Behold a Man!" *Hearst's Magazine*, November, 348–350.
"There's Another St. Nicholas," *New York Herald Tribune Magazine*, December 23, 11–12.

1919
"Labor as it Used to Be and as It is Now," March 23; "War Revelations about Labor," March 30; "A Reasonable Position of American Labor about the Present High Wage Scale," April 6; "Educational and Other Reforms that Are Most Needed," April 13; "The Great Need of Co-operation," April 20; "The Danger of Bolshevism in the United States," April 27; "Bolshevism and the United States" May 4; all *McClure's Syndicate*.
"Radical Press in America," *Bookman*, July, 513–518.

1920
"All for Belgium," *Hearst's*, March, 5.
"Hamstringing Shakespeare," *Bookman*, November, 207–212.

1922
"The Philippines: Independent of Vassal?" *The Nation*, April 26, 487–488.

1924
"Is the World Going Dry?" *Century*, January, 323–333.
"The True Dimensions of the Irish," *American Irish Review*, February, 1,7.
"British Propaganda in America," *American Irish Review*, March, 1,7.
"Is Woman Suffrage a Failure?" *Century*, March, 724–730.
"The Growing Shadow of Imperialism," *American Irish Review*, April, 3, 7–8.

1925
"At the European Switchboard," *Century*, February, 452–463.
"New Phases in the Italian Struggle," *Century*, April, 744–755.

1926
"The Case of the Paying Teller," *Elk's*, April, 14–16, 63–65.
"It's the Little Things that Count," *Elk's*, 14–16.
"The New Industrial Era," *Century*, May, 1–11.

1927
"The Nordic Goes Safer-Rattling," *Century*, April, 685–694.

1928
"The American Grand Orchestra," *Century*, June, 167–175.

1929
"The Age of Detraction," *New York Herald Tribune*, November 18, 12–13.

"The Navy's Heritage of Glory," *New York Herald Tribune*, January 13, 1–3.
"Washington's Neglected Heroes," *New York Herald Tribune*, February 17, 1–3.

1930

"Haym Salomon and the Revolution," *The Jewish Tribune*, October 10, 3–7.

1931

"The Frightening Grip of the Utilities," *Public Utilities Fortnightly*, August 6, 138–148.

1932

"Orchestral Dividends," *The Review of Reviews*, February, 55–56.

1933

"Old Reporter Looks at the Mad-House World," *Scribner's*, October 1933, 225–230.

1936

"Hark! From the Caves," *Real America*, February, 20–24, 81.

1938

"Toward the American Commonwealth: Social Democracy: Constant Gradualism as the Technique for Social Advance," *Social Frontier*, October 1938, 22–24.

INDEX